Improving the Odds

BURT S. BARNOW
AND
CHRISTOPHER T. KING,
EDITORS

IMPROVING THE ODDS

Increasing the Effectiveness of Publicly Funded Training

THE URBAN INSTITUTE PRESS
Washington, D.C.

HD
5715.2
.I58
2000

THE URBAN INSTITUTE PRESS
2100 M Street, N.W.
Washington, D.C. 20037

Library of Congress Cataloging in Publication Data

Improving the Odds: Increasing the Effectiveness of Publicly Funded Training [Burt S. Barnow and Christopher T. King, editors].

Includes bibliographic references and index.

1. Occupational training—United States.   I. Barnow, Burt S.   II. King, Christopher T.

HD5715.2.I58   1999   99-043470
331.25'92'097321—cd21   CIP

ISBN 0-87766-689-X (paper, alk. paper)

-Printed in the United States of America

THE URBAN INSTITUTE is a nonprofit policy research and educational organization established in Washington, D.C., in 1968. Its staff investigates the social and economic problems confronting the nation and public and private means to alleviate them. The Institute disseminates significant findings of its research through the publications program of its Press. The goals of the Institute are to sharpen thinking about societal problems and efforts to solve them, improve government decisions and performance, and increase citizen awareness of important policy choices.

Through work that ranges from broad conceptual studies to administrative and technical assistance, Institute researchers contribute to the stock of knowledge available to guide decisionmaking in the public interest.

Conclusions or opinions expressed in Institute publications are those of the authors and do not necessarily reflect the views of staff members, officers or trustees of the Institute, advisory groups, or any organizations that provide financial support to the Institute.

DEDICATION

We dedicate this book to the memory of Daniel Friedlander, who died during its preparation. Dan was an excellent economist, friend, and colleague who will be sorely missed by all who knew him.

Financial support for the volume was provided by the National Council on Employment Policy, which received its endowment from a bequest from the estate of Sar A. and Brita Levitan. The Council has endeavored to support projects that continue Sar's lifelong interest in fostering effective social policies and programs for those in need.

Finally, we would like to express our appreciation to our families, Joyce and Adrienne and Cody and Piper, who tolerated, sometimes cheerfully, our work on this volume.

CONTENTS

List of Tables

List of Appendix Tables

List of Figures

List of Exhibits

The labor market has changed dramatically in recent decades. In the 1980s, an average of 2 million workers each year lost their jobs permanently because of the increasingly global economy, rapid advances in technology, and corporate downsizing; by the 1990s, those laid off included large numbers of older, college-educated white-collar workers. During the same period, immigration increased, most workers under age 25 with no college education experienced lower real earnings and little hope of a rewarding career, and the percentage of young black men in the job market declined steadily. In the late 1990s, Congress passed welfare reform legislation that required many more Americans to join the workforce.

The U.S. economy, with its twin blessings of strong job growth and low unemployment, has been well positioned to absorb additional workers. Yet many of the people in need of jobs—whether dislocated older workers, low-income adults with limited skills and education, out-of-school youth, or welfare recipients—require training before they can be employed. What kind of training and for what kind of jobs are questions of great concern to policymakers.

Congress has looked closely at federal job training programs in recent years, particularly the Job Training and Partnership Act (JTPA), and in 1998 it passed the Workforce Investment Act and the Carl D. Perkins Vocational and Technical Education Act, both of which mandate changes in publicly funded job training. Chief among the changes are increased coordination among programs, greater consumer choice of services, universal availability of some services, and an emphasis on measuring outcomes. State and local governments are now examining their programs in light of both welfare reform and these new federal laws.

Into this auspicious policy environment editors Burt Barnow and Christopher King introduce *Improving the Odds: Increasing the Effectiveness of Publicly Funded Training*. The book explores the effects of current programs on earnings and employment, recommends improvements in programs, and assesses the methodologies used to measure effectiveness. It pays particular attention to promising approaches, such as customized training, in which JTPA participants are trained to employers' specifications for jobs that already exist.

Of particular interest to policymakers today are young people between the ages of 17 and 21 who are not in college and who may or may not have finished high school. These out-of-school youth tend to be poor and to have difficulty finding jobs because they lack educational and social skills, in addition to work experience. Many of the young women are single mothers, and many of the young men, particularly high school dropouts, have been imprisoned. Job training programs have generally been less effective for these young people than for other groups; *Improving the Odds* gives concrete examples of programs that appear to be improving that record.

For most people, having a job that enables them to provide adequately for themselves and their families is essential to their physical and emotional well-being. Well aware of both the individual and collective benefits of employment, the Urban Institute has for many years studied the issues surrounding workers and work. Two chapters in this book—on training for out-of-school youth and welfare recipients—are written by Institute researchers.

Training is essential if dislocated and disadvantaged workers, young and old, are to hold jobs that keep them out of poverty. The editors of *Improving the Odds* have laid out several strategies that should help policymakers design training programs aimed at getting workers those jobs.

William Gorham
President
The Urban Institute

Chapter One

PUBLICLY FUNDED TRAINING IN A CHANGING LABOR MARKET

Burt S. Barnow and Christopher T. King

The first public employment programs in the United States were created in response to the Great Depression. Although successful, these efforts, notably the Civilian Conservation Corps and the Work Projects Administration, were largely terminated when the country entered World War II and the Depression ended. The federal government did not become involved in training programs until 1961, with the enactment of the Area Redevelopment Act, followed quickly by the Manpower Development and Training Act in 1962. Subsequent legislation included the Economic Opportunity Act in 1964, the Comprehensive Employment and Training Act in 1973, the Job Training Partnership Act in 1982, and the Workforce Investment Act and the Carl D. Perkins Vocational and Technical Education Act in 1998. Over time, the groups targeted by federal programs have changed, from a focus on dislocated workers to economically disadvantaged adults, youth, and welfare recipients.

Today, the United States finds itself in a global, highly interdependent economy in which labor market events in one nation have immediate and often pronounced implications for workers in another. The U.S. economy currently supports a labor market that by nearly all accounts is more robust than it has been in nearly three decades, with unemployment rates averaging at or below 4.5 percent, strong employment growth, and very modest rates of inflation, both in terms of consumer and producer prices. This remarkable set of circumstances is bolstering consumer confidence, leading to earlier-than-expected reductions in the federal deficit and allowing the traditionally conservative leadership of the Federal Reserve Board to maintain low interest rates.

As this volume was being prepared, the nation was giving considerable thought to how our employment and job training system should be structured, which groups of workers should be targeted, and what types of activities should be offered. Some of the biggest changes so far have been in programs for welfare recipients.

A dramatic round of welfare reforms swept the nation in 1996 and late 1997. The Personal Responsibility and Work Opportunity Reconciliation Act of 1996 has largely "ended welfare as we know it." It drastically changed the way welfare is financed, imposed lifetime limits on receipt of benefits, and added work requirements far greater than those in any other program in the nation. The act replaced the Aid to Families with Dependent Children (AFDC) program with Temporary Assistance for Needy Families (TANF) and dropped the Job Opportunities and Basic Skills (JOBS) training program for welfare recipients. The Balanced Budget Act, signed in December 1997, created the Welfare-to-Work Block Grants program, which further changed programs for welfare recipients. The program provides subsidized employment and job-related activities for hard-to-serve welfare recipients. In addition, it stresses *post*employment services for recipients and can serve noncustodial parents whose children receive TANF benefits. For people who are or even may be on welfare, it is truly a new world.

For the past several years, bills have been introduced in both houses of Congress to replace the Job Training Partnership Act (JTPA) and consolidate many of the smaller training programs. In the latter half of 1998, Congress passed and President Bill Clinton signed into law both the Workforce Investment Act (WIA) and the Carl D. Perkins Vocational and Technical Education Act, commonly referred to as Perkins III, mandating major changes in the nation's job training and vocational and technical education. Included in WIA are reauthorizations of the Adult Education and Family Literacy Act (Title II) and the Rehabilitation Act (Title IV) as well. Finally, after years of reduced funding, there is renewed interest in providing training to disadvantaged youth.

With so many changes under way, the time is ripe for assessing what we know about targeted employment and training programs. Our goal in this volume is to determine how effective current training programs have been and to provide recommendations on how the nation's employment and training system could be improved. We are not just interested in the extent to which the current mix of programs has increased earnings and employment and reduced the receipt of welfare, however. We also want to know what particular approaches to training seem to be most effective. Thus, most of the chapters focus on programs for particular groups or on particularly promising approaches to training.

TRAINING PROGRAMS AND THEIR EFFECTS

Frank Bennici, Stephen Mangum, and Andrew Sum provide a context in chapter 2 for our discussion of publicly funded training in
the United States. They analyze labor market projections, assess
some of the realities of training as it is now conducted in both the
public and private sectors, and pose future challenges and possible
strategies.

The authors identify familiar trends in the labor market—a changing industrial employment structure, technical advancement and
organizational restructuring, and reduced employment security[1]—
and suggest that these trends have contributed to human resource
problems "of critical importance to the ongoing debate over the
appropriate direction and structure of future training policies" in the
United States today.

Welfare Recipients

In chapter 3, Lisa Plimpton and Demetra Smith Nightingale review
experimental and rigorous quasi-experimental evaluations of
14 welfare-to-work programs that have operated around the country
from the mid-1970s to the present. They begin with the intensive
National Supported Work demonstration of the late 1970s, continue
with the Work Incentive program that operated through 1988, and
conclude with the labor force attachment and human capital development sites of the ongoing national evaluation of welfare-to-work
programs. The authors summarize the evaluations of these efforts,
focusing on the programs' impacts on employment, earnings, and
welfare receipt, and highlight key design issues.

Jodi Nudelman, in chapter 4, analyzes a sample drawn from the
National JTPA Study, consisting of 1,862 adult women who were
receiving AFDC at the time they applied to JTPA, between November
1987 and September 1989. She found that a substantial portion of
the experimental group did not enroll in JTPA. She examines four
issues of interest to policymakers, especially in light of national and
state welfare reforms and the recent implementation of the Welfare-to-
Work program: (1) JTPA's net impacts on earnings and on welfare
receipt; (2) its impacts on various subgroups of welfare recipients;
(3) the impacts of various JTPA services; and (4) the relationship
between impact on earnings and impact on receipt of welfare.

Disadvantaged Adults and Youth

Chapters 5 and 6 address training and related interventions for disadvantaged adults and out-of-school youth. The first, by Christopher T. King, with colleagues Jerome A. Olson, Leslie O. Lawson, Charles E. Trott, and John Baj, focuses on the effects of training programs for the economically disadvantaged. The authors analyze data on out-of-school youth and adult JTPA participants in Texas and Illinois to identify the demographic characteristics and the program and environmental variables associated with key measures of long-term success. Their field studies of seven of the most successful programs in the two states show the program characteristics and practices that are associated with success. From these the authors develop a series of policy recommendations and practical guidance for local programs.

Drawing on both his own and others' research, Robert Lerman, in chapter 6, describes what we know about out-of-school youth and the serious labor market problems they face. Out-of-school youth—whose numbers may be rising in the immediate future—tend to belong disproportionately to minority groups, are more prone to involvement with the criminal justice system, are more likely to become early parents, are seriously short of job skills, live in areas largely lacking good jobs, and lack either appropriate attitudes, reliability, and basic work preparation *or* the networks they need to find and retain good jobs. Lerman reviews the effectiveness of the broad types of publicly funded interventions that have served these youth over the past three decades: education, training, and job search and direct job creation.

Customized Training

Customized training is typically characterized by the following features: the curriculum is employer-specific and designed with company input; JTPA pays for some or all of the training cost; trainees are JTPA participants; and JTPA recruits and screens applicants but allows employers to select trainees. Kellie Isbell, John Trutko, and Burt Barnow, in chapter 7, provide findings and recommendations from case studies of nine companies whose customized training was financed in part with JTPA dollars. The projects studied were chosen to represent diversity of industry and occupation, employer size and geographic location, and types of training provided; participation in the study was entirely voluntary for employers.

Dislocated Workers

In chapter 8, Duane E. Leigh reviews what we know about dislocated workers, the various programs and approaches that have been developed since the early 1960s to assist them, and what effects these effects have had. According to Leigh, dislocated workers, probably the least disadvantaged subpopulation served by publicly funded training programs, tend to be distinguished by three interrelated characteristics: they have been laid off from jobs they have held for some time; they have significant work experience and firm-specific skills; and they are unlikely to be recalled to their old jobs or other jobs in the same industry. Leigh finds that dislocation has been and continues to be a large problem, with an average of 2 million full-time workers permanently displaced from their jobs annually between 1984 and 1992. The groups displaced have changed somewhat over time, however, with older, college-educated, white-collar workers from non-goods-producing industries now being disproportionately affected.

Review of Training Evaluation Methodologies

Daniel Friedlander, David Greenberg, and Philip Robins review in chapter 9 the methodologies used to conduct impact evaluations of training programs and offer suggestions for future evaluations based on the lessons learned. The basic problem in conducting impact evaluations is that we cannot observe the participants with and without training at the same time. Evaluators get around that problem by assigning eligible individuals at random to treatment or control groups and ensuring that the groups are similar except for receipt of the treatment. In such an experiment, a training program's impact on earnings can be estimated without bias simply by measuring the difference between the treatment and control groups' mean earnings in the period after the program.

In nonexperimental situations, individuals enter a program on their own or are selected by program officials, or both, and failure to control statistically for the selection process can lead to bias in the impact evaluation. The authors describe a number of ways to deal with nonrandom selection and suggest that more effort be given to implementing differential impact studies, in which the efficacy of various treatment strategies can be compared and the impact of treatment on different subgroups can be compared.

The Long-Term View

In chapter 10, Garth Mangum—one of the founders of what in the 1960s was called simply manpower policy—reflects on almost four decades of federal and state policymaking. He points out that "on average, the only people who maintained the level of their real earnings from the early 1970s to the late 1990s were those with college education, and only those with graduate degrees, again on average, experienced real increases in their standard of living." Mangum then assesses the budgetary consequences of stagnant or falling expenditures on programs serving the disadvantaged and reviews recent programs for disadvantaged adults and youth, as well as dislocated workers. These programs reinforce his observations about patterns in workforce policy since the early 1960s and the "essentiality of occupational preparation."

The concluding chapter, by the book's editors, distills from the research presented earlier a series of strategies that should greatly improve the odds of success—as measured by increased employability and earnings and reduced dependence on public assistance—with publicly funded training. We then offer an agenda for future research in this policy area.

RECENT REFORMS IN WORKFORCE PROGRAMS

In contrast to the dramatic reforms in welfare policy enacted recently, national workforce policy is continuing on a categorical, program-by-program, target group–by–target group basis, paying little attention to the larger picture. Even when we consider recent programs such as Perkins III, 1994's School-to-Work Opportunity Act, and other federal legislative vehicles for workforce development, the existing framework has been largely ad hoc and fragmented, driven by the perceived needs of specific groups (National Commission for Employment Policy 1991; U.S. General Accounting Office 1993, 1994).

National Workforce Reforms in the 1990s

Serious efforts to reform workforce development programs at the national level were initiated in 1995 with the passage of the Kennedy-Kassebaum bill (S. 143, the Workforce Development Act) and the

McKeon-Goodling bill (H.R. 1617, Consolidated and Reformed Education, Employment and Rehabilitation Systems—or CAREERS). The bills approached reform in quite different ways,[2] but they were left as works in progress when the appointed conference committee was unable to reach consensus.

Workforce reform efforts in the 105th Congress enjoyed greater success, namely, the Workforce Investment Act of 1998, but some of the changes effected may be more apparent than real. Despite the rhetoric of this act, funding streams for the various federal and federal-state programs are kept largely separate, and many restrictions on eligibility and allowable services remain—but in the form of quasi block grants.[3] WIA also retains separate national programs, such as those for migrants and seasonal farmworkers and for veterans, and continues the four rural Concentrated Employment Programs.

Yet the act shows promise in several respects. First, it provides states greater leeway in preparing long-term, "unified" plans for their various workforce programs. Second, it builds upon the customer-friendly, one-stop service center approach that has evolved in recent years. Third, it deals more systematically with the wider workforce system, including adult and vocational education, employment and rehabilitation services, and job training programs. And fourth, it is more explicit about accountability, requiring common performance indicators and the disclosure of service provider performance information, among other provisions. Whatever else it may accomplish, however, the act will probably fall short of unifying the nation's workforce programs.[4]

So, what are the major elements of federal workforce reforms in the 1990s?

INCREASED COORDINATION

Both WIA and Perkins III strongly encourage or require increased coordination among the various program actors, especially at the state and local levels.[5] Examples include provisions for unified state-level planning across job training, labor exchange, adult/vocational education, and other workforce-related programs; one-stop career centers as key entry points for many, if not most, local workforce services; and common performance indicators across programs. For the most part, recent legislation has stopped short of calling for program consolidation or integration;[6] however, WIA restores once-standard provisions for inducing or rewarding collaborative efforts, including rehabilitation services.

GREATER RELIANCE ON MARKET MECHANISMS

WIA requires that a voucherlike instrument, the individual training account (ITA), be used to deliver services.[7] In practice, ITAs resemble the individual-referral model (described in chapter 5), in which individuals are assessed and counseled on available service options and their implications before being referred to a qualified provider or providers. Whatever the details of the service selection process, much greater weight is now given to mechanisms that seek to mimic the market. For example, WIA is quite clear about providing accurate, up-to-date performance information on providers to support informed consumer choice, an essential element in fostering reliance on market mechanisms.

UNIVERSAL SERVICE

Universal service, an important element in many recent proposals, is an interesting concept in theory, but it has not been particularly helpful in practice, because it suggests relatively unrestricted eligibility for workforce services. Given the very limited funding for these programs—federal expenditures on all forms of workforce development have never exceeded 0.85 percent of the gross domestic product or 2.4 percent of federal budget outlays (King, McPherson, and Long 1999: 3)—universal service remains largely rehetorical, though stressing it may help to remove some of the stigma associated with such programs over the years, both by potential participants and employers. Under WIA, core services, such as outreach, intake, initial assessment, job search, and provider performance information, are open to all applicants regardless of employment status, income, or other characteristics, while welfare recipients and the poor are given priority for training services.

INCREASED ACCOUNTABILITY AND CUSTOMER ORIENTATION

Workforce reforms in the last decade bear little resemblance to those of earlier periods in terms of accountability. Before 1990, only a few programs (for example, JTPA) had explicit performance management systems. Those that did often defined performance in terms of process rather than outcomes. Since then, there has been greater recognition that accountability, performance measurement, and management must be addressed systematically, *across* program services, rather than simply on a program-by-program basis.[8] Passage of the Government Performance and Results Act of 1993 constitutes a major step in this direction, although many agencies define performance in terms of process or change, with little effort to link the measures to

program outcomes. In addition, it is no longer unusual to see proposals and provisions referring to both participants (employees or
potential employees) and employers as "customers" of workforce services and viewing service providers (such as state and local agencies, community colleges, and community-based organizations) as
entities addressing their needs. WIA clearly reinforces this trend, calling for the establishment of a Performance Accountability System for
workforce services to maximize return on investment and promote
continuous improvement. Interesting features of this new system
include requiring indicators of performance (which differ for adults
and youth),[9] emphasizing longer-term (6- and 12-month) measures,
disseminating performance information widely, and applying measures at both the local and state levels. For the most part, this
approach is also reflected in Perkins III and the associated Adult Education and Family Literacy and Rehabilitation Act reauthorizations.[10]

Congress and various administrations have accompanied calls for
workforce reform with considerable rhetoric about increased state
or local control and greatly diminished federal responsibility. However, given that the federal government is still putting up most of
the funding for these services, the federal stakeholders (Congress and
the responsible cabinet agencies) still expect substantial control over
who gets served, how they get served, and the outcomes resulting
from such services.

State Reforms in the 1990s

Not content to wait for action at the federal level, many governors
and state legislatures proceeded with their own reforms in the
1990s.[11] Such developments can be expected in a dynamic federal
system. The states have often served as the nation's laboratories of
democracy, piloting numerous reforms that eventually became
national law, including many safety and health statutes in the early
years of this century, anti-injunction and other laws governing labor-
management relations (notably in Wisconsin), and, more recently,
welfare-to-work approaches.[12]

State reforms vary considerably in their breadth and scope; the
extent to which they appeal to employers or employees; the degree
to which they reflect bottom-up, customer orientation or top-down,
state direction; and other dimensions. These efforts appear to be
driven in part by a desire to rationalize their approach to delivering
workforce services—that is, designing and implementing approaches
to service delivery that are more appropriate to the skills, aptitudes,

and interests of the labor force and to the needs of employers, regardless of the strictures of federal and state funding sources. Some of the more noteworthy reforms from state laboratories, especially reforms that pursued more systemic change, are described here briefly.[13]

FLORIDA

Florida moved decisively toward reforming its workforce programs in 1992 with the creation of the Enterprise Florida initiative, which had a strong economic development emphasis and drew heavily from the high-skills, high-wages focus of the *America's Choice* report (Commission on the Skills of the American Workforce 1990). Florida worked to establish a single, coordinated, market-driven economic development strategy that would streamline its programs, eliminate customer confusion, increase efficiency, and provide a clear outcomes orientation. The redesign of its local system was well along in 1997, with 25 Jobs and Education Partnership boards formed to oversee, but not directly provide, workforce services with what they referred to as "simulated block grants" in a series of workforce funding "strands." Distinctive features of the system include the annual state Occupational Forecast Conference, which identifies emerging and high-growth, high-wage occupations that require less than baccalaureate-level preparation and for which local programs can train workers; and the Florida Education and Training Performance Improvement Program, which provides the labor market outcomes to support the award of incentive grants from the state's Performance-Based Incentive Fund.

MASSACHUSETTS

Massachusetts has been a leader in welfare and workforce reform since the late 1980s. In 1993, it adopted a comprehensive strategy for workforce development and economic growth aimed at building a highly skilled and educated workforce based conceptually on the reinventing government work of David Osborne. The Massachusetts Jobs Commission was created at the state level, along with strong Regional Employment Boards. This system was designed to be demand-driven, customer-oriented, performance-driven, locally administered, and centrally guided. It gave priority to school-to-work, one-stop, and welfare-to-work programs, all of which continued to be categorical federal-state workforce programs. In 1998, Massachusetts established an Executive Office of Labor and Workforce Development with responsibility for most workforce programs, as well as a new Corporation for Business, Work, and Learning, which replaced the Bay State Skills Corporation, JTPA, and several other program initiatives. Regional Employment Boards also may choose between competitive or collaborative approaches to service delivery.

MICHIGAN

In the late 1980s, Michigan began a series of cutting-edge reforms under former governor James Blanchard—reforms that eschewed the more traditional rewiring-the-state-organization-chart approach in favor of a technologically based, client-driven one featuring the Michigan Opportunity Card. Soon after, in the early 1990s under Republican governor John Engler, the state dove headlong into a sweeping set of top-down reforms. Engler established the Michigan Jobs Commission in 1993 and placed most programs—except for adult and vocational education—under its administrative purview, advised by the Governor's Workforce Commission. More than most other states, Michigan's approach is to serve the needs of its employers first; economic rather than workforce development is in the lead role, while firm-based training is the service of choice. Michigan's workforce system is three-tiered. Tier one services, including JTPA, stops, WorkFirst (under its TANF program), School-to-Work, and some state-funded training, are controlled directly by the local boards. Local boards have less influence over tier two services (including the employment service, adult and vocational education, and several others) in their area and plan jointly for their use. While local boards are expected to affect the provision of tier three services (such as public transit and K–12 public education), their influence is quite limited in practice. Workforce services (especially tier one services) are currently offered under the auspices of 26 local Workforce Development Boards, with service providers competing for subcontracts from the boards.

OREGON

In 1989, Oregon adopted a 20-year strategic plan, Oregon Shines, that set forth a strong human investment framework as the basis for much of its workforce and economic decisionmaking. Oregon was strongly influenced by the high-skills, high-wage vision articulated in the 1990 *America's Choice* report (Commission on the Skills of the American Workforce 1990) and has continued to pursue this vision under three governors, with widespread bipartisan support. Unlike most other states, Oregon has pursued an economic development strategy based exclusively upon workforce development. It focuses on the supply side of the market in what has been termed a field-of-dreams approach—educate and train them (workers), and they (businesses) will come. Oregon trains with a goal of living wages for all of its workers. A Workforce Policy Cabinet at the state level directs decisionmaking for most workforce development and related programs, while 15 regional Workforce Quality Commissions serve at the regional level. Oregon relies heavily on coordinated decisionmaking at all levels, with some block grant funding, but is ultimately seeking more fully integrated workforce services. A distinctive feature of its approach to workforce as well as other services is the Oregon Benchmarks initiative, instituted in 1991, which established performance goals across a broad array of programs and services. Oregon has since been developing a Shared Information System to support a more realistic (smaller) number of benchmarks.

TEXAS

Texas began confronting the fragmented array of workforce services in the late 1980s and early 1990s with a series of studies, some generated by state agencies and others by the state legislature. In 1993, the legislature created the Texas Council on Workforce and Economic Competitiveness (TCWEC), one of the earliest human resource investment councils, as an independent state agency charged with planning and overseeing most workforce services, as well as developing a plan for consolidating and integrating such services. However, the 1995 legislature passed a bill that created the Texas Workforce Commission (TWC), a superagency for workforce services. The new legislation strongly encouraged establishment of local workforce development boards and demoted TCWEC to advisory status within the governor's office. Some two dozen programs—including JTPA, ES, unemployment insurance, Food Stamp Employment and Training, JOBS, and child care services—were transferred to TWC, and 28 local workforce areas were designated. By the beginning of 1999, 26 of the 28 local boards were under contract to TWC, charged with serving its two primary customers: employers and residents. The Texas workforce system has several interesting dimensions. One is the explicit split—much like that called for in WIA—among the boards, the career centers, and other service providers. Boards are responsible for planning and oversight but cannot provide services directly; career centers, which are competitively bid, handle intake, assessment, and other front-end services before referring participants to service providers for more intensive workforce services. The workforce system in Texas is demand-driven, supported by one of the best labor market information efforts in the nation (see chapter 5), and among the first to have systemwide performance measures.

Wisconsin began addressing workforce and welfare reform issues early, having established its one-stop Jobs Centers in 1987; these centers now serve both workers and employers. Although threatened by the recent emphasis on WorkFirst, Wisconsin's workforce system is still considered one of the best in the nation.[14] This systemic approach to workforce development arose from a 1985 study documenting the chaos that existed in the state's various education, training, and related programs. Today's Department of Workforce Development presides over a strongly customer-oriented, demand-driven system with more than 60 local Jobs Centers that offer access to services under the state's W2, JOBS, vocational rehabilitation, JTPA, employment service, and adult and vocational education programs. The State Collaborative Planning Team helps to guide the workforce system at the state level, while its local counterparts do the job at the regional level. With the exception of its state-sponsored Regional Training Partnership programs, Wisconsin's approach to workforce development stresses local control. The state established a human resource investment council (the Council on Workforce Excellence) to address strategic planning and oversight across various workforce programs almost as soon as such councils were encouraged under the 1992 JTPA reform amendments, but only in the past few years has Wisconsin begun to address performance management and measurement in a more comprehensive, systematic way.

As this quick review illustrates, governors and legislatures have not shied away from developing and implementing substantive workforce reforms at the state and local levels, despite sometimes less-than-adequate federal support. Moreover, they have tackled workforce reform in often quite varying ways, even though some of the elements are similar. The United States still operates very much within a federal system for workforce development.

CONCLUSION

Labor markets have experienced dramatic change in recent decades. Publicly funded training programs, which respond to these market shifts, have been operating for the better part of four decades and have undergone numerous changes in mission, goals and objectives, target populations, service mix, administrative structure, funding, and many other facets of their operations. In the past few years, policymakers at the national and state levels have instituted sweeping reforms in these programs.

This book reviews what we know about many of the leading publicly funded training programs, offering a thorough look at who has been served, the types of services provided, and the impacts of participation in them. It also provides coherent recommendations for enhancing training policies and for improving the odds of success with publicly funded training—especially at the local level, where it matters most.

Notes

1. For related discussions of important labor market changes and what they might mean for workforce development strategies, see Marshall (1999); King, McPherson, and Long (1999); Cappelli (1995); and Cappelli et al. (1997).

2. A quick comparative review of the bills' major provisions can be found in Barnow and King (1996) and Sum and Harrington (1995).

3. Mangum et al. (1999) offer a detailed critique of the Workforce Investment Act.

4. The gap between rhetoric and reality is suggested by this quotation from one of the sponsors of S. 1186 and a leading advocate of workforce reform, Senator Paul Wellstone (D–Minn.): "The Workforce Investment Partnership Act ... incorporates adult and vocational education *without* threatening those programs' separate funding streams. [I]t will also include reauthorization and improvement of vocational rehabilitation programs, again *without* threatening separate funding for vocational rehabilitation programs.... It assures *separate funding* to adults, to youth, and to dislocated workers according to state formulae, and also according to formulae within states.... It does *not* block grant job training, adult education and vocational education programs [emphasis added]" (U.S. Senate, May 1, 1998, *Congressional Record,* p. S4024).

5. Interestingly, WIA and Perkins III largely fail to address one of the long-standing barriers to an improved workforce system, which is the incredibly fragmented rabbit warren of congressional authorizing committees for these efforts; so long as separate federal authority and funding streams for the various programs are maintained, separate authorizing committees will be writing the legislative language.

6. In this regard, federal proposals offer a sharp contrast to some of the more dramatic state-based reforms (e.g., Texas, Michigan).

7. Barnow and King (1996) and Barnow (1998) have offered a critical review of the evidence on vouchers and their effectiveness in the context of workforce program services. Trutko and Barnow (1999) also assess the experiences of local JTPA programs that have used vouchers and individual referrals.

8. King's (1988) report, prepared for the National Commission for Employment Policy, constitutes one of the earlier pieces in this regard. The National Governors' Association's 18-month project, sponsored by the U.S. Departments of Agriculture, Education, and Labor, to develop core data elements and standards for workforce programs in the mid-1990s represents another.

9. A curious omission in the act is any mention of employer-based performance measures. Texas, Oregon, and a few other states have been attempting to grapple with instituting employer performance measures, acknowledging that employers are one of the primary customers of workforce services. Such measures have included simple "satisfaction" measures, as well as ones designed to capture return business and market penetration.

10. The mandate for more detailed accountability provisions and accompanying processes may be the most important change in the vocational/technical and adult education programs.

11. Several recent reports have reviewed the more significant state reform efforts, including King and McPherson (1997) and Grubb et al. (1999).

12. See Osborne and Gaebler (1992).

13. These state descriptions are drawn primarily from two sources: a study of Texas's efforts to build its workforce development system with comparative research on six other states by King and McPherson (1997); and a monograph by W. Norton Grubb et al. (1999) for the National Center for Research in Vocational Education and the U.S. Department of Education that examines states in the process of revamping their systems. In addition, for one of the more thoughtful pieces on systemic workforce reform at the state and local levels, see McPherson (1992).

14. Despite the rise of WorkFirst and W2, Wisconsin's Governor Tommy Thompson is one of the leading proponents of investing in training for welfare recipients, having increased funding for workforce education and training as the state introduced a work-first approach and time limits on welfare receipt.

References

Barnow, Burt S. 1999. "Exploring the Relationship between Performance Management and Program Impact: A Case Study of the Job Training Partnership Act." *Journal of Policy Analysis and Management* 18 (4): 744.

———. 1998. "Vouchers for Government-Sponsored Targeted Training Programs," Baltimore: Johns Hopkins University. Unpublished manuscript.

Barnow, Burt S., and Christopher T. King. 1996. "The Baby and the Bath Water: Lessons for the Next Employment and Training Program." In *Of Heart and Mind: Social Policy Essays in Honor of Sar A. Levitan,* edited by Garth Mangum and Stephen Mangum. Kalamazoo, Mich.: W.E. Upjohn Institute for Employment Research.

Cappelli, Peter. 1995. "Rethinking Employment." *British Journal of Industrial Relations* 33 (4, December): 563–603.

Cappelli, Peter, Laurie Bassi, Harry Katz, David Knoke, Paul Osterman, and Michael Useem. 1997. *Change at Work*. New York: Oxford University Press.

Commission on the Skills of the American Workforce. 1990. *America's Choice: High Skills or Low Wages!* New York: National Center for Education and the Economy.

Grubb, W. Norton, Norena Badway, Denise Bell, Bernadette Chi, Christopher T. King, Julie Herr, Heath Prince, Richard Kazis, Lisa Hicks, and Judith Taylor. 1999. *Toward Order from Chaos: State Efforts to Reform Workforce Development "Systems."* MDS-1249. Berkeley, Calif.: National Center for Research in Vocational Education.

King, Christopher T. 1988. *Cross-Cutting Performance Management Issues in Human Resource Programs*. Research Report 88-12. Washington, D.C.: National Commission for Employment Policy.

King, Christopher T., and Robert E. McPherson, eds. 1997. *Building a Workforce Development System for Texas ... A Funny Thing Happened on the Way to Reform*. Policy Research Report No. 127. Austin: The University of Texas, LBJ School of Public Affairs.

King, Christopher T., Robert E. McPherson, and Donald W. Long. 1999. "Public Labor Market Policies for the 21st Century." In *Back to Shared Prosperity: The Growing Inequality of Wealth and Income in America,* edited by Ray Marshall. Armonk, N.Y.: M.E. Sharpe.

Marshall, Ray. 1999. "Overview." In *Back to Shared Prosperity: The Growing Inequality of Wealth and Income in America,* edited by Ray Marshall. Armonk, N.Y.: M.E. Sharpe.

McPherson, Robert E. 1992. *Building an Integrated Workforce Development System for Texas: A Radical Blueprint for the Future*. Austin: Center for the Study of Human Resources, Lyndon B. Johnson School of Public Affairs, The University of Texas at Austin.

Mangum, Garth, Stephen Mangum, Andrew Sum, James Callahan, and Neal Fogg. 1999. *A Second Chance for the Fourth Chance: A Critique of the Workforce Investment Act of 1998*. Policy Issues Monograph 99-01. Baltimore: Sar Levitan Center for Social Policy Studies, Institute for Policy Studies, The Johns Hopkins University.

National Commission for Employment Policy. 1991. *Coordinating Federal Assistance Programs for the Economically Disadvantaged: Recommendations and Background Materials, Special Report No. 31*. Washington, D.C.: NCEP.

Osborne, David, and Ted Gaebler. 1992. *Reinventing Government: How the Entrepreneurial Spirit Is Transforming the Public Sector*. New York: Plume.

Scrivener, Susan, Gayle Hamilton, Mary Farrell, Stephen Freedman, Daniel Friedlander, Marisa Mitchell, Jodi Nudelman, and Christine Schwartz. 1998. "Implementation, Participation Patterns, Costs, and Two-Year Impacts of the Portland (Oregon) Welfare-to-Work Program: Executive Summary, National Evaluation of Welfare-to-Work

Strategies." Washington, D.C.: U.S. Department of Health and Human Services, Administration for Children and Families and Office of the Assistant Secretary for Planning and Evaluation; and U.S. Department of Education, Office of the Under Secretary and Office of Vocational and Adult Education.

Secretary's Commission on Achieving Necessary Skills. 1991. *What Work Requires of Schools: A SCANS Report for America 2000.* Washington, D.C.: U.S. Department of Labor.

Sum, Andrew, Stephen Mangum, Edward De Jesus, Gary Walker, David Gruber, Marian Pines, and William Spring. 1997. *A Generation of Challenge: Pathways to Success for Urban Youth.* Baltimore: Sar A. Levitan Center for Social Policy Studies, Johns Hopkins University.

Sum, Andrew, and Paul Harrington. 1995. "Guiding Principles for National Employment and Training Reform." In *The Harassed Staffer's Guide to Employment and Training Policy,* edited by Marion Pines et al. Baltimore: The Sar A. Levitan Center for Social Policy Studies, Institute for Policy Studies, Johns Hopkins University.

Trutko, John, and Burt S. Barnow. 1999. *Experiences with Training Vouchers under the Job Training Partnership Act and Implications for Individual Training Accounts under the Workforce Investment Act: Final Report.* Washington, D.C.: U.S. Department of Labor, Employment and Training Administration.

[U.S. Department of Labor] Secretary's Job Training Partnership Advisory Committee. 1989a. *Working Capital: JTPA Investments for the '90s.* Washington, D.C.: USDOL.

———. 1989b. *Coordinating ETA-Administered Programs: Issues and Recommendations.* Washington, D.C.: USDOL.

U.S. General Accounting Office. 1993. *Multiple Employment Programs: National Employment Strategy Needed.* GAO/T-HRD-93-27. Washington, D.C.: GAO.

———. 1994. *Multiple Employment Training Programs: Overlapping Programs Can Add Unnecessary Administrative Costs.* GAO/HEHS-94-80. Washington, D.C.: GAO.

Chapter Two

THE ECONOMIC, DEMOGRAPHIC, AND SOCIAL CONTEXT OF FUTURE EMPLOYMENT AND TRAINING PROGRAMS

Frank Bennici, Stephen Mangum, and Andrew M. Sum

Employment and training programs operate within the context of existing labor markets, both those internal and external to firms. In evaluating the performance of these programs and identifying new directions for them, it is important to examine the labor market realities in which the programs are likely to operate in the future. This chapter identifies past labor market trends and describes how these are reflected in current human resource concerns. We then focus on labor market projections, defining these in terms of the challenges they portend for employment and training programs.

PAST LABOR MARKET TRENDS

The Changing Industrial Structure of Employment

Since the mid-1870s, agricultural employment in the United States has declined from 70 percent of total employment to less than 3 percent today. Jobs in the remainder of the goods-producing sector (primarily in manufacturing, mining, and construction) have been more stable, hovering between 20 percent and 30 percent of total employment since the 1870s. Goods-producing employment, nevertheless, has been declining as a share of total employment since World War II and is projected to continue to decrease at least through 2006. In contrast, employment in service industries (broadly defined) has grown from about 10 percent of total employment in 1870 to nearly 75 percent today. The real dollar value of output in the goods-producing sector, however, has expanded much more rapidly than has employment in this sector due to above-average gains in labor productivity, especially in manufacturing industries. In short, we have witnessed a deindustrialization of employment in America.

Globalization

Globalization of economic competition, another major trend, has ushered in an era in which national economies are increasingly integrated and interdependent. With globalization has come declining concentration of economic power and a diffusion of political force across the globe, in turn breeding less economic certainty and new sources of economic competition.

While often thought of in terms of the flow of goods and services across countries, globalization has important labor market dimensions as well. Economic interdependence is evident in sizable flows of human resources, both skilled and unskilled, across national boundaries. These flows take two forms: people migrating to wherever appropriate work can be found, and tasks flowing—often through advanced information technology—to wherever cost-effective human competencies are located.

In the marketplace for labor services, the impacts of globalization have been evident as real wage growth in developed countries has been below historical levels in recent years. In the face of increased competition, wage rates for given types of work in developed countries can differ from those in developing countries only to the degree in which real productivity differences exist among countries. Globalization has reduced the power of national institutions such as unions and protective legislation to independently regulate and control labor market conditions and to affect product markets. For such institutions to continue to have a substantial impact in today's world would require that their power extend broadly across national boundaries, an uncommon occurrence for them.

Increased global competitive pressures and a decline in oligopolies have made firms increasingly more vigilant cost managers in search of value creation. Watchwords of American business now include "core competencies" that establish "best-in-world" criteria and focus on what an organization does best by applying "make or buy" decisions to each activity in its value chain. The underlying rubric is for the company to examine each of its activities to determine if it can be one of the best in the world at that particular thing. Where the answer is no, the activity should be outsourced, with any freed resources used to concentrate on activities in which the firm is or can be best-in-class. Incumbent in this approach is the task of "managing a rapidly changing network of best-in-world suppliers for other [noncore] needs" (Quinn 1992: 49).

Technological Advance and Organizational Restructuring

Technological achievement also has fundamentally changed the nature of modern competition. Traditionally competitive arenas such as product quality and process technology have been reduced in influence by the increasing rapidity and completeness of information flows. Automation has forced "cost and physical quality standards toward a common norm" (Quinn 1992: 32), removing them as battlegrounds for advantage. Competitive pursuit of value creation has moved to other frontiers such as service quality and time-based strategies that shorten production and delivery cycles.

In this new era of increased competition, value creation relies increasingly on organizational capabilities involving human competencies. Organizational relationships that develop and sustain people in productive roles are increasingly critical to the value-creating ability of economic organizations in all sectors, government included (Kochan and Osterman 1994: 6). As stated earlier, competitive forces are pushing firms to identify and capitalize on their core competencies, so that they can reconceptualize themselves as "intelligent or intellectual enterprises" (Quinn 1992: 41) capable of thriving in a world of rapid change. Incumbent in most such strategies is increasing emphasis on the human input, what Marshall and Tucker (1992: 43) call human-resource capitalism.

Cost containment and a focus on core competencies have fueled "rightsizing" or "reengineering" trends, often leading to employment dislocation. Dislocation, long viewed as a natural element of capitalist economic activity, has increased significantly during the past two decades along with globalization, technological change, and corporate restructuring. Externalization of employment has been significant (Pfeffer 1995: 21), with outsourced business services, temporary help services, and employee leasing among the fastest-growing industries in terms of employment (von Hippel et al. 1997).

An Altered Employment Relationship

Globalization and technological advances have thus fundamentally altered organizational structures. Corporate hierarchies in some cases have been flattened to reduce cost, speed reaction time, generate a fresh flow of ideas, and put more decisionmaking responsibilities in the hands of workers with direct customer contact. Information sharing has expanded to assist front-line workers and to tap creative genius wherever it can be found. International partnering and joint ventures have become commonplace as corporations strive to conserve capital, gain access to locality-specific market knowledge, and exploit worldwide technological improvements and economies of scale.

With these changes, the meaning, extent, and source of labor market security have shifted. There is a lessened sense of job security, with individual mobility enhanced and organizations often appearing less committed to individual workers. Fewer workers can count on doing the same job for the same employer over their careers because of technological advancement, mergers and acquisitions, and the unpredictable nature of competitive advancement. Similarly, because of growing externalization of employment and dislocation, few workers can count on a career comprising a variety of jobs for the same employer. Economic security, to the extent that it exists, is increasingly defined in terms of "employability security," whose sources are found in individual competencies and the capability for self-improvement through lifelong learning, including on-the-job training and formal training from employers.

CURRENT HUMAN RESOURCE CONCERNS

These major trends have contributed to seven human resource problems of critical importance to the ongoing debate over the appropriate direction and structure of future training policies (in both the public and private sectors) for the United States. It is essential that such debates address these human resource concerns and the ways these are likely to change over the next decade:

- A steep deterioration in the real (after inflation) weekly earnings of the nation's youngest full-time workers (under age 25) over the past two decades and the continued depressed annual earnings and career prospects for many young men and women with no postsecondary schooling.[1]
- An increasing gulf in labor force participation and employment between young black males and their nonblack counterparts.[2]
- Declines in both the labor force participation rates and employment rates of older males (ages 45–64), especially those with no substantive postsecondary schooling, well before the "normal" retirement age (Sum and Fogg 1991).

- Continued high levels of worker dislocation, despite strong job growth and declining unemployment. Many older dislocated workers, especially those with long tenure and high amounts of firm-specific human capital, face limited reemployment prospects and steep real earnings declines when they are reemployed.[3]
- High levels of immigration and the reliance of many regions on immigrants for growth in their labor forces (Smith and Edmonstan 1997).
- New, strict time limits on receipt of public assistance income as a result of passage of national and state welfare reform that will increase the number of single mothers entering the labor market in search of unsubsidized employment. Since many of these women are undereducated and low skilled, their labor market entry places downward pressure on wages at the lower end of the labor market. Since most states are adopting a work-first approach, little progress is likely in increasing employability skills in the near term.[4]
- Growing concerns over the high degree of wage and income inequality among U.S. workers and the absence of sustained real wage growth for many workers in the 1990s. The inequality in the wage distribution among full-time wage and salary workers in the United States grew considerably between the late 1970s and the mid-1990s.[5]

THE FUTURE LABOR MARKET

Against this backdrop of key human resource challenges, we look to what national labor market projections forecast for the next decade.[6] The U.S. Department of Labor's Bureau of Labor Statistics (BLS) projects a continued slowing of aggregate labor force growth in the United States—specifically, a predicted growth of 15 million workers between 1996 and 2006 compared to 16 million between 1986 and 1996 and 21.7 million between 1976 and 1986. This predicted slowing results primarily from the slower projected population growth of the working-age population. Persons ages 16–24 and those ages 55 and older are expected to have faster annual rates of population growth (1.7 percent and 1.9 percent, respectively) than the projected 1.0 percent growth rate for the overall population.

The annual rates of population growth for Hispanics (3.3 percent), Asians and others (3.7 percent), and African Americans (1.2 percent) are projected to be much faster than for whites (0.8 percent), with immigration among Asians and Hispanics a key contributing factor. As a result, the white share of the population will decrease between 1996 and 2006, and the minority share of the labor force will increase during that period. African Americans are expected to add a net 2.1 million workers to the labor force by 2006, bringing their share of the nation's civilian labor force to 11.6 percent. An additional net 4.6 million Hispanics will enter the labor force by 2006, yielding a Hispanic labor force slightly higher in absolute size than the African American, non-Hispanic labor force. For both groups, labor force growth is attributed to population growth resulting from higher birthrates and from immigration. The "Asian and others" group is projected to add 2.3 million workers net to the labor force, representing an increase of 46 percent (from 4.3 percent of the total labor force in 1996 to 5.4 percent of it in 2006).

The aggregate labor force participation rate is expected to grow more slowly from 1996 to 2006 (.8 percent annual rate) than it did from 1986 to 1996 (1.5 percentage points), due to the aging of the population and slower forecast increases in labor force participation among younger women (2.2 percentage points for 1996–2006 compared to 4.0 percentage points in 1986–96 and 4.4 percentage points in 1976–86). The labor force participation rate of 16- to 19-year-old women is projected to decrease by 0.3 percentage points. In contrast the corresponding rate for women ages 55 and older is expected to increase by 6.0 percentage points (compared to a 1.8-percentage-point increase in 1986–96).

The aggregate labor force participation rate of men is projected to continue its long-term decline, decreasing by 1.3 percentage points. Women are projected to account for 49.6 percent of labor force entrants but only 44 percent of labor force leavers; therefore, they will increase their labor force share from 46.2 percent in 1996 to 47.4 percent by 2006.

Immigration has played a key role in contributing to the growth of the nation's civilian labor force over the past two decades and has been consistently underestimated by the U.S. Bureau of the Census.[7] New immigrants accounted for just under 30 percent of the net growth of 16.7 million persons in the U.S. civilian labor force between 1980 and 1990 and close to 39 percent of its growth between 1990 and early 1996. However, their actual share of the net change in the labor force over this most recent six-year period may actually have been several percentage points higher than this due to underestimates of the undocumented immigrant population.[8]

The impact of foreign immigration on civilian labor force growth has varied widely by region over the past two decades. During the

1980s, new immigrants increased the civilian labor force of each of the nine Census geographic regions; however, their share of net growth ranged from a low of 4 percent in the East South Central region to highs of 62 percent in the Middle Atlantic region and 43 percent in the Pacific region. In both the New England and Middle Atlantic regions, the resident labor force in early 1996 remained below that of 1990, despite continued foreign immigration. In the absence of this foreign immigration, New England's labor force would have declined by another 2 percent and the Middle Atlantic labor force by another 3 percent. Among the remaining regions, foreign immigrants accounted for only 4 percent of labor force growth in the East South Central region and only 13 percent of such growth in the Rocky Mountain region (the fastest-growing region), but they accounted for 34 percent of the South Atlantic region's growth and 93 percent of the labor force growth in the Pacific region (table 2.1).

The future growth of the immigrant workforce will depend heavily upon labor market conditions in the United States and abroad (especially in Mexico, Central America, the Dominican Republic, West Indies, and South Asia), as well as future national immigration policies and enforcement by the Immigration and Naturalization Ser-

Table 2.1 IMMIGRANTS' SHARE OF NET CHANGE IN CIVILIAN LABOR FORCE OF THE UNITED STATES AND NINE GEOGRAPHIC DIVISIONS: FEBRUARY–MARCH 1990 TO FEBRUARY–MARCH 1996 (IN THOUSANDS)

Geographic Area	Civilian Labor Force (seasonally adjusted)			New Immigrants in CLF, 1990–96	New Immigrants' Share of CLF Growth (%)
	Feb.–Mar. 1990	Feb.–Mar. 1996	Change: 1990–96		
United States	125,672	133,483	7,811	3,024	38.7
New England	7,159	6,956	−203	126	—
Middle Atlantic	18,762	18,493	−269	616	—
East North Central	21,186	22,483	1,297	228	17.6
West North Central	9,082	10,034	952	101	10.6
South Atlantic	22,328	23,737	1,409	478	33.9
East South Central	7,224	7,913	689	28	4.1
West South Central	13,003	14,515	1,512	342	22.6
Mountain	6,862	8,297	1,435	185	12.9
Pacific	20,066	21,055	989	920	93.0

Sources: U.S. Bureau of Labor Statistics, *Employment and Earnings* (Washington, D.C.: U.S. Department of Commerce, March 1997); and February and March 1996 Current Population Survey public-use tapes, tabulations by Center for Labor Market Studies, Northeastern University.

Note: CLF, civilian labor force.

vice of existing laws (Green 1997: 3–5).[9] The maintenance of low levels of unemployment and the existence of sizable wage differentials between the United States and other countries, particularly many of its southern neighbors, will undoubtedly provide continued economic incentives for migrants, both legal and illegal, to come to the United States. Given the young ages and relatively limited education of many new immigrants, their greater supply will continue to place downward economic pressures on the wages and employment opportunities of less-skilled younger native-born workers, particularly in many of the nation's large central cities.

Projected Employment by Industry and Occupation

Over the 1996–2006 period, total employment in the United States is projected to grow by 14.0 percent, substantially slower than the 18.8 percent growth during 1986–96. The number of jobs will increase by 18.6 million (table 2.2). However, the following industry groups will experience employment losses: mining (22.8 percent), durable manufacturing (2.3 percent), federal government (3.2 percent), agriculture (.7 percent), and private household (16.5 percent). The number of nonagricultural self-employed and unpaid family workers is expected to increase by 12.9 percent, adding 1.17 million jobs. By 2006, the service-producing sector's share of nonfarm wage and salary employment will increase from 79.4 percent in 1996 to 82.1 percent. With only a small agricultural sector in employment terms, continued growth in the share of service employment spells a loss of employment share for the goods-producing sector, which is projected to continue falling below its traditional 20 percent share of total employment (18.6 percent in 1996, decreasing to 16.2 percent by 2006).

The service-producing sector comprises six main divisions: wholesale trade; retail trade; finance, insurance, and real estate; private services; government; and transportation, communications, and utilities. Of these, only the private-services division is projected to increase its share of employment. By 2006, one-third (32.9 percent) of all nonfarm wage and salary employment is projected to be within this division, the largest concentration of any single division. Employment in private services is expected to grow 2.9 percent annually, more than twice the projected growth rate for all nonfarm wage and salary employment. Most of the anticipated growth within the division (59 percent) is in just two industry groups: business services (3.6 million) and health services (3.2 million).[10]

Table 2.2 PROJECTED EMPLOYMENT BY INDUSTRY, 1996–2006

Industry	1996	Projected Growth: 1996–2006 Number	Projected Growth: 1996–2006 Percentage	Percentage Distribution 1996	Percentage Distribution 2006
Total	132,352	18,575	14.0	100	100
Nonfarm wage and salary	118,731	17,587	14.8	89.7	90.3
Goods producing	24,431	20	.1	18.5	16.2
Mining	574	−131	−22.8	.4	.3
Construction	5,400	500	9.3	4.1	3.9
Manufacturing	18,457	−350	−1.9	13.9	12.0
Durable	10,766	−252	−2.3	8.1	7.0
Nondurable	7,691	98	1.3	5.8	5.0
Service producing	94,300	17,567	18.6	71.2	74.1
Transportation, communications, and utilities	6,260	851	13.6	4.7	4.7
Wholesale trade	6,483	745	11.5	4.9	4.8
Retail trade	21,625	2,250	10.4	16.3	15.8
Finance, insurance, and real estate	6,899	752	10.9	5.2	5.1
Private services	33,586	11.266	33.5	25.4	29.7
Federal government	2,757	−87	−3.2	2.1	1.8
State and local government	16,690	1,790	10.7	12.6	12.2
Agriculture	3,642	−24	−.7	2.8	2.4
Private household wage and salary	928	−153	−16.5	.7	.5
Nonagricultural self-employed and unpaid family workers	9,051	1,165	12.9	6.8	6.8

Source: *Monthly Labor Review* (November 1997: 40).
Note: Employment data for wage and salary workers are numbers of jobs, whereas self-employed, unpaid family worker, agricultural, and private household employment are numbers of workers. Nonfarm wage and salary excludes Standard Industrial Classifications (SICs) 074,5,8 (agricultural services) and 99 (nonclassifiable establishments). Agriculture excludes government wage and salary workers and includes private-sector SICs 08, 09. Nonagricultural self-employed and unpaid family workers excludes SICs 08, 09 (forestry and fisheries).

Employment growth in all but one major occupational group is projected to grow more slowly during 1996–2006 than it did over the previous 10 years (table 2.3). The one exception is precision production, craft, and repair, whose employment growth is projected to increase 6.9 percent, compared to the 4.4 percent increase during 1986–96. For some occupational groups, the rates of change are similar to the 1986–96 period, while others depart substantially. Another significant departure from the past is the slowing of employment

Table 2.3 EMPLOYMENT BY MAJOR OCCUPATIONAL GROUPS: 1986, 1996, AND PROJECTED 2006 (NUMBERS IN THOUSANDS OF JOBS)

Occupation	Employment			Employment Change				Employment Share (%)		
			Projection:	1986–96		Projection: 1996–2006				
	1986	1996	2006	Number	Percentage	Number	Percentage	1986	1996	2006
Total, all occupations	111,375	132,353	150,927	20,978	18.8	18,574	14.0	100	100	100
Executive, administrative, and managerial	10,568	13,542	15,866	2,974	28.1	2,324	17.2	9.5	10.2	10.5
Professional-specialty	13,589	18,173	22,998	4,584	33.7	4,826	26.6	12.2	13.7	15.2
Technicians and related support	3,724	4,618	5,558	894	24.0	940	20.4	3.3	3.5	3.7
Marketing and sales	11,496	14,633	16,897	3,137	27.3	2,264	15.5	10.3	11.1	11.2
Administrative support, including clerical	20,871	24,019	25,825	3,147	15.1	1,806	7.5	18.7	18.1	17.1
Service	17,427	21,294	25,147	3,867	22.2	3,853	18.1	15.6	16.1	16.7
Agriculture, forestry, fishing, and related	3,661	3,785	3,823	124	3.4	37	1.0	3.3	2.9	2.5
Precision production, craft, and repair	13,832	14,446	15,448	614	4.4	1,002	6.9	12.4	10.9	10.2
Operators, fabricators, and laborers	16,206	17,843	19,365	1,637	10.1	1,522	8.5	14.6	13.5	12.8

Source: *Monthly Labor Review* (November 1997: 59).

growth for administrative support/clerical occupations, reflecting the expected effect of increasing technological change in the office environment. Between 1986 and 1996, employment in this occupational group increased by 15.1 percent, while for 1996–2006 employment is expected to increase by only 7.5 percent.

Professional-specialty occupations are forecast by the Bureau of Labor Statistics to have the fastest projected growth, continuing the pattern of the 1986–96 period and providing the largest numerical increase in employment. Growth in technicians and related support occupations ranks second in the rate of growth, and service occupations rank second in numerical increase. Four occupational groups are projected to sustain a loss in their employment share: administrative support, including clerical; agriculture, fishing, forestry, and related occupations; precision production, craft, and repair; and operators, fabricators, and laborers.

Rates of projected employment growth by more-detailed occupational category range from an increase of 118 percent for database administrators, computer specialists, and all other computer scientists to a decline of 126 percent for sewing machine operators (garments). Twenty of the occupations with the largest expected job growth account for more than one-third of all projected employment growth between 1996 and 2006. Three of the top 10 occupations are health care occupations (registered nurses; home health aides; nursing aides, orderlies, and attendants), and 3 of the top 20 are education-related occupations (secondary school teachers; teacher aides and educational assistants; special education teachers). Generally, occupations with the fastest projected job growth do not add very large numbers of new jobs because these occupational categories tend to be the smallest in terms of numerical size. However, the 3 occupations with the fastest projected job growth (database administrators, computer specialists and all other computer scientists; computer engineers; systems analysts) are also among the top 20 occupations projected to have the largest increase in total employment. As stated, employment of database administrators, computer specialists, and all other computer scientists is expected to grow by about 118 percent, adding 249,000 jobs. Computer engineer jobs are projected to increase by 235,000, and systems analysts jobs by 520,000. Eleven of the top 20 fastest-growing occupations are in the health services industry.

Because workers leave jobs to enter other occupations or to leave the labor force entirely, replacement demand results in a large number of job openings. Total job openings are projected to reach near 50.6 million due to job growth and net replacement needs between

1996 and 2006, with replacement demand being the primary source of job openings.

ACCURACY OF OCCUPATIONAL
EMPLOYMENT PROJECTIONS

The accuracy of the BLS occupational employment projections has been a matter of recent debate. A number of labor market analysts, most notably John Bishop of Cornell University, have critiqued the BLS projections. Bishop and Carter (1990) have argued that BLS employment projections for the 1980s and the first half of the 1990s have consistently underestimated the growth of employment in professional, managerial, and technical occupations, thereby under-projecting the demand for college graduates.[11] In a recent evaluation of the 1995 occupational employment projections, the BLS revealed that it underestimated total employment by 7.25 million between 1984 and 1995. The two occupational groups with the largest relative errors were professional-specialty occupations (−11 percent) and management-related occupations (10 percent). The differences between actual and projected growth rates for these two educational groups were quite sizable (see table 2.4).

Between 1992 and 1996, the number of employed persons (ages 16 years or higher) in the United States is estimated to have risen by 8.22 million, or just under 7 percent, according to the findings of the Current Population Surveys (CPSs). Employment growth rates over this four-year period, however, have varied considerably across major occupational groups. Employment of administrative support/clerical (−2.2 percent) and technical (−8.2 percent) workers declined during this period, while the numbers of professional-specialty workers (14.6 percent) and executives/managers/administrators (20.5 percent) are estimated to have increased at double-digit

Table 2.4 ACTUAL AND PROJECTED GROWTH RATES FOR PROFESSIONAL-SPECIALTY AND MANAGEMENT-RELATED OCCUPATIONS: 1984–95

Occupational Group	Projected Growth Rate	Actual Growth Rate	Actual-Projected
Professional-specialty	20.6	35.9	+15.3
Executive, administrative, managerial	19.9	33.1	+13.2

Source: Carolyn M. Veneri, "Evaluating the 1995 Occupational Employment Projections," *Monthly Labor Review* (September 1997).

rates. Nearly 37 percent of the net job growth over the past four years took place in management and management-related occupations alone, and professionals and managers combined accounted for two-thirds of the net job growth in the entire nation.

While employment in the professional and managerial occupations is projected by the BLS to grow at above-average rates over the 1996–2006 period, the estimated growth rate in management-related occupations over the past four years has sharply exceeded growth rates projected by both the BLS and John Bishop. This explosive growth in management-related occupations also occurred in an economic environment in which major corporations claimed to be downsizing the number of middle-level managers, flattening corporate hierarchies, and delegating greater responsibilities for management functions to front-line workers. At the same time, while technical employment was projected to grow at above-average rates over the 1990s, the CPS findings suggest that technical employment has actually declined considerably during the past four years, with nearly all of this decline occurring outside of the allied health area, where employment in technical positions accounted for nearly one-half of total technical employment in 1994. Computer programming jobs and technician positions in manufacturing were estimated to have declined sharply.[12]

Occupational Earnings and Educational/Training Requirements

Using the median earnings of wage and salary workers who usually work full-time, the BLS develops occupation-based earnings quartiles. For 1994–96, these quartiles (given as hourly wage rates) were the following:

Highest quartile	$15.06 or higher
Second quartile	$10.61–$15.05
Third quartile	$7.48–$10.60
Lowest quartile	$7.47 or lower

Applying these occupation-specific earnings quartile designations to the 1996–2006 projection period, relatively high-paying occupations are projected to grow faster than low-paying occupations, with occupations in the top two quartiles accounting for nearly 60 percent of projected employment growth over the period. However, replacement needs are projected to be greater in occupations in the lower two earnings quartiles. Because greater numbers of job openings result from net replacement needs than job growth over the projection period, however, total job openings are projected to be greatest in the first and fourth quartiles (see table 2.5).

Table 2.5 DISTRIBUTION OF OCCUPATIONAL EMPLOYMENT BY EARNINGS CATEGORY: 1996 AND 2006
(EMPLOYMENT NUMBERS IN THOUSANDS)

Earnings Category (Quartile)	Number of Occupations	Employment: 1996		Change in Employment: 1996–2006		Average Annual Job Openings Due to Net Replacement		Average Annual Job Openings Due to Net Replacement and Job Growth	
		Number	Percentage Distribution	Number	Percentage Distribution	Number	Percentage Distribution	Number	Percentage Distribution
Total	508	132,353	100	18,574	100	3,054	100	5,056	100
First	137	32,976	25.0	6,308	34.0	675	22.1	1,313	26.0
Second	160	33,386	25.2	4,241	22.8	668	21.9	1,130	22.4
Third	153	32,829	24.8	3,918	21.1	711	23.4	1,157	22.9
Fourth	58	32,964	25.0	4,080	22.0	995	32.6	1,449	28.7

Source: Authors' calculations using *National Occupational Employment, Earning and Training Database, 1996–2006*, provided by the U.S. Bureau of Labor Statistics, March 1998.

The BLS also describes occupations by their typical education and training requirements, using a classification system comprising distinct categories of skill preparation (table 2.6).[13] For the 1996–2006 projection period, occupational employment patterns reflect movement toward higher levels of required education and training. The highest rates of growth in projected job openings due to employment growth are among occupations typically requiring academic degrees: doctorate degree (19.0 percent), master's degree (15.0 percent), bachelor's degree (25.4 percent), associate's degree (22.2 percent), and first professional degree (18.0 percent). Because occupations requiring less education and training typically have less job attachment and higher turnover than other occupations, these occupations have proportionately more total openings than their share of openings created by growth alone. Consequently, the largest single education and training category of job openings (43.4 percent) is that for openings requiring only short-term on-the-job training. In contrast, occupations requiring a bachelor's or higher degree account for 24.4 percent of job openings, and occupations requiring either an associate's degree or some postsecondary vocational education account for 7.8 percent of job openings.

Having examined both the earnings and educational-requirement dimensions of the occupational employment projections separately, it is important to integrate them. Table 2.7 provides the distribution of total job openings for the projection period by earnings quartile and education/training category. Over the projection period, occupations requiring at least a bachelor's degree comprise the majority of the projected job openings among occupations in the highest earnings quartile. The majority share of projected employment growth in the second-highest earnings quartile is in occupations requiring moderate- to long-term on-the-job training, significant amounts of work experience, or postsecondary vocational training. The third earnings quartile primarily comprises occupations requiring short- to moderate-term on-the-job training. The fourth earnings quartile is dominated by occupations requiring only short-term on-the-job training. Among occupations in the fourth (lowest earnings) quartile, seven account for nearly 60 percent of employment growth: cashiers; nursing aides, orderlies, and attendants; food counter, fountain, and related workers; food preparation workers; child care workers; teacher's aides and educational assistants; and home health aides.

Tables 2.8 and 2.9 provide the education and training category assigned by the BLS and the relative rank of median earnings for the occupations projected to have the largest numerical increase (table 2.8) and the fastest projected employment growth (table 2.9) between 1996

Table 2.6 PROJECTED CHANGE IN EMPLOYMENT BY EDUCATION AND
TRAINING CATEGORY, 1996–2006 (NUMBERS IN THOUSANDS OF JOBS)

Education and Training Category	Job Openings Due to Employment Growth		Job Openings Due to Growth and Net Replacement Needs	
	Number	Percentage	Number	Percentage
Total	18,574	14.0	50,563	100
First professional degree	308	18.0	582	1.2
Doctorate degree	193	19.0	460	.9
Master's degree	206	15.0	430	.9
Work experience plus a bachelor's or higher degree	1,597	17.8	3,481	6.9
Bachelor's degree	4,017	25.4	7,343	14.5
Associate's degree	915	22.2	1,614	3.2
Postsecondary vocational education	598	7.4	2,329	4.6
Work experience in a related occupation	1,211	12.2	3,285	6.5
Long-term on-the-job training	879	8.0	3,466	6.9
Moderate-term on-the-job training	1,468	8.7	5,628	11.1
Short-term on-the-job training	7,183	13.4	21,944	43.4

Source: *Monthly Labor Review* (November 1997: 82).

Table 2.7 DISTRIBUTION OF PROJECTED TOTAL JOB OPENINGS (DUE TO
GROWTH AND NET REPLACEMENT NEEDS) BY EARNINGS QUARTILE
AND BY EDUCATION AND TRAINING CATEGORY, 1996–2006

Education and Training Category	Median Earnings Quartile			
	Highest	Second	Third	Lowest
Total	26.0%	22.4%	22.9%	28.7%
First professional degree	3.9	0.6	0	0
Doctorate degree	3.5	0	0	0
Master's degree	3.2	0.1	0	0
Work experience plus a bachelor's or higher degree	24.9	1.3	.3	0
Bachelor's degree	42.7	10.9	3.0	1.1
Associate's degree	8.2	4.0	0.8	0
Postsecondary vocational education	.7	14.4	3.1	1.7
Work experience	5.8	14.5	7.7	0
Long-term on-the-job training	6.4	14.8	6.9	4.3
Moderate-term on-the-job training	0.7	26.7	20.0	1.4
Short-term on-the-job training	0	12.7	58.2	91.5

Source: Authors' calculations using *National Occupational Employment, Earning and
Training Database, 1996–2006,* provided by U.S. Bureau of Labor Statistics, March
1998.

Table 2.8 OCCUPATIONS WITH LARGEST PROJECTED ABSOLUTE INCREASE IN
   EMPLOYMENT, 1996–2006

Occupation	Education and Training Category	Relative Rank of 1994–96 Median Earnings
Cashiers	Short-term OJT	Very low
Systems analysts	Bachelor's degree	Very high
General managers and top executives	Work experience in occupation requiring at least a bachelor's degree	Very high
Registered nurses	Associate degree	Very high
Salesperson, retail	Short-term OJT	Low
Truck drivers, light and heavy	Short-term OJT	High
Home health aides	Short-term OJT	Very low
Teacher's aides and educational assistants	Short-term OJT	Very low
Nursing aides, orderlies, and attendants	Short-term OJT	Very low
Receptionists and information clerks	Short-term OJT	Low
Teachers, secondary school	Bachelor's degree	Very high
Child care workers	Short-term OJT	Very low
Clerical supervisors and managers	Work experience in a related occupation	High
Database administrators, computer support specialists, and all other computer scientists	Bachelor's degree	Very high
Marketing and sales worker supervisors	Work experience in a related occupation	High
Maintenance repairers, general utility	Long-term OJT	High
Food counter, fountain, and related workers	Short-term OJT	Very low
Teachers, special education	Bachelor's degree	Very high
Computer engineers	Bachelor's degree	Very high
Food preparation workers	Short-term OJT	Very low

Sources: *Occupational Outlook Quarterly* (Winter 1997–98, vol. 41, no. 4: 15), and
   Employment Outlook, 1996–2006: Summary of BLS Projections, BLS Bulletin 2502
   (U.S. Bureau of Labor Statistics) (February 1998: 66–78).
Note: OJT, on-the-job training.

Table 2.9 OCCUPATIONS WITH FASTEST PROJECTED EMPLOYMENT GROWTH, 1996–2006

Occupation	Education and Training Category	Relative Rank of 1994–96 Median Earnings
Database administrators, computer support specialists, and all other computer scientists	Bachelor's degree	Very high
Computer engineers	Bachelor's degree	Very high
Systems analysts	Bachelor's degree	Very high
Personal and home care aides	Short-term OJT	Very low
Physical and corrective therapy assistants and aides	Moderate-term OJT	Very low
Home health aides	Short-term OJT	Very low
Medical assistants	Moderate-term OJT	Low
Desktop publishing specialists	Long-term OJT	High
Physical therapists	Bachelor's degree	Very high
Occupational therapy assistants and aides	Moderate-term OJT	Low
Paralegals	Associate's degree	High
Occupational therapists	Bachelor's degree	Very high
Teachers, special education	Bachelor's degree	Very high
Human services workers	Moderate-term OJT	Very low
Data-processing equipment repairers	Postsecondary vocational training	High
Medical records technicians	Associate's degree	High
Speech-language pathologists and audiologists	Master's degree	Very high
Dental hygienists	Associate's degree	High
Amusement and recreation attendants	Short-term OJT	Low
Physician assistants	Bachelor's degree	Very high

Sources: *Occupational Outlook Quarterly* (Winter 1997–98, vol. 41, no. 4: 14), and *Employment Outlook, 1996–2006: Summary of BLS Projections,* BLS Bulletin 2502 (U.S. Bureau of Labor Statistics) (February 1998: 66–78).
Note: OJT, on-the-job training.

and 2006. Among the 20 occupations expected to generate the largest absolute increase in employment, 10 require only short-term on-the-job training, of which all, except for truck drivers, provide low or very low earnings. Of the 11 occupations offering very high or high relative earnings, 8 require an associate's degree or higher academic credential or long-term on-the-job training (table 2.8). Among the 20 occupations with the fastest projected employment growth rates,

8 require at least a bachelor's degree, 3 require an associate's degree, 5 require moderate- to long-term on-the-job training, and 1 requires postsecondary vocational training (table 2.9).[14]

The picture that emerges from the review of demand-side projections is stark and straightforward. Long-term on-the-job training or an associate's degree or higher academic qualification is increasingly needed to gain access to occupations in today's economy offering relative wages above the lowest quartile.

TRAINING REALITIES

Demand-side occupational projections suggest moderate- to long-term on-the-job training or two or more years of postsecondary formal education as the most certain path to employment offering family-sustaining wage and salary levels. A brief review of paths of access to such training activities is included here. Subsequent chapters in this volume offer greater detail on the points made here.

A number of training activities both inside and outside of firms have consistently been found to be successful in raising the wages and productivity of U.S. workers. Formal company training programs and apprenticeship training that lead to journeyman status or licensing/skill certification frequently have been found to have large and sustained effects on the hourly earnings and estimated productivity of trainees.[15] Formal company training, however, tends to be provided only to a minority of workers and at much higher rates to workers who possess more years of formal schooling and higher literacy proficiencies, with four-year college graduates the most likely recipients of such training.[16] Less-educated, less-literate, and low-skilled workers are the least-likely recipients of formal employee-provided training.

The amount of formal and informal training received by workers from their employers also varies by firm size, type of industry, unionization status, degree of complexity of the organization, and demographic characteristics of the workers.[17] Larger establishments as measured by level of employment typically provide more formal training than do medium or small companies, but even here training hours per worker have been found recently to equal only 1 percent of annual work hours (U.S. Department of Labor 1996).

Apprenticeship training is quite limited in scale in the United States and is concentrated in construction and some manufacturing industries. Only 1 to 2 percent of U.S. high school graduates participate in such programs in the early years following high school, with only an additional 1 to 2 percent doing so in their early to mid-twenties. Recent efforts to develop new youth apprenticeships through the School-to-Work Opportunities Act of 1994 have met with only limited success.[18]

Despite fairly widespread concern by employers over the literacy skills of front-line workers, only a small fraction (11 to 13 percent) of adult workers with limited to moderate literacy and numeracy proficiencies report having received any basic skills training since leaving school, and a majority of those obtained it from public educational agencies or community-based organizations outside of the workplace. Findings from the 1992 National Adult Literacy Survey revealed that only 4 percent of 25- to 64-year-old labor force participants had ever received basic skills training from their employers or a labor union, and that workers in the lowest proficiency group were no more likely than their more literate counterparts to have received such training (Sum 1996: 142–44). Many enrollees in Job Training Partnership Act (JTPA) Title IIA and III programs have severe reading and mathematics deficiencies; however, many of them either do not receive literacy training or spend little time in such training during the course of their program participation. Scant evidence is available on the effectiveness of such instruction in either raising their literacy or math proficiencies or promoting their employability upon leaving the program.[19] Available research evidence on the effectiveness of literacy training in raising worker wages and earnings suggests that only basic skills training provided by employers has positive and significant wage effects.[20] Evaluations of literacy and general equivalency diploma education programs for welfare recipients also provide little positive evidence of favorable earnings effects.

A number of federally funded employment and training programs for unemployed and economically disadvantaged adults have been found to be moderately successful in raising the annual earnings of participants.[21] (Some of these are reviewed in detail in other chapters in this volume.) By way of generalization, analysis of the sources of improvement in these annual earnings often has revealed that the bulk of earnings gains were attributable to increases in labor force attachment and average time worked during the year, rather than to gains in average hourly earnings. These programs seem to have facilitated reentry into the labor force and perhaps have provided access to more-stable or more-satisfying jobs that increased incentives to work more hours. Such training, however, often has had little significant positive impact on average hourly earnings, a reasonable proxy for job productivity.

One likely reason for the restricted hourly earnings effects of federally funded employment and training programs and of literacy programs is the limited duration and intensity of much of the training provided. For example, in chapter 10 of this volume, Garth Mangum points out that JTPA adult training in the late 1980s achieved an average training duration of only 24 weeks. He presents more detailed data from 1993–94 reporting an average of 34 weeks and demonstrates a positive relationship between hours of training received, the hourly wage at training termination, and the weekly wage 13 weeks following completion of training. For the majority of program participants, the training enabled hourly wages barely sufficient to reach the federal poverty level for a family of four. A recent analysis (Mangum et al. 1999: 20), of the 1996 Standardized Program Information Report data for JTPA revealed that the average participant in a classroom training program reports only 325 hours of instruction. Total hours of instruction range from 120 for those at the 20th percentile to 564 for those at the 80th percentile. With an average academic year involving approximately 1,200 hours of classroom time, total hours of JTPA classroom and on-the-job instruction seem to be quite moderate for the typical JTPA enrollee (Mangum et al. 1999: 20).

The limited hourly earnings outcomes of such programs are also reflected in the occupations for which training has been provided. Eleven occupations have accounted for over half of the occupation-specific training provided by federally funded employment and training programs beginning with the Manpower Development and Training Act in 1962. These are clerk/typist/word processor, secretary, electronic assembler, machinist, custodian, nurse's aide, salesperson, licensed practical nurse, bookkeeper, food service worker, and computer operator. Most of these occupations appear in the "very low" and "low" categories on the BLS rankings of occupations by relative median earnings. It is this same class of occupations, and the people that hold them, that have experienced the undesirable side effects of U.S. economic and wage growth patterns over the past two decades.

THE CHALLENGE

The demographic and economic picture that we have painted constitutes a major challenge for federally funded training programs in the United States and for U.S. training policy in general. At the risk of being labeled pessimists, we believe that the challenge, while complex, is easier to define than to solve. The BLS forecasts above-average growth in both high- and low-skill job openings. If present wage trends continue, those in low-skill jobs will fall even farther behind because the relative demand for low-skill workers has fallen. Broadly, the challenges are:

- To navigate a changing terrain of occupational skill demands requiring either longer-term on-the-job training and work experience or more extensive postsecondary formal education, specifically an associate's degree or more advanced;
- To shift training to occupations offering significantly higher average hourly earnings than the occupations in which these programs have characteristically trained; and
- To leverage federal, state, and other funding sources to support the more-extensive training required by the realities of the job market for graduates to secure adequate annual earnings.

Again, we emphasize that we are more adept at posing the challenge than responding to it. While many of the chapters in this volume offer glimpses at responses, several comments regarding desirable overall strategies seem appropriate.

One strategy for public-funded employment and training programs is to focus on preparing clients to enter moderate or long-term on-the-job training in the private sector. Some School-to-Work (STW) programs are designed expressly for this purpose, and several demonstration programs have attempted to provide preapprenticeship training. However, little systematic evidence on the nature or effectiveness of services received by STW participants is available. Trends in private-sector investment on the results of training of so-called front-line workers have not been very optimistic, particularly for workers lacking postsecondary schooling. So, the question becomes: How can we expand the level of informal and formal training undertaken by firms, including apprenticeship training? The answer should entail both an increase in the number of firms, especially small and moderate-sized firms who have provided such training to workers at below-average rates in the past, and an expansion in the training provided by firms that already invest in such training. The Workforce Investment Act of 1998 (WIA) does allow for the use of adult training monies for incumbent worker training to promote the skills of already-employed workers. In addition, several states have recently enacted legislation that would allow unemployment insurance trust monies to be devoted to incumbent worker training for workers in state industries. Such training investments have been used in a very limited way in past federally funded employment and training programs and might usefully supplement other training efforts in this field.

A second strategy for responding to these challenges is to adopt a work-first perspective: the view that any job is a good job and that the best way to succeed in the labor market is to join it, developing work habits and skills on the job rather than in a classroom. Such an approach does not rule out future training, but it emphasizes work as a critical step in a "learn while earning" framework. Recent evidence from the Manpower Demonstration Research Corporation indicates that both training and work-first strategies can raise participants' post-program earnings.[22] Longer-term evidence on the effectiveness of these two approaches is clearly desirable, as well as further experimentation with longer-term training and education investments in public assistance and other economically disadvantaged individuals. Other questions then arise: To boost the hourly wages of lower-paid and less-skilled workers, how can firms be induced to provide more training opportunities to less-educated and less-skilled front-line workers? How can more effective links be built between community-based literacy programs and employers to increase the likelihood that gains in literacy and in formal educational credentials will be converted into long-term gains in employment, wages, and earnings?

A third strategy is to focus on human capital development by providing the education and job training necessary to raise skill levels and productivity in order to command family-sustaining earnings levels. Here the question is: How can future training programs for the economically disadvantaged, public assistance recipients, and dislocated workers be tied more closely to the employment needs of the nation's employers so that the economic impacts of such publicly funded investments can be improved? A number of complementary training and placement strategies will likely have to be implemented to achieve these desired objectives. As stated earlier, the mix of occupations for which training is provided must be altered if training under the Workforce Investment Act is to allow access to higher wages. The goal should be to train for occupations offering a family-sustaining wage.[23] This will involve more extensive and costlier training interventions that will have to be justified on the basis of higher future productivity, real wages, and annual earnings.[24] Further, such training will have to be geared closely to local labor market demands of employers to guarantee that program graduates obtain access to jobs in training-related occupations that increase prospects for wage and employment gains. Added emphasis needs to be given to job placement activities. Program performance standards must incorporate and meet these needed changes.

In sum, a number of problems exist at the lowest end of U.S. labor markets. In terms of the relationship between real earnings of workers and education and skills, only the most educated (those with advanced academic degrees) have managed real earnings gains in recent years.[25] The underskilled, low-wage end of the labor pool has fared particularly poorly—actually losing ground relative to its position in earlier years. It is this part of the workforce that now faces growing competition from renewed growth in the youth population and the continuation of large immigration flows, both legal and undocumented. Welfare reform will likely contribute to the dilemma by adding a couple of million low-educated, low-skilled welfare recipients—displaced by benefit time limits and stiff work requirements—to those needing employment at the low end of the labor market.

The distribution of projected job openings by occupation and earnings through 2005 is concentrated among occupations in the highest and lowest earnings quartiles. While occupations in the top two quartiles account for 60 percent of projected employment growth, these occupations generally require significant postsecondary formal education or long-term on-the-job training. Plenty of jobs will be available that require only short-term training, but these jobs offer very low earnings. The education and training required to assist individuals to achieve employment at nonpoverty wages necessitate greater training intensity, on average, than in years past. In today's environment, training programs—like Alice in Wonderland—must run faster just to stand still. Unless the United States wants increasingly to be engaged in preparing people for poverty-level jobs, society will have to financially underwrite preparation for higher-level occupations. This requires a financial and philosophical commitment well beyond that which is currently apparent in both practice and WIA. The WIA's primary emphasis seems to be on a work-first strategy and relatively short-term training—the latter of which will likely have a very limited effect in raising postprogram earnings of future participants. We strongly believe that training investments under the WIA should be targeted to longer-term training in occupations that allow enrollees to obtain access to jobs with earnings in at least the third earnings quartile as developed by the Bureau of Labor Statistics.

Notes

1. See Sum, Fogg, and Taggart (1996).

2. See Wilson (1997) and Holzer (1996).

3. See Jacobsen, LaLonde, and Sullivan (1993).

4. See Nightingale and Haveman (1995) and O'Neill and O'Neill (1997).

5. See Freeman and Katz (1994) and Blau and Kahn (1996). For an alternative view, see Lerman (1997).

6. The data referred to throughout this section are from the following publications: U.S. Department of Labor (1997; 1997–98; and 1998a, b); another source was the *National Occupational Employment, Earning and Training Database*, Bureau of Labor Statistics, March 1998.

7. In a recent evaluation of the accuracy of the 1995 national labor force projections, the BLS revealed that it underestimated the size of the civilian labor force by 3.136 million. All of the shortfall was attributable to underestimation of the 1995 civilian noninstitutional population due to undocumented immigration. See Fullerton (1997).

8. See Fullerton (1995). The U.S. Bureau of Labor Statistics' labor force projections incorporate Bureau of the Census assumptions regarding the expected levels of net immigration from abroad. These assume 820,000 net immigrants per year through 2005. In contrast, the "high growth" labor force scenario is based on the assumption of 1.37 million net immigrants per year. While BLS labor force projections incorporate information on expected levels of foreign immigration, the BLS does not explicitly project the numbers of foreign immigrants who will be active in the civilian labor force during any given future year or their geographic distribution across the country.

9. According to Green (1997), the estimated number of Hispanics in the civilian labor force in early 1997 was revised upward by 352,000, exceeding the total net adjustment in the nation's labor force. In early 1997, the U.S. Bureau of the Census adjusted upward its estimate of the number of persons in the civilian noninstitutional working-age population (ages 16 years or older) by 468,000 on the basis of revised estimates of the number of undocumented immigrants and the age distribution of emigrants. The BLS then revised upward its estimate of the civilian labor force by 317,000 in early 1997, nearly all of whom were Hispanic immigrants. Legal immigration into the United States also accelerated in 1996, with the Immigration and Naturalization Service reporting that just under 1 million new legal immigrants arrived in the United States during 1996, exceeding the previous year's total by nearly 200,000, or 27 percent. A substantial share of these new immigrants arrived in the Middle Atlantic and Pacific regions. The state of California alone was the destination for 210,000 of these new immigrants.

10. The groupings within the private-services division are business services; health services; social services; hotel and other lodging places; personal services; auto repair services and garages; miscellaneous repair shops; motion pictures; amusement and recreation services; legal services; educational services; membership organizations; museums, botanical gardens, and zoological gardens; and engineering, management, and related services.

11. The BLS, in turn, has critiqued some of Bishop's findings and his methodology. See Rosenthal (1997).

12. These findings on recent occupational employment trends are perplexing in a number of respects. The estimated high rate of growth of employment in management-related occupations may be partly associated with a growing tendency for employed

respondents to report themselves to Census interviewers as occupying management positions at a rate well above that reported by employers. A recent comparison by Neal H. Rosenthal of 1993 occupational staffing patterns based on the Current Population Survey (CPS) household survey and the Occupational Employment Survey establishment matrix revealed that respondents to the CPS household survey were about one-third more likely than employers to report themselves as holding management-related jobs (see Rosenthal 1995). A key question for labor market analysis is whether this tendency toward overreporting of management positions in the CPS survey has intensified in recent years or whether firms have truly increased the relative demand for management workers. In 1992, only 12.4 percent of the employed in the CPS survey classified themselves as holding a management-related job, whereas 14.0 percent did so in 1996.

13. Within-occupation changes in skill requirements are not captured in employment projections. Changes such as those due to the introduction of new technologies, reengineering of work processes, or implementation of new management systems are examples. Studies of the impact of such changes on skill requirements include Bailey (1991) and Cappelli et al. (1997).

14. Projections by education and training category and by median earnings assume no change will occur in the relative earnings across occupations or in the education and training requirements of the occupation. Projections also assume that training method patterns evident in 1994 will continue over the projected period.

15. See Lynch (1994); Bishop (1994); Mangum and Adams (1987); and Black and Lynch (1996).

16. See Veum (1993); Sum, Johnson, and Fogg (1996); and U.S. Department of Labor (1993a, b).

17. See Lynch (1988); Altonji and Spletzer (1991); Jacobs, Lukens, and Useem (1996); and Mangum (1989).

18. See Hollenbeck (1997).

19. See Mangum, Mangum, and Sum (1998: 98–99).

20. See Hollenbeck (1993) and Sum and Fogg (1997).

21. See Mangum and Walsh (1973); Bloom and McLaughlin (1982); Bloom et al. (1992); Bloom (1993); and Orr et al. (1996).

22. See Manpower Demonstration Research Corporation (1996).

23. A list of growing occupations accessible to workers with no more than two years of postsecondary education and paying wages consistent with the upper quartiles of the U.S. earnings distribution can be found in appendix I of Mangum et al. (1998).

24. See Heckman (1996).

25. See Mishel, Berstein, and Schmitt (1997).

References

Altonji, Joseph G., and James R. Spletzer. 1991. "Worker Characteristics, Job Characteristics, and the Receipt of On-the-Job Training." *Industrial and Labor Relations Review* 45 (1): 58–79.

Bailey, Thomas. 1991. "Jobs of the Future and the Education They Will Require: Evidence from Occupational Forecasts." *Educational Researcher* 20 (2, March): 11–20.

Bishop, John. 1994. "The Impact of Previous Training on Productivity and Wages. In *Training and the Private Sector: International Comparisons,* edited by Lisa M. Lynch (161–99). Chicago: University of Chicago Press.

Bishop, John H., and Shani Carter. 1990. *The Worsening Shortage of College Graduate Workers.* Ithaca, N.Y.: Center for Advanced Human Resource Studies, School of Industrial and Labor Relations, Cornell University.

Black, Sandra, and Lisa M. Lynch. 1996. "Human Capital Investments and Productivity." *American Economic Review: Papers and Proceedings* 86 (2, May): 263–67.

Blau, Francine, and Lawrence Kahn. 1996. *Wage Inequality: International Comparisons of Its Sources.* Washington, D.C.: American Enterprise Institute.

Bloom, Dan. 1993. *After AFDC: Welfare-to-Work Choices and Challenges for States.* New York: Manpower Demonstration Research Corporation.

Bloom, Howard S., and Maureen A. McLaughlin. 1982. *CETA Training Programs—Do They Work for Adults?* Washington, D.C.: Congressional Budget Office and National Commission for Employment Policy.

Bloom, Howard S., Larry L. Orr, George Cave, Stephen H. Bell, and Fred Doolittle. 1992. *The National JTPA Study: Title II-A Impacts on Earnings and Employment at 18 Months.* Bethesda, Md.: Abt Associates Inc.

Cappelli, Peter, Laurie Bassi, Harry Katz, David Knoke, Paul Osterman, and Michael Useem. 1997. *Change at Work.* New York: Oxford University Press.

Freeman, Richard B., and Lawrence F. Katz. 1994. "Rising Wage Inequality: The United States versus Other Advanced Countries." In *Working under Different Rules,* edited by Richard B. Freeman (29–62). New York: Russell Sage Foundation.

Fullerton, Howard N., Jr. 1995. "The 2005 Labor Force: Growing but Slowly." *Monthly Labor Review* 118 (11, November): 29–44.

———. 1997. "Labor Force Projections." *Monthly Labor Review* 120 (9, September): 5–9.

Green, Gloria Peterson. 1997. "Revisions in the Current Population Survey Effective January 1997." *Employment and Earnings* 44 (2, February): 3–5.

Heckman, James J. 1996. "What Should Be Our Human Capital Investment Policy?" In *Of Heart and Mind: Social Policy Essays in Honor of Sar A. Levitan,* edited by Garth Mangum and Stephen Mangum (323–42). Kalamazoo, Mich.: W.E. Upjohn Institute for Employment Research.

Hollenbeck, Kevin. 1993. *The Economic Payoffs to Workplace Literacy.* Kalamazoo, Mich.: W.E. Upjohn Institute for Employment Research.

————. 1997. *School-to-Work: Promise and Effectiveness.* Kalamazoo, Mich.: W.E. Upjohn Institute for Employment Research.

Holzer, Harry J. 1996. *What Employers Want: Job Prospects for Less-Educated Workers.* New York: Russell Sage Foundation.

Jacobs, Jerry A., Marie Lukens, and Michael Useem. 1996. "Organizational, Job, and Individual Determinants of Workplace Training: Evidence from the National Organizations Survey." *Social Science Quarterly* 77 (1, March): 159–76.

Jacobsen, Louis, Robert LaLonde, and Daniel Sullivan. 1993. *The Costs of Worker Dislocation.* Kalamazoo, Mich.: W.E. Upjohn Institute for Employment Research.

Kochan, Thomas, and Paul Osterman. 1994. *The Mutual Gains Enterprise.* Cambridge, Mass.: Harvard Business School Press.

Lerman, Robert I. 1997. *Is Earnings Inequality Really Increasing?* Washington, D.C.: Urban Institute.

Lynch, Lisa M. 1988. "Race and Gender Differences in Private Sector Training for Young Workers." In *Industrial and Labor Relations Research Association, 41st Annual Proceedings* (557–77). Madison, Wis.: Industrial and Labor Relations Research Association.

————. 1994. "Payoffs to Alternative Training Strategies at Work." In *Working under Different Rules,* edited by Richard B. Freeman (63–95). New York: Russell Sage Foundation.

Mangum, Garth, Stephen Mangum, and Andrew Sum. 1998. *A Fourth Chance for Second Chance Programs: Lessons from the Old for the New.* Policy Issues Monograph 98-01. Baltimore: Institute for Policy Studies, Johns Hopkins University.

Mangum, Garth, Stephen Mangum, Andrew Sum, James Callahan, and Neal Fogg. 1999. *A Second Chance for the Fourth Chance: A Critique of the Workforce Investment Act of 1998.* Policy Issues Monograph 99-01. Baltimore: Institute for Policy Studies, Johns Hopkins University.

Mangum, Garth L., and John Walsh. 1973. *A Decade of Manpower Development and Training.* Salt Lake City, Utah: Olympus Publishing Company.

Mangum, Stephen. 1989. "The Evidence on Private Sector Training." In *Report to the Secretary's Commission on Workforce Quality and Labor Market Efficiency.* Washington, D.C.: U.S. Department of Labor.

Mangum, Stephen L., and Arvil V. Adams. 1987. "The Labor Market Impacts of Post-School Occupational Training for Young Men." *Growth and Change* 18 (4, fall): 58–78.

Manpower Demonstration Research Corporation. 1996. *Welfare Reform: Lessons from MDRC's Research.* New York: Manpower Demonstration Research Corporation.

Marshall, Ray, and Marc Tucker. 1992. *Thinking for a Living: Education and the Wealth of Nations.* New York: Basic Books.

Mishel, Lawrence, Jared Berstein, and John Schmitt. 1997. *The State of Working America 1996–97.* Armonk, N.Y.: Economic Policy Institute and M.E. Sharpe.

Nightingale, Demetra Smith, and Robert H. Havemann, eds. 1995. *The Work Alternative: Welfare Reform and the Realities of the Job Market.* Washington, D.C.: Urban Institute.

O'Neill, David M., and June Ellenoff O'Neil. 1997. *Lessons for Welfare Reform: An Analysis of the AFDC Caseload and Past Welfare-to-Work Programs.* Kalamazoo, Mich.: W.E. Upjohn Institute for Employment Research.

Orr, Larry L., Howard S. Bloom, Stephen H. Bell, Fred Doolittle, Winston Lin, and George Cave. 1996. *Does Training the Disadvantaged Work? Evidence from the National JTPA Study.* Washington, D.C.: Urban Institute Press.

Pfeffer, Jeffrey. 1995. *Competitive Advantage through People: Unleashing the Power of the Workforce.* Boston: Harvard University Press.

Quinn, James Brian. 1992. *Intelligent Enterprise.* New York: Free Press.

Rosenthal, Neal H. 1995. "The Nature of Occupational Employment Growth 1983–92. *Monthly Labor Review* 118 (June): 45–54.

———. 1997. "Bishop's Article in New England Economic Review." BLS Memorandum for Commissioner Katherine Abraham, Washington, D.C.

Smith, James P., and Barry Edmonstan, eds. 1997. *The New Americans: Economic, Demographic, and Fiscal Effects of Immigration.* Washington, D.C.: Urban Institute Press.

Sum, Andrew. 1996. *Literacy in the Labor Force.* Washington, D.C.: National Center for Education Statistics.

Sum, Andrew, and Neal Fogg. 1991. "Labor Market Turbulence and the Older Worker." In *Turbulence in the American Workplace,* edited by Peter Doeringer (64–101). New York: Oxford University Press.

———. 1997. "Literacy Program Participation and Its Effect on Wages and Earnings of Workers." CLMS Working Paper. Boston: Center for Labor Market Studies, Northeastern University.

Sum, Andrew, W. Neal Fogg, and Robert Taggart. 1996. *From Dust to Dreams: The Deteriorating Labor Market Fortunes of Young Adults.* Baltimore: Levitan Center for Social Policy Studies, Institute of Policy Studies, Johns Hopkins University.

Sum, Andrew, Clifford Johnson, and Neal Fogg. 1996. "Young Workers, Young Families, and Child Poverty." In *Of Heart and Mind: Social Policy Essays in Honor of Sar A. Levitan,* edited by Garth Mangum and Stephen Mangum (63–91). Kalamazoo, Mich.: W.E. Upjohn Institute for Employment Research.

U.S. Department of Labor, Bureau of Labor Statistics. 1993a. *Work and Family: Changes in Wages and Benefits among Young Adults.* Report 849. Washington, D.C.: U.S. Government Printing Office.

———. 1993b. *Work and Family, Never Too Old to Learn.* Report 856. Washington, D.C.: U.S. Government Printing Office.

————. 1996. *BLS Reports on the Amount of Employer-Provided Formal Training.* Washington, D.C.: USDOL. July 10.

————. 1997. *Monthly Labor Review* (November).

————. 1997–98. *Occupational Outlook Quarterly* (winter).

————. 1998a. *Occupational Projections and Training Data.* Bulletin 2501 (January). Washington, D.C.: U.S. Government Printing Office.

————. 1998b. *Employment Outlook: 1996–2006: Summary of BLS Projections.* Bulletin 2502 (February). Washington, D.C.: U.S. Government Printing Office.

Veum, Jonathan R. 1993. "Training among Young Adults: Who, What Kind, and For How Long." *Monthly Labor Review* (August): 27–32.

von Hippel, Courtney, Stephen Mangum, David Greenberger, Robert Heneman, and Jeffrey Skoglind. 1997. "Temporary Employment: Factors That Influence Organizational Use and Benefits and Employee Satisfaction." *Academy of Management Executives* 11 (1, February): 93–104.

Wilson, William Julius. 1997. *When Work Disappears: The World of the New Urban Poor.* New York: Vintage Books.

Chapter Three

WELFARE EMPLOYMENT PROGRAMS: IMPACTS AND COST-EFFECTIVENESS OF EMPLOYMENT AND TRAINING ACTIVITIES

Lisa Plimpton and Demetra Smith Nightingale

This chapter synthesizes evidence on the effectiveness of employment programs for adult recipients of Aid to Families with Dependent Children (AFDC), emphasizing particularly the impacts on earnings, employment, and welfare receipt. The main goals of most employment programs for welfare recipients are to prepare participants for the labor market and to assist them in obtaining regular employment. Investing in skills training to help welfare families become self-sufficient is also a stated aim of many of these programs, but relatively few have emphasized education or occupational skills training. Instead, most have focused on low-cost services and immediate job placement.

Research indicates that welfare employment programs have made very modest progress toward achieving increasing earnings and employment among adult welfare parents. Taken together, program evaluations show that:

- Most welfare employment programs that offer low-cost, low-intensity services (like job search assistance and short-term unpaid work experience) have positive impacts on employment and earnings, and in some cases reduce welfare costs.
- More-comprehensive training programs offering services like supported, paid work experience and occupational training generally have larger and longer-lasting impacts.
- Even those interventions with the greatest impacts have been unable to move individuals and families out of poverty or permanently off the welfare rolls, nor have they produced economic self-sufficiency.

This chapter examines evaluations of 14 separate welfare employment programs.[1] The estimated net individual impacts on employment rates over follow-up periods of two to five years range from 2 to 10 percentage points. About half of the program evaluations found no statistically significant impact on employment, although the programs may have had other positive impacts. The net impacts on earnings are more consistent, ranging from about $25 to $85 per month for low-intensity services to $100 or $200 per month for the most comprehensive services, such as occupational training and supported, paid work experience. Earnings impacts appear to last for five years or longer for the more comprehensive programs, but generally wear off by the third or fourth year for less-comprehensive programs. A substantial portion of the earnings increases produced by less-comprehensive programs reflects an increase in hours worked rather than higher wages.

There is less consistency in impacts on welfare receipt, either in duration of time on welfare or overall grant payments. About half of the programs modestly reduced average monthly AFDC payments. Welfare employment programs have not substantially improved participants' incomes because earnings gains have been offset by reduced income from welfare. For the most part, participation in employment programs has not reduced the likelihood that a family will return to the welfare rolls.

In 1996, the Personal Responsibility and Work Opportunity Reconciliation Act (PRWORA) replaced AFDC, an open-ended matching entitlement grant to states, with Temporary Assistance for Needy Families (TANF), a capped block-grant program. As a result, states now face complex and even conflicting objectives as they redesign welfare-to-work programs. First, the TANF legislation includes federal incentives for states to emphasize rapid employment strategies rather than longer-term education or training; states must meet federally mandated work participation rates and enforce a work requirement for nearly all recipients within two years of their first receiving welfare. At the same time, a five-year lifetime limit on cash assistance for families makes promoting sustainable self-sufficiency essential. This self-sufficiency goal conflicts with that of moving participants quickly into the low-wage workforce, where jobs tend to provide little opportunity for advancement and few benefits.

It is not clear whether welfare employment programs will have the same results under TANF as those observed under AFDC. Clients now face very different expectations and alternatives. There is no federal entitlement to cash assistance for families that meet eligibility criteria, and welfare is no longer a permanent alternative to work for most parents with young children. Compared to the AFDC years, employment rates among welfare-eligible adults will probably rise, but without an investment in skills development, it is unlikely that wages or income will increase or that poverty will decrease.

BRIEF HISTORY OF FEDERAL POLICY

For three decades, federal policy and funding have supported employment activities for welfare recipients (Holcomb 1993). In 1967, Congress mandated that every state operate a Work Incentive (WIN) program. AFDC parents without children under the age of six—about one-third of all AFDC adults—were required to register with WIN, and about one-quarter of registrants, or one-tenth of AFDC adults, actually participated in a WIN activity. Federal WIN funding, though, was very limited, representing only about $100 per AFDC adult nationwide. WIN services and the program's priorities changed periodically over the years, from focusing on skills training and education until the mid-1970s to emphasizing immediate job placement in the 1980s.

Through the 1980s, political debate proceeded about how to reform welfare, but in the absence of legislative agreement, WIN funding was reduced yearly and the program languished. Federal funding for WIN, in real dollars, declined by over 70 percent between 1979 and 1988. The Omnibus Budget Reconciliation Act of 1981 (OBRA) and subsequent related legislation did, though, give states the option of operating "WIN Single-Agency Demonstration" programs, which allowed them more authority over the types of welfare employment programs they operated. States operating WIN Demonstrations were allowed to choose new program and financing options, including the Community Work Experience Program (CWEP, or workfare), whereby welfare recipients were to "work off" their welfare grants in public or community job assignments, and "grant diversion," whereby AFDC grants were converted into subsidies to employers to offset wages paid to welfare parents.

Eventually, the Family Support Act of 1988 eliminated the WIN program and replaced it with the Job Opportunities and Basic Skills (JOBS) training program, which (1) required states to provide a broad array of employment-related services; (2) increased federal funding for both work-related services and supportive social services such as child care; and (3) encouraged states to target resources on those considered less likely to leave welfare on their own, including those with little or no work experience, long-term recipients, and young high school dropouts. The work-mandatory population was expanded to include those parents with no children under the age of three, and states were required to meet minimum standards of participation (e.g., in 1995, 20 percent of the average monthly number of mandatory recipients had to be participating in some work-related activity). In 1995, about 13 percent of AFDC adults were enrolled in the JOBS program nationwide, participating in services that ranged from job search workshops to CWEP to education and skills training (Nightingale 1997).

A separate track of welfare reform developed in the 1980s and 1990s through a legislative process in Section 1115 of the Social Security Act (the legislation that authorized AFDC) that allowed states to receive waivers from certain federal welfare provisions. Section 1115 waiver authority became an increasingly common way for states to pursue their own welfare reforms. The Reagan administration established an interagency board to review and approve state requests for waivers from various federal provisions regarding AFDC, WIN, Medicaid, and the Food Stamp program. The Bush and Clinton administrations encouraged states to develop their own welfare reform demonstrations using interagency federal waivers. By summer 1993, 15 states had received waivers for such demonstrations, many focusing on work requirements and work incentives (Seefeldt and Holcomb 1994). The Clinton administration accelerated the approval process and actively encouraged states to submit waivers, particularly those that would test the time-limit concept. Between 1993 and 1996, 43 states had waiver packages approved, some waiving as many as 30 different federal rules, and several states received waivers for five or more years (U.S. Department of Health and Human Services 1997). The most common waiver requests included expanding earned income disregards, increasing asset limits for eligibility, liberalizing two-parent family eligibility, reducing exemptions from the JOBS participation requirement, and imposing limits on the amount of time families could receive welfare without working (Savner and Greenberg 1995).

The state welfare reform waiver demonstrations, particularly those of the 1990s, were in a real sense precursors to the sweeping national welfare reform embodied in PRWORA, in that these demonstrations generally increased the work expectations placed on recipients and experimented with various time limits. While, under the terms of PRWORA, states are no longer bound by JOBS program mandates, they must meet new conditions. To receive the full TANF block-grant amount, states must meet work participation rates, which increase from 25 percent of all TANF families in fiscal year 1997 to 50 percent in 2002, and from 75 percent of two-parent families in 1997 to 90 percent in 2002.[2] For a state to count a person's work-related participation, the individual must be involved at least 20 hours a week (with hours increasing each year until 2002), and only a limited number of persons in education and training can be counted by the state.

Unlike the earlier waiver demonstrations, which experimented with various time limits, federal law now strictly requires states to deny federally funded TANF assistance to the entire family of an adult who has received five cumulative years of assistance in a lifetime. All TANF adults must be "engaged in work" within two years. No more than 20 percent of a state's average monthly caseload can be temporarily exempted for serious hardships or domestic violence (Greenberg and Savner 1996).

While these changes may encourage states to invest a larger share of resources in welfare employment programs, the shift from a matching grant to a block grant, a mechanism designed to give states more freedom, weakens the federal government's ability to enforce work requirements. States are now free to redefine the population they will serve under TANF, and they can legally avoid expanding welfare employment programs. States can implement programs designed to divert families from welfare with one-time cash assistance and can create up-front requirements, such as job search or immediate cooperation with child support enforcement, that applicants must meet prior to receiving assistance.

Although the structure of welfare has changed, the findings of evaluations of WIN- and JOBS-era programs are still relevant, since the emphasis of welfare has now explicitly shifted from income support to moving recipients into work. Further, many states are continuing work programs begun under JOBS or AFDC waivers without major alterations.

THE PROGRAM EVALUATIONS

The impacts and cost-effectiveness of welfare employment programs discussed here are based on 14 program evaluations conducted over the past two decades or more. We include only evaluations that used experimental or rigorous nonexperimental research designs to measure individual impacts. Table 3.1 presents the key characteristics of these evaluations, whose services and program models range from comprehensive and high-cost skills development approaches to low-cost job search assistance and direct job placement.

The earliest study reviewed is that by Hollister, Kemper, and Maynard (1984), who evaluated the National Supported Work Demonstration, which operated between 1975 and 1980 and targeted four

Table 3.1 CHARACTERISTICS OF PROGRAM EVALUATIONS

Program/ Study Period	Evaluation Setting	Impacts Estimated	Treatment Intensity Level	Study Design	Sample Size	Source(s)
Arkansas WORK, 1982–87	2 county welfare offices	Employment, earnings, AFDC receipt rate, AFDC payments, duration of initial AFDC spell	Low	Random assignment	1,127	Friedlander and Burtless (1995)
Baltimore Options, 1982–87	10 city welfare offices	Employment, earnings, AFDC receipt rate, AFDC payments, duration of initial AFDC spell	Medium	Random assignment	2,737	Friedlander and Burtless (1995)
California GAIN, 1988–95	Welfare offices and community-based organizations in 6 counties	Employment, earnings, AFDC receipt rate, AFDC payments	Varied; medium at Riverside site	Random assignment	33,000	Riccio et al. (1994); Freedman et al. (1996)
Homemaker/Home Health Aide Demonstrations, 1983–86	Demonstration sites in 7 states	Employment, earnings, participation in other education and training, public benefit receipt	High	Random assignment	3,516	Enns, Flanagan, and Bell (1987); Gueron and Pauly (1991)
JOBS Evaluation, 1988–ongoing	Welfare offices in Atlanta, Georgia; Grand Rapids, Michigan; and Riverside, California	Employment, earnings, AFDC receipt rate, AFDC payments	LFA low; HCD medium	Random assignment	2,604	Freedman and Friedlander (1995)
Maine Training Opportunities in the Private Sector (TOPS), 1983–86	Local welfare offices	Employment, earnings, AFDC receipt	Medium	Random assignment	444	Auspos, Cave, and Long (1988)
Massachusetts Employment and Training (ET) Choices, 1987–88	58 local welfare offices	Employment, earnings, AFDC payments, duration of initial AFDC spell	Varied	Matched comparison	5,164	Nightingale et al. (1991)

Program	Location	Outcomes measured	Intensity	Design	Sample size	Citation
Minority Female Single Parent (MFSP) Demonstration, 1984–91	Community-based organizations in Atlanta, Providence, San Jose, and Washington, D.C.	Employment, earnings, public assistance receipt, total income, health insurance coverage	Varied; high at CET	Random assignment	3,352	Gordon and Burghardt (1990); Zambrowski and Gordon (1993)
New Jersey On-the-Job Training (OJT) Program, 1984–87	Local welfare offices	Employment, earnings, AFDC receipt	Medium	Random assignment	994	Freedman, Bryant, and Cave (1988)
New York Child Assistance Program (CAP), 1989–95	CAP offices in 3 counties	Household earnings, child support, public assistance receipt, administrative costs	N.A.	Random assignment	4,300	Hamilton et al. (1996)
San Diego Saturation Work Initiative Model (SWIM), 1985–89	2 city welfare offices	Employment, earnings, AFDC receipt rate, AFDC payments, duration of initial AFDC spell	Medium	Random assignment	3,210	Friedlander and Burtless (1995)
Supported Work Demonstrations, 1976–79	Community-based organizations in Atlanta, Chicago, Hartford, Newark, New York, Oakland, and Wisconsin	Employment, earnings, AFDC receipt rate, AFDC payments, criminal behavior	High	Random assignment	1,620	Hollister and Maynard (1984)
Virginia Employment Services Program (ESP), 1982–87	11 county welfare agencies	Employment, earnings, AFDC receipt rate, AFDC payments, duration of initial AFDC spell	Low	Random assignment	3,150	Friedlander and Burtless (1995)
Washington State Family Independence Program (FIP), 1988–93	Welfare offices in 5 counties	Earnings, employment, AFDC receipt	N.A.	Comparison sites	10 sites	Long, Nightingale, and Wissoker (1994)

disadvantaged groups, one of which was long-term AFDC recipients. Supported Work provided up to one year of paid work experience, gradual skill development, and extensive support services. The AFDC Homemaker/Home Health Aide Demonstrations, funded by the Health Care Financing Administration and evaluated by Abt Associates, also provided training and paid work experience, specifically in home health care occupations. The demonstrations operated in seven states during the early 1980s.

Manpower Demonstration Research Corporation's (MDRC's) evaluations of 11 WIN-era programs, summarized in Gueron and Pauly's 1991 book, *From Welfare to Work*, form the basis for much of the current knowledge on welfare employment programs. In the interest of brevity, we include here only the findings from six programs: four that were studied for five years and two that provided on-the-job training.[3]

Two of these six programs, Arkansas WORK and the Virginia Employment Services Program (ESP), were broad-coverage, low-intensity programs designed to move as many AFDC parents as possible into jobs. The Baltimore Options and San Diego Saturation Work Initiative Model (SWIM) programs were of medium intensity. Baltimore Options emphasized skill enhancement, targeted a smaller number of clients, and provided a wider array of services. SWIM preceded California's well-publicized Greater Avenues for Independence (GAIN) program; it offered a fixed sequence of activities, strong work requirements, and a limited amount of education and training. The two on-the-job training (OJT) programs, Maine Training Opportunities in the Private Sector (TOPS) and the New Jersey OJT program, offered services of medium intensity. Both were voluntary and relatively small-scale, providing a range of opportunities to participants varying from job readiness classes to full-time training placements in private-sector firms, as well as supportive services.

The Urban Institute's evaluation of the Massachusetts Employment and Training (ET) Choices program provides some of the earliest evidence on the impacts of different training and employment activities within a single program, including low-, medium-, and high-intensity activities.[4] The ET program was voluntary and featured a broad array of education and training services, aggressive marketing campaigns targeted to participants and employers, and generous child care assistance.

The Minority Female Single Parent (MFSP) Demonstration was implemented by community-based organizations at four sites around the country and was evaluated by Mathematica Policy Research. The evaluation included a five-year follow-up at the most successful site, the Center for Employment Training (CET) in San Jose, California, which provided high-intensity occupational training integrated with basic education and relatively comprehensive support services.

The findings from MDRC's evaluation of the California GAIN program, which operated as a JOBS demonstration, are also included in this review. The evaluation studied the program in six sites; one of these, the Riverside County, California, site, which provided medium-intensity services, has been touted as one of the most effective welfare employment programs. The evaluation is also notable because GAIN is a JOBS-era program, while many of the other programs that have been evaluated operated as WIN demonstrations. MDRC's preliminary findings from three sites—Riverside County; Fulton County, Georgia; and Grand Rapids, Michigan—provide initial evidence on the impacts of two different welfare employment strategies: a low-intensity labor force attachment (LFA) model offering mainly job search assistance, and a medium-intensity human capital development (HCD) model offering mainly basic education.

Finally, we include evaluations from two programs that incorporated financial incentives to increase participation in employment and training. These programs did not provide expanded employment services, but coupled traditional job search, counseling, and referral to education and training providers with financial incentives to work and supportive services. The Washington state Family Independence Program (FIP), evaluated by the Urban Institute, offered welfare recipients financial bonuses in addition to their regular grant if they worked in a regular job or participated in education or training. The New York Child Assistance Program (CAP), evaluated by Abt Associates, offered participants an alternative to AFDC that provided financial allowances for children of recipients who agreed to extensive coordination with child support enforcement efforts. CAP participants also received enhanced case management services designed to help them move into employment.

Research Design Issues

Most of the evaluations discussed here used an experimental design, in which participants were randomly assigned to a treatment (experimental) group that could participate in program activities or to a control group that was denied services through the program. This design was reliable for estimating net individual impacts because it compared two groups that were statistically identical except for having received the intervention. Program impacts were estimated by comparing mean outcomes for the two groups. This solved much of the problem of selection bias, which nonexperimental evaluations must attempt to overcome by using econometric techniques (Heckman and Smith 1995).

Experimental evaluations with random assignment also have shortcomings, which are often overlooked in interpreting their results. One primary shortcoming of employment and training programs is that the evaluations often treat the programs as "black boxes," that is, estimating the effects of a program's entire package of services. The random assignment designs used in the evaluations reviewed here do not allow comparisons of subgroups of participants, nor are they adequate for estimating separate effects of different services or activities. To address this weakness in other studies, some researchers have used econometric methods and combinations of experimental and nonexperimental analysis to provide separate impact estimates for participant subgroups or for different activities. A few studies, especially in more recent years, have used multiple treatment groups to more adequately measure differential impacts (see Bloom et al. 1994). Unfortunately, none of these evaluations was completed at the time of this review.

Impact estimates in the experimental demonstrations reviewed may also imperfectly measure the actual effects of welfare employment programs. All the evaluations discussed here calculated impact estimates per eligible individual, but the proportion of treatment group members who actually participated in one or more program activities was often quite low, even when the programs were mandatory, as shown in table 3.2. This is explained by a number of factors: random assignment occurred at different points in the enrollment process, enrollment processes varied among programs, and many programs did not have adequate funding to serve all of the eligible (or even mandatory) individuals. The evaluations measure impacts on those *targeted* for treatment, even those who did not participate, rather than on those who actually received the intervention (Greenberg and Wiseman 1992). Individual impact estimates are thus biased downward as estimates of the impact of the treatment, since they are not based solely on those who actually received services.[5]

Substitution bias is another problem that arises in experimental evaluations. Many control group members receive similar services from other community programs, meaning that their experience is often similar to that of treatment group members. To a great extent, experimental employment program evaluations measure program impacts relative to other employment programs in the community, rather than to an absence of services. This problem is especially complicated in longer-term studies. Service embargoes in experimental demonstrations typically last only two years, after which control group members become eligible to receive the same services as treatment group members. Program evaluators typically cautioned that the estimates of earnings impacts for years three through five—for example, in Arkansas, Baltimore, San Diego, and Virginia—"should be treated conservatively as lower-bound estimates of the longer-term effects of a permanent program" (Friedlander and Burtless 1995).

Finally, randomization itself may introduce bias by changing the mix of participants in a demonstration program from what it would be in actual operation. To form a control group, programs must expand recruitment and intake and may even modify eligibility criteria (Heckman and Smith 1995).

Despite the difficulties with experimental approaches, they do represent the best available designs for accurately measuring net individual impacts. But, in many instances, it is not possible to use a random assignment design (e.g., owing to systemwide change, program resistance, or legal prohibitions), and evaluators must then develop nonexperimental methods to answer the research questions of interest.

Different, and potentially more serious, design concerns arise in nonexperimental program evaluations. For instance, the Urban Institute's Massachusetts ET evaluation compared program participants to a sample of nonparticipants selected using statistical matching. The participant sample was specifically designed to allow comparisons of individuals who participated in different program activities. All participants were then compared to a group of AFDC recipients with similar demographic characteristics who had chosen not to participate in ET. Statistical analysis controlled for observed differences among participants in various program activities. The impact estimates, however, may still be subject to bias as a result of unobserved or unmeasured differences between the two groups. The estimates produced by nonexperimental evaluations are typically highly sensitive to the statistical methods used (Barnow 1989; Fraker and Maynard 1987; Heckman and Smith 1995). Because activity assignment is almost never randomized, however, nonexperimental designs have the significant advantage of allowing evaluators to estimate the impacts of each program's activities by comparing groups that actually received different services in a real program environment.[6]

The evaluation of Washington state's FIP, an alternative to the regular AFDC program, used a comparison site nonexperimental design. Five treatment sites were chosen and then paired with comparison sites based on geographic, caseload, and local area characteristics. Research samples were drawn over the same time period at each site

Table 3.2 ESTIMATED PROGRAM PARTICIPATION RATES

Program/Site	Any Program Activity (%)	JSA (%)	Work Experience		ABE/GED/ ESL (%)	Occupational Training	
			CWEP (%)	Supported Work (%)		Classroom (%)	OJT (%)
Voluntary Programs:							
Supported Work Demonstration	97			97			
Homemaker/Home Health Aide Demonstrations	84			84			
Maine TOPS	90	32	68		6		31
New Jersey OJT	84	33					43
Massachusetts ET	100			11	24	33[a]	
MFSP overall	77				17	60	
at CET	85				3	82	
New York CAP	16						

Mandatory Programs:

Arkansas WORK	38	27	3		
Baltimore Options	45	25	18		17[b]
San Diego SWIM	64	51	20		24[b]
Virginia ESP	58	51	10		12[b]
California GAIN overall	N.A.	44/21[c]		53	43[d]
at Riverside	N.A.	50/32[c]		41	
JOBS LFA group	55				
JOBS HCD group	64				

Sources: Auspos et al. (1988); Freedman and Friedlander (1995); Freedman et al. (1988, 1996); Gordon and Burghardt (1990); Gueron and Pauly (1991); Hamilton et al. (1996); Nightingale et al. (1991); Riccio et al. (1994).

Notes: Blanks indicate that data are not available. Follow-up periods for which rates are reported, where available, are as follows: 9 months, Arkansas, Virginia; 12 months, Maine, New Jersey, Baltimore, San Diego, MFSP. Table abbreviations: JSA, job search resistance; CWEP, Community Work Experience Program; ABE/GED/ESL, adult basic education/general equivalency diploma/English as a second language; OJT, on-the-job training; see table 3.1 for translation of welfare employment program names.

a. Occupational classroom training and OJT counted together.

b. Education and training counted together.

c. Proportion of clients determined not to need basic education/clients determined to need basic education.

d. Proportion of clients determined not to need basic education that participated in training or postsecondary education.

and aligned according to the length of time individuals had been on AFDC. Statistical analysis attempted to control for remaining differences between the treatment and comparison sites, including making site comparisons with data from a sample of AFDC recipients drawn from a preprogram period (a "difference in differences" approach). With this design, however, as with all nonexperimental designs, systematic unobservable or unmeasurable differences between treatment and comparison sites may remain (Greenberg and Wiseman 1992).

A number of problems are common to both the experimental and quasi-experimental evaluations reviewed here. In many programs, few slots were available for the more expensive activities that theoretically could improve skills the most, such as occupational training or postsecondary education. Selection of clients for these services is often done by program staff through a partially subjective and even unmeasurable process that makes generalizing program impact results to other sites problematic. In addition, many of the programs evaluated were studied during the early phases of operation, when they had the potential to be unusually dynamic and possibly less effective, rather than after they had reached "steady state" operations (Greenberg and Wiseman 1992).

We offer one final caveat. Regardless of the research designs used, impact estimates from evaluations of AFDC-era welfare employment programs are not directly applicable to the post-1996 context of welfare reform. Because welfare is now time-limited, many families will no longer have welfare as an alternative after 60 months of receipt. This suggests that any program intervention may have greater net employment impacts in the current environment than it would have had under AFDC, when individuals had the option of receiving cash benefits indefinitely.

Thus, the discussion following presents an imperfect guide to the differences in impacts among broad categories of employment and training activities for welfare parents. Our comparison of impact and cost estimates should be interpreted with caution. The welfare employment programs are categorized by primary employment or training activity provided, and these comparisons must be viewed critically. No two interventions were exactly alike, and the same types of activities varied in duration and intensity across programs. As the next section discusses, factors such as implementation and management, and labor market conditions at different sites, may be as important in producing impacts as the services provided. Since most of the evaluations analyzed programs as whole interventions, it is difficult to compare programs or to attribute impacts to the employment/training activity or to activities alone. However, this is the best evidence we have on the impacts of various types of activities. Evaluations differed according to research methodologies; length of follow-up periods; proportions of treatment group members who actually participated in program activities (see table 3.2); the labor market conditions, AFDC benefit levels, and available activities of the research sites.

IMPACTS BY EMPLOYMENT/TRAINING ACTIVITY

Welfare employment programs vary widely in the employment and training activities they provide to clients. Most offer a combination of activities—some programs require a fixed sequence of activities, while others conduct client assessment and then develop varying employment or training plans based on individual needs. For the most part, welfare employment programs have not directly provided participants with the most comprehensive and costly training services, but rather have referred some clients to more-intensive training and education provided by other programs and institutions.

As stated, our program evaluation findings are grouped, where possible, by the program's primary activity. Programs that offered more than one activity to a significant proportion of clients are compared in the subsection entitled "Mixed Strategies." Table 3.3 provides general descriptions of employment and training activities and shows the range of services that fall under the broad categories. Table 3.4 summarizes estimated employment and earnings impacts of the programs by program activity; table 3.5 shows earnings impacts over five years for selected programs; and table 3.6 shows impacts on welfare payment by employment/training activity.

Job Search Assistance

Job search assistance, a relatively short-term and low-cost intervention, is the primary component of programs that aim to move large numbers of welfare recipients quickly into employment. This has been termed a "labor force attachment" or, most recently, a "work-first" strategy. Welfare employment programs have job-search components with varying degrees of intensity. Low-intensity efforts range from unassisted individual job search to one week of group instruction followed by independent job search. Higher-intensity models offer two to four weeks of classroom instruction followed by staff-

Table 3.3 WELFARE EMPLOYMENT PROGRAM ACTIVITIES

Job Search Assistance	Low-Intensity	High-Intensity
	One to five days of counseling or group instruction followed by up to eight weeks of independent job search.	Two to four weeks of classroom instruction, including labor market information and occupational planning, followed by up to eight weeks of assisted job search; may include peer components, such as job clubs.
Work Experience	**Community Work Experience/Workfare**	**Subsidized Employment/ Supported Work**
	Participants "work off" their welfare grant in unpaid positions at public or nonprofit agencies.	Up to one year of paid work experience in a productive job combined with support services, counseling, and/or peer support.
Education	**Basic**	**Postsecondary**
	Adult basic education in literacy and numeracy; preparation for high school equivalency (GED) certification; English-as-a-second-language instruction.	Two-year or four-year college degree program.
Occupational Training	**Classroom Training**	**On-the-Job Training**
	Job skills training in a classroom setting.	Employer-provided, subsidized training in the workplace, often intended to lead to a permanent job.
Incentives	**Basic AFDC Income Disregards**	**Expanded Work Incentives and Benefits**
	Eligibility criteria and earnings disregard rules changed to encourage work; may offer more generous child care allowances, health insurance, and other benefits for those who exit welfare for employment.	

assisted job search and can include peer group components such as job clubs. While job search is the main activity of many work-first programs, these programs may also use strategies such as up-front job search requirements for applicants and one-time payments or benefits designed to divert applicants from going on welfare.

Virginia's Employment Services Program (ESP) and the Arkansas WORK program, both WIN-era programs evaluated by MDRC, provided mainly low-intensity job-search assistance. In Virginia (see table 3.2), 58 percent of the experimental group participated in at least one program activity; just over one-half (51 percent) participated in up to four weeks of individual job search; about 10 percent participated in unpaid work experience; and 12 percent participated in education or training activities. In Arkansas, 38 percent of the experimental group participated in at least one program activity; about one-quarter (27 percent) participated in two weeks of group job search, 60 days of individual job search, or both; only 3 percent participated in another employment-related activity; and 3 to 5 percent participated only in an initial assessment. As shown in table 3.4, MDRC's evaluations found that both programs had significant impacts on employment and earnings after two years. But, as indicated in table 3.5, the earnings impacts were not statistically significant by the end of five years (Friedlander and Burtless 1995).

Also, as suggested in tables 3.5 and 3.6, the impacts from these programs are small compared to those of the more comprehensive programs. Gueron and Pauly (1991) concluded that job search assistance generally increases employment but has no significant net impact on wages or number of hours worked. They found no evidence that job search assistance alone substantially reduces welfare dependence.

Work Experience

Welfare employment programs offer a variety of work experience activities designed to help those without recent job experience get accustomed to the world of work—that is, to regular hours, supervision, exhibiting appropriate attitudes, and routine. Work experience programs vary greatly in intensity. The low-intensity Community Work Experience Program (CWEP), or workfare, has perhaps been the most controversial welfare-to-work strategy. Workfare is distinguished from paid work experience in that, while it is purportedly intended to provide work experience, its main operating feature is usually the requirement that recipients "work off" their welfare grants. In contrast, the most comprehensive and costly form of work experience, supported work, offers both paid job assignments, designed to develop occupational skills, and integrated support services, often including job coaching or counseling. Work experience in the WIN and JOBS programs fell somewhere between workfare and supported work, providing 13-week unpaid assignments to a

Table 3.4 EMPLOYMENT AND EARNINGS IMPACTS AFTER TWO YEARS, BY EMPLOYMENT/TRAINING ACTIVITY (1995 DOLLARS)

Program/Site	Employment			Monthly Earnings		
	Treatment Group Mean (%)	Estimated Impact[a]	Percentage Change[b]	Treatment Group Mean ($)	Estimated Impact ($)	Percentage Change[b]
Job-Search Assistance						
Arkansas WORK	50.4	2.8	5.9	176	24	16.0
Virginia ESP	75.7	3.4**	4.8	326	29*	9.9
Work Experience						
Supported Work Demonstration	42.0	8.5*	20.3	664	215**	48.0
Homemaker/Home Health Aide Demonstrations	N.A.	8.0[c]	N.A.	N.A.	132[c]	N.A.
Basic Education						
JOBS HCD group	35.1	2.7	7.1	207	-2	0.0
Occupational Classroom Training						
MFSP at CET	52.6	2.8	5.6	724	103*	16.6
On-the-Job Training						
Maine TOPS	50.2	6.9	16.0	437	111*	34.0
New Jersey OJT	56.1	-1.7	-3.0	570	70*	14.0
Mixed Strategies						
Baltimore Options	48.7	1.5	3.2	391	47***	13.5
San Diego SWIM	33.7	1.7	5.3	329	43**	14.8

Massachusetts ET overall	44.5	10.1***	22.6	330	84***	34.0
Supported work experience	52.2	15.4***	41.8	N.A.	190****	N.A.
Basic education	32.2	−1.6	−4.7	N.A.	−24	N.A.
Postsecondary education	40.5	1.4	3.5	N.A.	−28	N.A.
Occupational training	43.3	6.5***	17.9	N.A.	111***	N.A.
MFSP overall	47.7	2.3	5.1	446	36	8.7
California GAIN						
Overall (six sites)	64.8	4.3***	7.2	251	48***	23.3
Riverside	72.2	9.9***	15.9	282	84***	42.2
JOBS LFA group	42.5	8.1**	23.5	285	58**	25.5
Incentives						
Washington state Family Independence Program						
New recipients	30.9	2.7	9.5	226	−37*	−13.9
Ongoing cases	20.7	0.5	2.3	129	−10	−7.1
New York CAP	29.4	3.3*	12.6	265	44**	19.7

Sources: Adapted from Maynard and McGrath (1997). Additional sources: Freedman and Friedlander (1995); Freedman et al. (1996); Friedlander and Burtless (1995); Gueron and Pauly (1991); Hamilton et al. (1996); Hollister and Maynard (1984); Nightingale et al. (1991); Riccio et al. (1994); Zambrowski and Gordon (1993).

Note: Postprogram periods for which impacts are reported are: Arkansas and Virginia, years 1–5; Supported Work, months 25–27; JOBS, year 2; MFSP at CET, year 5; Maine, year 2; New Jersey, year 3; Baltimore and San Diego SWIM, years 1–5; Massachusetts ET, month 18 (month 15 for JSA); MFSP overall, year 1; GAIN, years 1–5; Washington FIP, year 2; New York CAP, years 1–5.

*Denotes statistical significance at 10 percent level; **at 5 percent level; and ***at 1 percent level.

a. Percentage points.

b. Calculated as percentage change from the control or comparison group mean.

c. Average across sites; significance level unavailable.

Table 3.5 EARNINGS IMPACTS OVER TIME, SELECTED PROGRAMS
(1995 DOLLARS)

	Estimated Impact on Monthly Earnings ($)				
Program	Year 1	Year 2	Year 3	Year 5	5-Year Average
Job Search Assistance					
Arkansas WORK	19**	25	36**	10	24
Virginia ESP	8	32**	36*	22	29*
Work Experience					
Supported Work	678**	209**	N.A.	73**b	N.A.
Occupational Training					
MFSP at CET a	44	124**		103*	N.A.
Mixed Strategies					
Baltimore Options	15	44***	57***	53*	47***
San Diego SWIM	25**	70***	65***	24	43**
GAIN overall	22***	43***	53***	58***	48***
Riverside GAIN	77***	99***	84***	77***	84***
Incentives					
New York CAP	27**	47**	30	64**	44**

Sources: Freedman et al. (1996); Friedlander and Burtless (1995); Hamilton et al. (1996); Hollister and Maynard (1984); Zambrowski and Gordon (1993).
*Denotes statistical significance at 10 percent level; **at 5 percent level; and ***at 1 percent level.
a. Follow-up periods for MFSP at CET are year 1, 30 months, and year 5.
b. Year 8.

small number of clients who had no prior experience in the regular labor market.

In 1993, MDRC summarized the findings from its evaluations of workfare programs, which served small proportions of the AFDC caseload and limited the participation to one to three months. Annual cost per participant ranged from $2,000 to $4,000. Workfare programs were found to have no consistent impacts on either employment or earnings (tables 3.4 and 3.5) or welfare receipt (table 3.6). The demonstrations, though, did show that states could enforce workfare requirements and that welfare recipients generally accepted the policy and felt the workfare obligation was fair (Brock, Butler, and Long 1993).

Both the Baltimore Options and San Diego SWIM programs included unpaid work experience as an available activity, but the programs used very different program models. In Baltimore the goal was skill enhancement, while SWIM stressed participants' obligation to pay back their welfare grants. The evaluators concluded that there was no evidence that short-term work experience had net impacts on employment or welfare receipt (Gueron and Pauly 1991).

In contrast, the National Supported Work demonstration of the late 1970s provided comprehensive supported work experience assignments and had very strong net impacts. At 15 sites around the country, participants received preassignment preparation and counseling, after which they were placed in wage-paying, subsidized jobs for up to 12 months, entailing closely supervised assignments, with ongoing support, and gradually increasing work demands. One of the four target groups in the demonstration was long-term AFDC parents who had been dependent on welfare for more than eight years, on average. In the second year after enrollment, mean treatment group monthly earnings exceeded the control group mean by more than $200, a 48 percent difference (table 3.5). Earnings impacts were sustained over many years; in the sixth, seventh, and eighth years after the demonstration, average annual earnings were approximately $1,000 higher than they would have been without the program (Couch 1992: 384). Supported Work also increased the likelihood of employment by 8.5 percentage points, or more than 20 percent (table 3.4), and reduced monthly AFDC payments by more than $100, or almost 25 percent (table 3.6) (Hollister and Maynard 1984).[7]

These employment, earnings, and welfare-reduction impacts are larger and longer-lasting than those of other welfare employment programs reviewed. Only the Massachusetts ET choices program and the Riverside GAIN site had greater net impacts on employment rates (see table 3.4). In fact, the Massachusetts program also offered paid, supported work experience, and the evaluation found that this supported work was the most effective program component in terms of increasing employment and earnings and reducing the duration of the spell on welfare and welfare payments. Approximately two years after enrollment, supported work participants' employment was 15 percentage points, or 42 percent, higher than that of nonparticipants (table 3.4); monthly earnings were $190 higher (table 3.4); and monthly AFDC payments were $135 lower (table 3.6) (Nightingale et al. 1991).

Evaluations of the Homemaker/Home Health Aide Demonstrations—which also involved paid, supported work experience—lend further credence to the positive impacts of this intensive program model. The demonstrations, which operated between 1983 and 1986, provided AFDC recipients with four to eight weeks of classroom training followed by 8 to 13 months of supported work, on average. In six of the seven sites, the program significantly increased earnings over a two-year study period;[8] it improved employment rates and reduced welfare receipt at four of the seven sites (Enns et al. 1987). After three years, annual earnings gains averaged about $1,500

Table 3.6 WELFARE IMPACTS BY EMPLOYMENT/TRAINING ACTIVITY (1995 DOLLARS)

Program/Site	Monthly AFDC Payments			Months of AFDC Receipt		
	Participant Group Mean ($)	Estimated Impact ($)	Percentage Change	Participant Group Mean	Estimated Impact	Percentage Change
Job Search Assistance						
Arkansas WORK	95	−16***	−14.3***	16.1	−3.0***	−15.8***
Virginia ESP	149	−8	−4.9	16.4	−1.0	−5.6
Work Experience						
Supported Work Demonstration	632	−119**	−23.2**			
Homemaker/Home Health Aide Demonstrations	N.A.	−41[a]	N.A.			
Basic Education						
JOBS HCD group	247	−38	−18.2			
Occupational Classroom Training						
MFSP at CET	300	−11	−3.5			
On-the-Job Training						
Maine TOPS	N.A.	9	4.0			
New Jersey OJT	N.A.	−28*	−11.0*			
Mixed Strategies						
Baltimore Options	251	−3	−1.0	17.9	−0.5	−2.7
San Diego SWIM	327	−38***	−10.3***	22.4	−3.9***	−15.1***

Massachusetts ET overall	395	−34***	−8.0***	10.2	−4.2***	−29.3***
JSA	315	−69***		6.8	−5.6***	−45.2***
Supported work	N.A.	−135***	−30.0***	8.8	−9.3***	−51.4***
Basic education	N.A.	34***	N.A.	21.5	4.6**	27.3**
Postsecondary education	N.A.	49***	N.A.	16.5	2.6	18.8
Occupational training	N.A.	−53***	N.A.	10.1	−6.1***	−37.8***
MFSP overall	307	24[a]	8.2			
California GAIN						
Overall (six sites)	336	−25***	−6.9***			
Riverside	261	−45***	−14.7***			
JOBS LFA group	216	−61**	−21.9**			
Incentives						
Washington FIP						
New recipients	245	41***	20.2***			
Ongoing cases	391	11***	2.9***			
New York CAP	499	−15	−3.0			

Sources: Adapted from Maynard and McGrath (1997). Additional sources: Freedman and Friedlander (1995); Freedman et al. (1996); Friedlander and Burtless (1995); Gueron and Pauly (1991); Hamilton et al. (1996); Hollister et al. (1984); Nightingale et al. (1991); Riccio et al. (1994); Zambrowski and Gordon (1993).

Note: AFDC receipt is reported as duration of initial spell (in months) for the Arkansas, Virginia, Baltimore, San Diego, and Massachusetts programs. Postprogram periods for which impacts are reported are: Arkansas and Virginia, years 1–5; Supported Work, months 25–27; JOBS, year 2; MFSP at CET, year 5; Maine, year 3; New Jersey, year 2; Baltimore and San Diego SWIM, years 1–5; Massachusetts ET, month 18 (month 15 for JSA); MFSP overall, year 1; GAIN, years 1–5; Washington FIP, year 2; New York CAP, years 1–5.

*Denotes statistical significance at 10 percent level; **at 5 percent level; and ***at 1 percent level.

a. Average across sites; significance level unavailable.

over all sites (Gueron and Pauly 1991: 195–98). Even after four and five years, annual earnings gains averaged $500 (U.S. Department of Labor 1995: 33).

Thus, the findings from the three paid, supported work experience program evaluations suggest that high-intensity supported work experience is one of the most promising activities in terms of improving employment and earnings and reducing welfare receipt. However, it is also the most costly activity that has been tested, as discussed below. The higher level of investment in skill development and comprehensive support results, though, in greater net impacts.

Education

The economic returns to education for the general population have been extensively analyzed. Educational attainment is positively correlated with lifetime earnings, and there is a clear correlation between low literacy levels and poverty. A national survey found that adults with the lowest literacy levels are 10 times more likely to be poor than those with the highest level (U.S. Department of Education 1989). Education is clearly important to economic security.

Research findings on the employment effects of remedial education for adults, however, are less conclusive. Two studies found no statistically significant difference between earnings of men or women with a general equivalency diploma (GED) and those who dropped out of high school (Cameron 1992; Cameron and Heckman 1993).[9] Murnane, Willett, and Boudett (1995) found, however, that the wages of male GED-holders, compared to men without a GED or a high school diploma, rose faster after they received the GED and that those with GEDs were more likely to subsequently participate in job training programs or postsecondary education. The researchers' most recent work has confirmed that male and female GED-holders are more likely than high school dropouts to pursue further training and education, but reported that few of them complete education programs (Murnane et al. 1997).[10]

Very little evidence is available on the effectiveness of basic or postsecondary education specifically for welfare recipients, possibly because so few welfare programs incorporate educational components. In programs that do provide education, activities have ranged from basic education—including adult basic education in literacy and numeracy, English-as-a-second-language instruction, and preparation for the GED high school equivalency test—to attendance at two- or four-year colleges. However, few welfare recipients in the demonstration programs evaluated participated in education;

more often, the focus was on either rapid entry into a job or occupational training.

Evaluations of programs that did provide, or allow, basic education for a substantial number of AFDC recipients, including Massachusetts ET Choices and the JOBS demonstrations, have found no impact on employment or earnings (table 3.4), possibly because the follow-up periods were not long enough to detect any effects. Findings of the Massachusetts ET evaluation suggest that both basic and post-secondary education increase welfare receipt, at least in the first two years, probably because they prolong the AFDC spell while participants are in school (table 3.6) (Nightingale 1991). Similarly, the California GAIN program, which assigned participants to basic education if they were determined to need it during initial assessment, did not have a measurable impact on academic skills or on earnings directly attributable to participation in education activities. However, Gueron theorized that education services at the Riverside site had "an indirect effect on people's self-confidence and unmeasured skills, factors that made subsequent job search services more effective" (1995: 12). Nonetheless, the overall GAIN evaluation did not find any correlation between the degree of emphasis on basic education and program impacts on earnings for participants with low literacy levels (Bloom 1997).

Other studies have also found limited effects of remedial education. The Baltimore Options program had greater impacts on AFDC applicants with lower educational attainment at enrollment, while the San Diego SWIM program did not. One evaluator has suggested that this may be the result of Baltimore's more readily available remedial education services (Friedlander 1988).

MDRC's JOBS Evaluation, which is ongoing, more directly examines the impacts of the human capital development approach, which provides some combination of skills training and education, postponing job entry in order to increase earning power. Evaluators found that, for a small sample of individuals, basic remedial education increased participants' high school diploma or GED receipt but did not improve earnings. Impacts on employment and AFDC receipt were similar to those of the labor force attachment approach in other JOBS sites (without education services), but earnings impacts were substantially lower (U.S. Department of Health and Human Services and U.S. Department of Education 1996). The authors of the JOBS Evaluation cautioned that the two-year follow-up period "[was] not long enough to capture the full or possibly even the initial effects of lengthy basic education or training activities" (Freedman and Friedlander 1995: 5).

There is also no evidence that postsecondary education has resulted in positive impacts either. Again, this probably reflects the fact that so few welfare-to-work programs have offered these services to a significant number of participants. A survey by the U.S. Department of Health and Human Services found that 15 states' JOBS programs restricted postsecondary education to associate degree programs, and only 9 states explicitly allowed AFDC recipients to enroll in four-year colleges.[11]

In summary, based on the prodigious findings pointing to the economic benefits of education for the general population, there are strong reasons to expect positive earnings impacts of education for welfare recipients. However, little evidence to date supports this premise. Disappointing results in the few evaluation studies that have estimated education's impacts for welfare recipients suggest that traditional stand-alone remedial education programs may not be particularly effective in increasing employment or earnings. The findings reviewed here should not be interpreted to mean that education is not a potentially effective strategy for welfare recipients. The programs in question aimed to improve participants' literacy and numeracy by, at most, a few grade levels. Such an increase is not likely to yield large employment and earnings impacts and should be viewed as only the start of a self-sufficiency strategy. As discussed below, some recent evidence indicates that integrating basic education with occupational training is more effective than providing education alone.

Occupational Training

Few welfare employment programs have provided occupational training—that is, instruction in specific job skills, either in the classroom, in the workplace, or in both settings—to a substantial proportion of participants. This type of training is available to some welfare recipients through JTPA (see chapter 4, by Nudelman, in this volume) and other programs. This section summarizes evidence from the few evaluations of welfare employment programs that did offer occupational training.

CET MODEL: CLASSROOM OCCUPATIONAL TRAINING AND EDUCATION

The most promising findings for classroom training come from the evaluation of the Center for Employment Training (CET) program. CET operates training programs at 30 sites on the West Coast, and the model is currently being replicated in several other sites nationwide with funding from the U.S. Department of Labor and the Rockefeller

Foundation. An individualized training plan is developed for each participant based on an intensive assessment. Clients begin occupational classroom training immediately, and, if they have educational deficiencies, simultaneously pursue basic or remedial education. CET has developed strong ties with local employers, offering training in specific job skills that are in demand in the local labor market and aggressively marketing its trainees to employers. The program also offers extensive supportive services, including on-site child care.[12]

The San Jose CET program was one of four sites in the Minority Female Single Parent (MFSP) demonstration, which tested employability development for low-income minority single mothers, both AFDC recipients and those at risk of becoming AFDC recipients. CET and three other community-based organizations each developed its own MFSP service model. In two of the other sites, participants were required to meet basic academic requirements before pursuing specific occupational training; in the third site, improving clients' employability was emphasized over specific skills training (Gordon and Burghardt 1990). Only CET provided education and occupational training concurrently. Of the four models, CET produced the most positive impacts and was the most cost-effective.

To learn more about the long-term impacts of integrating education and training, the MFSP sponsors funded a five-year follow-up study of CET alone. The program's impact on employment remained significant after 12 months and after 30 months (10.3 and 8.6 percentage points, respectively), but, like most other demonstrations, the effect declined by the fifth year. However, the evaluation found that CET's earnings gains held up better than other programs, as shown in table 3.5. After 30 months, CET had a large, statistically significant impact on monthly earnings of $124; by the fifth year, the earnings impact was still significant, although it had decreased slightly to $103 per month and was concentrated mainly among participants who had a high school degree or equivalent. The impact on earnings persisted during a period of high unemployment and despite the availability of education and training services to control group members through the newly implemented GAIN[13] (Zambrowski and Gordon 1993).

ON-THE-JOB TRAINING

Of the many employment strategies evaluated, on-the-job (OJT) training has had the most consistently positive results for increasing the earnings of disadvantaged workers, including welfare recipients. Research on programs of both the Comprehensive Employment and Training Act (CETA) and its successor—the Job Training Partnership Act (JTPA)—found that on-the-job training was the most effective training activity for welfare mothers (Barnow 1987; Bloom et al. 1994; see also Nudelman, chapter 4, this volume). An early evaluation of WIN employment programs also found that the largest impacts on earnings came from OJT (Burtless 1989). Several features of OJT probably contribute to the positive earnings impacts, including the fact that many OJT programs require a commitment on the part of the employer to hire participants, which helps maintain both employment and earnings after the subsidy period ends. It may also be that actual work experience is as important as the formal training provided.

MDRC evaluated two WIN-era programs that stressed OJT: the Maine Training Opportunities in the Private Sector (TOPS) and New Jersey OJT programs. Both evaluations found substantial earnings impacts. The Maine program offered a fixed sequence of three activities: job readiness training, full-time on-the-job training with grant diversion to subsidize wages, and part-time unpaid work experience for those not ready to enter OJT. The evaluators found that program staff selected the most motivated clients as well as those with high school degrees to participate in OJT (Friedlander and Gueron 1992: 163). This is consistent with the findings of Lurie and Hagen's (1993) 10-state JOBS implementation study; both program staff and employers deemed OJT an inappropriate strategy for most welfare recipients, who are widely perceived to be poorly prepared for work. Over three years, Maine TOPS increased average monthly earnings by more than $100 (table 3.4), a relatively large impact, though smaller than those of Supported Work and the Riverside GAIN site. The program had no statistically significant employment impact (table 3.4), and it did not reduce welfare receipt (table 3.6), probably for the same reason as for the MFSP at CET—most earnings gains accrued to participants who would not have been receiving welfare for long even without the program. This suggests that while the OJT program was intended to provide training, it may have provided a simple wage subsidy in some cases. Three-quarters of the earnings impact was attributable to higher wages or more weekly hours, rather than to increased employment (Friedlander and Gueron 1992: 186).

The New Jersey OJT program, which was evaluated between 1984 and 1987, offered enrollees training placements with local employers for an average of 10 weeks, as well as access to other activities such as job search, unpaid work experience, and referral to education or vocational training. About 43 percent of enrollees were hired into OJT positions (Freedman et al. 1988). New Jersey's program had positive, but smaller, earnings impacts after two years ($70 per month) than Maine's three-year impact and, like Maine, did not significantly impact employment rates. About 90 percent of the earnings gains in New Jersey were explained by higher wages and more hours worked, similar to the findings in Maine (186). Unlike Maine TOPS, New Jersey OJT substantially reduced welfare payments (table 3.6), which suggests that some of the earnings gains it caused accrued to participants who would have remained on welfare longer without the program.

While the earnings impacts of these two programs are substantial and larger than most programs that offered less-intensive treatments, the OJT programs did not result in a net increase in employment. Impacts on earnings were more consistent than those of the less-intensive interventions (job search and unpaid work experience). Some analysts suggest that OJT may be effective because it is a workplace-based activity, providing real work experience and employer-directed training for persons with some minimal work skills or characteristics (i.e., "soft skills") employers desire.

Mixed Strategies

Many welfare employment programs, including most of those referred to in the previous sections, offer some mix of activities, rather than one single activity. In many programs, activities are sequential. For example, SWIM and GAIN required a fixed sequence of activities, usually job search assistance followed by unpaid work experience, basic or remedial education, and referral to occupational training for those who do not find jobs. Other programs, such as Baltimore Options, CET, and Massachusetts ET Choices, allowed clients to choose among employment or training activities, offered multiple activities simultaneously, and often assigned clients to activities based on individual assessments. The evaluations reviewed here suggest that both types of programs can have relatively large impacts. However, programs that recognize that the welfare population is diverse and offer a range of different components to meet varying client needs seem more promising than those that provide the same intervention for all clients.

SAN DIEGO SWIM: FIXED SEQUENCE OF ACTIVITIES

The San Diego SWIM program, evaluated beginning in 1985, required clients to pursue a fixed sequence of activities, starting with job search assistance. Those who did not find jobs within eight weeks were then placed in unpaid work experience slots or referred to education or training. Half of the experimental group participated in job search assistance, one-fifth in unpaid work experience, and one-quarter in education or training. The evaluators found that many control group members participated in the same education and training programs and concluded that the program impacts were largely attributable to the mandatory job search activities. SWIM's employment, earnings, and welfare impacts were substantial after two years, although here, too, the impacts disappeared by the fifth year (table 3.5). Over the five-year follow-up period, SWIM's aggregate impacts on employment and earnings were substantial (about 15 percent) (table 3.4); the program also decreased monthly AFDC payments by 10 percent (table 3.6) (Friedlander and Burtless 1995).

BALTIMORE OPTIONS: ASSESSMENT-BASED MIX OF SERVICES

Like most other WIN demonstration programs in the 1980s, the Baltimore Options program was technically mandatory, but sanctions were rarely imposed for failure to participate (Friedlander and Gueron 1992: 176). The Baltimore program differed from the other programs in that it stressed long-term economic security rather than rapid job entry and did not require a fixed sequence of activities starting with job search. It offered a wider range of services than SWIM and provided more services in-house as opposed to referring clients elsewhere. Service options included job search, remedial education, classroom occupational training, OJT, and 13 weeks of unpaid work experience. Enrollment in the Baltimore demonstration was limited to 1,000 participants per year. The program had greater aggregate earnings impacts over five years ($47 per month) than any of the other WIN programs that MDRC studied for five years (tables 3.4 and 3.5) (Friedlander and Burtless 1995). Table 3.5 shows that the earnings impacts in Baltimore also persisted longer than those of the Arkansas, Virginia, and San Diego WIN programs. Baltimore Options did not significantly reduce welfare receipt (table 3.6), however, which suggests that earnings gains were concentrated among enrollees who would have left welfare for employment even without the program. In addition, increases in welfare receipt for experimental group members who stayed on AFDC longer than they would have otherwise in order to participate in Baltimore Options may have canceled out welfare savings for other experimental group members (Friedlander and Gueron 1992: 176). That is, while broad-based Baltimore Options showed some success for some participants, it came at the cost of longer periods of welfare recipiency.

GAIN: WORK FIRST, BASIC EDUCATION, AND TRAINING

The evaluation of California's GAIN program began in 1988 and studied the program in six sites around the state. The general GAIN model required AFDC recipients to participate in a sequence of activities based on their employability and education. Those who had educational deficiencies were required to enroll in remedial education. While all six sites offered the same activities, administration and service emphasis, as well as measured impacts, differed by site.

The Riverside County GAIN site had larger impacts on earnings and employment (table 3.4) and on welfare receipt (table 3.6) than any of the other sites and also had the lowest net cost per treatment group member, as discussed below. Riverside's success has been attributed to the fact that it placed "more emphasis on moving registrants into the labor market quickly than did any other site" (Riccio et al. 1994). The GAIN evaluators also reported that while Riverside followed the state policy of enrolling educationally deficient clients into education programs, it also required job search. The monthly earnings gains produced by Riverside over five years were $84, much higher than the six-site average of $48 (table 3.4). Employment rates at Riverside were increased by 10 percentage points, or about 16 percent, compared to 4 percentage points, or 7 percent, over the six sites (table 3.4). GAIN also reduced monthly AFDC payments by $45, compared to $25 over the six sites (table 3.6). The earnings impacts at Riverside were highest in the second follow-up year and persisted for five years of follow-up (table 3.5).

The GAIN evaluation found that another site, Alameda County, also produced large earnings gains, the largest financial gains overall being for those participants who had a high school diploma and basic literacy (the group targeted for training rather than basic education). Treatment group members at this site had the largest increase over control group members in participation in vocational training and postsecondary education. In contrast to the Riverside site, for example, Alameda placed greater emphasis on preparing participants for jobs by improving skills through education and training (Riccio et al. 1994). The Riverside site produced a larger impact on employment, but employed participants in Alameda earned significantly higher hourly wages and worked more hours than employed control group members (Bloom 1997: 46). Thus, the Alameda GAIN findings suggest that if the goal is to move participants, particularly high school graduates, out of poverty, more-comprehensive interventions such as vocational training may be more effective than rapid job placement. The Riverside findings, however, suggest that a rapid job entry strategy may be more effective if the goal is maximizing welfare savings in the short term.

JOBS: LABOR FORCE ATTACHMENT MODEL

MDRC's JOBS Evaluation includes studies of the impacts of a labor force attachment strategy that provides job search assistance and unpaid work experience. The Riverside GAIN site plus two other programs—in metropolitan Atlanta and Grand Rapids, Michigan—were included in this evaluation. After two years, this work attachment approach significantly increased employment by 24 percent, increased monthly earnings by $58 (26 percent), and reduced monthly AFDC receipt by $61 (22 percent). Unlike the GAIN evaluation, in which Riverside's results were unique, the subsequent JOBS Evaluation has generally found that impacts appear to be fairly similar across research sites (Freedman and Friedlander 1995), possibly reflecting the fact that other sites had by then followed Riverside's lead. These JOBS impacts, though, are moderate relative to those of the other earlier studies included in this synthesis, as shown in tables 3.4 and 3.6, suggesting that over time they too will decline.

MASSACHUSETTS ET: VOLUNTARY CHOICES

The Massachusetts ET Choices program for AFDC recipients was voluntary, provided a wide variety of services, and offered clients a choice among several options. The Urban Institute evaluation studied AFDC recipients who participated in ET in 1986 and 1987. In 1987, about 70 percent of AFDC adults enrolled in ET, and 50 percent participated in at least one activity beyond assessment. About 40 percent of the participant group studied were in more than one education, employment, or training component. Participation in activities to develop occupational skills was particularly high compared to other JOBS programs—one-third received occupational training either in a classroom setting or on the job, and more than 1 in 10 pursued supported work experience. Almost one-quarter of ET participants were in basic education, and more than one-quarter pursued postsecondary education. ET significantly increased employment (table 3.4); during the study period, almost one-half of the participant group got jobs, compared to less than one-fifth of nonparticipants. The average monthly earnings impact was $84, a 34 percent increase over the comparison group mean. ET also produced a slight decrease in the amount of welfare received, about 8 percent per month, and reduced the median duration of AFDC receipt by more than four months, or 29 percent (table 3.6).

The ET evaluation found that the supported work component had the greatest employment, earnings, and welfare impacts. Other components with substantial and statistically significant impacts were, in order of magnitude, occupational training (classroom and OJT were analyzed together) and intensive job search assistance. However, the evaluation found no significant impacts on the employment, earnings, or welfare receipt for participants in basic or postsecondary education. The study followed clients for only two years after program enrollment, which was probably not long enough to capture benefits of education (Nightingale et al. 1991).

WASHINGTON FIP: WORK, TRAINING, EDUCATION, BONUSES

For over 30 years, various forms of financial incentives have been used to encourage welfare recipients to work. The Washington state Family Independence Program (FIP) operated as a demonstration from 1988 to 1993 in 15 counties. Five counties served as FIP research sites for the evaluation, and they were compared to five comparison counties that continued to operate the regular AFDC and WIN/JOBS programs. FIP provided financial bonuses in addition to the monthly cash grant to recipients who participated in education or training or who worked. FIP also used a higher earnings disregard than the AFDC program in determining welfare benefit levels. Clients' food stamps were converted to cash to increase family discretion in budgeting and to eliminate the stigma associated with food stamp coupons. The program also provided generous child care allowances, and those who left welfare for work were entitled to transitional benefits for the first year, including child care payments and Medicaid (also available to control group members) (Long et al. 1994). In addition to the attractive financial benefits, FIP clients could voluntarily participate in an employment and training program that included job search assistance, counseling, and referral to education and training services.

The impacts of FIP were not in the expected direction. FIP had no significant impact on employment and actually reduced monthly earnings by $28 (table 3.4). Clients in the treatment sites were no more likely to enter education or training than those in comparison sites. The program also increased welfare payments by about $40 per month for ongoing cases and $10 for new recipients (table 3.6). The evaluators provide several possible explanations for FIP's disappointing impacts. First, participants were not offered additional or more intensive employment, education, and training services beyond those available at the comparison sites. This, plus the income effect from increased program cash income, probably accounts for the perverse results. Second, the demonstration operated during a period of rapid caseload growth; although the intent was to have each staff member work continuously with small numbers of families, the number of cases per worker remained quite high, at over 200. Third, the federal government's requirement that the demonstration be cost-neutral compared to the regular AFDC program made state political leaders reluctant to devote new resources to fully incorporate the employment and services components as originally intended. Finally, evaluators found some evidence that participants did not fully understand the program's complicated incentives and financial bonuses (Long et al. 1994). The authors caution readers not to conclude from the FIP experience that financial incentives do not work and suggest that simpler incentives along with stronger employment strategies may have produced different impacts.

NEW YORK CAP: ASSURED CHILD SUPPORT AND WORK INCENTIVES

New York's Child Assistance Program (CAP) was also a voluntary alternative to AFDC, with different rules on disregarding earnings and assets designed to help families end welfare dependence through work. CAP paid a lower basic benefit level than AFDC, but it reduced benefits based on earnings at a much lower rate than under AFDC (i.e., increased the earnings disregard). Unlike AFDC, CAP allowed families to combine benefits and earnings to achieve incomes above the poverty level. The program did not impose limits on assets or the value of clients' cars. Like the Washington program, CAP cashed out food stamp benefits (Hamilton et al. 1996).

CAP began in 7 counties in 1988 and was then expanded to 14. Three counties served as research sites for the experimental evaluation, and the study follow-up period was five years. To participate in the CAP demonstration, a woman's children had to be covered by court-issued child support orders. Those families opting to enter CAP rather than AFDC went to special offices separate from the regular welfare office and were assigned to CAP caseworkers who only served about 40 families at a time.

Although just one in six families in the treatment group participated in CAP during the five-year study period, the evaluation found that CAP increased employment over five years by 3.3 percentage points (measured over all treatment members, whether they participated or not) (table 3.4), an impact that exceeds that of the Baltimore Options and San Diego SWIM programs and is comparable to that of the Virginia ESP (job search assistance) program. CAP's aggregate earnings impact over five years was $44 per month (tables 3.4 and 3.5), which is comparable to the earnings impacts of the Baltimore and SWIM programs. CAP also reduced monthly public assistance receipt by about $15 (table 3.6), but this estimate was not statistically significant. In addition, CAP produced significant savings in food stamp and Medicaid payments (Hamilton et al. 1996). The CAP evaluation findings are important because they suggest that a model that emphasizes changing the structure of cash welfare programs to provide clients incentives to change behavior, combined with intensive case management, may be as effective at increasing employment and earnings as programs that offer job search assistance or job training activities. This contrasts with findings from earlier demonstrations such as FIP, which suggest that behavioral incentives in welfare rules had little effect on client behavior (Moffitt 1992).

NEW CHANCE: COMPREHENSIVE SERVICES FOR MOTHERS AND CHILDREN

Although the final report from the New Chance program evaluation was not available at the time of this volume's publication, some impact estimates have been released and deserve mention here. The New Chance demonstration was implemented at 16 sites to serve economically disadvantaged teenage mothers and their children (nearly all of whom received welfare at some point). The program provided high-intensity employment preparation services, case management, subsidized child care, and services designed to enhance personal and child development. Over a three-and-one-half-year follow-up period, the program increased the level of GED receipt but did not have significant impacts on employment, earnings, or welfare receipt. A nonexperimental analysis of the combined treatment and control groups found that those who received skills training or attended college (through New Chance or another source) earned higher wages than those who did not (Quint, Bos, and Polit 1997).

COST-EFFECTIVENESS

The major welfare employment program evaluations focus mainly on individual impacts, particularly economic impacts such as employment and earnings. Understanding a program's net individual impacts is important to program managers: Did this program make a difference to the individual clients? Another perspective often of interest to policymakers is whether the program's benefits exceed the costs. Cost-benefit analysis measures and indexes costs and benefits in dollar terms (e.g., program expenditures and earnings). A vast evaluation literature exists for distinguishing among different cost-benefit perspectives, including individual participant costs and benefits, government or taxpayer costs and benefits, and social costs and benefits. In many cases, the benefits or outcomes cannot be easily monetized, in which case cost-effectiveness analysis can be useful in relating the costs of the program to particular objectives (e.g., costs per person placed in a job). No single consistent cost-benefit methodology has been used in the studies reviewed, but all include some form of analysis that relates costs and benefits. At a minimum, the welfare employment evaluations reviewed include cost analysis, where the net marginal costs of the demonstration are compared to the counterfactual program or treatment. Most studies also estimate the program's cost per participant, some calculate a ratio of benefits to costs or estimate the rate of return from the investment, and a few estimate social costs and benefits.

Often impact estimates are considered in relation to program costs. For instance, costs per participant or experimental group member are usually compared to the estimates of program impacts on earnings or AFDC payments, or the marginal costs and benefits associated with the program are estimated by measuring the differences between the treatment and control groups. Not surprisingly, program cost is directly related to the types of employment and training activities provided (Friedlander and Gueron 1992). This is illustrated in table 3.7, which shows the costs and impacts as estimated by the respective evaluators; programs are listed in order from most expensive to least expensive. While program costs were calculated somewhat differently across studies, and problems in comparing impacts were discussed earlier, the table gives a rough idea of relative costs compared to impacts of different programs.

The Supported Work and Homemaker/Home Health Aide Demonstrations made a much greater investment per client than did the other welfare employment programs. Both programs also had among the greatest impacts of any that have been evaluated. The cost-benefit analysis in the Supported Work evaluation report indicates that this relatively expensive program produced a high rate of return. Its estimate of the program's value to society, obtained using a real discount rate of 5 percent per year, was more than $20,000, much larger than the estimate for Riverside GAIN ($4,705). A number of alternate assumptions were used to test the sensitivity of the Supported Work estimate, and all combinations yielded positive estimates of net benefits. It took more than three years after client enrollment for Supported Work's benefits to exceed its costs (Kemper, Long, and Thornton 1984), reinforcing the importance of having long follow-up periods in evaluations. Supported Work's program cost per treatment group member was more than $25,000 (Gueron and Pauly 1991), compared to $1,686 at the Riverside GAIN site. The program costs of Supported Work were substantially offset by revenues generated by participants, and a substantial portion of the costs were in the form of wages paid to participants.[14] The Home Health Aide demonstrations cost on average more than $13,000 per treatment group member (Gueron and Pauly 1991) and produced positive net social benefits at six of the seven sites (U.S. Department of Labor 1995).

The California GAIN program, the MFSP demonstration, and Washington's FIP are the only programs other than Supported Work for which cost-benefit analysis estimates of net benefits to society were calculated. FIP resulted in a net social cost of $1,828 per client (i.e., negative present value), but in both the GAIN and MFSP evaluations, some net benefits were identified. The cost-benefit analysis of GAIN determined that, overall, the program resulted in a slight loss to society over five years, including a two-year projection period. The analysis used a real discount rate of 5 percent. Three of the six sites, however, produced net benefits to society. Riverside, which had the lowest net cost per participant ($1,686), produced the greatest net social benefits, $4,705. The Riverside site was clearly very cost-effective relative to other programs of comparable intensity; its net cost per participant of $1,686 was much lower than the six-site average, and its impacts were substantially larger.

A cost-benefit analysis of the MFSP based on impacts estimated at 30 months found that CET (in San Jose) was the only one of four sites that would result in net benefits to society if impacts were projected for five years. This finding led to the funding of a five-year follow-up study, which confirmed the conclusion that CET's MFSP program resulted in net benefits to society of $1,356 per participant.[15] The program's cost per participant was more than $5,000. For each dollar spent, evaluators estimated that $1.23 was returned to society. Most of the benefits of the CET MFSP program accrued to participants in the form of increased earnings, rather than to the government in the form of reduced public assistance costs. The evaluators concluded that the CET site achieved economies of scale by integrating the MFSP with its ongoing training programs.

From available data, it appears that the Massachusetts ET program was also relatively cost-effective. While the evaluation did not include a formal calculation of costs and benefits because the follow-up period was too short to allow estimation of program benefits, especially for the education components, the researchers did estimate costs of the different services. The average cost per participant was $1,845. Supported work was the most costly service, at $4,939 per participant, and also produced the greatest earnings impact ($1,144 for a six-month period). The evaluators concluded that if the average earnings gains ($502 for six months) continued for

Table 3.7 PROGRAM COSTS AND IMPACTS (1995 DOLLARS)

Program/Site	Cost per Participant Group Member ($)	Annualized Earnings Impact ($)	Annualized Impact on AFDC Payments ($)	Net Present Value to Society ($)
Supported Work Demonstration	25,488[a]	1,909**	-2,600**	21,861
Homemaker/Home Health Aide Demonstrations	13,476	2,123[b]	-895[b]	
MFSP at CET	5,425	1,236***	-132	1,356
GAIN overall[†]	3,610	576***	-300***	-67
Washington state FIP	2,944			-1,828
New recipients		-444*	492***	
Ongoing cases		-120	132***	
Maine TOPS[†]	2,862	1,323*	82[c]	
Massachusetts ET overall	1,845	1,004***	-408***	
Job search assistance	1,625	1,692***	-828***	
Supported work	4,939	2,279***	-1,620**	
Basic education	2,138	-294	408***	
College	1,310	-340	588***	
Occupational training	2,236	1,334***	-639***	

Riverside GAIN[†]	1,686	1,008***	-540***	4,705
Baltimore Options[†]	1,398	564***	-36	
San Diego SWIM[†]	1,278	516**	-456***	
New Jersey OJT[†]	1,116	838*	-303*	
Virginia ESP[†]	610	352*	-92	
New York CAP[†]	237	528**	-180	
Arkansas WORK[†]	167	291	-189**	

Sources: Freedman and Friedlander (1995); Freedman et al. (1996); Friedlander and Burtless (1995); Gueron and Pauly (1991); Hamilton et al. (1996); Kemper at al. (1984); Long et al. (1994); Nightingale et al. (1991); Riccio et al. (1994).

Note: Postprogram periods for which impacts were estimated are as follows: Supported Work, 25 to 27 months; Homemaker/Home Health Aide, months 1–18; MFSP, year 5; GAIN, years 1–5; Washington FIP, years 1–2; Maine TOPS, years 1–3; Massachusetts ET, a 6-month period beginning 12 to 24 months after enrollment; Baltimore, San Diego, Virginia, and Arkansas, years 1–5; New Jersey, year 2 for earnings and years 1–2 for AFDC; New York CAP, years 1–5.

*Denotes statistical significance at 10 percent level; **at 5 percent level; and ***at 1 percent level.

[†]Program costs calculated as net of average cost per control group member.

a. Average per-client revenues of $4,352 not subtracted.

b. Estimated across state-specific impacts; significance level unavailable.

c. Average of separately calculated annual impacts over years 1–3; significance level unavailable.

16 months, or the average welfare grant reduction ($198 for six months) continued for four years, either of these benefits would have offset average program cost (Nightingale et al. 1991).

While none of the other studies included social cost-benefit analysis, the evaluators did report some comparison of costs and impacts, and even programs that appeared similar in terms of services offered differed in terms of costs related to individual impacts. For instance, although the Maine and New Jersey programs both offered on-the-job training, their costs and impacts differed substantially. The cost per participant of the Maine program, $2,862, was more than twice that of the New Jersey program, $1,116. Maine's annualized earnings impact, $1,323, was considerably greater than New Jersey's, $838. In addition, the New Jersey program significantly decreased welfare receipt, whereas the Maine program did not. While both programs can be considered cost-effective, it would take longer for Maine's impacts than for New Jersey's to surpass program costs.

In addition, different types of programs have been found to produce individual benefits that exceed costs. Five-year findings from the MDRC evaluations of the Arkansas, Baltimore, San Diego, and Virginia WIN programs, which differed considerably in types and intensity of services provided, also showed that aggregate earnings gains exceeded program net costs several times over. Although net impacts were smaller at the lower-intensity programs, net costs were also much lower. Reductions in AFDC payments, while smaller than earnings increases, exceeded costs for one low-intensity program, Arkansas WORK, and one high-intensity program, San Diego SWIM (Friedlander and Burtless 1995). These findings suggest that a wide variety of welfare employment programs are cost-effective.

The net cost per treatment group member of the New York CAP program was lower than those of all the other programs reviewed except Arkansas WORK, a low-intensity WIN program. CAP's earnings impact compares to those of programs like Baltimore and SWIM, which had much higher costs. This suggests that a well-designed incentive program may be at least as cost-effective as programs that provide employment and training services directly.

There is also a critical benefit-related distinction between the less-expensive programs that featured job search assistance and the few more-expensive programs that offered supported work experience and occupational training services: most of the benefits of the latter accrue to participants in the form of higher earnings, whereas in the former, most immediate savings accrue to the government (or taxpayer) in terms of reduced welfare costs. Benefits from increased wages (to both the individual and the government) begin to count at different time intervals in high-intensity and low-intensity programs. Participants in low-cost, low-intensity programs generally find low-paying jobs fairly quickly, and welfare costs begin to decline immediately as individuals start to receive earnings. Higher-cost and more-intensive programs are more likely to eventually increase wage rates and hours of work, even though it may take individuals longer to obtain a regular job. Because participants may be in training or school, they forgo individual wages and the government continues to incur welfare costs.

A full determination of net program benefits would require a decision about the relative priority, or weights, that should be attached to the benefits that accrue to society as a whole versus those that accrue to the individual or family, and about short-term versus long-term costs and benefits. For example, if one assumes that achieving a more equitable distribution of income is valuable, a strong case could be made for assigning more weight to benefits that accrue to welfare recipients directly (e.g., increased income) and less weight to benefits that accrue to the taxpayer (e.g., decreased welfare costs). While measuring benefits and costs is largely empirical and objective, assigning weights would be subjective, and thus is controversial (Boardman et al. 1996). In any case, the benefits of high-cost programs tend to accrue to the participants. If these benefits received more weight, this would, at least in part, offset the diminishing returns to higher-cost services.

OTHER FACTORS AFFECTING IMPACTS AND COST-EFFECTIVENESS

The findings summarized in the previous sections should be interpreted within a programmatic context that is broader than just the treatments, services, or interventions tested in demonstrations. Most of the evaluations reviewed here as well as other research on program performance and aggregate outcomes devote considerable attention to discussions of other factors, including program implementation, labor market conditions, and changing public policies, that may have influenced the operations of the demonstrations and the impacts observed. The implications of the individual net impacts and the generalizability of the findings from program evaluations must be analyzed within this broader context.

Implementation and Management

Program implementation and management have been recognized as important determinants of impacts. One study estimated that 50 to 70 percent of the variation in performance among WIN programs was explained by differences in program operations and management (Mitchell, Chadwin, and Nightingale 1979). This is illustrated by the striking impacts at the CET site of the MFSP demonstration, as well as at the Riverside GAIN site, compared with the impacts at other sites that offered comparable employment or training activities.

Similarly, Gueron asserted that success of welfare employment programs requires competent administration, including "articulating a clear mission; explaining to staff how this mission affects what should happen between welfare recipients and staff; getting people into quality services; monitoring their participation; [and] addressing problems quickly when they arise" (1995: 13). Evaluators attributed some of the success at CET, Riverside GAIN, Massachusetts ET, San Diego SWIM, and New York CAP to factors including organizational culture, clear objectives, goal consistency, and management priority.

Another service delivery feature that is now increasingly recognized as contributing to program performance is case management, which generally was not examined in the earlier welfare employment program evaluations reviewed. For example, recent findings from an ongoing case management experiment in Ohio suggest that integrated case management leads to higher rates of participation in employment services among welfare clients. Those clients served by a single worker who performed both welfare eligibility and employment functions were much more likely to attend a JOBS orientation session (86 versus 65 percent) and to participate in employment services (52 versus 34 percent) than those served by separate eligibility workers and employment case managers (the traditional arrangement) (Brock and Harknett 1996). Future findings from the study will estimate the impacts of integrated case management on earnings, employment, and welfare receipt.

Mandates and Sanctions

Nearly all of the programs included in the evaluations reviewed in this chapter were part of the federal-state WIN, WIN-Demonstration, or, after 1988, JOBS programs for AFDC recipients. As already noted, federal law required that recipients who were not otherwise exempt (usually because they had very young children) had to register and cooperate with WIN and, later, JOBS. That is, unlike other employ-

ment and training programs such as those funded by JTPA, participants in WIN and JOBS were mandated to participate and could face
sanctions (reductions in welfare benefits) for failure to do so. Under
JOBS, federal mandates also required states to ensure that certain
proportions of their nonexempt AFDC caseload participate in education, work, or training activities for at least 20 hours a week.

In practice, programs' enforcement of this work requirement varied widely. Some programs, including Massachusetts ET and Washington FIP, registered all AFDC clients for the WIN or JOBS programs,
but participation in program activities was purely voluntary. Even
among programs that took mandated participation seriously, there
was variation in enforcement of requirements and application of
sanctions. Sanction rates appear to be related to welfare impacts; programs that actually carry out sanctions have reduced welfare caseloads, expenditures, or both. Sanction rates do not, however, seem
to predict employment or earnings impacts, nor are they correlated
with aggregate participation rates. Participation rates in the Baltimore Options program, which made very limited use of sanctions,
were no lower than those in the Arkansas, San Diego, and Virginia
programs, which used sanctions much more aggressively (Friedlander and Burtless 1995). While the early impact on earnings (for the
program as a whole) was larger in San Diego, where about 10 percent of the treatment group were sanctioned, Baltimore had longer-
term earnings impacts that resulted in higher earnings on the job.
The Baltimore program, however, had no significant impact on AFDC
receipt, while San Diego reduced average AFDC payments by about
$2,000 over five years.

Voluntary programs, including Supported Work, Massachusetts
ET, the MFSP at CET, Maine OJT, and New Jersey TOPS, produced
individual net impacts and participation rates comparable to those of
mandatory programs. About half of the AFDC caseload in Massachusetts, for example, chose to participate in ET (beyond attending
orientation and assessment), and those who chose to participate were
largely representative of the AFDC population as a whole.[16]

The findings from the pre-TANF evaluations reviewed suggest that
mandates and sanctions have not significantly influenced participation rates and impacts. Nathan Glazer concluded that "adding sanctions does not add much" to welfare employment programs and
noted that sanctions are difficult to administer (1995: 27). They are
also costly to administer. Under the new TANF program, early evidence suggests that states are applying the work requirements and
sanctions more aggressively than under AFDC, but that the new time
limit is simultaneously influencing the behavior of individual

clients. Because participation rates among eligible individuals have in the past been comparable for voluntary and mandatory programs, it is unlikely that mandates and sanctions alone (e.g., without employment assistance, case management support, or the fear of reaching a time limit) will increase program participation or entered-employment rates, particularly if additional investments are not made in welfare employment programs. Past experience does suggest that mandates and sanctions will reduce welfare caseloads.

The Labor Market

The earnings impacts of welfare employment programs have been significant in many studies. Even the large Supported Work earnings impacts, however, only covered about one-quarter of the gap between the 1990 poverty line and the earnings of the former welfare parents who participated. It is unlikely that employment and training programs alone will succeed in moving many families out of poverty. Gary Burtless has pointed out that even if programs doubled or tripled earnings, most families would still have had below-poverty incomes (1995: 100).

In large part this probably reflects the fact that skills have become increasingly important in determining earnings (Blank 1995: 43). In fact, many economists assert that much of the rising wage inequality in the United States is explained by growing employer demand for more highly skilled workers. Research on the labor market and on the employment prospects for welfare recipients suggests that programs that do not invest in developing occupational skills cannot be expected to greatly improve earnings. The fairly modest employment and earnings impacts of the evaluations reviewed confirm this point. Women on welfare, most of whom have low skills, face a labor market "with low-paid jobs, relatively high unemployment and high turnover, and few fringe benefits" (Blank 1995: 63) and "a surplus of low-skilled workers in a market requiring more skill than ever" (Burtless 1995: 94). Combined with the limited nature of opportunities for low-skill workers, the fact that few of the welfare employment programs evaluated invested in skill development may help explain the relatively modest impacts achieved.

Public Attitudes and the Welfare Stigma

A number of past studies have documented the stigmatizing effects of employment and training programs for disadvantaged people. Evidence from a study by Burtless (1985) of targeted wage subsidies suggested that employers use information provided by wage subsidy vouchers to discriminate against welfare recipients. In the study, a sample of welfare recipients eligible for the Targeted Jobs Tax Credit was randomly assigned to treatment and control groups; treatment members were given tax credit vouchers to show employers during their job search, and control members were not informed of their eligibility for the credit. More than 20 percent of controls found jobs, while only 13 percent of treatments did, a statistically significant difference. These findings substantiate anecdotal evidence that many employers have regarded welfare recipients as poor risks and have been reluctant to hire them. A number of job placement programs Burtless studied avoided notifying potential employers of clients' eligibility for tax credits or training subsidies because they found that this information actually discouraged employers, particularly small businesses, from hiring their clients.

Welfare employment programs may have a similar stigmatizing effect. Bishop has argued that "training programs develop local reputations that in turn influence the wage offers their graduates receive" (1989: 210). He suggested that earnings impacts are not a reliable measure of training programs' productivity because "a systematic bias results from the fact that participating in a program often informs employers that the trainee is a member of a stigmatized target group" (212). The relatively short time period during which impacts are observed may not be long enough for any stigma to wear off, so estimated earnings impacts may underestimate the actual productivity effects of welfare employment programs.

More recent evidence suggests that employer attitudes in the mid-1990s have tempered somewhat. Many employers who have hired TANF recipients report that they are quite satisfied with their new workers and that they compare favorably with other new employees (Myers and Regenstein 1998). It is not clear whether this reflects a real change in employer attitudes toward welfare recipients, possibly because of the public information campaigns associated with welfare reform, or whether this simply is related to the very tight labor market and to the difficulty firms are having in finding workers.

POLICY IMPLICATIONS

The findings synthesized here suggest that a welfare-to-work strategy that focuses exclusively on placing welfare recipients into private-sector jobs will have modest positive impacts and will likely be cost-effective, but will not move AFDC families permanently out of poverty. Low-intensity welfare employment programs that offer mainly job search activities have small, significant impacts on employment and earnings and can reduce welfare receipt. But these impacts generally appear to last no more than three or four years. Most past programs did not reduce the likelihood of returning to AFDC. Programs that offer higher-intensity, more-expensive, and more-comprehensive training activities have greater impacts on earnings, but they still fall short of moving families out of poverty.

These findings have important implications, given the recent changes in federal welfare rules. Many states are now pursuing a work-first approach featuring job search assistance and limited unpaid work experience for those who do not find jobs, in an attempt to meet TANF work requirements. Although most recipients may eventually find jobs, many will not stay employed, and few will earn enough to escape poverty. This is particularly important now, with the federal time limit of 60 months for cash assistance. Even with the added value of the expanded Earned Income Tax Credit, only those welfare recipients who maintain employment continuously for several years will be able to remain permanently out of poverty.

The most salient factor to consider when choosing a welfare employment and training strategy may be the program goal. Programs aimed at lifting families out of poverty will likely place greater value on benefits that accrue to participants in the form of greater earnings than on short-term savings to government budgets. More-comprehensive programs providing skills training and support services and requiring greater investments are the best choice to meet this long-term goal. If the primary goal is to move families into work and off welfare quickly, a strategy providing mainly job search assistance may be sufficient. The impacts of these low-intensity programs, however, have disappeared within three to five years, so this is likely only a short-term solution.

Finally, the welfare population is not homogeneous, and there is clear evidence that welfare employment programs should allow for a broad range of integrated services. The programs with the largest and most-lasting impacts have provided comprehensive support services in conjunction with intensive employment activities, including paid work experience and integrated education and occupational training. Other promising features of welfare employment programs are ties with employers and integrated case management.

The lessons from past welfare-to-work programs are not simple, but they do suggest that investments in well-designed employment and training activities can pay off, at least in terms of earnings to individuals. Even low-intensity employment services can increase employment rates and earnings, at least in the short run. Achieving long-lasting benefits, such as the permanent removal from poverty, though, probably requires more investment in developing skills than has occurred thus far.

Notes

1. Services for welfare recipients through programs funded under the Job Training Partnership Act are examined in Nudelman's chapter 4 in this volume.

2. Caseload reductions not due to changes in eligibility criteria reduce states' required work participation rates.

3. The program evaluations not discussed in this chapter include two Louisville WIN Laboratory Experiments; the Cook County WIN demonstration; the San Diego I Program; and the West Virginia Community Work Experience Program. While the evaluations of the programs omitted here do not appear to reach different conclusions than those that are included, it is difficult to compare their findings since they cover a much shorter time period (one or two years). Gueron and Pauly (1991) do not divulge the criteria they used to choose the four programs for longer-term study; they may have been considered the most promising.

4. The Massachusetts ET Choices program was also evaluated by the Pioneer Institute, whose study we did not review because it examined program impacts on the AFDC caseload, rather than impacts on individual participants (see O'Neill 1990).

5. However, if one were primarily interested in understanding the costs and benefits of the program, rather than just the individual impacts, and if the marginal costs and benefits do not vary between treatment and control groups, then the fact that not all eligibles participated is irrelevant.

6. Nonexperimental methods could also be used to estimate the impacts of different activities within an experimental program evaluation.

7. The Supported Work program's employment and earnings impacts were not substantial for the other three target groups: ex-offenders, ex-addicts, and out-of-school youth.

8. Results from the Homemaker/Home Health Aide Demonstrations are not disaggregated in tables 3.4, 3.5, and 3.6 because the date were not presented in the evaluation report in a form that allowed site or treatment breakouts.

9. Pavetti (1993) found that, while AFDC women with higher basic skills are more likely to leave welfare permanently, acquiring a GED had no independent effect on these welfare outcomes.

10. Less than one-fifth of the adult GED holders studied had completed one year or more of postsecondary education by the time they reached their late twenties (Murnane et al. 1997).

11. A California study found that in many welfare offices, caseworkers counted student financial aid as income, causing recipients in college to lose welfare benefits (Spatz 1997).

12. King and colleagues, in chapter 5 in this volume, while looking at outcomes rather than impacts, find that many of these features distinguish successful JTPA programs.

13. In fact, about three-fifths of the control group participated in an employment and training program at some time during the five-year follow-up period, so the substantial impact estimates of the CET MFSP program are relative to other employment services rather than to no services. Also, CET did not significantly reduce welfare receipt. The evaluators suggested that this is due to the fact that most of the earnings gains accrued to participants who would not have received welfare even in the absence of the intervention (Zambrowski and Gordon 1993).

14. The Urban Institute's evaluation (Nightingale et al. 1991) of the Massachusetts ET Choices program also found that supported work was the most cost-effective of the components offered in that program.

15. This estimate for CET's MFSP program was obtained using a 5 percent real discount rate. These figures cannot be directly compared to those of the program evaluated by MDRC, because the cost per control group member has not been subtracted, meaning that the estimated treatment costs in the MFSP program are relatively higher than they would be using MDRC's calculation method.

16. In comparing impacts, it must be noted that higher proportions of treatment groups actively participated in program activities in voluntary than in mandatory program evaluations, so mandatory program impacts may be biased downward in comparison.

References

Auspos, Patricia, George Cave, and David Long. 1988. *Maine: Final Report on the Training Opportunities in the Private Sector Program.* New York: Manpower Demonstration Research Corporation. April.

Barnow, Burt S. 1987. "The Impacts of CETA Programs on Earnings." *The Journal of Human Resources* 22 (2, spring): 157–93.

Bishop, John H. 1989. "Toward More Valid Evaluations of Training Programs Serving the Disadvantaged." *Journal of Policy Analysis and Management* 8 (2): 209–28.

Blank, Rebecca. 1995. "Outlook for the U.S. Labor Market and Prospects for Low-Wage Entry Jobs." In *The Work Alternative: Welfare Reform and the Realities of the Job Market,* edited by Demetra Smith Nightingale and Robert H. Haveman. Washington, D.C.: Urban Institute Press.

Bloom, Dan. 1997. *After AFDC: Welfare-to-Work Choices and Challenges for States.* New York: Manpower Demonstration Research Corporation.

Bloom, Howard, Larry L. Orr, George Cave, Stephen H. Bell, Fred Doolittle, and Winston Lin. 1994. *The National JTPA Study. Overview: Impacts, Benefits, and Costs of Title II-A.* Bethesda, Md.: Abt Associates Inc.

Boardman, Anthony, David Greenberg, Aidan Vining, and David Weimer. 1996. *Cost-Benefit Analysis: Concepts and Practice.* Upper Saddle River, N.J.: Prentice Hall.

Brock, Thomas, David Butler, and David Long. 1993. *Unpaid Work Experience for Welfare Recipients: Findings and Lessons from MDRC Research.* New York: Manpower Demonstration Research Corporation.

Brock, Thomas, and Kristen Harknett. 1996. "Separation Versus Integration of Income Maintenance and Employment Services: Which Model Is Best? Findings from a Case Management Experiment in Columbus, Ohio." Paper presented at annual conference of the Association for Public Policy Analysis and Management.

Burtless, Gary. 1985. "Are Targeted Wage Subsidies Harmful? Evidence from a Wage Voucher Experiment." *Industrial and Labor Relations Review* (October): 105–14.

Burtless, Gary. 1989. "The Effect of Reform on Employment, Earnings, and Income." In *Welfare Policy for the 1990s,* edited by Phoebe H. Cottingham and David T. Ellwood. Cambridge, Mass.: Harvard University Press.

Burtless, Gary. 1995. "Employment Prospects of Welfare Recipients." In *The Work Alternative: Welfare Reform and the Realities of the Job Market,* edited by Demetra Smith Nightingale and Robert H. Haveman (71–106). Washington, D.C.: Urban Institute Press.

Cameron, Stephen. 1992. "Assessing High School Certification for Women Who Drop Out." New York: Columbia University. September; revised January 1994 and May 1996.

Cameron, Stephen, and James Heckman. 1993. "The Nonequivalence of High School Equivalents." *Journal of Labor Economics* 11 (1): 1–47.

Couch, Kenneth. 1992. "New Evidence on the Long-Term Effects of Employment Training Programs." *Journal of Labor Economics* 10 (4): 380–88.

Enns, John H., Kathleen L. Flanagan, and Stephen H. Bell. 1987. *Evaluation of the AFDC Homemaker-Home Health Aide Demonstrations: Trainee Employment and Earnings.* Cambridge, Mass.: Abt Associates Inc.

Freedman, Stephen, Jan Bryant, and George Cave. 1988. *New Jersey: Final Report on the Grant Diversion Project.* New York: Manpower Demonstration Research Corporation.

Freedman, Stephen, and Daniel Friedlander. 1995. *The JOBS Evaluation: Early Findings on Program Impacts in Three Sites.* Washington, D.C.: U.S. Department of Health and Human Services.

Freedman, Stephen, Daniel Friedlander, Winston Lin, and Amanda Schweder. 1996. "The GAIN Evaluation: Five-Year Impacts on Employment, Earnings, and AFDC Receipt." New York: Manpower Demonstration Research Corporation.

Friedlander, Daniel. 1988. *Subgroup Impacts and Performance Indicators for Selected Welfare Employment Programs.* New York: Manpower Demonstration Research Corporation.

Friedlander, Daniel, and Gary Burtless. 1995. *Five Years After: The Long-Term Effects of Welfare-to-Work Programs.* New York: Russell Sage Foundation.

Friedlander, Daniel, and Judith Gueron. 1992. "Are High-Cost Services More Effective Than Low-Cost Services?" In *Evaluating Welfare and Training Programs*, edited by Charles F. Manski and Irwin Garfinkel (143–98). Cambridge, Mass.: Harvard University Press.

Glazer, Nathan. 1995. "Making Work Work: Welfare Reform in the 1990s." In *The Work Alternative: Welfare Reform and the Realities of the Job Market*, edited by Demetra Smith Nightingale and Robert H. Haveman (17–32). Washington, D.C.: Urban Institute Press.

Gordon, Anne, and John Burghardt. 1990. *The Minority Female Single Parent Demonstration: Short-Term Economic Impacts*. New York: The Rockefeller Foundation.

Greenberg, David, and Michael Wiseman. 1992. "What Did the OBRA Demonstrations Do?" In *Evaluating Welfare and Training Programs*, edited by Charles F. Manski and Irwin Garfinkel (25–75). Cambridge, Mass.: Harvard University Press.

Greenberg, Mark, and Steve Savner. 1996. *A Detailed Summary of Key Provisions of the Temporary Assistance for Needy Families Block Grant of H.R. 3734*. Washington, D.C.: Center for Law and Social Policy.

Gueron, Judith. 1995. "Work Programs and Welfare Reform." *Public Welfare* (summer): 7–16.

Gueron, Judith, and Edward Pauly. 1991. *From Welfare to Work*. New York: Russell Sage Foundation.

Hamilton, William L., et al. 1996. *The New York State Child Assistance Program: Five-Year Impacts, Costs, and Benefits*. Cambridge, Mass.: Abt Associates, Inc.

Heckman, James J., and Jeffrey A. Smith. 1995. "Assessing the Case for Social Experiments." *Journal of Economic Perspectives* 9 (2, spring): 85–100.

Holcomb, Pamela H. 1993. *Welfare Reform: The Family Support Act in Historical Context*. Washington D.C.: Urban Institute.

Hollister, Robinson G., Jr., and Rebecca Maynard. 1984. "The Impacts of Supported Work on AFDC Recipients." In *The National Supported Work Demonstration*, edited by Robinson Hollister, Peter Kemper, and Rebecca Maynard (90–135). Madison: The University of Wisconsin Press.

Hollister, Robinson, Peter Kemper, and Rebecca Maynard, eds. 1984. *The National Supported Work Demonstration*. Madison: The University of Wisconsin Press.

Kemper, Peter, David A. Long, and Craig Thornton. 1984. "A Benefit-Cost Analysis of the Supported Work Experiment." In *The National Supported Work Demonstration*, edited by Robinson Hollister, Peter Kemper, and Rebecca Maynard (239–85). Madison: The University of Wisconsin Press.

LaLonde, Robert J. 1995. "The Promise of Public Sector-Sponsored Training Programs." *Journal of Economic Perspectives* 9 (2, spring): 149–68.

Long, Sharon K., Demetra Smith Nightingale, and Douglas A. Wissoker. 1994. *The Evaluation of the Washington State Family Independence Program*. Washington, D.C.: Urban Institute Press.

Lurie, Irene, and Jan Hagen. 1993. *Implementing JOBS: The Initial Design and Structure of Local Programs.* Albany, N.Y.: Rockefeller Institute of Government.

Lurie, Irene, and Colletta Moser. 1996. "Welfare Reform: Lessons from the JOBS Program." In *Of Heart and Mind: Social Policy Essays in Honor of Sar A. Levitan,* edited by Garth Mangum and Stephen Mangum (301–21). Kalamazoo, Mich.: W.E. Upjohn Institute for Employment Research.

Manpower Demonstration Research Corporation. 1980. *Summary and Findings of the National Supported Work Demonstration.* Cambridge, Mass.: Ballinger Publishing Company.

Maynard, Rebecca. 1995. "Subsidized Employment and Non-Labor Market Alternatives." In *The Work Alternative: Welfare Reform and the Realities of the Job Market,* edited by Demetra Smith Nightingale and Robert H. Haveman (109–36). Washington, D.C.: The Urban Institute Press.

Maynard, Rebecca, and Douglas McGrath. 1997. "The Social Benefits of Education: Family Structure, Fertility, and Child Welfare." In *The Social Benefits of Education,* edited by Jere Behrman and N. Stacey (125–74). Ann Arbor: The University of Michigan Press.

Meyers, Jack, and Marsha Regenstein. 1998. " What Employers Say about Welfare Reform." Washington, D.C.: Urban Institute.

Mitchell, John, Mark Lincoln Chadwin, and Demetra Smith Nightingale. 1979. *Implementing Welfare-Employment Programs: An Institutional Analysis of the Work Incentive Program.* Washington, D.C.: Urban Institute.

Moffitt, Robert. 1992. "Incentive Effects of the U.S. Welfare System: A Review." *Journal of Economic Literature* 30: 1–61.

Murnane, Richard, John Willett, and Kathryn Parker Boudett. 1995. "Do High School Dropouts Benefit from Obtaining a GED?" *Educational Evaluation and Policy Analysis* 17 (2, summer): 133–47.

———. 1997. "Does Acquisition of a GED Lead to More Training, Post-Secondary Education, and Military Service for School Dropouts?" Cambridge, Mass.: National Bureau of Economic Research.

Nightingale, Demetra Smith. 1997. *Work-Related Resources and Services: Implications for TANF.* New Federalism Issues and Options for the States, Policy Brief A-7. Washington, D.C.: Urban Institute.

Nightingale, Demetra Smith, Douglas A. Wissoker, Lynn C. Burbridge, D. Lee Bawden, and Neal Jeffries. 1991. *Evaluation of the Massachusetts Employment and Training (ET) Program.* Washington, D.C.: Urban Institute Press.

O'Neill, June. 1990. *Work and Welfare in Massachusetts: An Evaluation of the ET Program.* Boston: Pioneer Institute for Public Policy Research.

Pavetti, LaDonna. 1993. "Dynamics of Welfare and Work: Exploring the Process by Which Women Work Their Way Off Welfare." Presentation at the John F. Kennedy School of Government, Harvard University, Cambridge, Mass.

Quint, Janet, Johannes Bos, and Denise Polit. 1997. "Executive Summary: New Chance: Final Report on a Comprehensive Program for Disadvantaged Young Mothers and Their Children." New York: Manpower Demonstration Research Corporation.

Riccio, James, Daniel Friedlander, and Stephen Freedman. 1994. *GAIN: Benefits, Costs, and Three-Year Impacts of a Welfare-to-Work Program.* New York: Manpower Demonstration Research Corporation.

Savner, Steve, and Mark Greenberg. 1995. *The CLASP Guide to Welfare Waivers: 1992–1995.* Washington, D.C.: Center for Law and Social Policy. May 23.

Seefeldt, Kristin S., and Pamela A. Holcomb. 1994. *Welfare Reform in 1993: State JOBS Programs and Waivers.* Washington, D.C.: Urban Institute.

Spalter-Roth, Roberta, Beverly Burr, Heidi Hartmann, and Lois Shaw. 1995. *Welfare That Works: The Working Lives of AFDC Recipients.* A Report to the Ford Foundation. Washington, D.C.: Institute for Women's Policy Research.

Spatz, Diana. 1997. "Welfare Reform Skips School." *The Nation* 264 (June 2): 21.

Urban Institute. 1986. *A Compendium of Selected Employment and Training Services for Food Stamp Applicants and Recipients.* Washington, D.C.: U.S. Department of Agriculture, Food and Nutrition Service, Office of Analysis and Evaluation.

U.S. Department of Education. 1989. "National Assessment of Vocational Education."

U.S. Department of Health and Human Services. 1997. *Setting the Baseline: A Report on State Welfare Waivers.* Washington, D.C.

U.S. Department of Health and Human Services and U.S. Department of Education. 1996. *The JOBS Evaluation: Early Lessons from Seven Sites.* Washington, D.C.: U.S. Government Printing Office.

U.S. Department of Labor. 1995. *What's Working (And What's Not): A Summary of Research on the Economic Impacts of Employment and Training Programs.* Washington, D.C.: U.S. Government Printing Office.

U.S. General Accounting Office. 1995. *Welfare to Work: Most AFDC Training Programs Not Emphasizing Job Placement.* Washington, D.C.: GAO.

Zambrowski, Amy, and Anne Gordon. 1993. *Evaluation of the Minority Female Single Parent Demonstration: Fifth-Year Impacts at CET.* Princeton, N.J.: Mathematica Policy Research, Inc.

Chapter Four

THE IMPACT OF JOB TRAINING PARTNERSHIP ACT PROGRAMS FOR ADULT WELFARE RECIPIENTS

Jodi Nudelman

The role of employment and training programs in implementing welfare reform has become increasingly important in recent years. With the implementation in 1996 of the Temporary Assistance for Needy Families (TANF) program, states began to focus their efforts on moving welfare recipients off assistance and into jobs as quickly as possible.[1] In 1998, the passage of the Workforce Investment Act (WIA) consolidated the nation's myriad training and employment programs and created a system of one-stop service-delivery centers. These changes provide an important opportunity to rethink the role of employment and training programs in helping TANF recipients prepare for and find work.

Employment and training agencies can assist TANF recipients and help implement welfare reform initiatives in several ways. In many states, employment and training agencies have formal responsibility for work-related activities of TANF programs, including job search, job placement, and employer outreach. Employment and training agencies are also responsible for operating the Welfare-to-Work Grants that provide additional assistance for the hardest-to-employ recipients of TANF.

The passage of WIA has further increased the ability of employment and training agencies to work with TANF agencies to help move individuals from welfare to work. The focus of this legislation is to build a more integrated system in which employment and training initiatives and other programs such as TANF complement one another. Under WIA, for example, states must create one-stop career centers and team up with different agencies to provide information and services to employers and job seekers. Further, WIA encourages states and localities not only to help individuals find work but also to develop skills of newly hired workers and to upgrade skills of existing employees. This is particularly important to TANF programs that now face the challenges of keeping individuals employed and of moving them beyond entry-level jobs to self-sufficiency.

As states and localities design and implement their employment and training and TANF programs and policies, it is an important time to examine the experience of past employment and training programs in helping welfare recipients. The most prominent program that served welfare recipients prior to WIA was the Job Training Partnership Act of 1982 (JTPA), which provided training for economically disadvantaged adults and youth. According to program data, approximately one-third of adults who completed JTPA were welfare recipients. Despite the significance of JTPA for welfare recipients, little is known about the effectiveness of JTPA programs in helping welfare recipients become self-sufficient. This lack of information is somewhat surprising because JTPA had been the nation's largest system of job training and employment programs.

This chapter therefore begins to explore this largely uncharted territory. It reexamines the data from the National JTPA Study, which randomly assigned participants from November 1987 to September 1989. It looks at the impacts of the Title II-A program, the main component of JTPA, for women receiving Aid to Families with Dependent Children (AFDC) (the welfare program that preceded TANF).[2] Although the National JTPA Study briefly examined this subgroup, this chapter provides a more in-depth analysis that addresses four questions:

- What are the impacts of the program on earnings and welfare receipt for adult women on welfare?
- For which subgroups is the program most effective?
- Which services (e.g., classroom training, on-the-job training) are most effective for women on welfare?
- Do services that increase earnings also decrease welfare dependency for these women?

This chapter examines, in an introductory way, several basic relationships between training, employment, and welfare dependency.[3] It then tests the statement that if the program is effective for adult women receiving AFDC, those who have access to JTPA services will have increased earnings and be less dependent on welfare. Next, it previews the impact of training on different subgroups of the welfare population to determine who can benefit most from the program. The chapter concludes by assessing which services (such as classroom training and on-the-job training) are effective in promoting work and reducing welfare dependency.

The results of this analysis should be viewed in the context of past research on welfare-to-work initiatives and other programs (see Plimpton and Nightingale, chapter 3, in this volume). According to a review by Friedlander, Greenberg, and Robins (1997), employment and training and welfare-to-work programs consistently increased earnings for adult women. The authors also noted that despite the multitude of evaluations, "considerable uncertainty remains about the types of training that work best and the effectiveness of training for certain demographic groups." This chapter's analysis builds on past work in this area and attempts to provide further insight about what works best for whom.

METHOD OF ANALYSIS

The following analysis is based on a subsample of the National JTPA Study data that includes 1,862 adult women 22 and older who were receiving AFDC when they applied to the JTPA program. Like those in the larger study sample, these women were from 16 Service Delivery Areas (SDAs) located throughout the country and were randomly assigned to either the treatment or control group between November 1987 and September 1989.[4] Members of the treatment group had access to Title II-A services, whereas those in the control group were not allowed to receive JTPA services for 18 months after being randomly assigned. Control group members, however, had access to, and in many cases obtained, other services that were available in their communities.

The following analysis compares the treatment group to the control group over 30 months of follow-up to determine the program's impact on two key outcomes: earnings and welfare receipt. To increase the precision of the estimates and reduce bias due to differences between the treatment and control groups, ordinary least squares (OLS) was used to estimate average impacts of the program.[5] The program outcomes (for example, earnings) were regressed on a dummy variable indicating whether the person received treatment or not and on a number of baseline characteristics likely to affect the outcomes that were being estimated.[6] Dummy variables for the sites were also included in the model to control for variations—such as the population served and quality of service—so that these factors would not influence the outcomes being measured.

Like the National JTPA Study, this analysis presents two estimates of the program impact for each outcome. The first estimate is the *impact per assignee,* which represents the average impact of the program on all members of the treatment group, whether or not they actually enrolled in the program. This estimate is the result of having access to JTPA services. Because enrollment in the program was low, a second estimate is presented, referred to as the *impact per enrollee.* This estimate takes into account only participants in the sample who actually enrolled and received some type of JTPA service. The estimate is based on the assumption that the program had no effect for those who did not enroll and is also adjusted for the small percentage of control group members who enrolled in JTPA despite the rules of the experiment.[7]

LIMITATIONS

Before proceeding, the reader should be warned about the limits of this analysis. First, the data from the National JTPA Study have been criticized by the research community from several standpoints. The most significant concern is that the study sites were not randomly selected, and therefore the ability to generalize the findings to the JTPA program nationwide is limited. As argued by the authors of the National JTPA Study, however, the 16 sites that volunteered and were selected represent a broad range of administrative arrangements, program services, participant characteristics, and labor market conditions and display characteristics common to many of the SDAs.[8]

Another unforeseen problem with the initial study was that a substantial percentage of the treatment group never enrolled in the JTPA program.[9] This issue is addressed in the National JTPA Study and in this analysis by providing the per-enrollee impacts as described earlier. In addition, because control group members were able to obtain non-JTPA employment and training services, the estimates do not capture the impact of the program compared to no services. Rather, they represent the incremental effect of JTPA services relative to services available elsewhere in the community.

The reader should also keep in mind that the National JTPA Study data predate the 1992 JTPA Amendments that altered the program in several ways. The earlier program placed less emphasis on longer-term training for hard-to-serve groups. It also had not fully implemented some important policy shifts, including performance standards that placed less emphasis on cost per placement and more emphasis on postprogram earnings and employment.

Finally, caution is needed not to overgeneralize the results to estimate the effectiveness of similar services provided by state welfare-
to-work programs. It is important to note that welfare recipients who
participated in JTPA differ from those who were served by the past
welfare programs and from those now subject to TANF. Welfare
recipients in the JTPA program represented a small percentage of
the welfare population, were usually volunteers, were screened by
the JTPA program, and, at the time, were not subject to time limits.

Despite these limitations, the National JTPA Study data are highly
valued. Unlike many other evaluations, the data are experimental,
are from sites across the nation, and refer to a recent program. The
benefits and limits of the study are best summarized by Friedlander,
Greenberg, and Robins (1997): "The JTPA experiment has provided
the most credible evidence to date about training program effectiveness, but the estimated effects pertain only to the practices and scale
typified by the programs actually evaluated."

PROGRAM IMPACTS ON EARNINGS

The following sections examine program impacts on earnings and
welfare dependency. As stated in the JTPA legislation (Section 106),
the return on investment in job training was to be measured by
increased employment and earnings of participants and reductions
in welfare dependency.

Accordingly, as shown in table 4.1, Title II-A achieved gains in
earnings for adult women on welfare. Over 30 months, the control
group earned an average of $8,604, whereas the treatment group
earned $10,190. For those who actually enrolled, the program
increased earnings by an average of $2,411, or 28 percent more than
what recipients would have earned in the program's absence. All
impact estimates were statistically significant for the entire 30-month
period as well as for each of the program intervals.[10]

A closer look shows that JTPA's impact on earnings varied over
the 30-month period. During the in-program period, the first six
months after random assignment, earnings for treatment group program enrollees exceeded the control group's earnings by $321, or 29
percent. This was a lower dollar increase than the other periods
because many of the treatment group members were enrolled in the
program and not working. In the first year following program participation, earnings gains were the largest. During this period, JTPA
significantly increased average earnings by about $1,200 per enrollee,

Table 4.1 IMPACT OF JTPA TITLE II-A ON EARNINGS FOR ADULT WOMEN ON WELFARE

	Mean Earnings		Impact per Assignee		Impact per Enrollee	
	Treatment Group	Control Group	Dollars	Standard Error	Dollars	Standard Error
In-program period	$1,308	$1,097	$211.12**	95.67	$320.98**	145.45
First postprogram year	4,150	3,359	790.03***	244.21	1,201.12***	371.29
Second postprogram year	4,733	4,148	584.75**	293.12	889.03**	445.65
Total	10,190	8,604	1,585.90***	552.94	2,411.13***	840.66

Sources: Estimates are based on earnings data from state unemployment insurance (UI) agencies and responses from the First and Second Follow-up Surveys.

Notes: Estimates are based on a sample of 1,862 women receiving AFDC at the time of application. Estimates are regression-adjusted to control for differences in background characteristics between the treatment group and the control group. Statistically significant using a two tailed-test: *at the .10 level; **at the .05 level; ***at the .01 level.

or 36 percent, compared to the control group. In the second year of participation, earnings gains were still statistically significant but were somewhat lower. For program enrollees, earnings rose by about $890, or 21 percent more than what recipients would have earned had they not enrolled.[11]

An analysis of quarterly earnings shows that the treatment group's average earnings were consistently higher than the control group's. As figure 4.1 and table 4.2 indicate, the impact of having access to the program—the difference between the treatment group and control group lines in the figure—was significant for most quarters in the follow-up period.

In general, these results follow the pattern one would expect. For the first two quarters, the program's impact was not significant because the majority of the treatment group was enrolled in the program. However, in all but one of the remaining quarters, the program achieved statistically significant earnings gains, ranging from an average of $219 per enrollee in the ninth quarter to $342 in the sixth quarter. The influence was largest in the 4th, 5th, and 6th quarters, which correspond to the first postprogram year. It was also statistically significant in the 9th and 10th quarters, indicating that the program may have some lasting effects on earnings for at least this duration.

The upward trend in the control group's earnings, also shown in figure 4.1, suggests that even without access to JTPA services, women

Figure 4.1 JTPA TITLE II-A QUARTERLY EARNINGS FOR ADULT WOMEN ON WELFARE FOLLOWING RANDOM ASSIGNMENT

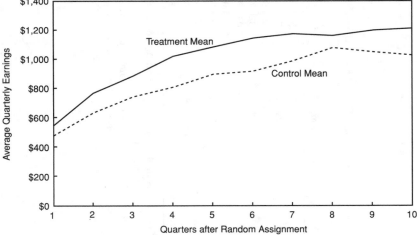

Table 4.2 IMPACT OF JTPA TITLE II-A ON QUARTERLY EARNINGS FOLLOWING RANDOM ASSIGNMENT

Quarter	Control Mean ($)	Treatment Mean ($)	Impact per Assignee ($)	Standard Error	Impact per Enrollee ($)	Standard Error
1	472.05	534.58	62.52	45.34	95.05	68.93
2	624.52	773.12	148.60	56.60	225.92	86.05
3	739.32	890.88	151.56**	61.53	230.42**	93.55
4	803.71	1,026.79	223.07***	68.58	339.15***	104.27
5	895.65	1,085.86	190.21***	69.69	289.19***	105.95
6	920.80	1,145.99	225.19***	72.45	342.37***	110.15
7	988.39	1,168.63	180.24**	74.02	274.03**	112.54
8	1,077.65	1,155.86	78.21	76.75	118.91	116.69
9	1,056.28	1,200.61	144.34*	80.85	219.45*	122.92
10	1,025.48	1,207.44	181.96**	82.87	276.64**	125.99

Sources: Estimates are based on earnings data from state unemployment insurance (UI) agencies and responses from the First and Second Follow-up Survey.

Notes: Estimates are based on a sample of 1,862 adult women receiving AFDC at the time of application. Estimates are regression-adjusted to control for differences in background characteristics between the treatment group and the control group.
Statistically significant using a two tailed-test: *at the .10 level; **at the .05 level; ***at the .01 level.

on welfare would have increased their average earnings over the 30-month period. This trend may reflect the impact of receiving non-JTPA services. It may also indicate that people tend to enroll in job training when they have reached a low point and their earnings are at a minimum and/or that those who elect to participate in the program are highly motivated to improve their situation.

PROGRAM IMPACTS ON WELFARE DEPENDENCY

Another measure of effectiveness is the JTPA's impact on welfare dependency. For this analysis, welfare dependency is measured in terms of average AFDC payments and average number of months spent on welfare over the 30-month follow-up period. Usable data on AFDC benefits were available from only 6 of the 16 sites.[12] These findings are therefore based on a subsample of 437 women in these 6 sites who were receiving AFDC when they applied to JTPA.

As shown in table 4.3, JTPA significantly decreased welfare dependency for adult women on AFDC. Over the 30-month follow-up period, the control group received an average of $5,203 in AFDC payments, whereas the treatment group received significantly less, about $4,476. For participants who actually enrolled in the program, AFDC payments were reduced by nearly $1,300, or about 25 percent, compared to control group members. This estimate was statistically significant at the .10 level.

The Title II-A program also had a marked effect on the average number of months that participants spent on welfare. As also shown in table 4.3, the control group spent an average of 15 months on AFDC during the 30-month follow-up period, whereas the treatment group spent an average of only 12.7 months. Time spent on welfare for those who enrolled in the program was decreased by more than 4 months, or 27 percent, compared to their counterparts in the control group.

In this analysis, the findings on AFDC payments and length of time on welfare are mutually reinforcing, demonstrating that JTPA can reduce welfare dependency for this population. The success of the program, particularly in reducing the length of time spent on welfare, highlights JTPA's potential role in a welfare system that limits cash assistance to a total of five years or less over an individual's lifetime.

In reviewing these results, it is important to keep in mind that several factors influence impacts on welfare savings and time spent on the welfare rolls. For one thing, state grant levels directly affect the

Table 4.3 IMPACT OF JTPA TITLE II-A ON WELFARE DEPENDENCY FOR 30 MONTHS FOLLOWING RANDOM ASSIGNMENT

	Treatment Group	Control Group	Impact per Assignee	Standard Error	Impact per Enrollee	Standard Error
AFDC payments	$4,476.11	$5,203.14	$-727.03*	391.64	$-1,299.47*	700.00
Number of months on AFDC	12.73	15.03	-2.30**	1.01	-4.11**	1.81

Sources: Estimates are based on state welfare agency records and responses from the First and Second Follow-up Survey.

Notes: Estimates are based on a total sample of 473 adult women receiving AFDC at the time of application: treatment group = 303; control group = 170. Estimates are regression-adjusted to control for differences in background characteristics between the treatment group and the control group.

Statistically significant using a two tailed-test: *at the .10 level; **at the .05 level; ***at the .01 level.

amount of welfare savings that can be achieved, as well as the length of time recipients may spend on welfare. For example, in a high-grant state, an individual working part-time may remain eligible for some welfare benefits, whereas in a low-grant state that individual may no longer be eligible. Among the sites in the study, the level of benefits varied widely, from $288 in Indiana to $663 in California.

Rules affecting earnings and other income also influence welfare impacts. At the time of the study, all states were required by law to disregard certain earned income when calculating an AFDC grant.[13] In some states, "fill-the-gap" budgeting was also employed, under which AFDC recipients could earn up to the difference between a financial "standard of need" and their AFDC grant without experiencing a reduction in their grant.

It should also be noted that the findings on welfare savings in this analysis differ from the widely cited findings of the National JTPA Study, which concluded that welfare savings over 30 months were small and not statistically significant.[14] The differences are due, at least partly, to the different subgroups that were analyzed; the National JTPA Study examined the impact on welfare receipt for all adult women, whereas this analysis takes into account only women who were actually receiving benefits when they applied to the program. Because the majority of adult women in the study sites never received AFDC during the follow-up, decreases in AFDC payments would be difficult to detect for all adult women. This chapter's approach therefore measures the more direct effects of JTPA on welfare payments. The estimates are also unbiased because AFDC status was determined prior to random assignment and is therefore not affected by having access to the program.[15]

PROGRAM IMPACTS FOR SUBGROUPS

This section explores whether the JTPA Title II-A program is more effective for specific subgroups of the welfare population. Two findings are presented for each subgroup: whether the impact of the program on earnings is significant for a particular subgroup (the *t*-statistic) and whether the program's impact differs significantly for one particular subgroup as compared to another (the *F*-test).

As table 4.4 shows, the program achieved statistically significant earnings gains for white women on welfare but not for black or Hispanic women. Over 30 months, the program increased earnings per enrollee by $3,493 for white women but only $2,107 for black

Table 4.4 IMPACT OF JTPA TITLE II-A ON 30-MONTH EARNINGS BY SUBGROUPS

	Sample Size	Impact per Assignee ($)	Standard Error	Impact per Enrollee ($)	Standard Error
Ethnicity					
White and other	785	2,413***	851	3,493***	1,233
Black	799	1,308	851	2,107	1,371
Hispanic	278	82	1,409	264	4,516
F-test, difference between subgroups			N.S.		
Education					
No high school diploma or GED certificate	555	1,906	1,011	3,127	1,659
High school diploma or GED certificate	1,207	1,067*	685	1,583*	1,015
F-test, difference between subgroups			N.S.		
AFDC history					
AFDC case less than two years	760	238	871	361	1,321
AFDC case two to five years	497	2,999***	1,086	4,577***	1,657
AFDC case more than five years	583	1,893*	979	2,887*	1,493
F-test, difference between subgroups			++		
Status of participation					
JTPA required	443	692	1,137	1,184	1,945
JTPA not required	1,360	1,577**	651	2,324**	960
F-test, difference between subgroups			N.S.		

Notes: Statistically significant using a two tailed-test: * at the .10 level; ** at the .05 level; *** at the .01 level. F-test is the ratio of between-group variance to within-group variance; N.S. indicates the F-test is not statistically significant; ++indicates the F-test is significant at the .10 level.

women and $264 for Hispanic women. The latter two estimates were not statistically significant, however. Further, as indicated by the *F*-test, the impacts of the program for these three groups were not significantly different from one another. Together, these data show that the evidence is not strong enough to determine the program's effects on earnings for black and Hispanic women relative to white women. In addition, because Hispanic and black women were concentrated at certain sites, the effects of race and ethnicity are difficult to disentangle from the effects of the different sites.

The data also show that the program achieved statistically significant gains in earnings for women who had a high school diploma or a general equivalency diploma (GED). For these women, the program raised earnings by more than $1,580 for enrollees over the 30-month follow-up period. Earnings gains for enrollees who had neither of these credentials were about $3,130, but this estimate was not statistically significant. In addition, the *F*-test showed that the program's impact on earnings was not statistically different for these two groups, indicating that we do not have enough evidence from the National JTPA Study data to determine the program's impact for women without a GED or high school diploma.

The data are most convincing for longer-term welfare recipients, showing that the program increased earnings by $4,577 for enrollees who had been on AFDC from two to five years prior to being randomly assigned and by nearly $2,890 for enrollees who had been on AFDC for more than five years. Both of these estimates were statistically significant. In contrast, the program did not achieve statistically significant gains for women who had been on AFDC for less than two years. As indicated by the *F*-test, the significant difference in program impact for these groups suggests that the program was more effective for women who had been on AFDC for at least two years. This subgroup, however, may not represent the most disadvantaged segment of the welfare population. Although these women had been on welfare for a long period of time, they volunteered for JTPA and may be somewhat more motivated to improve their situation than others on the welfare rolls.

Finally, for the subgroup of women who were not required to participate in the program, the analysis shows that the program achieved statistically significant earnings gains (nearly $2,325). Earnings also increased for women who were required to participate in the program, although this estimate was not statistically significant. The impacts for these two groups were not statistically significantly different from each other, however.

PROGRAM IMPACTS FOR DIFFERENT SERVICE STRATEGIES

Another fundamental question for policymakers, evaluators, and local program administrators is whether certain services are more effective than others for different segments of the welfare population. To respond to this question, the following analysis evaluates the impacts on earnings and welfare dependency for three different service strategies. These strategies were developed in cooperation with program operators and policymakers at the start of the study. They are based on services that were *recommended* for each participant, rather than on services that participants actually received. Because random assignment occurred after JTPA staff recommended a particular service strategy, control group members can be matched to treatment group members according to services recommended. The categories used in this analysis are the same as those used in the National JTPA Study and are described next.

- *Classroom training in occupational skills* includes in-class training in specific job skills such as word processing, electronics repair, and home health care. This category includes all women in the sample who were recommended for classroom occupational skills training and not for on-the-job training (OJT). Women in this category may have also been recommended for other services such as job search assistance, basic education, or work experience.
- *On-the-job training/job search assistance* (OJT/JSA) includes all women in the sample who were recommended for OJT but not for classroom occupational skills training. These women may have also been recommended for other services such as job search assistance.
- *Other services* includes women in the sample who did not fit into either of the previous two categories. It offers services such as basic education, job search assistance, and other services that range from further assessment and preemployment skills preparation to work experience.[16]

Overall, women on welfare were more likely to be recommended for classroom training than for other service strategies. Specifically, JTPA intake staff recommended nearly half of women in the sample for classroom training, compared to about 27 percent for OJT/JSA and 24 percent for other services. These service recommendations are not surprising, given the initial employability levels of women receiving cash assistance.

An analysis of the services actually received by the three service strategies shows that many participants in each category did not receive the primary service. Nevertheless, those assigned to each service strategy received distinctly different mixes of services that reflect service approaches commonly used in JTPA.[17] As shown in table 4.5, more recipients assigned to classroom training actually received classroom training (62 percent) than did those assigned to OJT/JSA (15 percent) or other services (19 percent), although some also received job search assistance and other services. Recipients assigned to OJT/JSA were more likely to be oriented toward immediate employment, either through on-the-job training or job search assistance, although some received classroom training. The other services category is somewhat more difficult to interpret. It includes both participants needing supplementary, quick job services and those needing more in-depth training and skill development. As a result, recipients in this category were more likely to receive other services, but some received job search assistance and/or classroom training.

As also shown in table 4.5, the service strategies varied by number of participants who actually enrolled in the program. Women assigned to classroom training were more likely to enroll in the program than those assigned to OJT/JSA and to other services. Differences in enrollment can possibly be attributed to the fact that OJT requires the cooperation of employers and is more difficult to arrange than services such as classroom training. Moreover, as described later, participants assigned to OJT/JSA tended to be more employable

Table 4.5 SERVICES RECEIVED BY TREATMENT GROUP MEMBERS IN EACH SERVICE STRATEGY

	Services Assigned		
Services Received	Classroom Training	OJT/JSA	Other Services
Never enrolled	22.3%	37.0%	38.6%
Classroom training	61.8%	15.2%	18.6%
Basic education	9.2%	3.0%	5.4%
On-the-job training	5.3%	30.1%	2.4%
Job search assistance	19.5%	19.1%	14.2%
Work experience	8.7%	4.8%	3.1%
Other	13.3%	8.4%	35.6%

Sources: Estimates are based on responses from the First Follow-up Surveys.
Notes: Estimates are based on a total sample of 1,862 adult women receiving AFDC at the time of application. Number of participants receiving classroom training equaled 912; OJT/JSA, 507; and other services, 443.

than did those assigned to classroom training—and may have had other options besides JTPA.

Importantly, the three strategies served women with somewhat different characteristics.[18] As expected, participants assigned to OJT/JSA were more job-ready than those assigned to the other two service strategies. OJT/JSA participants were also more likely to have ever been employed and to have worked during the past year, and they were less likely to have been receiving food stamps when they applied to JTPA. In contrast, participants assigned to classroom training and to other services were more disadvantaged. In particular, participants recommended for other services were the least likely to have a GED or high school diploma or to have received past vocational or occupational training. In addition, they were more likely to have been required to participate in the program than participants assigned to OJT/JSA and to classroom training.

These differences have several implications for the service strategy analysis. Because each service strategy served somewhat different populations, their impacts cannot be solely attributed to effects of the different services. The impact estimates for each service strategy are, rather, an indication of how well a certain set of services worked for the distinct group that was assigned to it.

Earnings by Service Strategy

Analysis of earnings reveals that the JTPA program had different consequences for those assigned to the three service strategies. The largest impact was seen for participants recommended for OJT/JSA. In fact, this was the only service strategy that consistently achieved statistically significant earnings gains over the total 30-month period, as well as during the first and second postprogram years and the in-program period.[19]

As shown in table 4.6, for enrollees assigned to OJT/JSA, the program significantly increased earnings over the 30-month follow-up period by an average of $5,461, or 55 percent, compared to control group members similarly assigned. The impact of the program also grew over time. Earnings increased by about $2,070 in the first postprogram year and by nearly $2,600 in the second postprogram year, suggesting that the program may have an extended effect on earnings for those assigned to OJT/JSA.

In addition, the program had a significant impact for participants assigned to the other services strategy. For enrollees in this service strategy, the program increased earnings over the 30-month follow-up period by an average of $4,178, or 54 percent, compared to control

Table 4.6 IMPACT OF JTPA TITLE II-A ON 30-MONTH EARNINGS BY SERVICE STRATEGY

	Mean Earnings		Impact per Assignee		Impact per Enrollee	
	Treatment Group ($)	Control Group ($)	Dollars	Standard Error	Dollars	Standard Error
Classroom training						
In-program	936	910	26.30	111.85	35.87	152.55
First postprogram year	3,579	3,117	461.18	317.76	628.99	433.38
Second postprogram year	4,252	4,293	−40.64	409.73	−55.43	558.82
Total	8,767	8,320	446.84	732.91	609.43	999.60
OJT/JSA						
In-program	2,035	1,553	481.33**	205.28	793.91**	338.59
First postprogram year	5,296	4,042	1,254.27**	523.37	2,068.79**	863.24
Second postprogram year	5,874	4,299	1,575.31***	601.35	2,598.31***	991.86
Total	13,205	9,894	3,310.91***	1,165.06	5,461.01***	1,921.65
Other services						
In-program	1,405	990	415.26*	232.04	737.81*	412.28
First postprogram year	4,117	3,038	1,078.81*	552.09	1,916.78*	980.92
Second postprogram year	4,576	3,718	857.55	629.22	1,523.65	117.97
Total	10,098	7,746	2,351.62*	1,239.19	4,178.23*	2,201.73

Sources: Estimates are based on earnings data from state unemployment insurance (UI) agencies and responses from the First and Second Follow-up Surveys.

Notes: Estimates are based on a total sample of 1,862 adult women receiving AFDC at the time of application. Number of participants receiving classroom training equaled 912; OJT/JSA, 507; and other services, 443. Estimates are regression-adjusted to control for differences in background characteristics between the treatment group and the control group.

Statistically significant using a two tailed-test: *at the .10 level; **at the .05 level; ***at the .01 level.

group members. Unlike OJT/JSA, the program's impact for this sub-group peaked in the first postprogram year and then declined some-what in the following year, suggesting that other services may not have a long-term effect on earnings for this population.

In contrast, classroom training did not significantly impact earn-ings. None of the estimates for classroom training was statistically significant, so we cannot be confident that this service had any effect on earnings for these participants. As one would expect, during the in-program period, the impact of the program was minimal because most participants were attending training. Earnings increased in the first postprogram year once participants completed training but declined in the second postprogram year. Although the training was more intensive than OJT/JSA and sought to improve human capital, it did not achieve earnings gains that were statistically significant or gains that persisted over time.

One explanation may be that classroom training was generally short-term, lasting from 3 to 6 months. As described in the National JTPA Study, the median length of enrollment for all adult women who received classroom training was 5.2 months (Kemple, Doolittle, and Wallace 1993). In addition, information about the content of the train-ing and its applicability to the workplace was not collected and most likely varied by site.[20] Thus, given the nature of the classroom train-ing provided, modest impacts may be a more reasonable expectation.

It is also important to note that the level of earnings differed across the three service strategies. As shown in table 4.6, average earnings for control group members assigned to OJT/JSA were higher than earnings for control group members assigned to the other two service strategies for the entire 30 months, as well as for each interval. These variations support the finding that the three strategies served differ-ent subpopulations. Those directed to OJT/JSA tended to be more job-ready and were able to earn more money without JTPA services than participants assigned to classroom training or other services.

AFDC Payments by Service Strategy

Analysis of AFDC payments reinforces the positive impacts on earn-ings found for those assigned to OJT/JSA. As shown in table 4.7, for enrollees assigned to this service strategy, the program dramatically decreased welfare payments by an average of $2,354, which repre-sented close to a 60 percent decrease in AFDC payments over 30 months.

The results are less convincing for those assigned to classroom training or to the other services subgroup. These service strategies

Table 4.7 IMPACT OF JTPA TITLE II-A ON 30-MONTH AFDC PAYMENTS BY SERVICE STRATEGY

	Treatment Group	Control Group	Impact per Assignee	Standard Error	Impact per Enrollee	Standard Error
Classroom training	$6,648	$7,308	$-660.12	975.66	$-957.34	1,414.95
OJT/JSA	2,723	3,960	-1,236.67**	564.94	-2,354.43**	1,075.56
Other services	4,049	4,601	-551.85	629.63	-1,088.64	1,242.07

Sources: Estimates are based on state welfare agency records and responses from the First and Second Follow-up Surveys.

Notes: Estimates are based on a total sample of 473. Number of participants receiving classroom training equaled 130; OJT/JSA, 150; and other services, 193. Estimates are regression-adjusted to control for differences in background characteristics between the treatment group and the control group.

Statistically significant using a two tailed-test: *at the .10 level; **at the .05 level; ***at the .01 level.

reduced AFDC payments by an average of $957 and $1,089, respectively. These estimates were not statistically significant, however.

Similar to the findings on earnings, the data show that participants assigned to the different service strategies received varying levels of AFDC payments. Over 30 months, control group members assigned to OJT/JSA received the lowest amount of AFDC, about $3,960, whereas those assigned to classroom training received substantially higher benefits, about $7,310. Once again, these data show that different populations were assigned to each of the three service strategies and remind us that the impacts for the service strategies may be due to varying impacts for women with particular characteristics rather than to the impacts of the different services themselves.

Months on AFDC by Service Strategy

The impacts for the different service strategies on the length of time spent on welfare are consistent with the findings on AFDC payments (see table 4.8). For enrollees assigned to OJT/JSA, the program significantly reduced the time participants depended on AFDC by nearly seven months, representing over a 50 percent reduction in the number of months participants would have spent on welfare without the program.

The program was less successful in reducing welfare months for those recommended for classroom training or other services. These strategies reduced time spent on welfare by 2.2 months and about 4 months, respectively. Similar to the analysis on AFDC payments, these estimates were not statistically significant. As noted earlier, a number of factors such as grant levels and AFDC rules may have also affected impacts on welfare payments and months.

CONCLUSIONS

Overall, this reanalysis of the National JTPA Study data indicates that the JTPA Title II-A program was somewhat effective for adult women on welfare.[21] The program produced significant gains in average earnings and reductions in welfare payments across diverse sites, program environments, and populations. As discussed, the results are less clear as to which subgroups benefited most from the program. The most convincing evidence, however, shows that the program was more effective for welfare recipients who had spent at least two years on welfare.

Table 4.8 IMPACT OF JTPA TITLE II-A ON MONTHS ON AFDC BY SERVICE STRATEGY

	Treatment Group (months)	Control Group (months)	Impact per Assignee (months)	Standard Error	Impact per Enrollee (months)	Standard Error
Classroom training	15.88	17.40	−1.51	1.94	−2.20	2.81
OJT/JSA	9.59	13.23	−3.64*	1.87	−6.92*	3.56
Other services	12.52	14.54	−2.02	1.72	−3.98	3.39

Sources: Estimates are based on state welfare agency records and responses from the First and Second Follow-up Surveys.

Notes: Estimates are based on a total sample of 473. Number of participants receiving classroom training equaled 130; OJT/JSA, 150; and other services, 193. Estimates are regression-adjusted to control for differences in background characteristics between the treatment group and the control group.

Statistically significant using a two tailed-test: *at the .10 level; **at the .05 level; ***at the .01 level.

A more in-depth look at the different types of services provided by JTPA indicates that all three service strategies—classroom training, OJT/JSA, and other services—were somewhat effective for this population. Although not all of the estimates were statistically significant, overall they show that the impact of these services was generally positive. The analysis also suggests that certain services may be more effective than others for subgroups of the welfare population. Specifically, OJT and job search assistance achieved positive results for welfare recipients who were more job-ready. The impact of other services, which included a wide range of activities, was more mixed. Finally, classroom training was not found to be particularly effective for women who were referred to this activity.

From another perspective, the analysis shows that impacts on earnings and welfare dependency were generally consistent with one another. This finding demonstrates that programs that increase earnings can also decrease welfare payments and time spent on the rolls for this population. These dynamics, however, also highlight the limits of such a program, indicating that earnings gains were at least partially offset by reductions in welfare benefits. Thus, the program was somewhat successful in replacing benefits with earnings but, most likely, did not increase recipients' total income. Nevertheless, one should keep in mind that the government's financial investment in the program was relatively small and should not be expected to produce large returns. According to the National JTPA Study, for example, the incremental training cost for adult women was $1,171 per enrollee over 30 months.

What is, perhaps, most striking about the findings discussed here is how low the earnings were for this population. In the second year following program participation, for example, average earnings for treatment group members were about $4,730, which is well below the 1990 Census poverty threshold of $9,885 for a three-person family. Consistent with other research, the earnings level for this population was extremely low both with and without the program. This finding demonstrates that although gains in average earnings were statistically significant, the increases were clearly not sufficient to lift these women and their families out of poverty.

POLICY IMPLICATIONS

Taken together, these findings provide some evidence that employment and training programs can help some welfare recipients. They also suggest that these programs can play an important role in implementing TANF initiatives. Although this finding seems overly simple, it is an important message for states and localities as they design and implement employment and training and welfare programs and policies.

The findings relating to the different services have more specific implications for policymakers and administrators. The success of OJT and job search for job-ready welfare recipients demonstrates that these are important activities that case managers can use to move some recipients from welfare to work. These results also underscore the importance of linking employment activities to the needs of employers. This, in turn, has implications for helping newly employed welfare recipients and other low-income populations upgrade skills and advance on the job, an important next step for both employment and training programs and welfare initiatives.

In contrast, the somewhat disappointing results for classroom training forewarn employment and training programs that short-term classroom training may not provide answers for some welfare recipients. Specifically, this finding signals the need for employment and training programs to reexamine these services, learn from other programs, and, perhaps, lengthen services and make them more relevant to the local labor market.

More importantly, these results suggest that employment and training programs may not be adequately meeting the needs of recipients who are more disadvantaged and less employable. This finding highlights the need for such programs to experiment with a wide range of new services and mixes of approaches, perhaps taking advantage of the Welfare-to-Work Grants. It also challenges programs to try innovative administrative practices, such as integrated case management.[22]

These results also have significant implications for the implementation of TANF. Time limits encourage states to implement a work-first approach that offers job search assistance and less-intensive activities. While this approach may work for some, the results discussed here do not indicate that these types of activities will work for those who are less job-ready. In effect, these results demonstrate that a time-limited welfare system is a wake-up call not only for welfare recipients but also for states. The results should serve as a caution to states concerning the limits of such programs and the fact that these services may not be enough for everyone.

On another level, these findings suggest that neither welfare programs nor employment and training programs alone can overcome the barriers to work faced by the most-disadvantaged recipients. Effective partnerships between employment and training agencies,

TANF agencies, and others are required to address complex barriers, such as child care and transportation, that will be increasingly difficult to surmount under time-limited welfare. The new legislation in both arenas greatly increases the decisionmaking power of states and localities. Collaboration between TANF and employment and training agencies at all levels can help meet the challenges of these reforms and should be particularly considered as states and localities structure their one-stop career centers.

As this analysis has shown, JTPA was effective for some women on welfare. Employment and training programs need to learn from the experience of JTPA and to take the next step. They must carefully rethink the content and type of services they offer as well as the way they provide these services, particularly for those who are likely to be left behind. In doing so, they will be able to provide a broader spectrum of the welfare population an opportunity to obtain employment and a permanent exit from welfare.

Notes

This chapter was written by Jodi Nudelman in her private capacity. No official support or endorsement by U.S. Department of Health and Human Services, Office of Inspector General is intended or should be inferred.

1. In August 1996, block grants to states for Temporary Assistance for Needy Families (TANF) replaced Aid to Families with Dependent Children (AFDC) and the Job Opportunities and Basic Skills (JOBS) programs.

2. The data analyzed in this chapter precede the 1992 JTPA Amendments. Prior to these amendments, Title II-A authorized training for both adults and youth. The 1992 Amendments separated the programs for these two populations. Title II-A authorized training only for adults who are 22 or older. Title II-B offered economically disadvantaged youth jobs and training during the summer, whereas Title II-C provided year-round training and employment programs for in-school and out-of-school youth.

3. For a more detailed description of the analysis presented in this chapter, see Nudelman (1995).

4. For more information on the design and implementation of the study, refer to Bloom et al. (1993). For a description of the 16 study sites and program characteristics, see Kemple, Doolittle, and Wallace (1993). Note that the study sites were a judgmental, not a random, sample.

5. Note that average impacts can obscure details about how the program is working and do not always give a complete picture of program accomplishments.

6. The model incorporates dummy variables for demographic characteristics including the participants' ethnicity, age, household composition, past education, training, employment experience, and dependence on public assistance. The baseline information was collected at the time the participant applied to the program.

7. For a more detailed explanation, see Bloom (1984).

8. See Doolittle and Traeger (1990) for additional information about site selection.

9. The data show that about 31 percent of adult AFDC women in the treatment group never enrolled in JTPA and generally did not receive any JTPA services.

10. Estimates are presented for different intervals in the follow-up period: the in-program period (the first 6 months), the first postprogram year (7 through 18 months), and the second postprogram year (19 through 30 months). These intervals are the same periods used in the National JTPA Study and are based on estimates of when most participants completed training. However, they are only rough guides since participation in the program varied.

11. An analysis of follow-up data of the National JTPA Study by the U.S. General Accounting Office (1996) found that impacts on earnings continued for all adult women in the fourth and fifth year following random assignment, although the difference in the fifth year was not statistically significant.

12. Usable data could not be obtained from the remaining 10 sites. See Orr et al. (1994).

13. States were required to disregard $30 plus work expenses ($90) and an additional one-third of earnings for a period of four consecutive months; and $30 plus work expenses ($90) for the next eight months of employment.

14. For 30-month impacts on earnings, employment, and welfare receipt for four main target groups, including adult women and men and female and male out-of-school youths, refer to Orr et al. (1994).

15. A more detailed analysis of adult women who were receiving AFDC at random assignment found sizable gains in earnings but no accompanying reductions in welfare receipt. See Orr et al. (1997).

16. Several groupings result from these definitions that are not immediately apparent. Individuals who were assigned to job search assistance only were not classified as OJT/JSA, but as other services. In addition, individuals who were assigned both classroom training and OJT were classified as other services.

17. This conclusion is the same as the findings for all adult women in the National JTPA Study. It is based on a more intensive analysis of treatment-control group differences in service receipt and mean hours of service (Orr et al. 1994).

18. Demographic differences highlighted in this section are statistically significant using an F-test at the .05 level.

19. The estimates for OJT also include wages paid to individuals who had on-the-job training positions.

20. Research from the Minority Female Single Parent (MFSP) Demonstration has shown that short-term classroom training can be successful when it is closely linked to work. This is best exemplified by the Center for Employment and Training (CET) in San Jose, which has effectively combined short-term classroom training with work by emphasizing specific skills needed by local businesses (Burghardt et al. 1992).

21. This overall conclusion is supported by a study that, using nonexperimental methods, found that JTPA programs were successful in employment outcomes for AFDC women who had not worked for at least one year prior to enrolling in the program (Romero 1994).

22. A preliminary analysis of data from the National Welfare-to-Work Evaluation (formerly the JOBS Evaluation) found that in Columbus, Ohio, integrated case management led to significantly higher rates of participation in program activities than traditional case management. Integrated case management also reduced welfare payments, although employment rates and earnings were no different than those in traditional case management (Brock and Harknett 1998).

References

Ashenfelter, Orley. 1978. "Estimating the Effect of Training Programs on Earnings." *Review of Economics and Statistics* 60 (1): 47–57.

Barnow, Burt. 1987a. "The Impact of CETA Programs on Earnings." *Journal of Human Resources* 22 (2).

Barnow, Burt. 1987b. "The Uses and Limits of Social Experiments." Proceedings of the Fortieth Annual Meeting, Industrial Relations Research Association Series.

Benson, Dennis. 1992. *Review of the National JTPA Study*. Columbus, Ohio: Appropriate Solutions, Inc.

Bloom, Howard. 1984. "Accounting for No-Shows in Experimental Evaluation Designs." *Evaluation Review* 8: 225–46.

Bloom, Howard, Larry Orr, George Cave, Stephen Bell, and Fred Doolittle. 1993. *The National JTPA Study: Title II-A Impacts on Earnings and Employment at 18 Months*. Bethesda, Md.: Abt Associates Inc.

Bowman, William. 1993. *Evaluating JTPA Programs for Economically Disadvantaged Adults: A Case Study of Utah and General Findings*. Washington, D.C.: National Commission for Employment Policy.

Brock, Thomas, and Kristen Harknett. 1998. "Welfare-to-Work Case Management: A Comparison of Two Models." New York: Manpower Demonstration Research Corporation.

Burghardt, John, Anu Rangarajan, Anne Gordon, and Ellen Kisker. 1992. *Evaluation of the Minority Female Single Parent Demonstration. Vol. 1: Summary Report*. New York: The Rockefeller Foundation.

Burtless, Gary. 1987. "Are Social Experiments a Useful Policy Technique?" Proceedings of the Fortieth Annual Meeting, Industrial Relations Research Association Series.

Burtless, Gary, and Larry L. Orr. 1986. "Are Classical Experiments Needed for Manpower Policy?" *Journal of Human Resources* 21 (4): 606–39.

Couch, Kenneth. 1992. "New Evidence on the Long-Term Effects of Employment and Training Programs." *Journal of Labor Economics* 10 (4): 380–88.

Doolittle, Fred, and Linda Traeger. 1990. *Implementing the National JTPA Study*. New York: Manpower Demonstration Research Corporation.

Friedlander, Daniel, and Gary Burtless. 1995. *Five Years After: The Long-Term Effects of Welfare-to-Work Programs*. New York: Russell Sage Foundation.

Friedlander, Daniel, David Greenberg, and Philip Robins. 1997. "Evaluating Government Training Programs for the Economically Disadvantaged." *Journal of Economic Literature* 35 (December): 1809–55.

Greenberg, David, and Philip Robins. 1986. "The Changing Role of Social Experiments in Policy Analysis." *Journal of Policy Analysis and Management* 5 (2): 340–62.

Gueron, Judith. 1987. "Reforming Welfare with Work." Occasional Paper. New York: Ford Foundation.

Gueron, Judith. 1990. "Work and Welfare: Lessons on Employment Programs" *Journal of Economic Perspectives* 4 (1): 79–98.

Gueron, Judith, and Edward Pauly. 1991. *From Welfare to Work*. New York: Russell Sage Foundation.

Heckman, James. 1992. "Randomization and Social Policy Evaluation." In *Evaluating Welfare and Training Programs*, edited by Charles F. Manski and Irwin Garfinkel (201–30). Cambridge, Mass.: Harvard University Press.

Heckman, James, and V. Joseph Hotz. 1987. "Are Classical Experiments Necessary for Evaluating the Impact of Manpower Training Programs? A Critical Assessment." Proceedings of the Fortieth Annual Meeting, Industrial Relations Research Association Series.

Hollister, Robinson, Peter Kemper, and Rebecca Maynard. 1984. *The National Supported Work Demonstration*. Madison: The University of Wisconsin Press.

Hotz, V. Joseph. 1992. "Designing an Evaluation of the Job Training Partnership Act." In *Evaluating Welfare and Training Programs*, edited by Charles Manski and Irwin Garfinkel (76–114). Cambridge, Mass.: Harvard University Press.

The JTPA Advisory Committee. 1989. *Working Capital: JTPA Investments for the 90's*. Washington, D.C.: U.S. Department of Labor.

The JTPA Advisory Committee. 1989. *Working Capital: Coordinated Human Investment, Directions of the 90's*. Washington, D.C.: U.S. Department of Labor.

Kemple, James, Fred Doolittle, and John Wallace. 1993. *The National JTPA Study: Site Characteristics and Participation Patterns*. New York: Manpower Demonstration Research Corporation.

Levitan, Sar. 1992. "Evaluation of Federal Social Programs: An Uncertain Impact." Occasional Paper. Washington, D.C.: Center for Social Policy Studies.

Levitan, Sar, and Frank Gallo. 1988. *A Second Chance: Training for Jobs*. Kalamazoo, Mich.: W.E. Upjohn Institute for Employment Research.

Manpower Research Development Corporation. 1980. *Summary and Findings of the National Supported Work Demonstration*. Cambridge, Mass.: Ballinger.

Nathan, Richard, and Thomas L. Gais. 1998. *Overview Report: Implementation of the Personal Responsibility Act of 1996*. New York: The Nelson A. Rockefeller Institute of Government, State University of New York. Http://www.rockinst.org/appam.html.

National Commission for Employment Policy. 1987. *The Job Training Partnership Act*. Washington, D.C: National Commission for Employment Policy.

Nudelman, Jodi. 1995. "The Impacts of Job Training for Women on AFDC: An Analysis of Title II-A of the Job Training Partnership Act." Master's thesis, The Johns Hopkins University, Baltimore, Md.

Orr, Larry, Burt Barnow, Robert Lerman, and Erik Beecraft. 1997. *Follow-up Analyses of the JTPA Study Sample: Final Report.* Bethesda, Md.: Abt Associates Inc.

Orr, Larry, Howard Bloom, George Cave, Stephen Bell, Fred Doolittle, and Winston Lin. 1994. *The National JTPA Study: Impacts, Benefits, and Costs of Title II-A.* Bethesda, Md.: Abt Associates Inc.

Pavetti, LaDonna. 1993. "The Dynamics of Welfare and Work: Exploring the Process by Which Women Work Their Way Off Welfare." Ph.D. diss., Harvard University, Cambridge, Mass.

Riccio, James, Daniel Friedlander, and Stephen Freedman. 1994. *GAIN: Benefits, Costs, and Three-Year Impacts of a Welfare-to-Work Program.* New York: Manpower Research Development Corporation.

Romero, Carol. 1994. *JTPA Programs and Adult Women on Welfare: Using Training to Raise AFDC Recipients above Poverty.* Washington, D.C.: National Commission for Employment Policy.

Romero, Fred. 1990. "The National JTPA Study: Lessons Not Learned."

U.S. Department of Labor. 1995. *What's Working (and What's Not): A Summary of Research on the Economic Impacts of Employment and Training Programs.* Washington, D.C.: U.S. Department of Labor.

U.S. Department of Labor, Employment and Training Administration. 1994. *Training and Employment Report of the Secretary of Labor.* Washington, D.C.: U.S. Department of Labor.

U.S. Department of Labor, Employment and Training Administration. 1998. "Overview of the Workforce Investment Act of 1998." Http://usworkforce.org/runningtext2.htm.

U.S. General Accounting Office. 1989. *Job Training Partnership Act: Services and Outcomes for Participants with Differing Needs.* Washington, D.C.: GAO.

U.S. General Accounting Office. 1996. *Job Training Partnership Act: Long-Term Earnings and Employment Outcomes.* Washington, D.C.: GAO.

Chapter Five

TRAINING SUCCESS STORIES FOR ADULTS AND OUT-OF-SCHOOL YOUTH: A TALE OF TWO STATES

Christopher T. King, with Jerome A. Olson,
Leslie O. Lawson, Charles E. Trott, and John Baj

Several decades ago, federal agencies responsible for administering the diverse array of workforce training programs in this country, along with a number of foundations, often commissioned careful implementation or "best-practice" studies in an attempt to understand how programs were being run and to ferret out and document effective practices in the field.

At the time, however, there was simply no way of knowing with any certainty whether the efforts they touted did in fact yield the desired results—that is, whether they were successful over some longer-term period. Examples of such efforts include studies of training under the Comprehensive Employment and Training Act (CETA) (Levitan and Mangum 1981), of welfare-to-work efforts under the Work Incentive (WIN) program (Mitchell, Chadwin, and Nightingale 1980), and of youth programs (Hahn and Lerman 1985).

In the second half of the 1980s, the same agencies began to devote an increasing share of their research and evaluation dollars to supporting large-scale experiments and demonstrations, following the recommendations of both the U.S. Department of Labor's Job Training Longitudinal Survey Research Advisory Committee (Stromsdorfer et al. 1985) and the National Research Council's report on the youth demonstration projects of the late 1970s (Betsey, Hollister, and Papageorgiou 1985).[1] Latin evaluations using experimental designs (i.e., random assignment) have yielded a wealth of information on the impacts of participation in training programs, including those funded under the Job Opportunities and Basic Skills (JOBS) training

Research for and preparation of this chapter were supported with funding from the National Commission for Employment Policy, the U.S. Department of Labor's Employment and Training Administration, and the Sar Levitan Institute for Policy Studies at The Johns Hopkins University. Views expressed herein are the authors' and do not represent those of their respective institutions or the sponsors.

and related programs for welfare recipients (Friedlander and Burtless 1995), the Food Stamp Employment and Training program (Puma and Burstein 1994), and the Job Training Partnership Act (JTPA) programs (Bloom et al. 1997; Orr et al. 1995). Policymakers at all levels are now relatively well informed about the impacts on employment, earnings, and welfare receipt that can be expected for most target populations from participating in employment and training efforts.

Impact evaluations, however, typically have treated the intervention (e.g., training) largely as a "black box."[2] They also have tended to measure impacts based upon necessarily artificial constructs of the interventions, such as the strategies (e.g., the combined job search/on-the-job training stream) used in the JTPA experiment (Orr et al. 1995). The result is that such studies have offered little practical guidance to policymakers or program operators. There are notable exceptions in this literature, including the evaluations of the Minority Female, Single-Parent Demonstration (Burghardt and Gordon 1990; Hollister 1990) and some of the emerging welfare-to-work strategies evaluation reports from the Manpower Demonstration Research Corporation (MDRC), especially those for Portland, Oregon (Scrivener et al. 1998).

There has been a resurgence of best-practices research in the 1990s, as evidenced by studies of JTPA training (Kogan et al. 1991) and assessment and case management (Dickinson, Kogan, and Means 1994). In addition, both the U.S. General Accounting Office (GAO) (1996a) and the Chief Economist's Office at the U.S. Department of Labor (1995) have recently offered contributions. Yet most of this research has been performed independent of longer-term outcomes data for the programs in question. For the most part, state and local policymakers and local service providers still encounter a void concerning the factors that might contribute to operating successful training programs for disadvantaged adults and youth.[3]

This section begins with a brief summary of the available evidence on the effectiveness of training for disadvantaged adults and youth. It continues with a report on findings and their implications and associated recommendations for training policies and programs based on research the authors conducted on more than 50 local JTPA programs for adults and out-of-school youth in two large and diverse states, Illinois and Texas (King et al. 1995).[4] The authors had the benefit of readily available, longer-term labor market performance data derived from unemployment insurance (UI) wage records, both pre- and postprogram, for JTPA programs in the two states. The data permitted the researchers to focus on local programs in each state that had attained some degree of longer-term success, as measured in terms of employment and earnings outcomes, for a significant share of its participants.

THE EFFECTIVENESS OF TRAINING FOR DISADVANTAGED ADULTS AND YOUTH

So, what does the evaluation literature tell us about the impacts of training participation on key outcomes of interest? For this discussion, findings are grouped into pre-JTPA and JTPA findings.

Barnow (1987), LaLonde (1995), and others have synthesized the evidence on the impacts from pre-JTPA training for disadvantaged adults and youth in the period that preceded widespread use of experimental designs and their associated evaluation methodologies. Barnow (1987, p. 189) concluded:

> "Thus, a reasonable assessment of the impact of the CETA programs studied is that the programs probably had a modest impact of several hundred dollars on earnings for men and a somewhat greater effect on women. However, the confidence interval surrounding these estimates must be considered quite large considering the sensitivity to alternative specifications and the lack of any strong reasons to accept findings from one study over those of another."

Treatment impacts were typically estimated relative to the experiences of comparison group members, some of whom may have participated in similar activities available in their communities. Thus, impacts should be viewed conservatively as incremental relative to other services rather than the complete absence of services. CETA programs then encompassed public service employment (PSE), work experience, classroom training, and on-the-job training (OJT). The greatest estimated earnings impacts by activity were from participation in PSE and OJT, and the smallest impacts (including some negative impacts) were from work experience, with those for classroom training in between (Barnow 1987, p. 159 and table 3, pp. 182–85).

LaLonde's (1995) review concurs with Barnow's, finding that for the pre-JTPA nonexperimental evaluations, training raised participants' postprogram earnings by $1,000 to $2,000 annually (or about $1,180 to $2,362, if expressed in 1996 dollars).[5] He states that "[g]iven the modest cost of these programs, if these impacts were to persist throughout participants' careers, they would imply a substantial rate of return to training" (p. 156). Earnings gains were found most consistently for disadvantaged adult women; for disadvantaged men and youth, training either had no effect or yielded negative results.

Bloom et al. (1997) and Orr et al. (1995) report findings from the National JTPA Experimental Study that was commissioned by the U.S. Department of Labor (DOL) to measure the net impact of JTPA Title II-A participation by disadvantaged adults (ages 22 and over) and out-of-school youth on employment, earnings, and welfare receipt. Participation in the evaluation was voluntary on the part of the local JTPA programs; only 16 Service Delivery Areas (SDAs) of the more than 600 nationwide opted to participate. Service strategies—that is, classroom training, OJT/job search assistance (JSA), and other services—were determined before random assignment, an arrangement that allowed researchers to estimate effects by service strategy, on both a per-applicant and a per-enrollee basis, for adult men, adult women, and male and female out-of-school youth.

Bloom et al. (1997, table 3, p. 562) report substantial incremental earnings impacts per enrollee over the 30-month postassignment period. Adult women experienced per-enrollee impacts of $1,837 (or almost 15 percent); adult men enjoyed impacts almost as large, $1,599 (or 8 percent) over the same period, the first solid evidence of statistically significant earnings gains for men. There was no sign of decay in the impacts for either men or women over the 30 months. GAO (1996b), estimating impacts with five full years of postassignment data, reported that earnings of adult male and female treatment group members remained above those of controls at the end of the period, but asserted that fifth-year differences were not statistically significant (using only a 5 percent test of significance). For adult women, the incremental training cost was $1,324, while for men, the added cost was $1,076 (Bloom et al. 1997, table 5, p. 567). Friedlander, Greenberg, and Robins (1997, table 2, pp. 1830–31) estimate rates of return of 74 percent for adult men and 41 percent for women, if the mean impacts last for as long as three years.

Further, earnings impacts for adult women derived primarily from participation in the other services and OJT/JSA service strategies, which produced highly significant 30-month impacts (per enrollee) of just under $4,000 and $2,300, respectively. Classroom training yielded positive but insignificant impacts over the period. Friedlander, Greenberg, and Robins (1997) suggest that "the effectiveness of classroom training may depend crucially on the relative emphasis placed on upgrading general academic skills versus training for a specific occupation" (p. 1836). For men, although all the 30-month activity impact estimates were positive—$2,109 for OJT/JSA, $1,287 for classroom training, and $941 for other services—none were statistically significant.

For out-of-school youth, the JTPA study offered little to cheer about. As with most previous studies, "there was virtually no sign of a positive impact on earnings, either during the in-program period or during the two postprogram years" (Bloom et al. 1997, p. 563). A faint glimmer of hope is suggested in the GAO results: for both male and female youth, treatment group earnings continued to grow over the postprogram period; by the fifth year, they exceeded those of controls in both cases (GAO 1996b, pp. 6–7). Earnings impacts for male youth, in particular, showed signs of trending upward.

After reviewing both experimental and nonexperimental training evaluations over the past several decades, LaLonde (1995, p. 149) concludes:

> "The best summary of the evidence about the impact of past programs is that we got what we paid for. Public sector investments in training are exceedingly modest compared to the magnitude of the skill deficiencies that policymakers are trying to address. Not surprisingly, modest investments usually yield modest gains—too small to have much effect on poverty rates. There also is evidence that existing services are ineffective for some groups."

Thus, even when participation in training has been effective in enhancing employment experiences and increasing earnings, most of those benefiting have remained in or very near poverty status, a point reiterated by Heckman, Roselius, and Smith (1994). Few participants have emerged from training to secure stable, full-time jobs earning wages that would render them and their families economically self-sufficient.

Approach and Data Sources

The research reported in this chapter is based on neither an experimental nor a quasi-experimental design and thus differs from the studies reviewed in the previous section. In this research,[6] the authors utilized program year (PY) 1990 JTPA Title II-A termination and associated program participation records for all adults and out-of-school (O/S) youth, both groups for whom the expected results of training should primarily be more stable work and higher earnings.[7] These records were matched to longer-term pre- and postprogram UI employment and earnings records in two of the nation's most populous states, Illinois and Texas.[8] Instead of pursuing the research from the entering participant's point of view as with most experimental and quasi-experimental evaluations, this study design began with successful outcomes and worked backwards to explain them. That is, given successful employment and earnings outcomes, it sought to determine who attained them, in what occupations and industries they were initially placed, which JTPA activities and services they received, what labor market conditions they encountered, and in which SDAs they occurred. Fieldwork was then conducted with selected local JTPA programs that were successes, and discussions were held with knowledgeable state JTPA administrators and staff to validate and ferret out programmatic explanations for the results and to draw salient policy implications.

MEASURES OF PROGRAM SUCCESS

There are many ways of measuring the success of publicly funded training. One important approach is to measure the net societal benefits (i.e., benefits less costs) of training (Gramlich 1990). Another is to determine whether the local job training program met or exceeded its program performance standards, numerical targets established by the Secretary of Labor and typically adjusted further by governors (e.g., Barnow 1992). In fact, most local JTPA programs have been awarded cash incentives each year for meeting or exceeding their outcomes-based standards. Yet another way of gauging success is by estimated net impacts on participants' employment and earnings following program participation. Such impacts on earnings have ranged from negative and large to modestly positive as discussed above. Nor do the measures of success appear to be as well correlated as most policymakers would hope (e.g., Barnow 1999). But none of these mechanisms for assessing program performance addresses the issue of whether participation has led to a successful result in absolute terms for the participants and their families, whether immediately or over the longer run. Doing so requires establishing a conceptual framework, associated measures, and criteria for gauging success.

It is important to note that measures of participant success and associated criteria were established ex post facto for this research. Neither of the states' JTPA programs was explicitly pursuing the success measures as defined here, nor were any of the local programs doing so. Instead, state and local programs were largely pursuing the federally established, state-adjusted performance standards and, in all likelihood, hoping to produce the desired net impacts on employment, earnings, and welfare receipt for their participants.

Concepts and measures of economic self-sufficiency have changed over time (e.g., Schwarz and Volgy 1992; Citro and Michael 1995). Recent work by the authors has explored this concept in different contexts—the University of Texas at Austin's Center for the Study of Human Resources (1993) in terms of successful exits from Texas's Aid to Families with Dependent Children (AFDC) program, and the Chicago Urban League, the Latino Institute, and Northern Illinois University (1993) in the context of "making work pay" in Chicago. Mangum et al. (1999) also recognize that poverty concepts and measures have become outdated and suggest a range of earnings for gauging economic self-sufficiency from 113 percent to 200 percent of the existing poverty standard, with a recommended level of 165 percent (pp. 21ff.)

We considered several measures of success for both adults and out-of-school youth terminees but ultimately used only two principal measures in this analysis, as follows:

- *155 percent of poverty,* an earnings measure based on the economic self-sufficiency concept developed by Schwarz and Volgy (1992). The measure essentially applies a factor of 1.55 to each of the existing federally defined (before-tax) poverty income levels; thus the measure varies by family size.[9] The rationale for using such an adjustment is that existing federal poverty measures have become outdated. They fail to account for many new items that are now an important part of the average consumer's market basket, as well as for the far greater share of total expenditures that housing constitutes.

- *Strict-steady employment,* that is, continuous employment, potentially with several different employers, in which an employment quarter is defined as one with UI-covered earnings greater than or equal to working 20 hours each week in the quarter at the federal minimum wage. This measure mimics the employment definitions that have been used by the U.S. Department of Labor's Employment and Training Administration for the national JTPA performance standards since 1994 (DOL 1994).

The measures were analyzed over two postprogram time frames, that is, the first and second full years following an individual's program termination quarter. Earlier research has focused on such measures as attaining earnings above the federal poverty level or employment retention (Romero 1994). The two success measures used here are more difficult to attain. Although quarterly data are available and were analyzed, the emphasis is on annual patterns.

Illinois and Texas are two of the country's most populous states, ranking sixth and third, respectively, in 1990.[10] They share many characteristics but reflect important differences as well. Illinois's 1990 population of around 11.6 million was approximately 78 percent white, 15 percent black, and 8 percent Hispanic. Texas's population of nearly 17 million was 61 percent white, 12 percent black, and 26 percent Hispanic, nearly all of whom were Mexican-American. Of the two state populations, the Illinois population was slightly better educated.

Although both states are highly urbanized—83 to 84 percent of the people reside in metropolitan statistical areas (MSAs)—their population distributions were markedly different. The Illinois portion of the Chicago MSA accounts for two-thirds of all Illinois residents and almost four of every five of its urban dwellers, while the Dallas, Houston, and San Antonio MSAs account for just over half the Texas population. Illinois outside the Chicago area is predominantly rural, but Texas features many other MSAs as well as vast rural areas.

Illinois and Texas faced broadly comparable labor market situations during the time frame encompassed by this study, whether expressed in unemployment rates, employment-to-population ratios, or the share of employment in key sectors and industries.[11] Of the two states, a higher share of Illinois's nonfarm employment was in manufacturing. Illinois also had much higher median household incomes and higher shares of its population on some form of public assistance, but much lower poverty rates. Poverty rates in Texas were especially high for single-parent families, children, nonwhites, and residents of communities near the Mexican border.

JTPA has established statewide delivery systems that provide job training and related services for unskilled adults and youth who are economically disadvantaged and for others who face serious barriers to employment. Private Industry Councils (PICs) in SDAs, of which there were 35 in Texas and 26 in Illinois in PY 1990,[12] oversaw local JTPA operations, including the development, coordination, and delivery of training programs. JTPA Title II-A was the core training program for adults and both in-school and out-of-school youth during the period.[13] During PY 1990, Title II-A programs in those states served 38,386 adults and youth in Illinois and 67,122 in Texas.

Characteristics of the Study Population

This study focuses on adults and out-of-school youth (18 and older) who were enrolled in JTPA for at least seven days and who also terminated sometime during PY 1990. The majority of the 20,126 Illinois and 24,919 Texas JTPA Title II-A adult and out-of-school youth terminees studied were female, as were terminees nationwide (table 5.1).[14] They also tended to be young—approximately 60 percent under age 30—and minorities: slightly over 53 percent in Illinois (mostly black) and almost 69 percent in Texas. Hispanics were by far the largest racial or ethnic group in Texas (45 percent). Nationally, whites constituted the largest group.

One of the sharpest differences between Texas and Illinois was in the reported education levels of their terminees. While close to half of all terminees in both states had just completed high school or received a general equivalency diploma (GED), only 25 percent of Illinois terminees but fully 40 percent of those in Texas had not graduated or received a GED.

Although family status was not available for Illinois (or national) JTPA terminees, well over half of all Texas terminees had some parental responsibility, whether single parents (32 percent) or parents in two-parent families (24 percent). The vast majority of Texas terminees lived with at least one other family member; nearly 40 percent lived in families with four or more members. In Illinois, by contrast, nearly 43 percent were in one-person families.

Nearly one-quarter of terminees in each state and nationally were AFDC recipients at enrollment, and 40 to 50 percent received some other form of public assistance, including food stamps, Refugee Cash Assistance, or Supplemental Security Income. The categories are not mutually exclusive, of course, as nearly all AFDC recipients also receive food stamps.

In line with the late 1980s national policy shift away from relative quick-fix approaches and toward more intensive services, JTPA programs in the two states emphasized longer-term, more substantive interventions. Enrollments in basic education activities continued to increase, and average program stays (not shown) were longer in PY 1990 than in previous years. Nationally, length of stay for all terminees rose by 26 percent from PY 1987 to PY 1990, to 129 days. Moreover, the mix of activities, as indicated by major program activity,[15] appears to reflect the differences in their terminee populations. OJT accounted for around 28 percent in each. Basic skills training (BST) was limited in Illinois but represented the most common activity (33 percent) for Texas's less-educated terminees. Occupational skills training (OST) and job search assistance (JSA) accounted for a greater share of Illinois than Texas terminees. Nationally, JTPA programs appeared to place more emphasis on JSA and other services, including work experience—likely reflecting the inclusion of in-school

Table 5.1 CHARACTERISTICS OF ILLINOIS, TEXAS, AND U.S. JTPA TITLE II-A
ADULT AND OUT-OF-SCHOOL YOUTH TERMINEES IN FY 1990

Characteristic	Illinois	Texas	United States*
Gender			
Male	45.3%	39.7%	43.0%
Female	54.7	60.3	57.0
Age Group			
18–21	26.4%	30.1%	41.0%
22–29	31.8	30.7	
30–39	26.8	26.0	59.0
40–49	10.0	9.9	
50+	5.1	3.2	
Race/Ethnic			
White	46.6%	29.8%	52.0%
Black	40.9	24.0	33.0
Hispanic	12.4	44.6	12.0
Other	2.1	1.5	4.0
Education			
Less than high school	25.3%	40.5%	
High school/GED	52.7	48.8	
More than high school	22.5	10.7	
Family Status (Texas only)			
Single parent		31.9%	
Parent in two-parent family	N.A.	23.5	
Other family member		20.8	
Nondependent individual		23.9	
Persons in Family			
1	42.9%	23.0%	
2	19.0	17.6	
3	16.0	20.7	
4	11.1	17.0	
5 or more	11.0	21.7	
Welfare Status			
AFDC recipient	24.1%	21.5%	24.0%
Other public assistance	39.9	50.0	46.0
Major Program Activity			
Basic skills training	8.5%	32.9%	—
Occupational skills training	40.9	28.5	40.0%
On-the-job training	28.4	27.8	18.0
Job search assistance	10.8	5.1	16.0
Other	11.3	5.6	26.0

Table 5.1 CHARACTERISTICS OF ILLINOIS, TEXAS, AND U.S. JTPA TITLE II-A
ADULT AND OUT-OF-SCHOOL YOUTH TERMINEES IN FY 1990
(*continued*)

Characteristic	Illinois	Texas	United States*
Preprogram Work History			
Earnings first year prior	$817	$936	
Earnings second year prior	261	761	
Average quarters employed—first year	1.7	1.8	
Average quarters employed—second year	1.6	1.8	
Termination Status			
Not employed at termination	35.7%	26.3%	45.0%
Minimal employment at termination	1.2	1.4	
Substantial employment at termination	16.7	12.9	55.0
Full-time employment at termination	52.4	59.3	
Occupation at Termination			
Management/administration	2.4%	1.4%	
Professional	6.0	7.1	
Sales	7.9	8.9	
Clerical	23:4	22.3	
Service	27.5	25.7	
Agriculture	0.7	1.7	
Precision production	8.3	10.8	
Operator	23.8	22.1	
Industry at Termination			
Agriculture	4.0%	1.4%	
Mining	3.4	0.7	
Construction	2.7	6.1	
Manufacturing	20.5	15.8	
Transportation, electric, gas, etc.	5.1	5.2	
Wholesale	3.5	2.0	
Retail	15.6	18.4	
Finance, insurance, real estate	4.2	2.6	
Services	38.9	40.8	
Other	2.2	7.0	
Percent of Total JTPA Title II-A Adult and Out-of-School Youth Terminees	100.0%	100.0%	100.0%
n	20,126	24,919	550,400

*Estimates of adult and all youth based on Job Training Quarterly Survey figures
where comparable (DOL 1992).

youth in the national figures—and less emphasis on OJT and class-room training.

Recent work experience in the two years preceding program entry was limited for terminees in both states; mean preprogram earnings were well under $1,000 annually for both preprogram years. Most terminees were reported as employed at termination from JTPA—about 65 percent in Illinois and 75 percent in Texas (compared to 55 percent nationally)—and roughly four of five of those were employed full-time (at least 35 hours per week). At least 70 percent of all term-inees with a job at termination were clustered into clerical, service, and operator occupations. Three-quarters were employed in the ser-vice, manufacturing, and retail trade industries. Service industry jobs alone accounted for about 40 percent of all termination jobs.

GENDER COMPARISONS

For some of the major demographic characteristics, including age, race/ethnicity, and education, male and female terminees appeared similar (table 5.2). However, other gender differences were marked, especially those for family status and size. Nearly 71 percent of Texas's female terminees were parents, primarily (51 percent) single parents; fewer than one-third of males were parents, and most of those were parents in two-parent families. In both states, female par-ticipants were part of much larger families and were far more likely to be receiving AFDC and other forms of public assistance at entry.

Male terminees also were more likely to have been enrolled in OJT (about 38 to 39 percent) as their major program activity than were females (at 20 to 21 percent), while females tended to have been enrolled in basic skills (36 percent) and occupational skills training (32 percent) in Texas and occupational skills training (52 percent) in Illinois.

Males had a sizable work and earnings advantage over females upon entering JTPA. Males also worked more quarters on average and, depending on the preprogram year selected, posted median UI earnings from 1.7 to 3.5 times (Illinois) to about 2.5 times (Texas) those of their female counterparts.

Female terminees were less likely to be employed at termination than males, and, if employed, were more likely to be employed less-than-full-time. JTPA administrative records shed no light on the rea-sons for part-time employment at termination. Male terminees were employed disproportionately in operator, precision production, and, to a lesser extent, agricultural occupations. Generally, female termi-nees worked more in clerical, sales, and professional occupations. Male terminees were also disproportionately employed in traditional goods-producing industries—especially manufacturing—as well as in transportation and public utilities. Females tended to be employed disproportionately in services industries.

Descriptive Results

Success rates for both the employment and earnings measures vary by state. The share of terminees who were continuously employed using the strict-steady employment definition increased from almost 25 percent to 28 percent from the first to the second postprogram year in Illinois, but remained roughly constant in Texas at about 35 percent (table 5.3). Earnings success rates, however, rose from the first to the second postprogram year in both states, from 20 percent to 31 percent in Illinois and from 22 percent to 25 percent in Texas (table 5.4).

Longer-term program success rates for both measures tended to move in consistent and expected ways with the usual array of demographic, program, and employment variables. Success rates were consistently higher for males, adults, whites, those with greater educational attainment, and those not receiving any form of public assistance at enrollment. In addition, those with more quarters of employment and higher earnings in the two years before entering the program also experienced greater postprogram success. Preprogram earnings levels were low even for those judged to be postprogram earnings successes; they ranged from about $1,600 to $3,000 annually depending on the preprogram year. Such earnings would hardly qualify the participants as preprogram successes.

Parents in two-parent families (available for Texas only) tended to post higher employment and earnings success rates than all other groups. Adjusting earnings for family status and size produced substantial effects on earnings success rates in Texas.[16] Those with greater family responsibilities and larger family sizes—including women, minorities, and those with less education—faced even more difficulty reaching real levels of economic self-sufficiency when their earnings were adjusted to account for differences in family status and size. There appears to be a family-size employment success effect in Illinois—larger families being associated with higher success rates—but not in Texas.

Success rates also were noticeably higher for participants who were enrolled in OST and OJT, as well as for those who secured full-time jobs at program termination. Having a full-time job at termination conveyed a considerable employment and earnings advantage over those without any job and those with only minimal (less than

Table 5.2 CHARACTERISTICS OF PY 1990 ILLINOIS AND TEXAS JTPA TITLE II-A
ADULT AND OUT-OF-SCHOOL YOUTH TERMINEES, BY GENDER

	Male		Female	
Characteristic	Illinois	Texas	Illinois	Texas
Age Group				
18–21	26.2%	31.0%	26.5%	29.6%
22–29	32.3	29.0	31.4	31.9
30–39	26.8	26.1	26.8	26.0
40–49	10.1	10.4	9.8	9.5
50+	4.6	3.5	5.5	3.1
Race/Ethnic				
White	46.0%	31.0%	43.5%	29.1%
Black	38.8	20.7	42.6	26.1
Hispanic	12.8	46.3	12.1	43.5
Other	2.4	2.0	1.8	1.2
Education				
Less than high school	28.5%	41.5%	22.7%	39.9%
High school/GED	50.8	47.1	53.3	50.0
More than high school	20.8	11.4	24.0	10.2
Family Status (Texas only)				
Single parent		3.0%		50.9%
Parent in two-parent family	N.A.	29.1	N.A.	19.7
Other family member		28.2		15.9
Nondependent individual		39.6		13.5
Persons in Family				
1	59.1%	38.2%	29.5%	12.9%
2	10.7	11.9	25.8	21.4
3	10.8	15.6	20.8	24.1
4	9.1	13.7	12.7	19.2
5 or more	10.1	20.7	11.2	22.3
Welfare Status				
AFDC recipient	6.8%	4.3%	38.4%	32.8%
Other public assistance	31.2	34.9	47.1	60.0
Major Program Activity				
Basic skills training	7.9%	28.4%	9.0%	35.8%
Occupational skills training	28.3	23.2	51.5	32.1
On-the-job training	38.9	37.9	19.6	21.2
Job search assistance	12.2	4.9	9.6	5.3
Other	12.6	5.7	10.3	5.6
Preprogram Work History				
Earnings first year prior	$1,066	$1,578	$632	$621
Earnings second year prior	467	1,258	132	534
Average quarters employed— first year	1.8	2.0	1.7	1.7
Average quarters employed— second year	1.7	1.9	1.5	1.7

Table 5.2 CHARACTERISTICS OF PY 1990 ILLINOIS AND TEXAS JTPA TITLE II-A
ADULT AND OUT-OF-SCHOOL YOUTH TERMINEES, BY GENDER
(*continued*)

Characteristic	Male		Female	
	Illinois	Texas	Illinois	Texas
Termination Status				
Not employed at termination	32.1%	22.2%	38.6%	29.1%
Minimal employment at termination	0.8	0.8	1.6	1.8
Substantial employment at termination	8.9	9.7	12.3	15.1
Full-time employment at termination	58.3	67.4	47.5	54.0
Occupation at Termination				
Management/administration	2.1%	1.4%	2.5%	1.5%
Professional	3.4	4.2	8.5	9.3
Sales	5.0	6.1	10.5	11.0
Clerical	10.3	7.9	35.4	32.6
Service	26.9	21.2	28.0	29.0
Agriculture	1.1	3.2	0.3	0.6
Precision production	14.8	22.3	2.4	2.4
Operator	36.3	33.8	12.4	13.7
Industry at Termination				
Agriculture	4.6%	2.3%	3.4%	0.8%
Mining	4.2	1.2	2.7	0.4
Construction	4.2	12.5	1.2	1.5
Manufacturing	26.5	20.2	15.0	12.7
Transportation, electric, gas, etc.	6.9	7.1	3.5	3.8
Wholesale	4.1	2.6	3.0	1.5
Retail	15.9	16.8	15.3	19.5
Finance, insurance, real estate	2.2	1.1	6.0	3.7
Services	29.2	28.3	47.8	49.8
Other	2.1	8.0	2.2	6.4
Percent of Total JTPA Title II-A Adult and Out-of-School Youth Terminees	100.0%	100.0%	100.0%	100.0%
n	9,112	9,902	11,015	15,017

20 hours/week) or substantial (20 to 35 hours/week) part-time
employment. Type of job at termination was also important for success. Those placed in less seasonally oriented employment tended to
be more successful by these measures as well. Not surprisingly, success rate variation tended to be more pronounced for earnings than
for employment success.

Table 5.3 PERCENT OF PY 1990 ILLINOIS AND TEXAS JTPA TITLE II-A
ADULT AND OUT-OF-SCHOOL YOUTH TERMINEES
CONTINUOUSLY EMPLOYED DURING THE FIRST AND
SECOND POSTPROGRAM YEARS

| | Postprogram Year | | | |
| | First | | Second | |
Characteristic	Illinois	Texas	Illinois	Texas
Gender				
Male	24.9%	36.3%	27.7%	36.2%
Female	24.2	33.5	28.3	33.7
Age Group				
18–21	21.6%	26.9%	25.4%	28.4%
22–29	25.1	37.3	28.8	36.9
30–39	26.6	38.4	29.3	37.6
40–49	27.5	38.8	29.8	39.2
50+	23.1	37.3	26.8	34.7
Race/Ethnic				
White	28.2%	37.4%	31.6%	36.5%
Black	18.6	29.2	21.8	30.2
Hispanic	29.7	35.5	35.3	35.2
Other	31.7	39.7	31.2	37.9
Education				
Less than high school	16.6%	22.8%	18.9%	24.0%
High school/GED	25.7	41.4	29.7	41.0
More than high school	30.7	47.8	34.3	46.3
Family Status (Texas only)				
Single parent		32.8%		33.2%
Parent in two-parent family	N.A.	41.2	N.A.	41.1
Other family member		31.5		32.0
Nondependent individual		33.2		32.5
Persons in Family				
1	23.0%	33.5%	25.6%	32.8%
2	23.8	34.3	28.3	33.8
3	26.2	35.2	30.7	35.7
4	28.3	34.9	32.6	35.4
5 or more	25.7	35.2	30.9	35.8
Welfare Status				
AFDC recipient	18.2%	25.3%	22.1%	25.8%
Other public assistance	19.7	31.2	22.8	31.7
Major Program Activity				
Basic skills training	11.9%	20.2%	14.9%	23.1%
Occupational skills training	24.8	41.8	29.6	42.5
On-the-job training	31.0	44.4	33.2	39.8
Job search assistance	23.5	36.3	26.3	38.0
Other	18.0	31.9	20.9	33.3

Table 5.3 PERCENT OF PY 1990 ILLINOIS AND TEXAS JTPA TITLE II-A
ADULT AND OUT-OF-SCHOOL YOUTH TERMINEES
CONTINUOUSLY EMPLOYED DURING THE FIRST AND
SECOND POSTPROGRAM YEARS (*continued*)

| Characteristic | Postprogram Year | | | |
| | First | | Second | |
	Illinois	Texas	Illinois	Texas
Preprogram Work History				
Earnings first year prior	$2,434	$2,406	$2,314	$2,343
Earnings second year prior	1,479	2,093	1,476	2,052
Average quarters employed—first year	N.A.	2.2	N.A.	2.2
Average quarters employed—second year	N.A.	2.2	N.A.	2.2
Termination Status				
Not employed at termination	8.6%	16.8%	14.1%	21.1%
Minimal employment at termination	17.5	17.4	28.5	23.7
Substantial employment at termination	23.2	28.9	26.2	31.4
Full-time employment at termination	35.9	44.2	37.9	41.6
Occupation at Termination				
Management/administration	39.7%	39.8%	42.3%	38.6%
Professional	53.2	61.0	56.7	59.8
Sales	34.8	35.8	30.0	35.1
Clerical	36.7	45.4	40.9	44.7
Service	27.3	35.0	28.7	34.1
Agriculture	14.4	27.3	18.9	28.9
Precision production	36.3	40.1	34.0	38.4
Operator	34.0	40.7	36.1	37.3
Industry at Termination				
Agriculture	30.7%	25.1%	31.7%	25.5%
Mining	33.7	44.2	43.5	44.2
Construction	22.8	33.8	26.0	31.3
Manufacturing	37.3	45.2	39.5	42.0
Transportation, electric, gas, etc.	34.3	40.9	35.3	39.7
Wholesale	41.1	39.9	40.9	36.8
Retail	26.2	37.2	27.1	33.7
Finance, insurance, real estate	34.5	44.8	44.1	43.6
Services	34.0	42.6	46.1	41.6
Other	30.8	47.7	34.8	45.9
Percent of Total JTPA Title II-A Adult and Out-of-School Youth Terminees	24.5%	34.6%	28.0%	34.7%
n	20,127	24,919	20,127	24,919

Table 5.4 PERCENT OF PY 1990 ILLINOIS AND TEXAS JTPA TITLE II-A
ADULT AND OUT-OF-SCHOOL TERMINEES WITH EARNINGS THAT
EXCEEDED 155 PERCENT OF POVERTY DURING THE FIRST AND
SECOND POSTPROGRAM YEARS

| | Postprogram Year | | | |
| | First | | Second | |
Characteristic	Illinois	Texas	Illinois	Texas
Gender				
Male	22.0%	27.3%	32.5%	29.1%
Female	17.8	19.1	29.8	22.0
Age Group				
18–21	13.3%	13.8%	26.9%	17.3%
22–29	21.3	24.5	32.5	27.1
30–39	22.8	27.4	32.8	29.1
40–49	24.3	27.6	34.8	29.7
50+	17.8	23.4	26.3	24.0
Race/Ethnic				
White	22.1%	29.6%	33.4%	30.9%
Black	14.5	18.1	25.1	20.8
Hispanic	26.1	19.3	41.3	22.6
Other	32.4	35.3	36.8	34.5
Education				
Less than high school	11.1%	11.7%	20.1%	14.0%
High school/GED	20.7	27.5	33.2	30.4
More than high school	27.0	39.2	38.4	40.6
Family Status (Texas only)				
Single parent		19.7%		22.0%
Parent in two-parent family	N.A.	28.8	N.A.	32.0
Other family member		17.6		20.5
Nondependent individual		23.7		25.2
Persons in Family				
1	17.6%	24.2%	27.9%	25.6%
2	18.7	20.7	30.7	23.3
3	21.5	22.3	33.7	25.1
4	24.1	22.3	36.4	25.7
5 or more	22.5	21.6	34.5	24.3
Welfare Status				
AFDC recipient	13.9%	13.1%	25.0%	14.5%
Other public assistance	14.7	17.7	24.3	20.3
Major Program Activity				
Basic skills training	6.5%	10.3%	16.3%	13.1%
Occupational skills training	20.3	31.9	32.5	34.9
On-the-job training	26.2	27.5	37.0	28.6
Job search assistance	18.5	18.4	28.8	25.1
Other	12.1	21.8	23.8	23.2

Table 5.4　PERCENT OF PY 1990 ILLINOIS AND TEXAS JTPA TITLE II-A
ADULT AND OUT-OF-SCHOOL TERMINEES WITH EARNINGS THAT
EXCEEDED 155 PERCENT OF POVERTY DURING THE FIRST AND
SECOND POSTPROGRAM YEARS (*continued*)

| | Postprogram Year | | | |
| | First | | Second | |
Characteristic	Illinois	Texas	Illinois	Texas
Preprogram Work History				
Earnings first year prior	$2,827	$3,075	$2,342	$2,940
Earnings second year prior	1,798	2,961	1,617	2,874
Average quarters employed— first year	N.A.	2.3	N.A.	2.3
Average quarters employed— second year	N.A.	2.3	N.A.	2.3
Termination Status				
Not employed at termination	6.5%	10.0%	17.2%	13.1%
Minimal employment at termination	10.6	9.7	22.0	12.8
Substantial employment at termination	9.6	11.3	25.1	16.7
Full-time employment at termination	31.0	30.5	41.9	32.1
Occupation at Termination				
Management/administration	36.4%	29.7%	46.9%	29.7%
Professional	59.4	56.5	63.7	56.8
Sales	12.9	13.3	27.5	16.6
Clerical	30.4	30.5	43.1	33.8
Service	15.8	15.9	28.8	19.5
Agriculture	10.0	12.4	25.6	16.5
Precision production	33.6	33.4	43.7	33.6
Operator	30.4	29.0	41.1	30.1
Industry at Termination				
Agriculture	26.7%	15.6%	34.5%	20.2%
Mining	30.9	45.0	43.5	42.6
Construction	25.4	32.3	35.6	31.3
Manufacturing	34.5	32.5	45.8	33.4
Transportation, electric, gas, etc.	31.8	31.5	40.6	32.2
Wholesale	35.9	30.8	44.5	30.8
Retail	12.6	13.6	25.6	17.7
Finance, insurance, real estate	32.4	33.4	46.6	33.8
Services	26.0	27.7	30.0	30.7
Other	31.5	34.1	40.7	26.9
Percent of Total JTPA Title II-A Adult and Out-of-School Youth Terminees	19.7%	22.3%	31.0%	24.8%
n	20,127	24,919	20,127	24,919

The effects of employment status at termination on earnings success are also visible through their postprogram success transition rates. Figures 5.1 and 5.2 show earnings success transition rates for Illinois and Texas using two different termination-status configurations; the left panel in each figure contrasts rates for those with *any* employment at termination versus all others, whereas the right panel provides transition rates for those employed *full-time* at termination versus all others. Having a job—any job—at termination clearly contributes to earnings success, with some 80 percent and 92 percent of second-year successes having had a job when they left the program in Illinois and Texas, respectively. But having a full-time job at termination was even more critical: 71 percent and 81 percent of all year-two earnings successes in each state had been employed full-time when they exited JTPA. Note that this is far higher than their respective shares of all terminees: 52 percent in Illinois and 59 percent in Texas.

Multivariate Findings

Descriptive statistics can take the analysis only so far. Multivariate analysis was performed to isolate independent influences on outcomes, modeling successful outcomes as a function of demographic, program participation, and local population/economic variables for each year. Both ordinary least squares (OLS) and logistic regression were performed. Logistic regression is the more appropriate estimation technique when the outcome of interest is a dichotomous variable, such as success/nonsuccess; in such cases, OLS sometimes provide misleading results. The models presented in this section were estimated using both techniques and then compared. There were no substantive differences in the results. Thus, only OLS results are presented here.[17] Dependent variables for the regressions were dummy variables for the two success measures: strict-steady employment, and earnings greater than 155 percent of poverty. Separate regressions were run for each postprogram year. Appendix table 5A.1 defines the variables used in these regressions.

EMPLOYMENT SUCCESS

Table 5.5 summarizes the OLS results for employment success in the first and second postprogram years for all PY 1990 Illinois and Texas terminees. Variables indicated with a + or − had statistically significant,[18] positive or negative effects on employment success when controlling for the effects of other factors. Variables indicated

Figure 5.1 PERCENT OF ILLINOIS PY 1990 JTPA TITLE II-A ADULT AND OUT-OF-SCHOOL YOUTH TERMINEES BY SELF-SUFFICIENCY EARNINGS LEVEL IN THE FIRST AND SECOND POSTPROGRAM YEARS, BY EMPLOYMENT STATUS AT TERMINATION

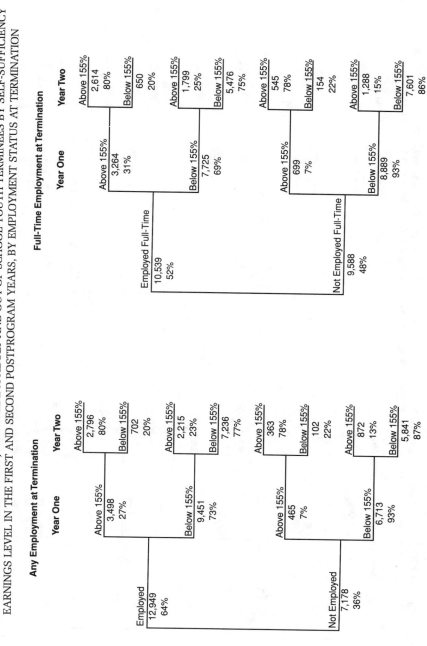

Figure 5.2 PERCENT OF TEXAS PY 1990 JTPA TITLE II-A ADULT AND OUT-OF-SCHOOL YOUTH TERMINEES BY SELF-SUFFICIENCY
EARNINGS LEVEL IN THE FIRST AND SECOND POSTPROGRAM YEARS, BY EMPLOYMENT STATUS AT TERMINATION

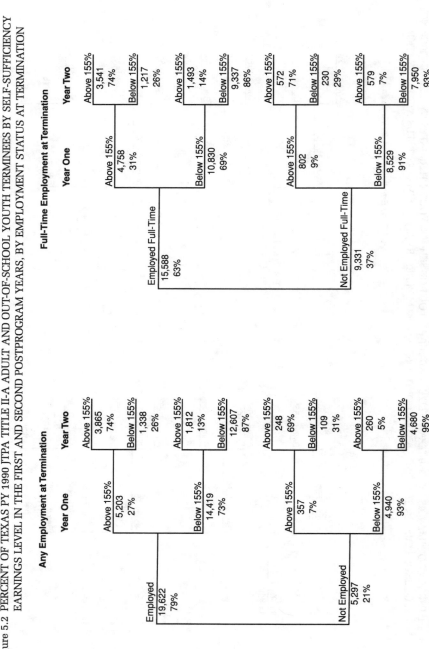

Table 5.5 EXPLAINING THE EMPLOYMENT SUCCESS OF PY 1990 ILLINOIS AND TEXAS OUT-OF-SCHOOL YOUTH AND ADULT JTPA TERMINEES IN THE FIRST AND SECOND POSTPROGRAM YEARS

Characteristic/Variable	Illinois		Texas	
	Postprogram Year		Postprogram Year	
	First	Second	First	Second
Female	+***	+***	+***	
Ages 18–21			−***	−*
Ages 30–39				
Ages 40–49				
Ages 50+	−**	−**		
Black	−***	−***	−***	−*
Hispanic		+***	+***	+***
High school dropout	−***	−***	−***	−***
Post–high school	+***	+***	+***	+***
Single parent	N.A.	N.A.	+***	+***
Parent in two-parent family	N.A.	N.A.	+***	+***
Other family member	N.A.	N.A.		+*
Two-person family	+*	+***		
Three-person family	+***	+***		
Four-person family	+***	+***		
Five-person family	+***	+***		
AFDC recipient	−***	−***	−***	−***
Other public assistance recipient	−***	−***	−***	−***
Basic skills training				
Occupational skills training	+***	+***	+***	+***
OJT	+***	+***	+***	+*
Job search assistance	+*			
Average prior earnings, years 1–2	+***	+***	+***	+***
Minimal employment at termination	N.A.	N.A.		
Substantial employment at termination	+***	+***	+***	+***
Full-time employment at termination	+***	+***	+***	+***
Percent families in poverty				
Median area rent	−**		−*	
Average area unemployment, 1991–92				
Per capita income, 1991–92		−***		
Employment growth, 1990–92			+**	+***
R-square	0.13	0.11	0.13	0.10
n	20,126	20,126	23,091	23,091

Source: Appendix table 5A.2.

with a blank space had no statistically significant effects. A reference group has been selected for each set of regressions, with variable coefficients indicating effects relative to that group. In most cases, the reference group is implicit but relatively unambiguous, for example, terminees ages 22 through 29, whites, those with just a high school education in table 5.5. Detailed regression results for both states are provided in the chapter appendix (appendix tables 5A.2 through 5A.5).

There are few differences between the two postprogram years in the way most of the demographic characteristics, program participation, and environmental factors affect employment success in Texas and Illinois. Females are more likely to be continuously employed than males. Blacks face significantly lower chances of employment success, while Hispanics tend to face higher ones relative to whites/others, mirroring their experiences in the labor market generally. High school dropouts were significantly less likely and post–high school graduates significantly more likely to succeed in both years than those with just a high school diploma. Terminees who received public assistance at enrollment in any form were significantly less likely to find and keep jobs in both years.

The two training activities, OST and OJT, had significant positive effects on employment success in both years, although the OJT coefficient for Texas was marginally significant but still positive in year two. Job search assistance was marginally significant in Illinois in the first year.

The prior earnings coefficient was highly significant and positive in both years, indicating that one of the indicators of postprogram employment success was preprogram success. This is the case despite the fact that the preprogram earnings of the successes were low (see table 5.3). In addition, the results for termination employment status variables show significant positive effects from having either substantial part-time or full-time work at termination. The effects are strong and consistent across both postprogram years.

As for noteworthy differences between the states, being an out-of-school youth is associated with significant reductions in the chances of employment success in both years in Texas but not in Illinois, as is being 50 or older in Illinois but not Texas. Such differences are not easily explained. Also, family status and size results are particularly interesting. Texas offered the opportunity to control for family status as well as size, while Illinois could adjust only for family size. In Texas, parents—whether single parents or parents in two-parent families—were significantly more likely to succeed than others, whereas family size was not associated with employment success either positively or negatively, because of the previous adjustment for family status. In Illinois, however, increasing family size, unadjusted for family status, was associated with increased employment success. This suggests that family size variables may be carrying some of the weight that is more appropriately placed on family status.

Surprisingly, few of the local economic and population variables produced strong significant effects on terminees' postprogram employment success. Median area rents, a cost-of-living proxy, negatively affected employment success in both states, but only in the first year. In Illinois, per capita incomes exerted a negative influence in year two only, while area employment growth rates were positively and significantly associated with employment success in both years only for Texas terminees.

The factors affecting continuous employment success for males and females exhibit important similarities as well as differences (table 5.6). The factors having the most significant positive effects on postprogram employment success for both males and females were Hispanic ethnicity, prior earnings, and termination employment status (both substantial and full-time employment). Receipt of other public assistance and having less than a high school education had significant negative effects on employment success.

There were also interesting differences. First, being a parent in a two-parent family positively affected employment success for males but not for females. Second, for females, receiving any form of public assistance lowered their chances for success, while for males, only other public assistance did.[19] Third, males apparently benefited from participating in all activities (relative to participation in other) in year one, whereas there was only one significant year two activity coefficient for females, OST (in Illinois). And fourth, area economic variables largely appeared to influence employment success for females but not for males, a result consistent with research on labor force participation that indicates that males have fewer nonwork alternatives than females, regardless of the state of the local economy.

EARNINGS SUCCESS

Earnings results for PY 1990 Illinois and Texas JTPA terminees are summarized in table 5.7. Most of the variable coefficients had the expected signs and either produced consistent effects across both postprogram years or had effects that were significant in one year but not the other. Being an out-of-school youth, black, and a high school dropout and receiving other public assistance all were associated with significantly lower earnings success rates in both postprogram years in Illinois and Texas. Other variables with primarily negative effects on earnings success in both states were being female, being 50 or older, living in areas with larger shares of families in poverty, and living in high-rent areas. Similarly, being a parent (whether single or in a two-parent family, Texas only), having some

Table 5.6 EXPLAINING THE EMPLOYMENT SUCCESS OF MALE AND FEMALE PY 1990 ILLINOIS AND TEXAS OUT-OF-SCHOOL YOUTH AND ADULT JTPA TERMINEES, BY GENDER, IN THE SECOND POSTPROGRAM YEAR

| Characteristic/Variable | Illinois | | Texas | |
| | Gender | | Gender | |
	Male	Female	Male	Female
Ages 18–21	+*	_*		_***
Ages 30–39			_***	
Ages 40–49	_*			
Ages 50+		_***	_*	
Black	_***	_***	_***	+*
Hispanic	+***	+*	+***	+***
High school dropout	_***	_***	_***	_***
Post–high school	+*	+***		+***
Single parent	N.A.	N.A.		
Parent in two-parent family	N.A.	N.A.	+***	
Other family member	N.A.	N.A.		
Two-person family	+*	+***		
Three-person family	+***	+***		
Four-person family	+***	+***		
Five-person family	+***	+***		
AFDC recipient		_***		_***
Other public assistance recipient	_***	_**	_***	_***
Basic skills training			+**	
Occupational skills training	+***	+***	+**	
OJT	+***		+***	
Job search assistance	+**		+***	
Average prior earnings, years 1–2	+***	+***	+***	+***
Minimal employment at termination	N.A.	N.A.		
Substantial employment at termination	+***	+***	+***	+***
Full-time employment at termination	+***	+***	+***	+***
Percent families in poverty				
Median area rent			_*	
Average area unemployment, 1991–92				
Per capita income, 1991–92		_***		
Employment growth, 1990–92				+***
R-square	0.10	0.13	0.09	0.11
n	9,111	11,015	9,413	13,677

Source: Appendix table 5A.3.

post–high school education, participating in OST and OJT, having prior earnings, and having a full-time job at termination were associated with significantly higher earnings success rates.

There were key differences by state as well. Being Hispanic was positively associated with earnings success in Illinois but not in

Table 5.7 EXPLAINING THE EARNINGS SUCCESS OF PY 1990 ILLINOIS AND TEXAS OUT-OF-SCHOOL YOUTH AND ADULT JTPA TERMINEES IN THE FIRST AND SECOND POSTPROGRAM YEARS

Characteristic/Variable	Illinois		Texas	
	Postprogram Year		Postprogram Year	
	First	Second	First	Second
Female	−***		−***	−***
Ages 18–21	−***	−*	−***	−***
Ages 30–39				
Ages 40–49				
Ages 50+	−***	−***		−**
Black	−***	−***	−***	−***
Hispanic	+**	+***		
High school dropout	−***	−***	−***	−***
Post–high school	+***	+***	+***	+***
Single parent	N.A.	N.A.	+***	+***
Parent in two-parent family	N.A.	N.A.	+***	+***
Other family member	N.A.	N.A.	+***	+*
Two-person family	+***	+***		
Three-person family	+***	+***		
Four-person family	+***	+***		
Five-person family	+***	+***		
AFDC recipient				−***
Other public assistance recipient	−***	−***	−***	−***
Basic skills training				
Occupational skills training	+***	+***	+***	+***
OJT	+***	+***	+***	+***
Job search assistance	+*		−*	
Average prior earnings, years 1–2	+***	+***	+***	+***
Minimal employment at termination	N.A.	N.A.		
Substantial employment at termination	+***	+***	−***	
Full-time employment at termination	+***	+***	+***	+***
Percent families in poverty	−***		−***	−**
Median area rent		−**	−***	−**
Average area unemployment, 1991–92				
Per capita income, 1991–92			+***	+**
Employment growth, 1990–92			+***	+***
R-square	0.16	0.14	0.16	0.14
n	20,126	20,126	23,091	23,091

Source: Appendix table 5A.4.

Texas, as was larger family size in Illinois, perhaps because of the absence of a family status variable in Illinois. Receiving AFDC adversely affected earnings success in Texas but only in year two. Participation in JSA, though marginally significant, was found to affect success positively in Illinois and negatively in Texas (again, relative to participation in other), as was having substantial part-time employment at termination, puzzling results to say the least. Finally, area economic variables appear to have exerted greater influence on earnings success rates in Texas than in Illinois, for reasons that are not clear. In Texas, higher per capita incomes and employment growth rates were significantly associated with greater earnings success in both years, while higher shares of families living in poverty and area rents were negatively related to earnings success. Only the unemployment rate variable failed to exert a statistically significant effect in Texas.

Similar factors affected male and female earnings success in the second postprogram year (table 5.8), largely mirroring the results for employment success. Variables with highly significant negative effects on postprogram (second-year) earnings success, regardless of gender, were being black, having less than a high school education, and receiving other public assistance. Similarly, variables with highly significant positive effects on second-year earnings for both males and females were having some post–high school education, participating in OST, prior earnings, and having a full-time job at termination.

There were interesting differences by gender as well. First, being an out-of-school youth (ages 18 through 21) had a strong negative influence on earnings success only for females. Second, it is curious that being a parent and, to a lesser extent, another family member had significant positive effects on earnings success for males, while none of the family status variables are significant for females (Texas only). Recall that only about one in three males had (or admitted having) parental responsibilities, while most females were parents. Third, although all program activities (except basic skills training) were associated with earnings success for males, OST was the sole activity associated with highly positive earnings effects for females in year two. Fourth, although securing a full-time termination job retained its power for explaining positive earnings success regardless of gender, for females minimal part-time employment had a significant negative effect on earnings success. Finally, in contrast to the employment success results, to the extent that area variables played a significant role in explaining earnings success variations, they did so more for males than for females.

In sum, the multivariate statistical analysis provides the basis for the following observations.

• Most of the standard demographic variables examined play a fairly consistent role in both continuous employment and self-

Table 5.8 EXPLAINING THE EARNINGS SUCCESS OF MALE AND FEMALE
PY 1990 ILLINOIS AND TEXAS OUT-OF-SCHOOL YOUTH AND
ADULT JTPA TERMINEES, BY GENDER, IN THE SECOND
POSTPROGRAM YEAR

| | Illinois | | Texas | |
| | Gender | | Gender | |
Characteristic/Variable	Male	Female	Male	Female
Ages 18–21		_**		_***
Ages 30–39				
Ages 40–49	_*			
Ages 50+	_**	_***	_***	
Black	_***	_***	_***	_***
Hispanic	+***	+***		
High school dropout	_***	_***	_***	_***
Post–high school	+***	+***	+***	+***
Single parent	N.A.	N.A.	+***	
Parent in two-parent family	N.A.	N.A.	+***	
Other family member	N.A.	N.A.	+*	
Two-person family		+***		
Three-person family	+***	+***		
Four-person family	+***	+***		
Five-person family	+***	+***		
AFDC recipient				_***
Other public assistance recipient	_***	_***	_***	_***
Basic skills training			+*	
Occupational skills training	+***	+***	+***	+***
OJT	+***		+***	
Job search assistance	+*		+**	
Average prior earnings, years 1–2	+***	+***	+***	+***
Minimal employment at termination	N.A.	N.A.		_**
Substantial employment at termination	+*	+***		
Full-time employment at termination	+***	+***	+***	+***
Percent families in poverty			_*	
Median area rent	_***		_***	
Average area unemployment, 1991–92				
Per capita income, 1991–92			+*	
Employment growth, 1990–92			+**	+**
R-square	0.14	0.14	0.14	0.14
n	9,111	11,015	9,413	13,677

Source: Appendix table 5A.5.

sufficiency earnings success, including gender, age, race or ethnicity, education, and welfare receipt.

- The effect of prior earnings is also strong and consistent: higher
  preprogram earnings are significantly associated with higher
  employment and earnings success as measured here. Although

this finding raises traditional concerns that training programs may be "creaming" from the eligible population, it should be pointed out that prior earnings for these participants, nearly all of whom are economically disadvantaged, are quite low, well under $1,000 annually on average. Moreover, the local programs selected for field visits (see below) were standouts even after adjusting for participants' previous earnings.

- Having a job at termination, especially a full-time job, appears to contribute substantively toward postprogram employment and earnings success as well. Immediate success appears to breed further success. This finding is consistent with Romero's (1994) research on the outcomes for welfare recipients served by JTPA programs. This issue merits further research.

- In contrast to the net impact findings of the National JTPA Study (e.g., Bloom et al. 1997), participation in OST is associated with employment and earnings success for both males and females, while participation in OJT and JSA seems to have such association only for males. Clearly, such results beg for validation using more rigorous experimental or quasi-experimental designs.

- Area economic variables are probably less important in constraining or contributing to postprogram success than has been generally thought, at least as long as programs are operating on a relatively modest scale: regardless of area pay scales, unemployment rates, employment growth, and other conditions, a substantial share of trainees in these states obtained steady jobs and higher-paying earning opportunities.[20]

- Additional research should be done on the role played by family status and size in contributing to postprogram employment and earnings success. The differences between the Texas and Illinois findings raise interesting issues that should be examined further. The Texas results suggest that family status—especially being either a single parent or a parent in a two-parent family—may be an important factor in explaining the longer-term success of training, most likely because of the added motivation that parenting imparts to participation and subsequent labor market success.

Views from the Field

A handful of successful SDAs were selected for intensive field visits in each state—four in Texas and three in Illinois[21]—to help the researchers validate and better understand the statistical findings, as well as to assist in the formulation of policy implications and recommendations. Those SDAs were selected through a process analogous to the DOL/Employment and Training Administration (ETA) performance standards model (e.g., DOL 1994), but substituting our employment and earnings success measures for the usual JTPA standards.[22] Employment and earnings success were modeled using the multivariate ordinary least squares regression models described above to determine the predicted rate of success, which was then compared to the actual rate for that measure. SDAs in each state were subsequently ranked by the actual-predicted success residuals: SDAs with larger positive actual-predicted residuals ranked higher and were designated successes in each state.[23]

Field interviews were conducted with program administrators and staff in the selected SDAs, based upon a common interview guide. (Key state JTPA officials also were consulted.) The Illinois and Texas research teams determined results and wrote them up independently. Although the terminology and the implicit weight given each factor identified in the interviews differed somewhat, the conclusions both research teams reached in their respective states are remarkably similar.

Results of the field interviews in both states showed that a number of factors were associated with the success of local JTPA programs.

1. The selected programs offered their participants *constrained choice* among the available training activities, featuring strong emphasis on individualized programming and reliance on individual training referrals to a set of approved providers and in-demand or emerging occupations and industries only. In some instances (e.g., the Central Texas SDA), the local programs had even conducted their own longer-term tracking studies to identify those occupations that were affording participants the capacity to attain economic self-sufficiency, after taking into account family status and size.

2. The SDAs also *stressed intake, assessment, and counseling* as key up-front program components. Their counselors were empowered with considerable discretion. The counselors often were responsible for and authorized to commit their own budget resources for individuals in need of training, in line with what might be viewed as a vocational rehabilitation approach to case management not typically seen in job training. Counselors in some of the selected SDAs even conducted provider approvals as well.

3. Successful programs also *prioritized occupational skills training* over other employment and training interventions as the activity of choice. Local program administrators and staff felt that the principal route to success for participants was through investing in

their human capital, in particular through training in higher-paying, demand occupations. Those programs had begun down-playing OJT and stand-alone job search assistance as their primary activities well before reliance on those activities came under fire nationally.

4. The programs also used *highly structured processes* to determine the demand and emerging occupations and industries for which to train in their areas. Too many training programs over the years have tended to select training fields for their participants without sufficient forethought and especially without considering the types of jobs likely to be available or the wages they might pay. Some training programs have lacked all but the most tenuous of relationships with the employers that actually control the jobs in question. More-successful training programs have made the "training-for-what" question the very heart of their approach.

5. The programs have offered *case management* by trained, professional case managers who were valued highly by the local SDA administrators. Such case management services were described as continuing through program participation and into the post-program period. More recent research on training programs has lent credence to the value of this program component.

Three features common to these SDAs should be highlighted here as well. First, they tended to be small- to mid-sized in annual funding allocations or numbers of participants served.[24] These programs may have enjoyed the luxury of being small enough to have more easily managed programs generally. Second, they appeared largely to have avoided politics in the awarding of provider contracts or the allocation of funds within the SDA, largely by adopting policies that precluded having providers serve on the local PIC. These SDAs did so long before that became an issue with the Office of the Inspector General or the object of DOL/ETA regulation. Third, all the SDAs valued staff continuity and retention highly.

For lack of a better term, a few "nonfindings" are worth noting as well. One was that not one of the field interviews produced a comment about the importance of national (or state) JTPA performance standards or their accompanying performance incentives or sanctions. National JTPA standards, pegged as they are to relatively low average levels of performance, were not viewed as having much practical relevance for day-to-day program performance management, nor were they seen as posing significant challenges to the programs. Another was that, while considerable discussion surrounds which local employment and population factors to employ in the national performance standards models as control factors, these SDAs operated quite successfully relative to their peers despite facing quite varied labor market situations.

The research did not explore to any great extent why other training programs in the two states were not as successful or why they were not adopting similar policies and practices for their areas. In fact, although their lack of success has been documented, many of them may have been attempting to institute improved strategies along the lines suggested here. However, decisionmaking in the larger training programs in these states traditionally has been more political in nature. In addition, larger SDAs have tended to set aside shares of their training allocations for key providers and groups in ways that preclude more effective performance management, a practice that may reflect the political nature of the funding process in training programs.

It is important to note that Texas—and Illinois to a lesser extent—instituted major workforce development reforms soon after the research was completed. Several of the policies and practices found to be associated with greater training success in the research were incorporated into those reforms and were subsequently implemented statewide. For example, Texas House Bill 1863, which became effective in 1995, among other provisions

- Explicitly recognized employers as well as residents (participants) as the primary customers of the workforce system;
- Strengthened reliance on training for demand and emerging occupations and industries through enhanced labor market information;
- Separated strategic planning and oversight from the provision of training services locally;
- Called for the creation of one-stop career centers to provide front-end eligibility, assessment, and job readiness services; and
- Mandated that local programs adopt an individual-referral model for accessing training services.

Many of these provisions are reflected in the Workforce Investment Act of 1998.

POLICY AND PROGRAM RECOMMENDATIONS

Several recommendations for federal, state, and local workforce development policy result from this research. Some of these rest on the assumption that there is a positive correlation between the gross program outcomes—employment and earnings success rates up to two years postprogram—observed for Illinois and Texas adult and out-of-school youth terminees and real net impacts on their employment and earnings.[25] The Workforce Investment Act of 1998, which some states, including Texas, began to implement as early as July 1, 1999, supports many, but not all, of the following recommendations.

1. *Training programs (e.g., JTPA) should place greater emphasis on real training, especially occupational skills training.* Participation in occupational skills training appears to yield sustained employment and earnings success, a finding that is strongly supported in field interviews with high-performing SDAs in varying labor market contexts. In particular, it appears that local programs that have focused their efforts on demand/emerging occupations and industries and that have counseled participants (through intake and structured assessment) about the merits of pursuing jobs with high pay and decent employee benefits have done especially well in the more stringent, longer-term success measures applied here. This is not to say that training is a panacea for all participants or that only training should be provided. Nevertheless, training offerings can be expanded considerably in the country's existing job training programs.

   Enthusiasm for this recommendation, of course, must be tempered by the experimentally based findings from the National JTPA Study (Bloom et al. 1997) that, although participation in classroom training yielded positive impacts for adult men and women over the 30-month follow-up period, the impacts were not statistically significant. Per LaLonde (1995), and others, it may well be that our investments in training to date have been too modest or, per Friedlander et al. (1997 and their chapter in this volume), it has been poorly linked to the labor market. When training is systematically linked to jobs in growth industries and higher-paying, demand occupations, it may yield greater impacts, a result that is further bolstered by MDRC's recent Portland findings (Scrivener et al. 1998). Mathematica's evaluation of the Minority Female, Single-Parent Demonstration also suggests that combining remedial education and training for some of the more disadvantaged participants may be preferable to the common approach of having months of remediation precede entry into training (Burghardt and Gordon 1990).

   Moreover, local programs should be encouraged to avoid committing additional public funds to training for traditionally low-paying fields (e.g., cosmetology). Such programs have been the bane of training programs as well as career and technical education for decades, as Mangum's chapter in this volume also suggests. Programs allowing participants to pursue such training only put off the day when they must confront the realities of the job market and are wasting scarce public resources. High-performing SDAs declined to support such training with their scarce public training dollars.

Whether or not WIA (Workforce Investment Act) will foster use of occupational skills training largely depends upon the U.S. Department of Labor's regulatory interpretation of key provisions of the act. Mangum et al. (1999) and others suggest that a strict reading of the act would restrict access to training to those (1) unable to secure a job, regardless of wage level, and (2) lacking non-WIA financing for such training (e.g., a Pell grant). Training under WIA under such an interpretation is thus seen more as an activity of last resort within a "work-first" approach than as the centerpiece of the nation's workforce development programming. However, high-level officials within the DOL have made it clear that they will pursue a flexible interpretation of the key provisions that will be fully supportive of local decisionmaking and the provision of occupational training to those who require it to perform well in the labor market.

2. *Access to and understanding of labor market information regarding employment and earning opportunities should be enhanced.* All the successful local JTPA programs in these two states relied heavily on labor market information (LMI) to identify which occupations and industries to train for and place their participants in. Given the central role the two states and their successful SDAs accorded to the use of LMI, and especially given the national and state movement toward block grants and even vouchers for workforce development programs, policymakers should ensure that appropriate information regarding opportunities for work and earning is readily accessible.

But Texas and Illinois have gone well beyond mere access to LMI. State Occupational Information Coordinating Committees (SOICCs) in both states, working closely with their various education, employment, and training agency partners, have developed and supported model tools for program planners, counselors, and participants themselves to use when attempting to take advantage of and apply such information. For example, the Texas SOICC first developed the Standardized Occupational Components for Regional Analysis of Trends in Employment System (SOCRATES) in the late 1980s to put labor market planning tools and counseling information at the fingertips of the front-line staff who most needed them. And, more recently, it designed and instituted Texas CARES, the Career Alternative of Resource Exploration System, which provides students and counselors with visually oriented tools for exploring key aspects of occupations of interest. Similar LMI-related efforts were under way in Illinois.[26]

Moreover, Congress appropriated funds to the U.S. Department of Labor in 1994 to launch the America's Labor Market Information System (or ALMIS) project. The ALMIS effort comprised state-led consortia around the country, including a Michigan- and Missouri-led consortium that created a nationwide electronic talent and help-wanted bank; and a Maryland-led consortium (in which Texas is a partner) that sought ways to make UI wage records more useful and supportive tools for LMI. Those efforts, some of which are ongoing, were intended to enhance the nation's LMI system to provide better, more accessible information for those who require it. Based on our research findings, ALMIS merits continuing support from the Congress and the various state partners in the consortia.

3. *Federal and state workforce development policy should give more attention to day-to-day performance management practices of its local job training system to ensure that such practices are implemented systematically.* Although performance standards, per se, are apparently not "driving" the more successful training programs, sensible day-to-day performance management is playing a strong role. Programs examined for this research clearly are carrying out their performance-oriented functions within the context of a wider management system that encompasses longer-term economic self-sufficiency as the goal for their participants.

Key elements and features of such policies include the following:

- Open, nonpolitical processes for determining which providers will be approved to provide training services in the area for a given period;
- Precluding of service providers from serving on policy and program boards—whether existing Private Industry Councils or the emerging local workforce boards in states like Texas that have since moved to integrate many of the employment and training programs at the state and local level—that are allocating funds and selecting training providers;[27]
- Individual-referral, rather than standing subcontract, approaches for delivering training services locally, to foster greater reliance on training in demand occupations and indus-

tries and quicker responses to changes in labor market demand; and

- Federal and/or state technical assistance and training to foster local evaluations of training outcomes, which might include longer-term tracking of employment, earnings, and welfare receipt via administrative records, as well as greater sharing and discussion of such evaluation results; the ultimate aim of these efforts clearly should be to enhance the capacity of localities for assessing their own programs and their efficacy and for designing and implementing improved training strategies as a result.

Although voucher-based approaches to education and training have entered the national and state policy limelight again recently, this research offers little evidence to support them.[28] It is a big leap—probably an unwarranted one—from arguing for the use of an individual-referral approach to training coupled with intensive career counseling and individualized assessment based on accessible, leading-edge labor market information, to urging adoption of a pure voucher system. The Chicago-area Service Delivery Area often has been characterized as a voucher-based program, but in fact it more closely resembles the enhanced, individual-referral approach just described.

Performance standards have a vital role to play in federal and state policies regarding workforce development initiatives, including JTPA.[29] Among other things, outcome-based standards have provided, and continue to provide, concrete guidance to state and local programs as to the centrality of employment and earnings as the end-purpose of their services. It may be that performance standards and their associated policies play a more important role, as currently structured, for low- to mid-performing programs than for the high-performing SDAs observed in this research. Despite advances in performance standards policies since the early 1980s, a clearly articulated, comprehensive performance management philosophy applicable to all workforce development programs in the United States remains elusive. It will be interesting to see whether the new Workforce Investment Act's provisions requiring a series of core standards for adults and youth groups will improve this situation.

WIA, as well as the reauthorization of the Adult Education and Family Literacy Act (Title II of WIA) and related provisions in the Carl D. Perkins Act of 1998 (Perkins III, passed in late October), effect important changes in the delivery, as well as performance measurement and management, of workforce education and training programs. Many of the changes are consistent with this research-based recommendation. For example, WIA calls for separating assessment and intake for core services (via one-stop centers) and training provision (via certified training providers) from strategic planning and oversight (which are now board functions). WIA and Perkins III also mandate the establishment of "core indicators of performance" on a more systematic basis (e.g., employment and earnings indicators as reflected in UI wage records). WIA also institutes a system of training and related service provision that resembles the individual-referral model used in Illinois and Texas during the period of this research more closely than it does a pure voucher system.

4. *Federal and state policy also should give special attention to ensuring that those with pressing family and parenting demands are able to participate effectively in training programs and ultimately secure jobs at wages that allow them to become self-sufficient.* Those with pressing family and parenting responsibilities arrive with even greater burdens and barriers to training program participation than do (most) other family members or nondependent individuals. They also have more pressing demands to work and earn when they exit the programs than do other participants. Limited analysis conducted here on the impact of adjusting for family status and size on success rates suggests that JTPA and related programs have a long way to go to ensure that such efforts are accessible, participation is effective, and the earnings outcomes are sufficiently successful.

5. *Expanding the current Earned Income Tax Credit should receive priority on the nation's policy agenda.* Although a number of JTPA terminees have left the program and found their way to successful employment and earnings outcomes, too many have not. And clearly not all of those counted as successes here in this gross outcomes analysis would have been successes if measured in terms of net employment and earnings impacts. The overwhelming majority of the JTPA terminees were severely disadvantaged economically when they enrolled—even when they earned wages before program entry, their earnings were quite low—and they managed to work hard following their exit even if they did not qualify as successful.

National policymakers should acknowledge that work effort by ensuring that work truly does pay. The most efficient way yet devised in this country, whatever its administrative and related problems (e.g., GAO 1993), is the Earned Income Tax Credit (or

EITC). If work is to be sufficiently rewarded, expansion of the EITC should receive greater policy priority.

It is unlikely that pursuing the strategies outlined here—such as proactively using labor market information to identify and train for high-paying jobs in demand occupations and growth industries and managing for performance on a more aggressive and more timely basis—will lead to universally better outcomes if workforce development program operations approach full scale and every local program adopts such practices. More-appropriate supply-side practices fostering program improvements are not a sinecure or substitute for, but rather a complement to, effective demand management strategies. As the Commission on the Skills of the American Workforce (1990) pointed out, the United States is one of the few postindustrial nations lacking a national policy of consciously pursuing high-skills, high-wage employment.

This research took place during a period of far-reaching state reform. Many states were in the process of revamping both their welfare and workforce development systems (Grubb et al. 1999; King and McPherson 1997), even as Congress and the Clinton administration struggled to enact their own reforms at the national level. Many, but certainly not all, of the important changes being ushered in by the Workforce Investment Act (and Perkins III) are broadly consistent with the recommendations stemming from this research. As states implement WIA and other legislative provisions in the near future, it will be interesting to see just how much the new world of workforce training and education created in the states resembles the one outlined here.

Notes

Author's Note: Dr. Carol J. Romero, then with the National Commission for Employment Policy, and Ray Uhalde and Karen Greene, with the U.S. Department of Labor's Employment and Training Administration, supported and guided this research. In Texas, Jim Boyd, Jim Gaston, Bill Grossenbacher, and Mark Anderberg (in state government) and Tom Smith, Mary Ross, Susan Kamas, H.W. Streitman, and Monette Molinar (with local JTPA programs) offered their support and insights. Their counterparts in Illinois were Tim Harmon and Gerry Snyder in state government and Bashir Ali, Mike Arnett, and Mary Pepperl at the local level. Burt Barnow, Norton Grubb, Garth Mangum, Patricia McNeil, Blair Potter, and an anonymous reviewer provided helpful comments and suggestions on earlier drafts. Deanna Schexnayder, Diane Tucker, Karen Franke, Chris Young, and Michelle Segal (at the Center for the Study of Human Resources) and Rhonda Mollet and Rima Roy (at the Center for Governmental Studies) provided their assistance as well.

1. Public education has a 30-year tradition of applied research identifying effective schools that even has both quantitative (e.g., Coleman 1966, Murnane 1981) and more qualitative (e.g., Edmonds 1979) branches. The "first-class" institutions apparently have taken this much more seriously than have "second-chance" programs.

2. Grubb (1996, pp. 24–25) has remarked on the potential contribution of nonimpact studies to better understanding program success or failure.

3. The National Governors' Association established the Center for Best Practices in the mid-1990s, and many federal (e.g., DOL) and state agencies have begun actively disseminating information on "best practices," typically via training and technical assistance activities as well as Web sites. However, it still requires a considerable investment in resources to determine what those practices are before findings about them can be disseminated.

4. Together, Illinois and Texas accounted for almost one-tenth of the nation's local JTPA programs and contained a number of its largest urban programs (e.g., Chicago, Dallas, Houston) during this period. The chapter by Robert Lerman offers a more in-depth look at what we know about the impacts of program participation on youth both in school and out.

5. For comparability purposes, earnings impacts have been converted to 1996:III dollars using the GDP Implicit Price Deflator series. This procedure facilitates comparisons with the recent evaluation review by Friedlander, Greenberg, and Robins (1997) and their chapter in this volume.

6. This chapter is based on more extensive research performed for the National Commission for Employment Policy and the U.S. Department of Labor's Employment and Training Administration by King et al. (1995).

7. The JTPA program year runs from July through June of each year; PY 1990 began on July 1, 1990.

8. In most states, employers covered by the federal/state UI program are required to report the earnings of their employees quarterly. Baj and Trott, in earlier work performed for the National Commission for Employment Policy (1992), demonstrated the feasibility of using employment and earnings records in support of performance management. Romero (1994) and others, including the authors, have shown that they are also invaluable for various forms of policy research.

9. As a pretax earnings measure, this does not account for the effects of the Earned Income Tax Credit.

10. State population figures are drawn from the 1990 Decennial Census of Population and Housing.

11. Based on U.S. Bureau of Labor Statistics *Employment and Earnings* information for 1991.

12. JTPA information for both states is based on a combination of program records and State Job Training Coordinating Council briefing materials. In September 1995, Texas began implementing the provisions of House Bill 1863 that was passed by the Texas legislature in May and signed by Governor George W. Bush in June of that year. HB 1863 simultaneously reformed the state's welfare system and consolidated most federal and state workforce development programs (excluding adult and vocational education) in a single state agency, the Texas Workforce Commission (TWC). Local areas that establish workforce development boards may receive what amount to employment and training "block grants" from the governor by way of the newly created TWC. Illinois also enacted major changes to its workforce programs in 1995, creating a new human resource investment council.

13. Before implementation of the 1992 JTPA Reform Amendments in July 1993, Title II-A programs served both adults and youth. Youth are now served under Title II-C of JTPA. The Workforce Investment Act of 1998 is now replacing JTPA.

14. In-school youth, those with fewer than seven days' program participation, and those for whom insufficient (fewer than four) preprogram UI wage quarters were available were excluded from the study population. National figures for disadvantaged adults and youth, both in and out of school, are drawn from the Job Training Quarterly Survey (DOL 1992).

15. Major program activity was computed using an algorithm developed by Bill Bowman of Annapolis Economic Research in Annapolis, Maryland.

16. These results are available from the authors on request. Earnings adjustments based on family status and size were made treating the participating parent in both single- and two-parent families as the sole earner and the earnings of nondependent individuals and other family members as those of a single individual.

17. Direction of influence and significance levels did not differ noticeably between the two procedures.

18. Statistical significance was measured at the 10 percent (*), 5 percent (**), or 1 percent (***) levels.

19. Very few males in JTPA were AFDC caretakers in either state (e.g., 4 percent in Texas).

20. Numerous studies have reported that JTPA programs have seldom had funding sufficient to serve more than a small fraction (i.e., 5 to 8 percent) of those eligible for services (e.g., Mangum et al. 1999).

21. The successful SDAs were Central Texas (Belton), West Central Texas (Abilene), Concho Valley (San Angelo), and Golden Crescent (Victoria) in Texas; and North Cook County SDA (SDA #8, the Chicago suburbs), Central Illinois PIC (SDA #15, Peoria), and PIC, Inc. (SDA #21, an eight-county rural area around Carlinville). The West Central Texas Council of Governments—then the JTPA entity and now the one-stop manager for the West Central Texas Workforce Development Board—became the first winner of the Enterprise National Award for Performance Excellence in Process Management in October 1998; it was also one of only four entities considered as an overall award winner and received honorable mention as such. Enterprise awards result from a selective applications and review process based on the seven Malcolm Baldrige Award principles for creating high-performance organizations. West Central's awards lend further credibility to the findings reported in this chapter.

22. Immediate program outcomes also were excluded from the model as being partially within the control of local program operators.

23. Details of this procedure are available from the authors on request.

24. Grubb (1996) makes a similar observation.

25. Barnow (1997) suggests this may be a heroic assumption, though Geraci (1984) was more sanguine, finding that near-term gross outcomes and longer-term net impacts were at least mildly correlated.

26. For example, HORIZONS is a hard-copy and software-based tool now available to counselors and planners in JTPA, high school, postsecondary institutions, and related programs from the Illinois Occupational Information Coordinating Committee. It includes information on employment by occupation and on programs available from various education and training institutions in Illinois.

27. For more on the Texas workforce system, as well as their counterparts in other leading states, see King and McPherson (1997) and Grubb et al. (1999).

28. Barnow and King (1996) and Trutko and Barnow (1999) review the evidence on vouchers.

29. For a discussion of some of the broader policy issues surrounding the role of performance standards, see Barnow (1992) and Barnow and King (1996).

References

Barnow, Burt S. 1987. "The Impact of CETA Programs on Earnings: A Review of the Literature." *Journal of Human Resources* 22 (spring).
———. 1992. "The Effects of Performance Standards on State and Local Programs." In *Evaluating Welfare and Training Programs,* edited by Charles F. Manski and Irwin Garfinkel. Cambridge, Mass.: Harvard University Press.
———. 1999. "Exploring the Relationship between Performance Management and Program Impact: A Case Study of the Job Training Partnership Act." *Journal of Policy Analysis and Management* 18 (4): 744.
Barnow, Burt S., and Laudan Y. Aron. 1989. "Survey of Government-Provided Training Programs." In *Investing in People: A Strategy to Address America's Workforce Crisis.* Washington, D.C.: Commission on Workforce Quality and Labor Market Efficiency, U.S. Department of Labor. September.
Barnow, Burt S., and Christopher T. King. 1996. "The Baby and the Bath Water: Lessons for the Next Employment and Training Program." In *Of Heart and Mind: Social Policy Essays in Honor of Sar A. Levitan,* edited by Garth Mangum and Stephen Mangum. Kalamazoo, Mich.: The W.E. Upjohn Institute for Employment Research.
Betsey, Charles L., Robin G. Hollister, Jr., and Mary R. Papageorgiou, eds. 1985. *Youth Employment and Training Programs: The YEDPA Years.* Washington, D.C.: National Academy Press.
Bloom, Howard S., Larry L. Orr, Stephen H. Bell, George Cave, Fred Doolittle, Winston Lin, and Johannes M. Bos. 1997. "The Benefits and Costs of JTPA Title II-A Programs: Key Findings from the National JTPA Study." *Journal of Human Resources* 32 (summer).
Bowman, William R. 1993. *Evaluating JTPA Programs for Economically Disadvantaged Adults: A Case Study of Utah and General Findings.* Report 92-02. Washington, D.C.: National Commission for Employment Policy Research. June.
Burghardt, John, and Anne Gordon. 1990. *More Jobs and Higher Pay: How an Integrated Program Compares with Traditional Programs.* New York: The Rockefeller Foundation, The Minority Female Single-Parent Demonstration.

Center for the Study of Human Resources. 1993. "Economic Self-Sufficiency for AFDC Families." Austin: Lyndon B. Johnson School of Public Affairs, The University of Texas at Austin. May.

Chicago Urban League; Latino Institute; and Northern Illinois University. 1993. "Making Work Pay: State and Local Responses to the Problems of the Working Poor." Policy issues for panel discussion, prepared for the Working Poor Policy Forum. December.

Citro, Constance F., and Robert T. Michael, eds. 1995. *Measuring Poverty: A New Approach*. Washington, D.C.: National Academy Press.

Coleman, James S. 1966. *The Equality of Educational Opportunity*. Washington, D.C.: U.S. Department of Health, Education, and Welfare, Office of Education.

Commission on the Skills of the American Workforce. 1990. *America's Choice: High Skills or Low Wages!* New York: National Center for Education and the Economy.

Dickinson, Katherine P., Deborah J. Kogan, and Barbara M. Means. 1994. *JTPA Best Practices in Assessment, Case Management, and Providing Appropriate Services*. Washington, D.C.: U.S. Department of Labor, Office of Strategic Planning and Policy Development, Employment and Training Administration. February. Draft.

DOL. See U.S. Department of Labor.

Edmonds, Ronald R. 1979. "Effective Schools for the Urban Poor." *Educational Leadership* 37 (1): 15–24.

Friedlander, Daniel, and Gary Burtless. 1995. *Five Years After: The Long-Term Effects of Welfare-to-Work Programs*. New York: The Russell Sage Foundation.

Friedlander, Daniel, David H. Greenberg, and Philip K. Robins. 1997. "Evaluating Government Training Programs for the Economically Disadvantaged." *Journal of Economic Literature* XXXV (December): 1809–55.

GAO. See U.S. General Accounting Office.

Geraci, Vincent J. 1984. "Short-Term Indicators of Job Training Program Effects on Long-Term Participant Earnings." Austin: Center for Economic Research, The University of Texas at Austin.

Gramlich, Edward M. 1990. *A Guide to Benefit-Cost Analysis, Second Edition*. Englewood Cliffs, N.J.: Prentice Hall.

Grubb, W. Norton. 1996. *Learning to Work: The Case for Reintegrating Job Training and Education*. New York: The Russell Sage Foundation.

Grubb, W. Norton, Norena Badway, Denise Bell, Bernadette Chi, Christopher T. King, Julie Herr, Heath Prince, Richard Kazis, Lisa Hicks, and Judith Taylor. 1999. *Toward Order from Chaos: State Efforts to Reform Workforce Development Systems*. MDS-1249. Berkeley, Calif.: National Center for Research in Vocational Education.

Hahn, Andrew, and Robert I. Lerman. 1985. *What Works in Youth Employment Policy? How to Help Young Workers from Poor Families*. National Planning Association Report No. 213, NAR Report No. 3.

Washington, D.C.: National Planning Association, Committee on New American Realities.

Heckman, James J., Rebecca L. Roselius, and Jeffrey A. Smith. 1994. "U.S. Education and Training Policy: A Re-Evaluation of the Underlying Assumptions behind the 'New Consensus.'" In *Labor Markets, Employment Policy and Job Creation,* edited by Lewis C. Solomon and Alec B. Levenson (83–121). Boulder, Colo.: Westview Press.

Hollister, Robinson G., Jr. 1990. *New Evidence about Effective Training Strategies.* New York: The Rockefeller Foundation. The Minority Female Single-Parent Demonstration.

King, Christopher T., and Robert E. McPherson, eds. 1997. *Building a Workforce Development System for Texas . . . A Funny Thing Happened on the Way to Reform.* Policy Research Project Report 126. Austin: Lyndon B. Johnson School of Public Affairs, The University of Texas at Austin.

King, Christopher T., Leslie O. Lawson, Jerome A. Olson, John Baj, and Charles E. Trott. 1995. *JTPA Success Stories in Texas and Illinois: The Who, How and What of Successful Outcomes.* Washington, D.C.: National Commission for Employment Policy.

Kogan, Deborah, Katherine Dickinson, Barbara Means, and Marlene Strong. 1991. *Improving the Quality of Training under JTPA.* Research and Evaluation Report Series 91-A. Washington, D.C.: U.S. Department of Labor, Employment and Training Administration.

LaLonde, Robert J. 1995. "The Promise of Public Sector-Sponsored Training Programs." *Journal of Economic Perspectives* 9 (2): 149–68.

Levitan, Sar A., and Garth L. Mangum, eds. 1981. *The T in CETA: Local and National Perspectives.* Kalamazoo, Mich.: The W.E. Upjohn Institute for Employment Research.

Mangum, Garth, Stephen Mangum, Andrew Sum, James Callahan, and Neal Fogg. 1999. *A Second Chance for the Fourth Chance: A Critique of the Workforce Investment Act of 1998.* Policy Issues Monograph 99-01. Baltimore: Sar Levitan Center for Social Policy Studies, Institute for Policy Studies, The Johns Hopkins University.

McKee, William L., and Nancy L. Harrell. 1989. *Targeting Your Labor Market: Using Labor Market Information in Regional Planning for Texas Jobs.* Austin: Texas State Occupational Information Coordinating Committee.

Mitchell, John J., Mark L. Chadwin, and Demetra S. Nightingale. 1980. *Implementing Welfare-Employment Programs: An Institutional Analysis of the Work Incentive (WIN) Program.* R&D Monograph 78. Washington, D.C.: U.S. Department of Labor, Employment and Training Administration.

Murnane, Richard J. 1981. "Interpreting the Evidence on School Effectiveness." *Teachers College Record* 83 (1): 19–35.

National Commission for Employment Policy. 1992. *Using Unemployment Insurance Wage-Record Data for JTPA Performance Management.* Research Report 91-07. Washington, D.C.: National Commission for Employment Policy. June.

Orr, Larry L., Howard S. Bloom, Stephen H. Bell, Fred Doolittle, Winston Lin, and George Cave. 1995. *Does Training for the Disadvantaged Work? Evidence from the National JTPA Study.* Washington, D.C.: The Urban Institute Press.

Puma, Michael J., and Nancy R. Burstein. 1994. "The National Evaluation of the Food Stamp Employment and Training Program." *Journal of Policy Analysis and Management* 13 (2, spring): 311–30.

Romero, Carol J. 1994. *JTPA Programs and Adult Women on Welfare: Using Training to Raise AFDC Recipients above Poverty.* Research Report No. 93-01. Washington, D.C.: National Commission for Employment Policy. June.

Schwarz, John E., and Thomas J. Volgy. 1992. *The Forgotten Americans.* New York: W.W. Norton and Company.

Scrivener, Susan, Gayle Hamilton, Mary Farrell, Stephen Freedman, Daniel Friedlander, Marisa Mitchell, Jodi Nudelman, and Christine Schwartz. 1998. "Implementation, Participation Patterns, Costs, and Two-Year Impacts of the Portland (Oregon) Welfare-to-Work Program: Executive Summary, National Evaluation of Welfare-to-Work Strategies." Washington, D.C.: U.S. Department of Health and Human Services, Administration for Children and Families and Office of the Assistant Secretary for Planning and Evaluation; and U.S. Department of Education, Office of the Under Secretary and Office of Vocational and Adult Education. May.

Stromsdorfer, E., H. Bloom, R. Boruch, M. Borus, J. Gueron, A. Gustman, P. Rossi, F. Scheuren, M. Smith, and F. Stafford. 1985. *Recommendations of the Job Training Longitudinal Survey Research Advisory Committee.* Washington, D.C.: Employment and Training Administration, U.S. Department of Labor.

Texas Education Agency. 1994. *Texas Quality Work Force Planning 1992–94: Results from the Field.* Austin: Division of Career and Technology Education, Quality Work Force Planning Unit. November.

Trutko, John, and Burt S. Barnow. 1999. *Experiences with Training Vouchers under the Job Training Partnership Act and Implications for Individual Training Accounts under the Workforce Investment Act: Final Report.* Washington, D.C.: U.S. Department of Labor, Employment and Training Administration.

U.S. Department of Labor. 1992. *Job Training Quarterly Survey: JTPA Title II-A and III Enrollments and Terminations during Program Year 1990 (July 1990–July 1991).* Washington, D.C.: DOL, Employment and Training Administration, Office of Strategic Planning and Policy Development, Division of Performance Management and Evaluation. January.

————. 1994. *Guide to JTPA Performance Standards for Program Years 1994 and 1995*. Washington, D.C.: DOL, Employment and Training Administration. July 29.

————. Office of the Chief Economist. 1995. *What's Working (and What's Not): A Summary of Research on the Economic Impacts of Employment and Training Programs*. Washington, D.C.: DOL. January.

U.S. General Accounting Office. 1993. *Tax Policy: Earned Income Tax Credit: Design and Administration Could Be Improved*. GAO/GGD-93-145. Washington, D.C.: GAO. September.

————. 1996a. *Employment Training: Successful Projects Share Common Strategy*. GAO/HEHS-96-108. Washington, D.C.: GAO. May.

————. 1996b. *Job Training Partnership Act: Long-Term Earnings and Employment Outcomes*. GAO/HEHS-96-40. Washington, D.C.: GAO. March.

Appendix Table 5A.1 DEFINITIONS OF VARIABLES IN REGRESSIONS

INTERCEP	The constant term
FEMALE	Dummy variable for female gender
AGE18–21	Dummy variable for individuals ages 18 to 21
AGE30–39	Dummy variable for individuals ages 30 to 39
AGE40–49	Dummy variable for individuals ages 40 to 49
AGE50–UP	Dummy variable for individuals ages 50 and over
BLACK	Dummy variable for black race
HISPANIC	Dummy variable for Hispanic ethnicity
DROPOUT	Dummy variable for last grade completed less than 12
POSTHS	Dummy variable for high school completed and attendance at academic, technical, or vocational school
SINGPNT	Individual was a single parent
DUALPNT	Individual was a parent in a two-parent family
OTHRFAM	Individual was a nonparent family member
FSIZE2	Dummy variable for individuals in families of two
FSIZE3	Dummy variable for individuals in families of three
FSIZE4	Dummy variable for individuals in families of four
FSIZE5	Dummy variable for individuals in families of five or more
INAFDC	Dummy variable for individuals receiving AFDC while in JTPA
OTHASST	Dummy variable for individuals receiving any other public assistance while in JTPA
MBST	Dummy variable for individuals for whom basic skills training was the major activity
MOST	Dummy variable for individuals for whom occupational skills training was the major activity
MOJT	Dummy variable for individuals for whom on-the-job training was the major activity
MJSA	Dummy variable for individuals for whom job search assistance was the major activity
PRESUM	Sum of UI wages for two years before JTPA
MINPTE	Individual was employed in minimal part-time job at termination
SUBPTE	Individual was employed in substantial part-time job at termination
FULLTE	Individual was employed in full-time job at termination
FAMINPOV	Percent of families in poverty in county
MEDRENT	Median rent in county
UN91–92	County unemployment rate averaged for 1991 and 1992
CAP91–92	Per capita income averaged for 1991 and 1992
EGROWTH	Growth rate of employment over the period 1990 to 1992

Appendix Table 5A.2 STRICT-STEADY EMPLOYMENT, ALL TERMINEES

R-Square	0.13	0.11	0.13	0.10
Number of Observations	20,126	20,126	23,091	23,091
Dependent Mean	0.24553	0.28041	0.33605	0.33496

	Illinois		Texas	
Variable	First Post-Program Year Coefficient (t-Statistic)	Second Post-Program Year Coefficient (t-Statistic)	First Post-Program Year Coefficient (t-Statistic)	Second Post-Program Year Coefficient (t-Statistic)
INTERCEP	0.210693	0.234777	0.145076	0.160285
	4.54***	4.811***	2.844***	3.091***
FEMALE	0.027118	0.03113	0.025305	0.009965
	4.189***	4.573***	3.539***	1.371
AGE18–21	−0.003881	0.000526	−0.025786	−0.015044
	−0.501	0.065	−3.24***	−1.859*
AGE30–39	0.004615	−0.002161	−0.002338	−0.007196
	0.615	−0.274	−0.298	−0.902
AGE40–49	0.001345	−0.014918	−0.007504	0.001407
	0.129	−1.363	−0.703	0.13
AGE50–UP	−0.032641	−0.033423	0.006323	−0.010726
	−2.322**	−2.261**	0.371	−0.619
BLACK	−0.059221	−0.052255	−0.031678	−0.01646
	−7.673***	−6.438***	−3.793***	−1.939*
HISPANIC	0.01302	0.042317	0.047401	0.047754
	1.216	3.759***	5.906***	5.853***
DROPOUT	−0.049471	−0.066165	−0.075592	−0.087065
	−6.716***	−8.542***	−9.657***	−10.942***
POSTHS	0.031892	0.030064	0.027145	0.022032
	4.389***	3.934***	3.509***	2.802***
SINGPNT	N.A.	N.A.	0.050118	0.05916
	N.A.	N.A.	2.588***	3.005***
DUALPNT	N.A.	N.A.	0.063134	0.065936
	N.A.	N.A.	3.31***	3.401***
OTHRFAM	N.A.	N.A.	0.028568	0.030667
	N.A.	N.A.	1.559	1.646*
FSIZE2	0.016023	0.036958	0.010852	0.003997
	1.879*	4.121***	0.58	0.21
FSIZE3	0.038487	0.059334	0.007057	0.009522
	4.278***	6.271***	0.371	0.492
FSIZE4	0.045232	0.063988	0.000158	0.005888
	4.486***	6.035***	0.008	0.298
FSIZE5	0.028943	0.055387	0.014057	0.017908
	2.888***	5.256***	0.737	0.923
INAFDC	−0.030841	−0.03564	−0.032139	−0.04107
	−3.61***	−3.967***	−3.464***	−4.354***
OTHASST	−0.018554	−0.026616	−0.046446	−0.038867
	−2.723***	−3.715***	−6.818***	−5.612***

Appendix Table 5A.2 STRICT-STEADY EMPLOYMENT, ALL TERMINEES
(*continued*)

Variable	Illinois		Texas	
	First Post-Program Year Coefficient (t-Statistic)	Second Post-Program Year Coefficient (t-Statistic)	First Post-Program Year Coefficient (t-Statistic)	Second Post-Program Year Coefficient (t-Statistic)
MBST	0.009096	0.006499	0.022405	0.011911
	0.679	0.462	1.531	0.801
MOST	0.03926	0.050871	0.050596	0.03949
	3.948***	4.865***	3.633***	2.789***
MOJT	0.043075	0.036425	0.084766	0.027195
	4.144***	3.332***	6.067***	1.915*
MJSA	0.020716	0.017845	0.025176	0.019844
	1.697*	1.39	1.394	1.081
PRESUM	0.000006723	0.000008186	0.000009504	0.0000101
	19.435***	22.505***	26.627***	27.838***
MINPTE	N.A.	N.A.	0.006316	0.021405
	N.A.	N.A.	0.251	0.837
SUBPTE	0.127815	0.099609	0.107084	0.075288
	12.799***	9.485***	9.742***	6.738***
FULLTE	0.233067	0.192922	0.202575	0.139115
	36.426***	28.673***	20.992***	14.181***
FAMINPOV	−0.000514	−0.000259	−0.059875	0.002354
	−0.509	−0.245	−0.514	0.02
MEDRENT	−0.003922	−0.002545	−0.000213	−0.000155
	−2.009**	−1.24	−1.812*	−1.3
UN91–92	−0.001388	−0.001508	−0.025528	0.106345
	−0.693	−0.716	−0.144	0.591
CAP91–92	−0.001334	−0.002284	0.000002573	0.000002496
	−1.58	−2.574***	1.093	1.043
EGROWTH	−0.00082	0.000252	0.19071	0.244014
	−0.754	0.22	2.253**	2.836***

Appendix Table 5A.3 STRICT-STEADY EMPLOYMENT, SECOND POSTPROGRAM
                     YEAR

	0.10	0.13	0.09	0.11
R-Square	0.10	0.13	0.09	0.11
Number of Observations	20,126	20,126	23,091	23,091
Dependent Mean	0.27681	0.28339	0.35649	0.32015

	Illinois		Texas	
Variable	Male Coefficient (t-Statistic)	Female Coefficient (t-Statistic)	Male Coefficient (t-Statistic)	Female Coefficient (t-Statistic)
INTERCEP	0.247265	0.247291	0.183885	0.182079
	3.358***	3.806***	2.165**	2.774***
AGE18–21	0.021359	−0.018197	0.010436	−0.036869
	1.764*	−1.648*	0.786	−3.598***
AGE30–39	−0.011597	0.007725	−0.033089	0.012863
	−0.988	0.724	−2.548***	1.273
AGE40–49	−0.027364	−0.003958	0.001893	−0.00083
	−1.692*	−0.265	0.11	−0.059
AGE50–UP	−0.011369	−0.051757	−0.048137	0.005457
	−0.501	−2.636***	−1.79*	0.239
BLACK	−0.062687	−0.041676	−0.071142	0.020705
	−5.215***	−3.753***	−5.217***	1.899*
HISPANIC	0.063988	0.027357	0.033993	0.058118
	3.912***	1.76*	2.642***	5.503***
DROPOUT	−0.073477	−0.062784	−0.085405	−0.089526
	−6.558***	−5.84***	−6.872***	−8.629***
POSTHS	0.021108	0.033476	0.011286	0.028048
	1.786*	3.338***	0.892	2.799***
SINGPNT	N.A.	N.A.	0.048513	0.035481
	N.A.	N.A.	1.35	1.205
DUALPNT	N.A.	N.A.	0.105157	0.034546
	N.A.	N.A.	3.969***	1.149
OTHRFAM	N.A.	N.A.	0.039923	0.010622
	N.A.	N.A.	1.644	0.36
FSIZE2	0.02518	0.036808	0.002842	0.000082609
	1.677*	3.148***	0.11	0.003
FSIZE3	0.065905	0.049385	0.001349	−0.001162
	4.232***	3.957***	0.051	−0.038
FSIZE4	0.06587	0.056438	0.005571	−0.006562
	3.986***	3.945***	0.202	−0.215
FSIZE5	0.058273	0.044479	0.003017	0.012052
	3.78***	2.997***	0.115	0.398
INAFDC	−0.026244	−0.035792	−0.031644	−0.03805
	−1.35	−3.326***	−1.292	−3.67***
OTHASST	−0.034027	−0.020305	−0.02677	−0.045438
	−3.23***	−2.067**	−2.448***	−5.06***
MBST	0.019694	−0.00456	0.055523	−0.014965
	0.933	−0.24	2.282**	−0.797

Appendix Table 5A.3 STRICT-STEADY EMPLOYMENT, SECOND POSTPROGRAM YEAR (*continued*)

Variable	Illinois		Texas	
	Male Coefficient (t-Statistic)	Female Coefficient (t-Statistic)	Male Coefficient (t-Statistic)	Female Coefficient (t-Statistic)
MOST	0.059823	0.034992	0.049422	0.029187
	3.854***	2.439***	2.151**	1.626
MOJT	0.066744	0.000725	0.061085	0.008084
	4.454***	0.045	2.759***	0.434
MJSA	0.036411	0.002962	0.085032	−0.023068
	2.014**	0.162	2.849***	−0.994
PRESUM	0.000007406	0.000009262	0.000009161	0.000010912
	15.316***	16.587***	18.207***	20.076***
MINPTE	N.A.	N.A.	−0.02101	0.020602
	N.A.	N.A.	−0.386	0.715
SUBPTE	0.089046	0.106527	0.062736	0.069775
	5.249***	7.971***	3.189***	5.145***
FULLTE	0.152679	0.225653	0.116036	0.141102
	15.086***	25.023***	6.889***	11.655***
FAMINPOV	0.000009935	−0.000818	−0.044051	0.053158
	0.006	−0.588	−0.225	0.359
MEDRENT	−0.00318	−0.001154	−0.00034	−0.000038235
	−1.036	−0.415	−1.743*	−0.254
UN91–92	−0.003532	0.000849	0.320603	−0.061545
	−1.125	0.298	1.082	−0.272
CAP91–92	−0.001147	−0.003389	0.000005856	0.000000618
	−0.874	−2.794***	1.444	0.209
EGROWTH	−0.001195	0.0013	0.102768	0.322562
	−0.678	0.864	0.734	2.961***

Appendix Table 5A.4 155 PERCENT OF POVERTY, ALL TERMINEES

R-Square	0.16	0.14	0.16	0.14
Number of Observations	20,126	20,126	23,091	23,091
Dependent Mean	0.19693	0.31038	0.20925	0.23389

	Illinois		Texas	
Variable	First Post-Program Year Coefficient (t-Statistic)	Second Post-Program Year Coefficient (t-Statistic)	First Post-Program Year Coefficient (t-Statistic)	Second Post-Program Year Coefficient (t-Statistic)
INTERCEP	0.072762	0.296871	0.138436	0.104677
	1.726*	5.984***	3.21***	2.307**
FEMALE	−0.016268	−0.005566	−0.050527	−0.037023
	−2.766***	−0.804	−8.358***	−5.822***
AGE18–21	−0.040712	−0.015794	−0.027805	−0.019746
	−5.79***	−1.908*	−4.131***	−2.789***
AGE30–39	0.008044	−0.006098	0.008076	−0.001697
	1.18	−0.76	1.217	−0.243
AGE40–49	0.005976	−0.004401	0.005485	−0.004045
	0.632	−0.396	0.607	−0.426
AGE50–UP	−0.033284	−0.06872	−0.01631	−0.034972
	−2.607***	−4.573***	−1.132	−2.308**
BLACK	−0.053929	−0.058981	−0.071264	−0.052322
	−7.692***	−7.148***	−10.092***	−7.043***
HISPANIC	0.020697	0.056596	−0.004418	0.006576
	2.128**	4.945***	−0.651	0.921
DROPOUT	−0.055231	−0.087897	−0.054761	−0.069964
	−8.255***	−11.162***	−8.274***	−10.048***
POSTHS	0.041348	0.035832	0.06198	0.047157
	6.264***	4.612***	9.475***	6.853***
SINGPNT	N.A.	N.A.	0.074296	0.064249
	N.A.	N.A.	4.537***	3.729***
DUALPNT	N.A.	N.A.	0.094554	0.086434
	N.A.	N.A.	5.863***	5.095***
OTHRFAM	N.A.	N.A.	0.046413	0.029716
	N.A.	N.A.	2.995***	1.823*
FSIZE2	0.026568	0.03572	−0.021161	−0.004118
	3.429***	3.918***	−1.338	−0.248
FSIZE3	0.045739	0.058965	−0.021653	−0.004689
	5.597***	6.13***	−1.344	−0.277
FSIZE4	0.053596	0.069107	−0.026346	−0.000847
	5.852***	6.411***	−1.603	−0.049
FSIZE5	0.045573	0.053966	−0.014223	0.0000503
	5.006***	5.037***	−0.881	0.003
INAFDC	−0.010055	−0.006753	−0.009181	−0.035554
	−1.296	−0.739	−1.17	−4.307***
OTHASST	−0.025349	−0.04574	−0.047519	−0.047645
	−4.096***	−6.28***	−8.249***	−7.862***

Appendix Table 5A.4 155 PERCENT OF POVERTY, ALL TERMINEES (*continued*)

| Variable | Illinois | | Texas | |
	First Post-Program Year Coefficient (t-Statistic)	Second Post-Program Year Coefficient (t-Statistic)	First Post-Program Year Coefficient (t-Statistic)	Second Post-Program Year Coefficient (t-Statistic)
MBST	0.015538	0.00586	−0.001967	0.007399
	1.278	0.409	−0.159	0.568
MOST	0.050714	0.05555	0.055252	0.062645
	5.614***	5.225***	4.692***	5.057***
MOJT	0.046306	0.038063	0.047196	0.034552
	4.904***	3.425***	3.995***	2.78***
MJSA	0.019873	0.011218	−0.0272	0.008583
	1.792*	0.86	−1.781*	0.534
PRESUM	0.000008103	0.00001005	0.000009426	0.000010513
	25.79***	27.178***	31.234***	33.114***
MINPTE	N.A.	N.A.	−0.030735	−0.027173
	N.A.	N.A.	−1.444	−1.214
SUBPTE	0.024097	0.067641	−0.024623	−0.007284
	2.656***	6.336***	−2.649***	−0.745
FULLTE	0.201542	0.193263	0.100893	0.094124
	34.676***	28.253***	12.364***	10.965***
FAMINPOV	−0.002172	0.000081626	−0.278324	−0.23257
	−2.371***	−0.076	−2.828***	−2.246**
MEDRENT	0.000037587	−0.004569	−0.00045	−0.000218
	0.021	−2.19**	−4.524***	−2.085**
UN91–92	0.001427	−0.003178	−0.127668	0.106501
	0.784	−1.485	−0.853	0.677
CAP91–92	−0.000149	−0.000317	0.000005915	0.00000425
	−0.194	−0.351	2.972***	2.03**
EGROWTH	−0.001071	−0.001735	0.201532	0.220306
	−1.083	−1.492	2.816***	2.926***

Appendix Table 5A.5 155 PERCENT OF POVERTY, SECOND POSTPROGRAM YEAR

R-Square	0.14	0.14	0.14	0.14
Number of Observations	20,126	20,126	23,091	23,091
Dependent Mean	0.32477	0.29847	0.28415	0.19930

	Illinois		Texas	
Variable	Male Coefficient (t-Statistic)	Female Coefficient (t-Statistic)	Male Coefficient (t-Statistic)	Female Coefficient (t-Statistic)
INTERCEP	0.359607	0.237317	0.146009	0.056417
	4.753***	3.62***	1.871*	1.02
AGE18–21	−0.00628	−0.025387	−0.000531	−0.035002
	−0.505	−2.278**	−0.043	−4.052***
AGE30–39	−0.015076	0.003556	−0.005904	0.002615
	−1.25	0.33	−0.495	0.307
AGE40–49	−0.027571	0.015022	0.010215	−0.016723
	−1.659*	0.999	0.648	−1.408
AGE50–UP	−0.05199	−0.083231	−0.072277	−0.016307
	−2.228**	−4.2***	−2.924***	−0.848
BLACK	−0.069986	−0.047458	−0.083794	−0.029639
	−5.666***	−4.235***	−6.688***	−3.226***
HISPANIC	0.062318	0.054418	0.001685	0.01091
	3.708***	3.469***	0.143	1.226
DROPOUT	−0.092843	−0.084917	−0.071587	−0.069468
	−8.064***	−7.827***	−6.269***	−7.944***
POSTHS	0.031043	0.038752	0.0337	0.054705
	2.557***	3.829***	2.899***	6.475***
SINGPNT	N.A.	N.A.	0.078085	0.029532
	N.A.	N.A.	2.364***	1.19
DUALPNT	N.A.	N.A.	0.137056	0.033265
	N.A.	N.A.	5.63***	1.312
OTHRFAM	N.A.	N.A.	0.040227	0.00687
	N.A.	N.A.	1.802*	0.276
FSIZE2	0.01898	0.036164	−0.005929	0.008576
	1.23	3.064***	−0.249	0.342
FSIZE3	0.060901	0.049978	−0.031802	0.012216
	3.806***	3.968***	−1.302	0.48
FSIZE4	0.087549	0.05154	−0.002487	0.004636
	5.156***	3.57***	−0.098	0.18
FSIZE5	0.062484	0.039784	−0.020788	0.015144
	3.945***	2.656***	−0.86	0.594
INAFDC	0.001703	−0.011174	−0.030806	−0.038975
	0.085	−1.029	−1.368	−4.46***
OTHASST	−0.056363	−0.035085	−0.049461	−0.046995
	−5.208***	−3.54***	−4.923***	−6.209***
MBST	0.02071	−0.006448	0.041268	−0.012986
	0.955	−0.336	1.846*	−0.82
MOST	0.06492	0.043443	0.077863	0.050485
	4.071***	3.001***	3.688***	3.337***

Appendix Table 5A.5 155 PERCENT OF POVERTY, SECOND POSTPROGRAM YEAR (*continued*)

Variable	Illinois		Texas	
	Male Coefficient (t-Statistic)	Female Coefficient (t-Statistic)	Male Coefficient (t-Statistic)	Female Coefficient (t-Statistic)
MOJT	0.062709	0.007181	0.074986	0.003133
	4.073***	0.443	3.686***	0.2
MJSA	0.035243	−0.008872	0.063399	−0.026784
	1.897*	−0.482	2.312*	−1.369
PRESUM	0.000009377	0.00001082	0.00001012	0.000010426
	18.873***	19.2***	21.89***	22.755***
MINPTE	N.A.	N.A.	0.025665	−0.048692
	N.A.	N.A.	0.513	−2.006**
SUBPTE	0.032865	0.090135	−0.016662	−0.007308
	1.885*	6.683***	−0.922	−0.639
FULLTE	0.167613	0.213237	0.08337	0.095405
	16.119***	23.431***	5.387***	9.349***
FAMINPOV	0.001122	−0.001038	−0.313302	−0.146253
	0.664	−0.74	−1.742*	−1.171
MEDRENT	−0.007743	−0.001581	−0.000526	0.000017483
	−2.456***	−0.563	−2.935***	−0.138
UN91–92	−0.002831	−0.003413	0.07101	0.104849
	−0.877	−1.187	0.261	0.549
CAP91–92	0.000039552	−0.000595	0.000007003	0.000003001
	−0.029	−0.486	1.879*	1.207
EGROWTH	−0.002731	−0.000993	0.260186	0.190932
	−1.509	−0.654	2.023**	2.079**

Chapter Six

EMPLOYMENT AND TRAINING PROGRAMS FOR OUT-OF-SCHOOL YOUTH: PAST EFFECTS AND LESSONS FOR THE FUTURE

Robert I. Lerman

The economic expansion of the 1990s has increased access to jobs for individuals from historically unemployed populations, but young adults with no more than a high school diploma—referred to here as out-of-school youth—still struggle to enter, and to remain in, the labor market. In October 1997, when the nation's unemployment rate was only 5 percent, young people who left high school as graduates or dropouts in the 1996–97 year experienced a 20 percent unemployment rate; over 40 percent of these youth were not working.[1] Although rapid job growth reduced the unemployment of 16- to 24-year-olds from 13.5 percent in 1991 to 10.4 percent in 1998, out-of-school youth with no more than a high school education still have trouble finding and keeping jobs.

The problems are most severe for young high school dropouts and minority youth. As of early 1999, their unemployment rates had declined but remained close to 20 percent, even as overall unemployment rates reached the 30-year low of nearly 4 percent. In April 1999, just over half of the out-of-school youth without a high school diploma held jobs, but the employed share of minority high school dropouts was only about 40 percent. In addition, given the problems of out-of-school youth vis-à-vis the job market, one might expect public policy to focus resources on improving their employment outcomes. Yet federal and state investments in young people go almost entirely to the college-bound. Through federal college grants and subsidized loans, along with direct state aid to community colleges and state universities, the U.S. government allocates billions of dollars to higher education; very little support goes to out-of-school youth to improve their employment possibilities (see table 6.1). The Clinton administration's 1998 budget, which called for over $4 billion in new tax credits and deductions for families with children attending college, widened the gap even further.

Table 6.1 PROPOSED 1998 OUTLAYS ON SELECTED FEDERAL EDUCATION AND
TRAINING PROGRAMS FOR YOUTH AFTER HIGH SCHOOL

Type of Program	1998 Proposed Funding (in billions of $)
Selected College Programs	
HOPE Scholarships	4.1
Pell Scholarship Grants	7.6
Interest Credits on College Loans	2.8
College Work-Study Programs	0.857
Other Campus-Based Support	0.771
Presidential Scholars	0.132
Total, Selected College-Oriented Programs	16.26
Selected Programs for Out-of-School Youth	
Youth Training	0.123
Opportunity Areas for Out-of-School Youth	0.250
Youth Build	0.030
Job Corps	1.250
Total, Selected Programs of Other Youth	1.653

Source: Demetra Nightingale (1996) and U.S. Office of Management and Budget
(1997).

One reason for the limited governmental effort is the perception
that programs for out-of-school youth have produced little positive
effect on employment and earnings. When the 1994 National Job
Training Partnership Act (JTPA) study provided evidence that JTPA
yielded no earnings gains for youth, Congress cut the program's funding. Federal spending on JTPA youth programs (other than the summer jobs program) fell from $659 million in 1994 to $77 million in
1995 (Nightingale 1996).

While spending on college-bound youth goes forward despite limited evaluative evidence, employment and training programs must
be proved effective to receive funding. This chapter examines the
record of past and current programs designed to address unemployment of out-of-school youth to identify promising strategies for the
future. I first take a closer look at out-of-school youth and their relationship with the job market.

OUT-OF-SCHOOL YOUTH AND THE JOB MARKET

Demographic studies of out-of-school youth report that this population is disproportionately poor and minority and that many have

criminal records. Their lack of both education and work experience makes finding lasting employment a difficult challenge (Grogger 1995).

In the past, the size of the out-of-school population has followed the arc of population growth. From the mid-1970s to the mid-1990s, the out-of-school youth population dropped along with the decline in the overall number of young people. The number of 17- to 21-year-olds who were not in school and did not have a college education dropped from 9.2 million to 5.4 million, coinciding with a 19 percent decline in the number of 18- to 21-year-olds between 1980 and 1993.[2] Today the number of young people is on the rise, an indication that the out-of-school population will soon follow. The U.S. Bureau of the Census projects a 4.5 million, or 14 percent, increase in 16- to 24-year-olds between 1994 and 2005.

A large share of out-of-school 17- to 21-year-olds, especially high school dropouts, were poor or near-poor in 1995. These proportions vary by sex, since many out-of-school women leave home after they become mothers. By 1995, about 44 percent of 17- to 21-year-old female dropouts and 30 percent of female high school graduates without a college degree had become mothers. Over half of these families with young mothers have low incomes. In comparison, about 40 percent of male dropouts and 20 percent of male high school graduates without a college degree came from poor or near-poor families, whether or not they head their own households.

The demographics of the out-of-school youth population have shifted substantially over the last two decades. In 1974, white youth comprised over 70 percent of high school dropouts; in 1995, they accounted for only 47 percent. In 1995, almost 50 percent were African American and Hispanic, up from roughly 30 percent in 1974 (Sum and Fogg 1996). About 15 percent of high school dropouts in 1995 were immigrants who entered the country after 1990. White, non-college-bound high school graduates also declined, from 84 percent to 70 percent between 1994 and 1995.

Dropouts are 10 to 20 times more likely to be imprisoned than high school graduates. Although only 3 percent of all 25- to 34-year-old men are in jail, nearly 12 percent of all dropouts and 34 percent of black male dropouts are incarcerated (Freeman 1996). Among males, especially young black men, involvement with the criminal justice system increased markedly during the 1980s. Twenty percent of black 18- to 29-year-old male dropouts were incarcerated in 1989, 12.7 percent more than in 1980 (Bound and Freeman 1992). According to Bound and Freeman, the rise in black dropouts with criminal records may have accounted for 70 percent of the decline in employment rates between 1979 and 1989. The proportion of youth reporting they could earn more from illegal activity than a legitimate job increased during the 1980s (Freeman 1996).

Out-of-school youth are a dynamic population that grows and shrinks depending on changing educational choices. As Klerman and Karoly (1994) report, over two-thirds of youth who drop out of high school ultimately return to school, with about one-third earning a high school degree and another one-third earning a general equivalency diploma (GED). Similarly, 61 percent of those who initially end their schooling after graduating from high school subsequently return to school, and about 8 percent of those returning obtain a bachelor's degree.

With little education and work experience, out-of-school youth have difficulty entering the labor market. Almost three-quarters of the jobs that do not require a college degree do require a high school diploma, and about one-third of the employers for these jobs check educational records. Even with a diploma or its equivalent, out-of-school youth face other hurdles. Employers screen prospective workers by checking criminal records and giving skills tests. Nearly all use personal interviews, for which adequate communications skills may be important (Holzer 1996).

It takes a wide range of skills to get a job in today's market. In the early 1990s, the U.S. Department of Labor (DOL) sponsored the Secretary's Commission on Achieving Necessary Skills (SCANS), a study to pinpoint the types of skills needed for employment. SCANS used a sample of 50 jobs and studied how proficient workers needed to be by asking 20 people to rate the skill levels required for job tasks identified by the job analysis. The SCANS report documented the importance of a range of generic skills in addition to basic reading, writing, and math ability. The study found that workers relied on such capabilities as listening, speaking, decisionmaking, problem solving, and mental visualization. To succeed in the workplace, the commission recommended teaching the following: how to manage time, money, material, and human resources; how to acquire, evaluate, organize, interpret, and communicate information; how to use computers to process information; how to participate as a member of a team; and how to teach others, serve clients, exercise leadership, and work with cultural diversity.

There may be a perception among employers that out-of-school youth lack some of these less-tangible job skills. Although evidence is limited, a study conducted in Chicago found that employers often state explicitly their concerns about poor attitudes and the absence of a strong work ethic when discussing why they do not hire inner-city black males, a group that overlaps demographically with out-of-school youth. When asked about why inner-city black males cannot find or retain jobs easily, 37 percent of the 179 employers in Chicago surveyed cited a lack of work ethic, 17 percent cited bad attitudes, and 17 percent cited a lack of dependability (Wilson 1996). Whether these assessments are true or not, it is a serious problem if employers believe they are accurate.

The role of attitudes is hard to quantify, and influencing attitudes in ways that improve job skills is not easy. Yet employers, some social scientists, and many program staff believe that attitudes play a significant role in how well workers perform in the job market. Some programs viewed as successful emphasize improving the attitudes of disadvantaged workers, including increasing their spirit of cooperation and their ability to take direction and constructive criticism.

EMPLOYMENT PROGRAMS FOR OUT-OF-SCHOOL YOUTH

There are two broad approaches to employment programs for out-of-school youth. The first focuses on providing education, training, and job search services. The second creates and places youth in jobs, usually temporary positions designed for training. Some programs incorporate elements of both approaches. Researchers have struggled to study each variety of employment program, sometimes with limited success.

One factor complicating evaluation is the lack of program consistency. Even in national programs, design, personnel, and delivery differ from one location to the next. In addition, community program locations are not the same with respect to the quality of their community colleges, the demand for workers, the role of unions, the degree of residential segregation, the availability of transportation, and the geographic dispersion of economic activity. Program adaptability, though desirable, makes evaluation difficult.

Evaluations often overlook important aspects of a program's methodology, another factor that makes assessment difficult. For example, research suggests that success in the job market for out-of-school youth hinges on their ability to not only achieve basic skills but also develop positive attitudes toward work and attain the competencies identified in the SCANS report. Yet few studies examine the extent to which programs teach, and participants acquire, these skills.

Despite difficulties, several national evaluations using experimental methods have yielded important findings about the overall effects of employment and training programs on the education and earnings of out-of-school youth. Findings for six programs are discussed below.

Education and Training Approaches

JOB TRAINING PARTNERSHIP ACT

Under the JTPA, the federal government sponsored job training programs for economically disadvantaged workers, including out-of-school youth.[3] Local Service Delivery Areas (SDAs), which are formed by one or more local governments, received JTPA funds and operated authorized programs with advice and supervision from Private Industry Councils (PICs). The PICs included representatives from local businesses, unions, social service agencies, and organizations providing employment and training services. SDAs provided or contracted for services to help workers raise their educational levels, upgrade their occupational skills, and find jobs. Local community-based organizations, community colleges, public schools, and private for-profit occupational schools had been among the frequent providers of services. After participants received an assessment, they participated in one or more of a variety of activities, such as basic education, job search assistance, classroom training in occupational skills, on-the-job training, or work experience through temporary, subsidized public jobs.

To determine the impact of JTPA on participants, the DOL funded the National JTPA study.[4] Evaluators compared the experiences of applicants randomly assigned to have access to JTPA with those of applicants assigned to control status. The study took place in 16 SDAs recruited from across the United States. Within each site, staff members assessed eligible applicants and recommended one of three service strategies: classroom training, on-the-job training and job search assistance, or other services, such as basic education, tryout employment, and job shadowing. After the staff recommended one of the three groups of services, they randomly assigned applicants to experimental status, where they would have access to program treatments, or to control status, where they would not have access to JTPA-sponsored services for 18 months after applying for the program.

The youth component of the study evaluated the year-round program participation of out-of-school 16- to 21-year-olds. The study described the JTPA services obtained by participants and the effects of access to JTPA on educational outcomes and earnings. The analysis dealt separately with female youth, male youth with prior arrest records (male arrestees), and other male youth (male nonarrestees).

The vast majority of youth had left high school before receiving their diploma.

The study showed that JTPA increased the utilization of education, training, and employment services. While control group members could not receive JTPA-sponsored services, they could obtain training assistance from other sources. The differentials were highest in components associated with government programs, such as on-the-job training contracts and job search assistance. Classroom training was also significantly higher for the experimental group. About 53 to 62 percent of the experimental group took advantage of at least one form of education, training, or employment assistance, a rate about 25 percent higher than the utilization of similar services by controls. The experimental group spent an additional 180 hours in training or related services as a result of their access to JTPA.

Despite JTPA's stimulus to participation in education and training, it exerted a modest effect on the attainment of a high school diploma or GED. Males in the treatment group had slightly lower rates of high school graduation than males in the control group, or about 30 to 37 percent. For females, on the other hand, JTPA raised graduation rates by nearly 11 percentage points, from 31.7 percent to 42.3 percent.

Another finding is that JTPA apparently did not reduce the arrest rates of enrollees. In fact, males who began without arrest records showed a statistically significant increase in arrests during the follow-up periods. In the three years following random assignment, the arrest rate was 26 percent among the experimental group and 19 percent among controls. Nearly 60 percent of experimentals with arrest records predating their enrollment in JTPA were arrested during the follow-up period, a rate slightly higher than the 56 percent rate among controls with a previous record.

The measured effects on earnings were disappointing. None of the three youth experimental groups saw their earnings rise relative to the earnings of those in the control group. In the period beginning 19 months after applying for JTPA, female experimentals showed earnings levels equivalent to the female control group. Using survey data, the researchers found that earnings among male youth arrestees were actually 22 percent lower than they would have been without JTPA for the entire 30 months after application for JTPA. Unfortunately, no statistically significant positive effects on wages were reported for females or males through the fifth year after signing up for JTPA (GAO 1996b).

Why did JTPA fail to raise the earnings of out-of-school youth? After all, JTPA did increase the amount of education and training, and previous research demonstrates that education and training lead to higher earnings. In considering JTPA's ineffectiveness, a number of hypotheses arise (Lerman 1996).

One possibility is that the study's timing did not allow it to capture increased earnings. For example, if program participants continued to receive training through much of the 30-month follow-up period, their earnings gains may have occurred after the experiment results were collected. In this case, JTPA succeeded in stimulating continued training that would reduce earnings temporarily but ultimately improve the success of participants in the job market. Estimates of earnings in the follow-up period 25 to 30 months after application did show that for each hour of training in the follow-up period, participants forfeited from $2.34 to $3.48 of pay. However, the difference in the amount of training or other employment services sought by the experimental and control groups took place almost entirely during the first 12 months after application. Thus, the absence of JTPA-induced earnings gains cannot be dismissed on grounds that the program stimulates added training.[5]

Another possibility is that the greater access to training provided to JTPA experimentals diverted some from taking jobs in the private market. Thus, while experimentals were more likely than controls to accumulate education, training, and other employment services, controls were more likely to gain work experience. There is clear evidence that assignment to experimental status reduced the amount of work experience received by male youth, especially male arrestees. For male arrestees, whose earnings after JTPA showed no positive gains, JTPA raised the amount of employment services by 176 hours but lowered the amount of work experience by 434 hours. The harmful effects of the diversion from work experience were less pronounced for females, whose JTPA participation resulted in positive earnings gains, and male nonarrestees, who showed modest pay gains. To the extent that the skills learned through work experience correspond with those identified in the SCANS report, it is not surprising that work experience seemed to be more effective than training in raising earnings.

JTPA services might also have diverted youth from higher-quality training. If so, we would expect higher earnings gains among controls who received training than among experimentals. However, estimates of effects of service hours do not support this hypothesis. In fact, the evidence suggests just the opposite for experimental females, whose earnings responded more to services than did the earnings of controls.

Perhaps the group most able to benefit from training would have obtained sufficient services in the absence of JTPA. In this case, additional services induced by JTPA would have no effect because they were received by youth unable to benefit from training. Another possibility is that the treatment group members not receiving services might have become frustrated by insufficient service options or spent time waiting for services and, as a result, performed worse than controls not receiving services. Some evidence emerged in support of these hypotheses. The study compared earnings gains among experimentals and controls receiving at least 150 hours of training or employment services. Among males, the change in earnings was higher for controls receiving services than for experimentals receiving services.

While JTPA services yielded no significant positive effects on any of the groups of out-of-school youth, the absence of experimental effects on females is most difficult to pinpoint. Experimental females received more training than controls and had a higher gain per hour of training than controls; however, it seems the untrained members of the control group earned more than the untrained members of the experimental group, offsetting the increased earnings associated with higher training among experimentals.

By the standards of training programs, JTPA is an inexpensive program, costing only about $1,900 to $2,800 per enrollee in 1996 dollars. Yet, despite its low cost, the benefits to youth enrollees were insufficient to make the program a sound government investment.[6]

JOB CORPS

The largest and most expensive intervention for youth sponsored by the federal government is the Job Corps. Initiated in the mid-1960s as part of President Lyndon Johnson's War on Poverty programs, the Job Corps is one of the few job training programs that has persisted for 30 years. The Job Corps provides education, training, health, and other services in a residential setting away from the homes of out-of-school youth who participate. The intention of the program was to take young people out of declining neighborhoods and rural areas and place them in facilities with continuous supervision and discipline. The Job Corps is the most intensive federally sponsored program aimed at helping out-of-school youth enter employment; it costs as much as 10 times the amount provided for JTPA. Unlike other federally sponsored programs that delegate funds to local and state governments, the federal government has retained the responsibility for operating the program, contracting with providers, and monitoring the results. Private firms operate a large share of the Job Corps sites.

The main evidence of the Job Corps' effectiveness comes from an evaluation (Maller et al. 1982) sponsored by the U.S. Department of Labor and conducted by Mathematica Policy Research, Inc., beginning in the 1970s. The study compared the experiences of about 5,000 youth enrolled in Job Corps centers throughout the country with those of similar youth who did not enroll. The study design did not rely on the experimental approach, in which applicants are randomly divided into treatment and control groups. As a result, it is difficult to place the same level of confidence in the findings as in the results from the other experimental-based findings.[7]

Despite the study's limitations, the authors developed well-documented estimates of the benefits and costs of Job Corps activities. The analysis included a large number of observations, the follow-up period was a lengthy 42 to 54 months after the program period, the attrition rate was low, and the data included information on social as well as economic outcomes.

The evaluation found that the Job Corps raised the rate of high school graduation or attainment of a GED by almost 20 percent, reduced criminal activity as indicated by arrest rates, and increased earnings per week by about 10 percent and employment per year by about 15 to 20 percent. As a result, overall earnings increased by about $600 per year, or 28 percent above what they would have been in the absence of the Job Corps. The estimates revealed a large and continuing advantage in employment rates of corpsmembers that did not appear to erode over the postprogram period. One element in the higher employment rate was the more than doubling of the probability of males entering military service. Yet, even excluding employment through the military, the proportion of time spent employed was about 12 percent higher.

One striking element was the fact that males gained as much or more from the Job Corps as females. In many other training programs, the employment and earnings tend to be much higher among females.[8] In this case, one group of females—those with children—actually lost in earnings and employment by participating in the Job Corps.

The evaluators calculated the benefits and costs of the program from the perspective of society as a whole and from the perspectives of corpsmembers. The key outlays for the program were the operations of the program, including the room and board provided to corpsmembers. Those costs amounted to about $5,700 per corpsmember (in 1977 dollars). On the benefit side, the gain in production resulting from the added employment and earnings of corpsmembers amounted to about $3,300 (or $4,000 if one includes production within the program). The other large social benefit was a

$3,000 reduction in the costs of crime, both through savings for the court system and lower costs to victims of crime. Taking all costs and benefits together, the evaluators estimated that the present value of the $5,000 social investment was about $2,300 above costs.

The evaluation of the program illustrates the importance of obtaining reliable values for what would have happened in the absence of the Job Corps. Because the Job Corps draws from a particularly disadvantaged population, the employment and earnings of corpsmembers are low even after a beneficial program effect. Overall, the employment rate of these out-of-school youth amounted to only about 52 percent even after the intervention.

For a number of reasons, one must remain somewhat cautious about the study's findings. First, the evaluation result is 20 years old. Second, the value of reduced criminal activity accounted for nearly half the benefits. Third, a good share of the employment gains came about through increases in military service. Both the crime reductions and military entry effects may be sensitive to the time period and to the use of a comparison group instead of a control group methodology. The study does not consider those who drop out of the program early, a group whose job earnings may or may not have been positively affected by participation in the Job Corps.

There are renewed efforts to improve the Jobs Corps, especially the linkage between training and private employers. In the absence of such connections, effectiveness in teaching skills to corpsmembers may not lead to success in the job market if the skills are not in demand in the communities where the corpsmembers live. Moreover, there continue to be concerns about the high costs per enrollee. Still, if a new Labor Department–sponsored evaluation yields results as positive as the previous one, Congress will no doubt continue to fund the Job Corps.

JOBSTART

Unlike the two ongoing programs, the Job Corps and JTPA, JOBSTART was a demonstration program that used random assignment of applicants to create a social experiment. A major purpose of JOBSTART was to determine whether a program that had the intensity of the Job Corps but was run in a nonresidential setting could be cost-effective. JOBSTART drew on JTPA and the Job Corps for its operating funds and used JTPA rules to determine the eligibility of applicants. Three of the 13 local operators running JOBSTART were Job Corps centers. The Manpower Demonstration Research Corporation (MDRC) designed JOBSTART in collaboration with other experts in employment and training and oversaw JOBSTART's implementation between 1985 and 1988.

The program embodied four central components: instruction in basic skills with self-paced learning; occupational training involving both classroom activity and hands-on experience in high-demand occupations; training-related support services including transportation, child care, and life skills training; and job placement assistance. The model required sites to offer at least 200 hours of basic education and 500 hours of occupational training. The program dealt with particularly disadvantaged youth. All were high school dropouts, 75 percent were between the ages of 16 and 19, 90 percent were minorities (black or Hispanic), 26 percent were women living with their own child, and only 35 percent lived with both parents at age 14. Of the 2,312 youth who applied for the program and were randomly assigned to experiment or control status, the evaluators managed to interview 84 percent of them, or 1,941 applicants.

As in the case of JTPA, JOBSTART substantially increased the receipt of education, training, and employment services, but almost the entire increase took place during the year after application. About 90 percent of experimentals and only 26 percent of controls received education and training in months 1 through 12 after application. In the first year, participants averaged 415 education and training hours, compared with 115 averaged by controls—a gap of 300 hours. By the second year, the gap had narrowed to 65 hours, and it declined to zero for the last two years of the follow-up period (Cave et al. 1993).

Education services raised the proportion of participants earning a GED (37 percent to 21 percent), though controls were more likely to earn a high school diploma (7.5 percent to 4.4 percent).[9] Occupational training yielded an increase in the receipt of trade certificates from 17 percent to 33 percent.

Unfortunately, the program yielded few or no gains in earnings, employment, reduced childbearing, or criminal activity. Even by the fourth year after the program (three years after the added training), the experimentals had virtually the same rate of employment and a slight, though statistically insignificant, rise in earnings. By this time, when the youth were between the ages of 20 and 25, over one-third did not work at all during the year, and average annual earnings were only about $5,600 (in 1988 dollars). Among males, the employment and earnings levels were higher; 79 percent worked at least some time during the year, and earnings for the experimental group averaged $7,600. Although experimentals earned about $500 more per year than controls, this difference was not statistically significant. Moreover, male experimentals gave up more in lost earnings during the first two years after entering the program than they gained in the last two years of the follow-up period.

The evidence on crime showed slight reductions in the proportion arrested or using any illegal drugs. Yet the only statistically significant positive was in a lower rate of using illegal drugs other than marijuana. Only 3.7 percent of experimentals as compared with 10.5 percent of controls admitted using such drugs.

The effects on childbearing and pregnancy reductions were disappointing. Among women who began JOBSTART as custodial mothers, experimentals experienced a higher rate of childbearing than controls. However, the rate of welfare receipt was significantly lower among experimentals than controls (31 percent compared with 39 percent) for women with no children at the start of the program.

The one group that appeared to gain substantially from JOBSTART was men arrested between age 16 and the time they entered the program. On average, experimentals in this category earned over $1,000 more per year than controls in both the third and fourth year after entering the program. The pattern of earnings gains grew over time, rising from $425 in the second year to $1,872 in the fourth year after random assignment. This result contrasts sharply with findings from the JTPA evaluation in which males with prior arrest records fared worst and apparently had lower earnings than they would have achieved in the absence of JTPA services.

In a reanalysis of JOBSTART, Cave and Bos (1996) attempted to determine whether experimentals who earned a GED in JOBSTART were also able to reap gains in earnings. Given that increases in educational levels generally raise earnings, the researchers wondered why no significant earnings gains emerged from JOBSTART despite the program's positive and significant impact on educational attainment. Their strategy involved developing matched pairs of treatment and control group members and then comparing earnings of four groups: experimentals who earned a GED when their matched control did not; experimentals who did not earn a GED when their matched control did; experimentals and matched controls with a GED; and experimentals and matched controls without a GED. Cave and Bos performed the matching process 100 times. Their simulations suggest that JOBSTART exerted a significant, positive impact on the earnings of the group induced to earn a GED but not on any of the other three groups. Since most of the sample falls into the three categories that did not benefit from the program, the overall impact turned out not to be statistically significant. Yet Cave and Bos conclude that programs able to engage young people enough to stimulate them to work hard toward their GED can be effective in improving job market outcomes.

Direct Job Creation

CONSERVATION AND YOUTH SERVICE CORPS

The National and Community Service Act of 1990 funded Conservation and Youth Service Corps, still in operation, as a way of expanding opportunities for 18- to 25-year-old out-of-school youth. More than half the corpsmembers were economically disadvantaged, and most did not have high school degrees or GEDs. The primary goals of these corps are to boost the work ethic, sense of public service, and skills of program participants while benefiting the public with goods and services. About 100 corps sites received funding in the 1993–94 program year.

Corpsmembers participated in projects that included tutoring children, assisting in child care, escorting patients to examinations, planting trees, rehabilitating housing, improving parks, and helping to clean up debris after a hurricane. About 70 percent of the work took place under the auspices of nonprofit institutions and the remaining 30 percent involved government agencies.

To determine the effectiveness of service corps programs, Abt Associates and Brandeis University's Center for Human Resources conducted an intensive evaluation of eight sites (Jastrzab et al. 1996). In four of the sites, the evaluation used a social experiment methodology, randomly assigning applicants to a treatment group or a control group. The evaluation examined the costs of the service corps program, the value of the output produced in the program, and the effects on participants over a 15-month follow-up period.

To examine the effectiveness of the service corps in producing valued outputs, evaluators interviewed beneficiaries of the projects and determined what it would cost a private, unsubsidized supplier to produce the output generated by the corps. The reports were largely positive. Over half the beneficiaries rated the quality of work by corpsmembers as excellent or very good; about 30 percent stated the work had some problems or was poor. Using data from a representative sample of projects, the evaluators estimated the value of program output per service hours as averaging $13.24, with individual project values ranging from $8.64 to $15.18 per hour.

The analysis of the program participants is limited to the period corpsmembers were still working on projects. Many remained with the corps for 12 months of the 15-month follow-up period. The corps did stimulate added employment, as participants worked almost 40 percent more hours than controls (2,030 hours, compared with 1,465 hours) and earned $83 more per month. In addition, participation in the service corps reduced arrest rates from 17 percent to 12 percent.

However, participation in the corps diverted members from obtaining certificates or diplomas from technical schools; 13 percent of controls but only 8 percent of corpsmembers earned such certificates.

The service corps results were particularly positive for black and Hispanic male corpsmembers. Work hours and earnings were especially large for both groups. In contrast, white male participants earned substantially less than their counterparts in the treatment group.

Evaluators analyzed the service corps in terms of social benefits and found that they exceeded the social costs. The operational costs of the program other than stipends or participant benefits were $9.66 per hour. While participants obtained $6.76 per hour in stipends or fringes, they gave up $2.92 per hour they would have earned outside the program. The largest benefit component was the program output, valued at $13.63 per hour. The monetary benefit exceeded the combined costs of $12.58 per hour (operational costs of $9.66 per hour plus $2.92 in forgone earnings) by $1.05 per hour.[10]

Overall, researchers found the Conservation and Youth Service Corps to be a cost-effective way to utilize out-of-school youth, especially minority males. The provision of low-wage jobs that give young people a chance to serve their communities is a sensible approach to improving job market capabilities of disadvantaged youth.

Supported Work

The National Supported Work Demonstration, no longer operating, began in 1975 to test whether a well-funded and well-designed work experience program could raise the earnings of hard-core unemployed workers. The project placed workers in jobs with graduated stress, peer support, and close supervision. Young high school dropouts were one of the four target groups included in the demonstration—along with unemployed welfare mothers, drug addicts, and former criminal offenders. Workers performed construction, manufacturing, business services, and clerical work. Although the program started during a recession, most participants exited during the recovery of 1977–78.

The demonstration used an experimental design, randomly assigning applicants to a treatment or control group. Supported Work clearly increased the share of dropouts obtaining employment during the program period. During the first three months after enrollment, over 90 percent of the treatment group had jobs, compared with only 29 percent of controls. This difference implies that for every nine jobs financed by the program, about six represented increased employment for young dropouts and about three replaced jobs that youth would have obtained in the absence of the program. As a result of increased employment, dropout youth produced output valued at over three times what they would have earned in the absence of the program (Kemper, Long, and Thornton 1981). But in the period after the program, the control group was able to work and earn as much as the treatment group. Evaluators found that the relatively steep costs of about $4,000 per participant exceeded the benefits of the program for youth (Maynard 1980).

A recent study (Couch 1992) examined the earnings of AFDC and youth participants in the Supported Work treatment and control groups data for eight years following training. While modest, statistically significant gains continued among AFDC women, youth in the Supported Work treatment group fared no better than youth in the control group.

YOUTH INCENTIVE ENTITLEMENT PILOT PROJECTS

In 1977, Congress mandated a major demonstration to test the impact on poor youth of providing jobs linked to staying in school or returning to school (Hahn and Lerman 1985). No longer in operation today, Youth Incentive Entitlement Pilot Projects (YIEPP) guaranteed part-time jobs during the school year and full-time jobs in the summer to all poor youth who stayed in school or returned to school. The goal of the YIEPP demonstration was to reduce youth unemployment while at the same time encouraging young people to graduate from high school. Although YIEPP was designated largely as a program to keep poor youth in high school until they graduated, the demonstration provided incentives for dropouts to return to high school. Evaluators examined the impact of YIEPP by studying communities operating the demonstration and comparison communities with no demonstration.

On the basis of the evaluation, YIEPP's record in dealing with the out-of-school group was mixed at best (Farkas et al. 1992; Farkas et al. 1984). By offering jobs to dropouts if they returned to school, YIEPP drew many dropouts back to school. The return-to-school rate rose by 55 percent in 1978 and by 10 percent in 1979. In addition, the program raised the employment rates of poor youth substantially. However, the program was unable to stimulate these dropouts to stay in school long enough to graduate. In the three YIEPP sites that fully implemented the program, only 47 percent of black 19- to 20-year-olds had graduated from high school as of fall 1981. The evaluators of YIEPP did estimate a postprogram gain in earnings of about $10 per week. Although positive and statistically significant, the results were based on comparisons of sites that are less reliable than comparisons of randomly assigned treatment and control groups. Moreover, well after YIEPP, the unemployment rates of YIEPP eligibles (most of whom participated) remained extremely high, reaching 60 percent among black young adults.

PROMISING STRATEGIES FROM SELECTED PROGRAMS

Well-designed job creation programs for out-of-school youth can produce useful community services and substantially raise the employment rate of participants during the program period. However, job creation programs for out-of-school youth have not exerted significant, positive impacts on postprogram earnings of the youth with access to subsidized employment. One recent study (Foster 1995) attempted to determine why public work programs have yielded so few gains for disadvantaged youth. Analyzing a national sample drawn from the Panel Study of Income Dynamics, Foster found that youth work experience from any type of employer is much less effective among poor and black youth than among youth as a whole. In attempting to explain these results, Foster speculates that disadvantaged youth may lack the foundation of skills on which work experience can build and that those with poor reading skills may be assigned to menial tasks that add little or nothing to the youths' productivity.

The limited success of several large, well-researched programs has led to pessimism about employment and training interventions aimed at helping dropouts and other disadvantaged out-of-school youth. The only program shown to produce statistically significant earnings gains is the Job Corps. But even the Job Corps had to rely on savings from reduced crime to yield enough social benefits to offset its costs. Further, the basis for claiming positive effects of the Job Corps is a study using a nonexperimental approach examining those entering the program over 20 years ago.

Fortunately, it is possible to look beyond the evidence from national demonstrations and observe specific sites and models that appear highly successful. Information on these programs comes from a report by the U.S. General Accounting Office (GAO 1996a) and from an expert review of promising youth programs (National Youth Employment Coalition 1996). While most of the programs described here have not been subject to rigorous evaluation, the case reviews add to our knowledge of what may or may not work when training youth for jobs.

One program cited in the GAO report is the Center for Employment and Training (CET). CET, in San Jose, California, was by far the most positive site in the JOBSTART demonstration. Since random assignment took place within JOBSTART sites, it is possible to compare the treatment and control samples site by site. CET raised earnings by an extraordinary 42 percent two through four years after program entry. CET's success carried over to an initiative for minority single parents (the Minority Female Single Parent demonstration). Five years after program entry, minority parents who went through the CET program earned nearly 20 percent more than the control group. Currently, the U.S. Department of Labor is sponsoring replications of the CET program in other sites throughout the country.

The CET model emphasizes a concurrent training and education design as well as learning in context rather than the common sequence of education first, training second. For example, participants may learn math in the context of a building maintenance program. The training simulates what actually takes place in industry and operates at several competency levels. CET also stresses the development of close linkages with the job market to ensure that trained workers obtain jobs. It eliminates programs when a local job market is unable to absorb its graduates. The program also offers supportive services, remedial education, and training in job-finding skills. Participants must demonstrate their willingness to come to training on time every day, to show responsibility, and to work effectively with instructors and fellow students.

STRIVE (Support and Training Results in Valuable Employment) is another promising program that emphasizes the improvement of job skills—dependability, teamwork, conflict resolution, and taking direction. Participants attend a demanding three-week workshop in which individual tardiness is brought to the attention of the entire group. Applicants who leave, unable to deal with the rigors of the program, are referred to other services. The STRIVE staff aim to find jobs with benefits and a chance for advancement; the program's philosophy is that no job should be considered a "dead end." In the Reno, Nevada, site, 80 percent of those who completed the full three-week program found jobs, 75 to 80 percent of whom retained their jobs for at least two years. The New York City site reports moving 11,140 men and women into unsubsidized jobs with a high retention rate.

The Focus: HOPE program in Detroit, Michigan, attempts to prepare workers for careers in manufacturing, especially in the machinist trades. A program component called FAST TRACK prepares mostly disadvantaged males, ages 17 to 23, for the Machinist Training Institute (MTI). The program provides instruction in math, reading, computer literacy, and other studies necessary for meaningful employment. Participants improve rapidly, raising their educational levels one to two grades during an intensive seven-week course. As with CET and STRIVE, Focus: HOPE attempts to improve the attendance, cooperation, interpersonal skills, and work performance of participants. The record appears excellent, with 75 percent of all participants completing the program, 99 percent of whom find jobs with an average wage of $9.50 per hour.

Other successful programs develop skills through job creation. A good example is the Casa Verde Builders AmeriCorps Youthbuild Program in Austin, Texas. The program is part of the American Institute for Learning, a nonprofit comprehensive education and employment training program mainly for young adults. In addition to emphasizing promptness, reliability, responsibility, and teamwork, the project has put participants to work building low-income dwellings to rehabilitate a small community. The housing is built with innovative, sustainable construction methods that result in lower utility costs and durable structures. Participants spend about half their time in on-site construction activities and half in educational activities, which include basic academic skills and career preparation. Nearly 80 percent of participants earned their GED from the program.

Another successful program, the Gulf Coast Trades Center, provides education and training in a residential setting for out-of-school youth, most of whom have criminal records. The program offers a range of services, including assessment, occupational training, academic training, social skills training, career counseling, work experience, and job placement. Students are expected to engage in community service, and many gain work experience through positions at local area nonprofit organizations. In five years, the center enrolled 1,700 youth, 80 percent of whom graduated with a certificate in an approved trade program. Sixty-two percent found trade-related jobs.

LESSONS FOR THE FUTURE

Deriving lessons from research on employment and training strategies is difficult. Evaluations pay little attention to the precise content of the program, ways operators of the program change in response to changing labor demand, and ways the program instills applicants with the incentive to learn and train intensively.

National programs have paid only modest attention to linking the specific content of programs to the main barriers found in the research literature. Few have emphasized the development and testing of the work-relevant skills highlighted in the SCANS report, developed clear incentives, or placed strong demands on the participants. Few use well-structured combinations of work-based and school-based learning leading to competence in a skill standard or discuss how they will overcome geographic barriers to employment. Few have close linkages with employers and local labor markets that ensure placement for successful graduates and that adapt program content to changing labor force demands.

Some basic lessons are emerging from successful and unsuccessful programs. First, stand-alone training programs for disadvantaged out-of-school youth rarely work, especially in the absence of a mentor or some other person who monitors and takes a serious and sustained interest in the participant's success. Second, job creation programs seem to create useful public outputs, with dollar value estimates that can be defended, and leave participants with a credible reference.

In separate studies, GAO and the Department of Labor found a similar set of components that contribute to program success. The two reports agree along major dimensions, yet few government programs actually include these components.

The keys from the perspectives of GAO and the DOL are as follows:

- Make sure that participants are committed to training and getting a job; programs can require a small payment by participants and strict discipline after initial counseling.
- Commit to removing all barriers—geography, family, attitudes—to finding and keeping a job.
- Improve the skills employers require of all workers, such as dependability, teamwork, taking instruction, and conflict resolution; some successful programs require participants to use a time card to clock in and out, sanctioning those who are late or miss days.
- Link occupational skills training with the job market to make sure that employers can absorb successful graduates.
- Integrate basic skills training with occupational training so that participants can learn by doing and can see the relevance of their skills.
- Use individual case management to mentor participants and to help them overcome temporary setbacks.

The next wave of research, development and evaluation activity should examine rigorously how well these techniques succeed for out-of-school youth. If the evidence regarding promising practices is as positive as I expect, the expansion and replication of training programs should become a priority for the Departments of Labor and Education.

Notes

1. Unless otherwise noted, the data reported here came from the U.S. Bureau of Labor Statistics as published in selected issues of *Employment and Earnings.* As background references, see, for example, Freeman and Wise (1982), Freeman and Holzer (1986), and Sum and Fogg (1996).

2. The statistics in this and the following two paragraphs come largely from Sum and Fogg (1996).

3. Federal funding for training began with the Manpower Development and Training Act of 1962. In 1973, the Comprehensive Employment and Training Act (CETA) decentralized the contracting and supervision of employment and training. JTPA replaced CETA in 1982.

4. For the complete impact evaluation of JTPA, see Orr et al. (1996).

5. To control for the possibility that the work experience effect resulted from a continuation of employment, the analyses controlled for the individual's employment status in the 24th month after application in regressions on earnings during the period 25 to 30 months after application.

6. JTPA appeared to generate earnings gains for adult men and women during the initial three years after entry into the program (Orr et al. 1996). However, a five-year follow-up conducted by the U.S. General Accounting Office indicated declines in the extent and significance of the gains by the fifth year.

7. The current evaluation of the Job Corps, which began enrolling treatment and control groups in 1995, uses an experimental design and should yield new findings by early 2000.

8. For example, females in JTPA achieved higher percentage earnings gains than did male JTPA participants.

9. The evidence suggests that attaining a GED yields much smaller earnings gains than earning a regular high school diploma. Indeed, some researchers find that the GED does not yield any increase in earnings.

10. One caution about these results is that the value of the program's output might be overstated. If the public places a low value on what the program produced, then the measure of value used by the evaluators (the costs of producing the services through normal channels) could well be an overestimate of the value of the program output.

References

Anderson, Elijah. 1994. "The Code of the Streets." *The Atlantic Monthly* (May): 80–94.

Bound, John, and Richard B. Freeman. 1992. "What Went Wrong? The Erosion of Relative Earnings and Employment among Young Black Men in the 1980s." *Quarterly Journal of Economics* (February): 201–32.

Cave, George, and Hans Bos. 1996. "The Value of a GED for School Dropouts Using a Random Assignment Experiment to Measure It." Unpublished manuscript. December.

Cave, George, Hans Bos, Fred Doolittle, and Cyril Toussaint. 1993. *JOB-START: Final Report on a Program for School Dropouts.* New York: Manpower Demonstration Research Corporation. October.

Couch, Kenneth A. 1992. "New Evidence on the Long-Term Effects of Employment Training Programs." *Journal of Labor Economics* (October): 380–88.

Duncan, Greg, and Rachel Dunifon. 1998. "'Soft Skills' and Long-Run Labor Market Success." Unpublished manuscript. Evanston, Ill.: Institute for Policy Research, Northwestern University.

Farkas, George, D. Alton Smith, Ernst Stromsdorfer, Gail Trask, and Robert Jerrett III. 1982. *Impacts from the Youth Incentive Entitlement Pilot Projects: Participation, Work, and Schooling over the Full Program Period.* New York: Manpower Demonstration Research Corporation. December.

Farkas, George, Randall Olsen, Ernst Stromsdorfer, Linda Sharpe, Felicity Skidmore, D. Alton Smith, and Sally Merrill. 1984. *Post-Program Impacts of the Youth Incentive Entitlement Pilot Projects.* New York: Manpower Demonstration Research Corporation. June.

Foster, E. Michael. 1995. "Why Teens Do Not Benefit from Work Experience Programs: Evidence from Brother Comparisons." *Journal of Policy Analysis and Management* (summer): 393–414.

Freeman, Richard B. 1996. "Why Do So Many Young American Men Commit Crimes and What Might We Do About It?" *Journal of Economic Perspectives* (winter): 25–42.

Freeman, Richard, and Harry Holzer. 1986. *The Black Youth Employment Crisis.* Chicago, Ill.: University of Chicago Press.

Freeman, Richard, and David Wise (eds.). 1982. *The Youth Labor Market Problem: Its Nature, Causes, and Consequences.* Chicago, Ill.: University of Chicago Press.

GAO. See U.S. General Accounting Office.

Grogger, Jeffrey. 1995. "The Effect of Arrests on the Employment and Earnings of Young Men." *Quarterly Journal of Economics* (February): 51–71.

———. 1997. "Market Wages and Youth Crime." NBER Working Paper W5983. Cambridge, Mass.: National Bureau of Economic Research.

Hahn, Andrew, and Robert Lerman. 1985. *What Works in Youth Employment Policy?* Washington, D.C.: National Planning Association.

Holzer, Harry J. 1987. "Informal Job Search and Black Youth Unemployment." *The American Economic Review* (June): 446–52.

———. 1996. *What Employers Want: Job Prospects for Less-Educated Workers.* New York: Russell Sage Foundation.

Jastrzab, JoAnn, Julie Masker, John Bloomquist, and Larry Orr. 1996. *Impacts of Service: Final Report on the Evaluation of American Conservation and Youth Service Corps.* Cambridge, Mass.: Abt Associates.

Kemper, Peter, David A. Long, and Craig Thornton. 1981. *The Supported Work Evaluation: Final Benefit-Cost Analysis.* New York: Manpower Demonstration Research Corporation. September.

Klerman, Jacob, and Lynn A. Karoly. 1994. "Young Men and the Transition to Stable Employment." *Monthly Labor Review* (August): 31–48.

Lerman, Robert I. 1996. "JTPA's Negligible Impacts on the Earnings of Out-of-School Youths." Washington, D.C.: Abt Associates.

Mallar, Charles, Stuart Kerachsky, Craig Thornton, and David Long. 1982. *Evaluation of the Economic Impact of the Job Corps Program. Third Follow-Up Report.* Princeton, N.J.: Mathematica Policy Research. September.

Maynard, Rebecca. 1980. *The Impact of Supported Work on Young School Dropouts.* New York: Manpower Demonstration Research Corporation. September.

National Youth Employment Coalition. 1996. *PEPNet '96: Promising and Effective Practices Network.* Washington, D.C.

Nightingale, Demetra. 1996. *Work-Related Resources and Services: Implications for TANF.* New Federalism: Issues and Options for States. Series A, No. A-7. Washington, D.C.: The Urban Institute.

Orr, Larry L., Howard S. Bloom, Stephen H. Bell, Fred Doolittle, Winston Lin, and George Cave. 1996. *Does Training for the Disadvantaged Work? Evidence from the National JTPA Study.* Washington, D.C.: Urban Institute Press.

Tierney, Joseph P., and Jean Baldwin Grossman, with Nancy L. Resch. 1995. *Making a Difference: An Impact Study.* Philadelphia: Public/Private Ventures.

Secretary's Commission on Achieving Necessary Skills. 1991. *What Work Requires of Schools. A SCANS Report for America 2000.* Washington, D.C.: U.S. Department of Labor.

Sum, Andrew and W. Neal Fogg. 1996. *The Labor Market Problems of the Nation's Out-of-School Youth Population.* Monograph 96-01. Baltimore: Sar Levitan Center for Social Policy Studies, Johns Hopkins University.

U.S. General Accounting Office. 1996a. *EMPLOYMENT TRAINING: Successful Projects Share Common Strategy.* Washington, D.C.

————. 1996b. *Job Training Partnership Act: Long-Term Earnings and Employment Outcomes.* GAO/HEHS 96-40. Washington, D.C.: U.S. Government Printing Office.

U.S. Office of Management and Budget. 1997. *Budget of the Government of the United States: Fiscal Year 1998.* Washington, D.C.: U.S. Government Printing Office.

Wilson, William J. 1996. *When Work Disappears: The World of the New Urban Poor.* New York: Alfred A. Knopf.

Chapter Seven

CUSTOMIZED TRAINING FOR EMPLOYERS: TRAINING PEOPLE FOR JOBS THAT EXIST AND EMPLOYERS WHO WANT TO HIRE THEM

Kellie Isbell, John Trutko, and Burt S. Barnow

Customized training, a collaboration between companies and Job Training Partnership Act (JTPA) Private Industry Councils (PICs) or Service Delivery Areas (SDAs), represents a new approach to training JTPA participants. By involving employers in the training process, JTPA can ensure that participants receive the training that companies want and are prepared for jobs that actually exist. Customized training is specifically acknowledged in the Workforce Investment Act (WIA) and is exempted from the requirement for individual training accounts.

Customized training is characterized by these features:

- The training curriculum is company-specific and is designed with company input.
- JTPA pays some or all of the training costs.
- Trainees are JTPA participants.
- JTPA screens and refers participants to the companies, but companies have the flexibility to choose the referrals who participate in the training.

Considerable research has been conducted on worker training in recent years. The research demonstrates that training is most effective when it takes place on the job or in a joblike setting and that the more training is linked to work, the better the result. Training received from an employer is also considerably more likely to be used on the job than is training obtained at a school (Bishop 1994). Basic skills training is most successful when used in combination with work-based training (Brown et al. 1998).

Despite this research, many gaps remain in our knowledge about training, particularly relating to effective methods for structuring training and the returns on investments in training for firms and workers. The study summarized in this chapter—funded by the Employment and Training Administration in the U.S. Department of Labor (DOL)—assesses nine exemplary customized training programs and provides recommendations on effective strategies for implementing such programs.

The study includes case studies of selected companies sponsoring exemplary customized training programs. The case studies are based on site visits to each firm that included interviews with company management, supervisors of workers in training, individuals providing instruction (including instructors at vocational training institutions), workers receiving training, and local JTPA administrators.

Nominations of companies with exemplary customized training programs were solicited from DOL regional offices, local JTPA SDAs, national organizations involved in employment and training issues, and customized training experts around the country. Selection of the companies to participate in the study was based on a range of criteria, including industry and occupations trained, characteristics of workers being trained, and structure of and types of training provided. The companies selected exemplify employer-based training programs; they are not necessarily the best training programs available. In addition, the sample of firms chosen was small (nine companies) and was not randomly selected; hence, it is not possible to make statistically valid generalizations to all firms. Table 7.1 provides an overview of the case study companies and their training programs.

STUDY FINDINGS

Reasons for Initiating EBT Programs and the Types of Workers Trained

All the JTPA-funded programs were created to recruit, screen, assess, and train new workers for employment with the sponsoring company. Companies typically faced a scarcity of a particular type of skilled, entry-level worker and so were interested in establishing a program that would both help with recruitment and offset training costs. JTPA was interested in sponsoring such customized initiatives because the initiatives were considered as an effective way to train, place, and retain workers in full-time, well-paying jobs.

In addition to filling job vacancies with workers with the requisite competencies and skills, companies also looked to the training program to

- Boost productivity and profitability,
- Improve the quality of goods and services,
- Ensure on-time production and delivery of goods and services,
- Improve the level of customer service,
- Facilitate hiring and training of workers within the community, and
- Increase worker morale and reduce turnover.

As shown in table 7.2, the customized training programs provided training to a variety of workers entering jobs in both the service and manufacturing sectors. Some examples of the types of workers trained follow.

- Faced with a shortage of skilled assembly-line workers, Solectron Corporation partnered with its local PIC and a local vocational training organization to establish a 26-week training program in the emerging field of surface mount/pin-through-hole assembly.
- With plans to open 40 to 60 new automotive parts and service stores in the Los Angeles area, Pep Boys collaborated with the City and County of Los Angeles PICs and the Urban League's Automotive Training Center to establish a five-week training program for cashiers and customer service representatives and an eight-week training program for sales and parts representatives. The program was also aimed at reducing employee turnover at area stores.
- Facing a critical need for 25 to 30 new school bus drivers each school year and difficulties finding drivers with appropriate training and licensing, the Yuma Public Schools Transportation Center teamed up with the Yuma PIC to establish a five-week training program that included two weeks of classroom instruction and three weeks of behind-the-wheel instruction.

Curriculum Development and Provision of Other Resources for Start-Up

A hallmark of customized training programs—and what sets them apart from more traditional JTPA training—is the active involvement of employers in customizing training so that trainees emerge from the training program with the skills and competences needed for a specific job. One of the key advantages of customized training—one cited by all the firms we visited—was that the employer had substantive input into the types of training provided and the instructional methods used.

Table 7.1 CASE STUDY COMPANIES AND THEIR CUSTOMIZED TRAINING PROGRAMS

Company	Location	Industry	Sector	Size of Company[a]	Description of Training Program
C.D. Baird	Milwaukee, Wisconsin	Manufacturing	For-profit	M	JTPA-funded training in printing, binding, and mounting. Graphics Art Institute, a private training institution, provides the training.
Harrington Hospital	Southbridge, Massachusetts	Health care	Nonprofit	M	Harrington Hospital trains JTPA participants to be home health care aides through classroom and on-the-job training using hospital staff
NeighborCare Pharmacies	Baltimore, Maryland	Health care/ retail sales	For-profit	L	JTPA-funded training for pharmacy technicians. Training provided by local community college. Training is customized to needs of the employer and focuses on recruiting and training new workers.
Pacific NW Federal Credit Union	Portland, Oregon	Banking	Nonprofit	S	JTPA-funded training for member services representatives for a consortium of five credit unions in Portland. Trainees are all older workers (over 55). Training provided by Goodwill Industries.
Pep Boys Corporation	Los Angeles, California	Retail sales	For-profit	L	JTPA-funded training for cashiers, customer service representatives, and sales representatives. Trainees are hired from local communities in which new Pep Boys stores are opened. The Urban League's Automotive Training Center provides the training.

	Location	Industry	Type	Size[a]	Description
Solectron	San Jose, California	Manufacturing	For-profit	L	JTPA-funded training in the field of surface mount/pin-through-hole assembly for electronics manufacturing. The Center for Training and Careers, a private training institution, provides the training.
TempsPlus/ Staffing Solutions	Cleveland, Ohio	Temporary services	For-profit	M	Job Opportunities and Basic Skills (JOBS) and JTPA-funded training for PC specialists. Training provided by TempsPlus's sister company, JPC Learning Centers.
Wisconsin Electric Power Company	Milwaukee, Wisconsin	Utility	Public	L	JTPA-funded training for entry-level line mechanics. Program intended to increase employee diversity and retention. Milwaukee Area Technical College provides the training.
Yuma Schools Transportation Consortium	Yuma, Arizona	Transportation	Public	S	JTPA-funded training for school bus drivers. School district provides the training and curriculum development; trainees receive commercial drivers' licenses at the end of training.

a. Classified as S, M, or L—small, medium, or large. Small firms have 100 or fewer employees, medium firms have 101 to 500 employees, and large firms have more than 500 employees. Firms are classified according to the size of the establishment we visited.

Table 7.2 CHARACTERISTICS OF CUSTOMIZED TRAINING PROGRAMS

Company	Occupations Trained For	Training Provider	Type of Training[a]	Number Screened/ Considered/ Applied	Number Enrolled in Training	Percent Completing Training (%)[b]	Percent Hired (%)[c]	Cost per Slot (Paid by JTPA, $)	Employer Contributions to Training ($)
C.D. Baird	Entry-level printing and binding	Union-sponsored industry school	P, CT-OS	50	20	90	n/a	2,650	0
Harrington Hospital	Home health aide	Nonprofit training organization	CT-OS, P, W	n/a	39	90	94	1,225[d]	In-kind (instructor time, labs for practicum, library access)
NeighborCare Pharmacies	Pharmacy technician	Community college	CT-OS, P, W	40	18	100	n/a	1,495	Some instructor time, labs for practicum
Pacific NW Federal Credit Union	Member services representatives	Nonprofit training organization	CT-OS, W, OJT	50–60	17	82	n/a	2,143	0
Pep Boys Corporation	Cashiers, customer service representatives, parts/sales associates	Nonprofit training organization	CT-OS, W, OJT	270	124	79	100	Parts/sales associates = 4,700; cashier/ customer service = 5,100	250,000 cash and in-kind over 3 years

		Vocational training provider							
Solectron	Electronic assembly workers	Company	CT-OS, P	n/a	40	90	82	n/a	40,000 in-kind (equipment and materials)
TempsPlus/ Staffing Solutions	PC specialist, office skills	Company	CT-OS, W, OJT	15–16	5	100	100	2,577	0
Wisconsin Electric Power Company	Line mechanics	Technical college	CT-OS, P	n/a	16^e	69	6	5,625	50,000 cash and 150,000 in-kind
Yuma Schools Transportation Consortium	School bus drivers	Company (i.e., school district)	CT-OS, P, W	450	90	90	100	1,300	Company developed curriculum and provides instructors

a. CT-OS = classroom training—occupational skills; P = practicum; W = workplace skills; OJT = on-the-job training.
b. Number includes those still in training at the time of the site visit.
c. Percent hired is of those completing training. Number hired is n/a if the course had not been completed.
d. JTPA and JOBS each pay 50 percent of the training cost. The total cost per slot, therefore, is $2,450.
e. These figures are for WEPCO's first training class. Although 11 graduated from the program, only 2 passed WEPCO's exam and only 1 was hired.

In all the programs visited, companies worked closely from the beginning with the education and training institutions providing the training (such as community colleges, vocational schools, and other educational providers such as Goodwill Industries and the Urban League) to develop curricula and instructional materials. Typically, the training vendor took the lead in the development of curriculum and instructional methods for the training program but consulted closely with the company throughout the development process. In most instances, the training vendor already had a core curriculum but needed input from the employer to tailor the curriculum and instructional methods to meet the employer's needs.

Recruitment, Eligibility Determination, and Selection of Training Candidates

Recruitment, eligibility determination, and selection of training candidates for customized training programs sponsored by JTPA were typically a shared responsibility of the company and JTPA. In most instances, the JTPA program or training vendor took the lead on recruitment and eligibility determination but received considerable input from the employer on the types of workers that should be considered for program participation.

With some exceptions, methods of recruitment for most programs were similar to those used by JTPA programs in their general recruitment of participants for Title II or III programs—word-of-mouth, referral from other human service agencies, and television, radio, and newspaper advertisements. JTPA or the training providers placed advertisements in local papers with diverse readerships, and some training providers (such as the Urban League) recruited participants through other programs they operated.

Once recruited, applicants for the training programs generally underwent a two-tiered selection process. First, recruits were screened by the PIC to determine their eligibility and appropriateness for the JTPA program. Second, JTPA-eligible applicants were screened according to the company's criteria (e.g., a high school education, specific reading or math levels, and specific work experience).

Types and Structure of Job-Specific Training Provided

Training offered by companies was usually job-specific and carefully customized to the specific training requirements of the employer and occupation. Under each of the programs examined, training was customized for the companies—generally with direct input from employers on the curriculum and instructional methods. Training was designed to prepare workers for a specific job opening at the company sponsoring the training.

The duration of training varied substantially across customized training programs. The training duration was as short as five weeks in Yuma's school bus driver training program and as long as 36 weeks for line mechanics in the WEPCO training program. The training was in the range of 80 to 1,260 hours but was generally shorter than that provided under JTPA Title II-A, which for program year (PY) 1996 averaged 435 hours for Title II-A terminees nationally.

The content of job-specific training varied substantially across training programs, but the instruction methods were similar. All the JTPA-sponsored customized training programs used a combination of classroom and laboratory ("hands-on") training. Emphasis was placed on (1) providing trainees with the job-specific knowledge they needed for the job through classroom instruction and (2) simulating specific job functions and tasks through laboratory workshops or OJTs. For example:

- C.D. Baird and Company's customized training program provides both classroom and hands-on training through the Milwaukee Graphic Arts Institute (MGAI), a local industry–sponsored training provider. MGAI uses state-of-the-art printing and binding equipment and provides practical training.
- NeighborCare's pharmacy technician training program includes 100 hours of classroom training and 40 hours of practicum in work settings. The classroom training takes place on the Baltimore City Community College campus. The practicum includes working in both retail and clinical pharmacy settings.
- After successfully completing classroom training, trainees were hired by Pep Boys in sales, cashier, or customer service positions. Most trainees started working for the company on five-week OJTs, during which JTPA subsidized half the trainees' wages.

Types and Structure of Basic Skills and Other Employability Enhancement Training

Companies and training providers found that in addition to job-specific skills training, many JTPA trainees needed training in basic skills, literacy, and workplace skills. Some trainees had never worked, and others had been out of the workforce for many months or years. Some had lost previous jobs because of a lack of workplace skills, such as an inability to get along with supervisors and coworkers, or because they failed to report to work on time.

Most of the JTPA-sponsored customized training programs included some type of preemployment and workplace skills training. That training included workshops on how to dress for work, arrive on time, develop a positive work attitude, use business English, work effectively with others, answer the telephone, and handle stress and time management. This type of instruction was either concentrated into a one- or two-week seminar before the start of the training (often as part of JTPA's objective assessment process) or incorporated into the curriculum over the course of the training.

Some participants also needed to address basic skills deficiencies to take full advantage of the training offered. All the JTPA-sponsored training programs built in testing of basic skills and interests as a screening device for program participation. From the perspective of companies sponsoring the customized training initiatives, one of the advantages of working with the JTPA system was that it provided basic skills screening and arranged for basic skills training before workers entered job-specific training. Basic skills training was generally provided by local nonprofit community organizations and paid for by the public sector.

Company Hiring Commitments

Most of the case study companies partnering with the JTPA system provided either a written or oral commitment that they would hire trainees who successfully completed the training program. Some PICs requested commitment of a certain wage level for trainees or that a certain percentage be retained for a specified number of months (e.g., six months or a year), or both. Most of the firms studied lived up to their commitments by extending job offers to successful graduates of the training programs.

Companies generally provided input to JTPA and the training provider on what constituted "successful" completion of the training. Often, companies wanted trainees to maintain excellent attendance records. Training curricula typically included a competence test at the end of the training, and some companies administered their own tests to trainees at the conclusion of training, with commitment to hire only those who passed the test.

Benefits of JTPA-Sponsored Customized Training

All the companies partnering with JTPA indicated that the returns on their investment in the customized training effort far outweighed costs. In fact, in our discussions with companies, PICs, and training participants, the customized training programs were cited as a "win-win-win" situation for everyone involved. The company sponsoring the training "wins" because

- Training costs are subsidized by the government.
- Training is customized to the company's needs, so workers emerge from the program with the skills they need to be productive from their first day on the job.
- JTPA and the training vendor can help with recruiting, assessing, and screening applicants.
- In addition to providing customized job-specific training, JTPA or the training vendor can provide basic skills remediation, workplace skills training, and case management to ensure that trainees perform well on the job.

Companies we interviewed also indicated that the training provided under their customized training programs had a positive and direct effect on the firm's bottom line by contributing to a high-performance workforce, a customer service focus, lower turnover, and improved morale.

The PIC wins because

- A high percentage of trainees complete training, in part because they are motivated by the possibility of jobs at the end of the training.
- Almost everyone who successfully completes the training obtains full-time work in jobs paying at or above the JTPA average wage.
- With appropriate training and other support services available through the JTPA program, retention rates for those entering training are high.

Overall, the high placement and retention rates achieved through customized training programs help the PIC in meeting JTPA performance standards and enhance its reputation as a resource for high-quality training services with employers, the training community, and prospective program participants.

Finally, the worker "wins" because

- Training enhances the trainee's skills and long-term employability both at the firm that sponsored the training and with other firms.
- Jobs are generally guaranteed if the trainee successfully completes training.

- The jobs are generally full-time, paying at least the average JTPA wage, and often include fringe benefits and career advance potential.
- Basic skill deficiencies and other barriers to employment are carefully assessed, and the JTPA program can provide or arrange for a variety of support services to assist the individual to complete training and secure employment.

Outcomes for JTPA-Sponsored Customized Training

All PIC administrators we interviewed indicated that the results of their customized training programs (both the ones that were the focus of this study and others they had initiated in their localities) were at least as good as, and generally substantially better than, those achieved under the more traditional types of JTPA training programs. The results reported for each of the JTPA-sponsored customized training programs visited in this study solidly support the contention that customized programs yield excellent results for companies, workers, and the JTPA system. Two factors seem to be paramount in the success of the programs:

- Training provided is customized to meet the needs of the company so trainees emerge with the skills they need to be productive.
- In exchange for the subsidized training, companies make a firm commitment to hire individuals who successfully complete training.

Although the sample of sites visited was small and programs were exemplary and still relatively new, the results for the customized training programs reviewed were impressive:

- In the nine programs visited, over 80 percent of those beginning training successfully completed it.
- Because most companies made a commitment to hire employees if they were successful in completing training, almost all successful trainees obtained jobs. In comparison, in PY 1996, 66 percent of JTPA terminees nationwide entered employment.
- The hourly starting wage generally ranged from $6.25 to $8.00 per hour for trainees hired by the case study companies (though it ranged as high as $16.46 for line mechanics trained under the Wisconsin Electric Power Company's customized program). In all nine firms studied, the starting wage exceeded the average hourly wage for Title II-A participants in the locality. Nationwide, the average hourly wage for JTPA Title II-A terminees in PY 1996 was $7.58.

- All of the trainees hired by case study companies received fringe benefits (including medical benefits), generally after an initial probation period (e.g., 90 days). Some companies even included benefits such as eye care and 401(k) programs.
- Although still early and not available for all firms studied, retention rates for those hired appeared to be high. For example, during its first training program for JOBS participants, TempsPlus/Staffing Solutions trained five participants, and all five successfully completed the training. Six months later (at the time of the site visit), all five were still employed by TempsPlus/Staffing Solutions. In comparison, for PY 1996, JTPA reported a 66 percent retention rate, with 46 percent employed with the same firm.

Costs of JTPA Customized Training

As shown in table 7.2, the JTPA reimbursement for training to training vendors under the program ranged from $1,300 to $5,625 per participant. Average tuition costs for most of the programs visited were about $3,000 per participant. The cost of training was typically negotiated between the JTPA program and the training vendor. If the program was open to non-JTPA participants, the tuition was the same as that charged to JTPA participants.

As noted earlier, companies often provided cash for start-up costs or in-kind contributions of equipment and instructional expertise. For example, Solectron provided computer boards and electronic components regularly for use in the laboratory portion of its training program. All the firms indicated that the returns on their investment in the customized training programs far outweighed their outlays.

Barriers to Establishing JTPA-Sponsored Customized Training Programs

Given such outcomes, why is customized training not used more often? Companies and PICs we interviewed identified a number of barriers to the establishment of customized training programs.

- The occupational areas in which training is to be provided must generally be ones in which there is unmet demand within the locality. Employers that can obtain skilled manpower with relative ease within their local labor market are unlikely to be interested in establishing customized training programs.

- Small and mid-sized companies—and even large firms—may lack the critical mass of workers and resources needed to establish a customized training program. For example, if a company needs only one or two new workers with a specific skill per year, the costs of customization are likely to outweigh the benefits.
- Companies may be reluctant to commit to hiring successful graduates of customized training programs because they are unsure about the number of openings they will have in the future.
- The time and effort involved in negotiating and establishing a customized training program can be considerable for both the firm and the SDA. For example, several of the customized programs included in this study took over a year to negotiate and become operational.
- Companies must commit some level of resources to get customized programs under way and keep them going. For example, to customize the training, it may be necessary to donate equipment and materials to the program. In addition, firms generally need to be actively involved in curriculum development and may need to commit to providing assistance with instruction. Small companies, especially, may not have the necessary working capital available for customized training programs.
- Companies may be wary of working with government programs because of fear of paperwork and red tape, as well as concerns over the possibility of future audits. They also may lack knowledge about government training programs and the time to find out about them.
- Lack of available JTPA funding and the occurrence of funding cycles can create uncertainty for SDAs as to their ability to support customized training programs from year to year.

STRATEGIES FOR BUILDING SUCCESSFUL CUSTOMIZED TRAINING PROGRAMS

Successful customized training programs can be implemented by a range of companies and can differ in a number of ways: size of company, amount expended on training, and type of training offered. There is no single method for structuring a successful training program. Discussions with companies and SDAs revealed several strategies that SDAs should undertake in establishing customized training programs.

Be visible. In almost every instance, case study companies and SDA staff met and began initial discussions at community meetings, such as business roundtables. SDA staff should be visible in the business community by attending meetings of local industry groups, business roundtables, or chambers of commerce to make presentations about JTPA and the opportunities for training. It also will be beneficial for JTPA programs to have ongoing representatives at meetings so that informal relationships develop between JTPA and businesses.

Target employers already involved. Often, the case study companies were involved throughout the community in business associations and roundtables, and many participated in the school-to-work initiative. Companies already involved in the community are more likely to be familiar with government training programs and interested in helping the community by hiring JTPA participants.

Market customized training by emphasizing its bottom-line benefits. Some companies will have to be sold on the idea of establishing a customized training program and hiring JTPA participants. Offer to put companies in touch with others that have had successful JTPA experiences. Stress these bottom-line benefits of training:

- Increased productivity,
- Increased profits,
- Improved employee morale,
- Higher retention for entry-level employees (lower labor turnover costs),
- Fewer accidents, and
- Fewer mistakes and scrap parts.

Stress these additional benefits of JTPA customized training:

- Costs of training are offset by JTPA.
- Customization of the training program ensures that companies have input into the curriculum and get workers who will be productive from Day 1 on the job.
- Customized training provides a flexible arrangement; companies can help choose the training provider, suggest selection criteria for training applicants, and provide their own instructors for the training.
- JTPA provides screening and assessment of trainees, resulting in excellent recruits for the firm.
- Supportive services, such as day care and transportation, are available to trainees to help them be consistent workers and retain their jobs.

- JTPA has the ability to work with trainees even after employment and provide case management to reduce absenteeism and turnover.
- JTPA has relationships with training organizations and can put companies in touch with excellent training institutions.
- In addition to job-specific skills, JTPA can provide job readiness training and basic skills remediation.

Establish customized training for consortia of businesses. Small and mid-sized firms often do not have sufficient numbers of job openings in specific occupations to justify the establishment of a customized program. In addition, small and mid-sized firms may lack the working capital and management time needed to customize the training program (e.g., design the curriculum). JTPA programs should consider establishing programs for consortia of similar businesses. A consortium of manufacturing companies or health care providers, for example, can work together to decide the type of training and develop a curriculum with the JTPA training provider. JTPA then provides one training session for a larger number of trainees who are hired by members of the consortium.

Ask for and receive commitments for employment. Companies may be reluctant to commit to hire trainees, but that commitment is essential to the success of customized training programs. Trainees, for example, are more motivated in training if a job depends on their success.

Carefully negotiate agreements. The agreements between companies, the SDA, and training providers take time to negotiate—sometimes a year or more. SDAs should not try to rush the negotiation process but should use it to ensure that there is a commitment to hire and that companies have the opportunity to contribute to the training program.

Look to the companies to provide resources. Companies should provide start-up and ongoing development assistance. SDAs should ask companies to provide equipment for training laboratories. Often, up-to-date equipment (especially in manufacturing processes) is expensive and can quickly become obsolete. Companies can donate equipment they have upgraded, and trainees will have the opportunity for hands-on experience.

Build in feedback, and expect to refine the program over time. Once a training program is established, it should not be static or it will fail to respond to companies' needs and they will withdraw support. SDAs should ask for feedback from companies regarding the trainees and the curriculum. SDAs may need to refine their selection criteria for trainees. For example, it may become apparent over time that trainees need to have a high school education before they begin training. Likewise, as companies gain more experience with the training program and the trainees who begin work, they may have suggestions for improving the curriculum. The curriculum also may need to be adjusted to respond to new technologies; as technology changes, the curriculum will need to change as well. Companies are in the best position to inform SDAs of technology changes.

Keep paperwork to a minimum. Many companies may be wary of working with JTPA because they believe government programs require burdensome paperwork. By keeping paperwork requirements to a minimum, SDAs can collect needed program data while encouraging companies to participate.

References

Bishop, John. 1994. "The Incidence and Payoff to Employer Training: A Review of the Literature." Ithaca, N.Y.: Cornell University School of Industrial and Labor Relations.

Brown, Rebecca, Evelyn Ganzglass, Susan Golonka, Jill Hyland, and Martin Simon. 1998. "Working Out of Poverty: Employment Retention and Career Advancement for Welfare Recipients." Washington, D.C.: National Governors' Association Center for Best Practices, Employment and Social Services Policy Studies Division.

Chapter Eight

TRAINING PROGRAMS FOR DISLOCATED WORKERS

Duane E. Leigh

Dislocated workers usually can be distinguished from other unemployed workers by three related characteristics. First, they have been laid off, often as a consequence of large layoffs or establishment closings. This fact distinguishes them from unemployed workers who quit earlier jobs and from unemployed new entrants and reentrants into the labor force. Second, dislocated workers accumulated significant work experience before they were laid off. Hence, they are typically adults strongly attached to their employer and industry. It is likely that they have built up substantial firm-specific skills. It is also likely that their job search skills are rusty from disuse.

Finally, dislocated workers face a low probability of being recalled to their old jobs—or perhaps even to jobs in their old industries. This last characteristic arises because of industrial restructuring, which, in turn, is the consequence of improvements in technology, expanded international trade, and shifts in government policies. The reemployment of dislocated workers therefore may require a change in occupation or industry, with the associated costs of retraining and, even then, a willingness to accept employment at a lower wage. In the words of the Secretary of Labor's Task Force on Economic Adjustment and Worker Dislocation (DOL 1986), "[J]obs lost [by dislocated workers] are often perceived as especially good jobs, for which the individual worked many years for one employer to achieve. Also, extraordinary emotional adjustments are required as life plans and goals are changed abruptly."

This chapter examines the evaluation evidence available for publicly funded programs designed to assist dislocated workers in obtaining new employment. First comes a discussion of the incidence and economic costs of worker dislocation and a consideration of the case for government assistance to the dislocated. An outline of the two major federal government programs currently providing services to dislocated workers follows. The heart of the chapter is an examination of the available quantitative and case study evidence; it includes a discussion of estimates of the labor market effectiveness of activities designed to expedite reemployment and a consideration of evaluation evidence for alternative adjustment assistance services, including retraining, intended to replenish dislocated workers' lost firm-specific human capital. The summary pulls together the policy implications of the chapter.

DISLOCATED WORKERS: WHO ARE THEY AND SHOULD THEY BE COMPENSATED?

Incidence and Seriousness of Dislocation

In 1984, the availability of the first Displaced Worker Survey (DWS) gave researchers and policymakers a much better understanding of the number and characteristics of dislocated Americans. DWS data sets are biannual supplements to the January Current Population Surveys produced by the Bureau of Labor Statistics. In those data, dislocated workers can be distinguished from other unemployed persons by affirmative answers to a question asking whether within the last five years the respondent was separated from his or her job because of a plant closing, an employer going out of business, or a layoff from which the respondent was not recalled. In addition to being laid off, displaced workers are characterized by substantial prelayoff labor market experience. Researchers differ as to exactly how to quantify a threshold level of labor market experience.[1] The "official" definition used in the benchmark analysis by Flaim and Sehgal (1985) defines dislocated workers as those who lost jobs that they had held for three or more years. Using this fairly restrictive threshold level of labor market experience, the authors calculate a population of 5.1 million dislocated workers during the January 1979 to January 1984 period.

Merging the five DWS data sets available for the 1984–92 period and defining the dislocated as all workers who lost full-time jobs (regardless of job tenure), Ross and Smith (1993) estimate that on average 2 million full-time workers were displaced from their jobs each year during the 1980s. Not surprisingly, they find that the annual number of displaced workers varies with the overall state of the economy. In the recession year of 1982, 2.7 million workers—about 1 of every 25 full-time wage and salary workers—lost their jobs and were not recalled. But even during the relatively strong labor market existing in 1988, 1.5 million workers—about 1 in every 50 full-time workers—are estimated to have permanently lost their jobs.

Farber's (1993) analysis of DWS data for the same 1984–92 period provides insight into whether worker dislocation is a growing labor market phenomenon. His evidence indicates that while job loss is still disproportionately concentrated in the goods-producing sector, dislocation in non-goods-producing industries was more common during the 1990–91 recession than during the decade-earlier 1982–83 recession. Moreover, he finds the rate of job loss among older workers during the 1990–91 recession to be higher than during the earlier recession, especially for college-educated men. Adding data from the 1994 and 1996 DWS surveys, respectively, Gardner (1995) and Hipple (1997) report that observed job losses continue to be spread more evenly across industries and occupations than was the case during the 1980s.

There is a substantial literature, much of it using DWS data, examining the postlayoff employment and earnings experience of dislocated workers. Fallick's (1996) and Kletzer's (1998) recent surveys point to the following conclusions:

- Dislocated workers experience much greater nonemployment than does the general working population, but differences appear to fade away after about four years.
- In contrast to the fading out of nonemployment differences, dislocated workers' earnings losses are large and persistent.
- Years of tenure on the old job, higher prelayoff earnings, and union membership increase length of postlayoff joblessness.
- Larger earnings losses upon reemployment occur for dislocated workers who change industries than for those reemployed in their old industries. Earnings losses also are greater for those who change occupation or region.
- Controlling for tenure, industry, occupation, and local labor market conditions, race, gender, and age are not important in explaining the adverse consequences of dislocation.

A study of dislocated Pennsylvania workers by Jacobson, LaLonde, and Sullivan (1993a, 1993b) dramatically underscores the second of these conclusions. Using state unemployment insurance (UI) records covering the 1980–86 period for workers with six or more years of job tenure, the authors find that earnings losses of dislocated workers average about 40 percent of prelayoff earnings in the year following displacement. The size of the losses declines somewhat over time, as almost all dislocated workers find stable employment after six quarters of unemployment. But even during the fifth year after job separation, lower-wage reemployment jobs led to earnings losses that average more than $6,500 or more than 25 percent of former earnings.[2] Moreover, earnings losses associated with temporary layoffs and wage reductions began even before permanent separations. Taking into account the prelayoff earnings dip, the period of postdisplacement joblessness, and lower reemployment wages, Jacobson et al. (1993b) calculate that the present value of earnings losses for a typical dislocated worker is on the order of $80,000.

Should the Dislocated Be Singled Out for Special Assistance?

Losses of this magnitude raise the possibility that dislocated workers are entitled to some form of compensation. In their analysis of this issue, Hamermesh (1987) and Hamermesh, Cordes, and Goldfarb (1987) suggest that the key question is whether the job loss could have reasonably been anticipated by affected workers. If the answer is "yes," then informed workers will require a wage premium to accept employment in less-stable industries. Then, since they already receive a wage premium for accepting a greater risk of job loss, compensation would be double payment and thus unjustified. In such industries, moreover, we would not expect workers and firms to invest heavily in specific training, the value of which is lost when permanent layoffs occur. If the answer to the anticipated job loss question is "no," on the other hand, uninformed workers are less likely to demand a wage premium to accept jobs in what turn out ex post facto to be unstable industries. At the same time, those workers will be more likely to overinvest in firm-specific training.

The authors argue that job loss is especially likely to be unanticipated by workers affected by government policy changes such as liberalization of trade laws, deregulation of major industries, or reductions in defense spending. Regarding other factors leading to job losses, those caused by plant closings are more likely to be unanticipated than are temporary layoffs associated with periodic downturns in the business cycle.

The major policy conclusion emerging from this discussion is that, for workers adversely affected by plant closings, compensation should be related to the lost present value of firm-specific training. Thus, our system of unemployment insurance is an appropriate first step because it is intended to provide no-fault transitional aid for job losers. However, UI is directed to all job losers, not just to dislocated workers. Moreover, UI payments are based on lost income while the worker is unemployed and generally bear little relationship to the size of the long-term loss suffered by the dislocated.

Hamermesh et al. (1987) argue that a more direct relationship between compensation and earnings losses can be accomplished with a severance payment–like scheme that makes total compensation paid to permanently laid-off workers hinge on their tenure and prelayoff earnings. Under this scheme, compensation would be low for workers with little tenure because they had little chance before being laid off to accumulate firm-specific skills. Payments would then increase with tenure but would peak at a tenure level such as 20 years, recognizing that firm-specific investments of senior workers nearing retirement are nearly fully depreciated. Jacobson et al. (1993b: 160–9) recommend that another form a cash payment scheme might take is as an earnings subsidy that pays reemployed dislocated workers some fraction of the gap between their pre- and postdisplacement earnings.

As an alternative to cash payments, Hamermesh et al. (1987) suggest that compensation could be offered in the form of either a training voucher or a hiring voucher. Training vouchers used to pay the direct costs of retraining courses help to replenish human capital lost when dislocated workers are permanently displaced from long-held jobs. The hiring voucher represents a subsidy to employers willing to hire and provide on-the-job training to targeted workers for a specified period.

CURRENT FEDERAL PROGRAMS

The federal government currently provides assistance to dislocated workers through two major programs and a host of minor programs. The two major programs are Title III of the Job Training Partnership Act (JTPA) and the Trade Adjustment Assistance (TAA) Act. JTPA was authorized in 1982 with the broad mandate to train and place unemployed workers—both the dislocated and the economically disadvantaged—in private-sector jobs. Title III of the act provides funds to state governments for establishing programs tailored to meet the reemployment needs of dislocated workers, while the Title II-A program was intended to prepare economically disadvantaged adults and youths for entry into the labor force.

Dating back to 1962, TAA was originally designed to provide income support (called Trade Readjustment Allowances or TRAs) and, to a much lesser extent, retraining and other forms of adjustment assistance to workers who lost their jobs as a consequence of trade agreement concessions. Legislation passed in 1974 removed the linkage between tariff reductions and job loss by making workers eligible for adjustment assistance if expanding trade alone was an important contributor to layoffs. While liberalized eligibility criteria and expanded program benefits increased the number of certifications for assistance and benefit payments by the later 1970s, relatively few participants received adjustment assistance services. Beginning in 1981, TRA benefits were restricted to the level of regular UI benefits and allowed to begin only after the UI entitlement period was exhausted. In 1982, the emphasis of the program began to shift away from income support and toward the provision of adjustment assistance services, particularly training.

Both Title III of JTPA and TAA were substantially altered by the Omnibus Trade and Competitiveness Act of 1988. Title III of JTPA was amended by a provision called the Economic Dislocation and Worker Adjustment Assistance (EDWAA) Act. Two years earlier in 1986, a task force appointed by the U.S. Secretary of Labor recommended development at the state level of the capacity to respond quickly to plant closings and mass layoffs with the delivery of reemployment services (DOL 1986). Following up on the task force's recommendations, Congress required in the EDWAA amendment that states develop displaced worker units capable of reacting to major layoffs and plant closures. EDWAA program services, many of which were also recommended by the task force, are described in the enabling legislation under the headings of "basic readjustment services" and "retraining services." Basic readjustment services include a range of job search assistance (JSA) services as well as relocation allowances and support services such as child care and commuting assistance. In addition to classroom training (CT) and on-the-job training (OJT), retraining services include remedial education, English programs for non-English speakers, and entrepreneurship training.

The 1988 legislation also made training an entitlement for all TAA-certified workers, with eligible workers given a good deal of discretion in choosing their own training programs. Hence, the training component of TAA became essentially a voucher-based system.[3] TAA-certified workers continued to be eligible for up to 18 months of income-maintenance support (six months of UI benefits plus an additional year of TRA assistance), but TRA recipients are required as of 1988 to participate in retraining unless they receive a waiver exempting them from this requirement.

Moving into the 1990s, much of the current thinking of federal policymakers regarding assistance to dislocated workers is captured in the proposed Reemployment Act of 1994. Although the act failed to receive congressional approval, its comprehensive scope and the widespread discussion it prompted warrant a brief mention of some of its major provisions. These include the following:

- One-stop career centers designed to facilitate access in one location to all available reemployment services;
- Early identification of displaced workers—termed "profiling"—that allows prompt referral to reemployment services;
- Payment of the costs of education and training for up to two years, and up to one year of income support beyond the usual six-month maximum for dislocated workers enrolled in an approved retraining program; and
- Changes in the UI system to expedite the return to work, including reemployment bonuses to claimants who find jobs quickly and measures to promote self-employment.

With the defeat of the Reemployment Act, assistance to dislocated workers continued to be provided by EDWAA and TAA programs. Assistance was also made available under separate legislation to dislocated workers whose job losses are specifically related to enforcement of the Clean Air Act, cuts in defense spending, and the North American Free Trade Agreement. Nevertheless, parts of the Reemployment Act have been authorized in recent federal legislation encouraging states to develop one-stop career centers and profiling systems. In addition, the Tax Relief Act of 1997 introduces two new tax credits for educational expenditures: Hope Scholarships providing up to $1,500 per year in tax savings for the first two years of college, and the Lifetime Learning Credit that can be used in subsequent years. The Lifetime Learning Credit saves $1,000 in taxes through 2002, after which it increases to an annual maximum of $2,000. Most recently, the Workforce Investment Act of 1998 mandates the one-stop delivery system as the access point for all employment-related and training services, with operators of one-stop centers to be determined through a competitive process. The 1998 legislation also establishes a voucherlike Individual Training Accounts program designed to allow participants greater choice among classroom training options supplied by qualified providers.

At present, however, dislocated workers undergoing retraining are not typically entitled to an additional period of income support except for TAA-certified workers undergoing retraining and workers eligible for certain state programs (such as the New Jersey WDPP, to be discussed in "Evidence on Activities to Replace Lost Earnings Capacity" later in this chapter).

EVIDENCE ON ACTIVITIES TO SPEED UP REEMPLOYMENT

Table 8.1 groups activities included in existing and proposed dislocated worker programs into two broad categories: services intended to speed up the job search process, and initiatives that provide compensation for earnings losses. The available empirical evidence measuring the effectiveness of the first of the service categories is considered here.

As noted earlier, dislocated workers are typically eligible for UI benefits to help them maintain family income during their spell of unemployment. During this period, they are required to meet work search requirements imposed by the UI system, and they are eligible for traditional labor exchange services provided by the U.S. Employment Service. Labor exchange in this context refers to matching unemployed workers who choose to sign up with local employment service offices to vacant jobs voluntarily listed by local employers. Job search assistance services are designed to go beyond the traditional labor exchange function of public employment agencies in reaching out to the unemployed, improving their job search skills, and assisting them to locate jobs that may not be listed or advertised by employers. A menu of specific JSA services is listed in table 8.1. Relocation assistance complements these services by providing additional financial resources to enable the dislocated to expand the geographic scope of their job search and, if successful, to move their families to the new location.

Reemployment bonuses are intended to at least partially offset the incentive of UI recipients to delay active job search until the end of their eligibility for benefits, because UI benefits cease once a new job has been found. Structured as either lump-sum or periodic payments, the key feature of reemployment bonus schemes is that bonuses are paid only to UI recipients who find jobs quickly.

The Dislocated Worker Demonstrations

During the early 1980s, rising unemployment and an increasing number of plant closures led to U.S. Department of Labor (DOL) funding of a series of demonstration projects intended to test the effectiveness of alternative reemployment services in placing dislocated workers in private-sector jobs. In chronological order, the projects are (1) the Downriver, Michigan, program; (2) the Buffalo program of the six Dislocated Worker Demonstration Projects;

Table 8.1 MAJOR TYPES OF DISLOCATED WORKER SERVICES

Type of Service	Description
Expediting reemployment	
Job search assistance	Refers to a sequence of services designed to enhance job search skills, thereby speeding up the reemployment process. JSA services typically include some combination of the following: outreach; orientation, assessment, and testing; job search workshops, resource centers, and job clubs; follow-up counseling; and job development and placement. Early intervention with JSA services to workers at risk of exhausting their UI eligibility is termed profiling.
Reemployment bonuses	Directed at the problem that the reemployment of dislocated workers may be delayed not by inadequate job search skills but by a lack of motivation to engage in search while drawing UI benefits. Reemployment bonus schemes are also intended to overcome the natural reluctance of the dislocated to accept new jobs offering lower wages and benefits than prelayoff jobs.
Relocation assistance	Designed to encourage relocation from depressed to expanding local labor markets. Financial assistance allows workers to travel to job interviews in geographically distant labor markets and, if successful, to relocate their families to the new location.
Compensation for earnings losses	
Classroom training	Classroom courses designed to restore lost earnings potential by providing the job skills necessary for dislocated workers to qualify for vacant jobs in expanding industries. Classroom courses may also provide training in basic skills. Government funding has traditionally flowed to postsecondary schools, allowing them to enlarge course offerings to targeted workers. Under the voucher system alternative, funding goes directly to workers, who make their own choices among available course offerings.
Wage subsidies	Employers receive a temporary subsidy to encourage the hiring of targeted workers. The objective of this activity is to make it attractive for employers to provide OJT that enhances workers' firm- and industry-specific job skills.
Earnings subsidies	The subsidy is directly paid to eligible workers. The objectives of this activity are to (1) increase the incentive to return to work, even at lower wages, for those who under the present UI system have a strong work disincentive, and (2) target assistance to those dislocated workers who have suffered the greatest losses in earnings.
Self-employment	Allows dislocated workers to continue receiving UI benefits while they acquire basic business skills and establish their own small businesses.

(3) the Texas Worker Adjustment Demonstration (WAD) projects; and (4) the New Jersey UI Reemployment Demonstration.

As described in table 8.2, individuals eligible for the first two of the demonstrations were predominantly dislocated auto and steel workers residing in the Detroit and Buffalo metropolitan areas, respectively.[4] In both demonstrations, program participants were enrolled in orientation and assessment sessions first, followed by mandatory four-day job search workshops. Selected participants then were channeled into classroom training slots or on-the-job training positions. Controlling for worker characteristics and plant-specific variables, the most striking aspect of the Downriver estimates presented by Abt Associates is their variability (see Kulik, Smith, and Stromsdorfer 1984). Depending on the particular plants from which treatment and comparison group members were selected, net weekly earnings estimates range from a negative $19 to a positive $122.

The incremental earnings effect of classroom training beyond that of job search assistance is not reported, but Kulik et al. (1984: 90–92) conclude that classroom training did not significantly improve participants' postprogram reemployment rates.

Program impact estimates for the Buffalo evaluation also are difficult to assess because of their variation in the two available samples. Nevertheless, the results considered more reliable by the authors of the Mathematica Policy Research report—the "target-plant sample" estimates—indicate a JSA effect on earnings of $134 per week for program participants (see Corson, Long, and Maynard 1985: table IV.4).[5] That positive and statistically significant effect is primarily due to a 33 percentage point increase in the proportion of time worked by JSA recipients. There is no evidence of an incremental earnings effect of classroom training above that of JSA, despite the much higher per participant cost of CT.

The Texas WAD projects offered JSA and limited vocational skill training to eligible workers under Title III of JTPA. At each of three program sites, eligible workers were randomly assigned to either of two treatment groups or to a control group. Members of the first treatment group were offered job search assistance services only, whereas the second treatment offered JSA followed, if necessary, by classroom training or on-the-job training. Bloom (1990) reports that the WAD mix of services has an appreciable but short-lived impact on the earnings of males. That early reemployment effect reduces UI benefits paid during a 30-week postassignment period by $207 (or 13 percent) per male participant.[6] Estimated earnings impacts for women are larger than those obtained by men, but they also diminish by the end of the one-year observation period. For the first 30 weeks, female participants receive on average $227 (or 19 percent) less in UI benefits than they would have in the program's absence. Bloom indicates that for women, increased tax revenues generated by program-induced earnings gains coupled with lower UI payments are likely to more than offset modest program costs, making WAD cost-effective from a government budgetary perspective. For men, lower estimated impacts on both earnings and UI payments mean that program costs and benefits are roughly offsetting for the government.

An emphasis on classroom training in the Houston WAD site allows the incremental effect of CT to be estimated for men. Despite its higher costs, researchers find essentially no additional gains when classroom training is added to job search assistance. Bloom (1990: 139) comments on this result and suggests that the blue-collar orientation of CT curriculums available at a local Houston community college was not well matched to the backgrounds and interests of the mostly white-collar participants.

Reemployment services offered in the New Jersey demonstration were targeted to UI claimants with characteristics common to dislocated workers, namely, individuals older than age 25 who had at least three years of tenure with their prelayoff employer and did not anticipate being recalled. A key objective of the New Jersey project was to assess the feasibility of an early intervention (or profiling) strategy in which the UI system is used to identify early in the claim period unemployed workers who, in the absence of intervention, are likely to face prolonged spells of unemployment and exhaust UI benefits. UI claimants who passed through a series of screens to determine those likely to exhaust benefits were assigned randomly to one of three treatment groups (JSA-only, JSA plus retraining, and JSA plus a reemployment bonus) or to a control group. After completing a common set of JSA services, those assigned to the JSA/retraining treatment were offered the opportunity to enroll in a CT or OJT program. Acceptable classroom training programs were subject to the restriction that expected duration not exceed six months. Employers willing to provide on-the-job training slots received a wage subsidy of 50 percent for up to six months.

Corson et al. (1989) present net impact estimates for the first year following the date of filing the initial UI claim. Quarterly estimates obtained for the JSA-only treatment indicate that program net impacts rise through the second quarter, peaking at $263 in additional quarterly earnings and a 4.3 percentage point increase in the employment rate. Thereafter, as in the Texas WAD projects, both outcome measures decline to nearly zero.

Table 8.2 CHARACTERISTICS OF MAJOR DISLOCATED WORKER PROJECTS OFFERING JOB PLACEMENT AND SKILL TRAINING SERVICES

Project	Workers Studied	Nature of Retraining Activity	Length of Observation Period	Evaluation Design
Dislocated Worker Demonstrations				
Downriver, Michigan	Experienced male workers laid off from auto assembly and parts plants.	Initial enrollment in JSA services followed, for about 60 percent of participants, by referral to CT or in some cases OJT.	2 1/2 years from date of layoff.	Comparison group of workers laid off from other auto assembly and parts plants in the area.
Buffalo	Experienced male workers laid off from auto and steel plants. Layoffs of 1+ years common for workers served.	JSA services followed by short-duration CT or OJT for about 45 percent of participants.	First 6 postprogram months.	Recruited workers from targeted plants who chose not to participate when offered services and individuals not offered services.
Texas WAD	Eligible for Title III of JTPA.	Two treatment groups: (1) JSA services only, and (2) JSA followed if necessary by CT or OJT.	4 quarters after random assignment.	Random assignment to treatment and control groups.
New Jersey UI	UI claimants with 3+ years of prelayoff tenure.	Three treatments: (1) JSA only, (2) JSA plus short-duration CT or OJT, and (3) JSA plus offer of a reemployment bonus. Relocation assistance also offered to treatment group 2 participants.	4 quarters after initial UI claim in Corson et al. (1989); 10 quarters in Anderson, Corson, and Decker (1991); and 6 years in Corson and Haimson (1995).	Random assignment.

Study				
TAA Study	Eligible for TAA assistance.	Longer-duration training designed to develop job-related skills in new occupations.	12 quarters following the initial UI claim.	Comparison groups of UI exhaustees and TRA recipients.
New Jersey Workforce Development Partnership Program (WDPP)	Unemployed workers who were employed at least 5 of the last 7 years.	Training programs that may exceed a year supplied by proprietary schools and community colleges.	9 quarters after claim date.	Matched comparison group of UI claimants.
Pennsylvania Displaced Worker Employment and Training Program (DWETP)	Workers displaced from a job that had lasted 3+ years.	Longer-term training courses offered by a large community college.	6 to 8 years after training ends.	Regression analysis of administrative data for DWETP enrollees who differ in number of courses completed.

As noted in table 8.2, claimants assigned to the JSA/retraining treatment received, as an alternative to skill training, an offer of relocation assistance consisting of payment for expenses associated with out-of-area job interviews and moving costs. Consistent with the lack of interest shown in earlier dislocated worker demonstrations, only about 1 percent of JSA/retraining claimants were recorded by counselors as interested primarily in relocation assistance.

The UI Reform Experiments

A second major source of evidence on the effectiveness of JSA and other reemployment services is a series of random-assignment experiments carried out during the late 1970s and 1980s to test proposed reforms of the UI system. Six job search experiments evaluate combinations of JSA services,[7] while evidence is available from four reemployment bonus experiments.[8] Two random-assignment experiments testing a third proposed UI reform, self-employment programs, will be discussed shortly.

Meyer (1995) provides a comprehensive survey of results of the job search and reemployment bonus UI experiments. To briefly summarize his conclusions, the job search experiments indicate that a wide range of JSA services including increased enforcement of work search rules is successful in speeding up reemployment. The evidence shows that weeks of UI benefits typically are reduced by about half a week. Since the costs of JSA services are generally low compared with savings in UI benefits, cost-benefit analyses from both the perspectives of the UI system and the government as a whole are strongly favorable.[9] Meyer (1995: 120) notes that imprecisely estimated earnings increases make cost-benefit analyses of the JSA experiments less conclusive from a social perspective. For the New Jersey demonstration, nevertheless, a large positive effect of JSA services on reemployment earnings leads to benefits exceeding costs by a wide margin.

The evidence is not as positive for reemployment bonus plans. The first bonus experiment carried out in Illinois paid a lump-sum bonus of $500 to claimants who found a job within 11 weeks. Results for the Illinois plan indicate that UI receipt declined by more than a full week. Put another way, UI benefits were reduced by a striking $2.32 for every $1 paid out in bonuses to claimants (Woodbury and Spiegelman 1987). This very favorable outcome led to additional bonus experiments conducted in New Jersey, Pennsylvania, and Washington state. In those three experiments, however, estimated net impacts tended to be much smaller, clustering around half a week.

That is, reemployment bonuses have about the same effect as that found in the JSA experiments, but at a much higher cost because of the bonuses.

The Worker Profiling Case Study

The New Jersey UI Reemployment Demonstration provided the empirical basis for federal legislation enacted in 1993 (the Worker Profiling and Reemployment Services initiative) requiring each state to establish a system for profiling new UI claimants. The intent of profiling systems is twofold: early identification of claimants who are at risk of long unemployment spells and exhausting their UI benefits, and prompt delivery to those claimants of appropriate reemployment services. The 1993 legislation also requires claimants referred to reemployment services to participate in the services as a condition of eligibility for UI benefits.

The U.S. Department of Labor recently initiated a major four-year study of state profiling systems. Decker et al. (1996) present interim findings from Phase I of the study focusing on the implementation of profiling systems in the first six states to implement such systems—Delaware, Florida, Kentucky, Maryland, New Jersey, and Oregon. (Phases II and III will present net impact estimates.) Drawing on case studies of the six states, the authors highlight the following findings:

- Although all six states had in place profiling systems, some sites encountered delays in providing the promised reemployment services.
- An array of services is supplied to referred claimants. All of the states require attendance at an orientation, either as a stand-alone service or as part of a workshop. Most states also require an individual or group assessment followed by the development of an individual service plan. Table 8.3 shows that nearly three-quarters of referred claimants in the case study states attended orientation. Assessment and job search workshops or job clubs are the second and third most frequently attended services. Only 19 percent of claimants participated in a retraining program.
- While DOL guidelines strongly encourage individualized service plans tailored to each claimant's needs, some local offices developed plans with minimal requirements. Staff members in those local offices expressed reluctance to add mandatory services beyond orientation and assessment for fear that they would jeopardize claimants' benefits.

Table 8.3 PERCENTAGES OF PROFILED AND REFERRED CLAIMANTS
ATTENDING VARIOUS SERVICES IN THE SIX CASE STUDY STATES,
SECOND QUARTER OF 1995

Service	Percent of Claimants Reporting
Orientation	73.6
Assessment	59.5
Job search workshop/job club	57.7
Job placement/referral	33.4
Counseling	27.3
Education and training	19.1
Self-employment program	0.0

Source: Decker et al. (1996: table 4).

- All administrators report that potential benefit denial is a crucial factor in encouraging claimant participation in reemployment services.
- An unexpected advantage of the participation requirement is that it eases enforcement of the "able and available" work requirement for maintaining benefit eligibility.

O'Leary, Decker, and Wandner (1998) assess the usefulness of profiling models similar to those in existing state systems to target reemployment bonuses to dislocated workers. In contrast to the rather negative results summarized earlier for the New Jersey, Pennsylvania, and Washington experiments, their simulation results indicate that targeting bonuses to claimants with high exhaustion probabilities can improve the cost-effectiveness of reemployment bonuses.

EVIDENCE ON ACTIVITIES TO REPLACE LOST EARNINGS CAPACITY

Table 8.1 outlines four activities intended to compensate dislocated workers for their earnings losses. Three of the activities—classroom training, on-the-job training supported by wage subsidies, and self-employment programs—provide alternative forms of training to replenish lost firm-specific human capital. Earnings subsidies combine compensation for lost earnings with an incentive to return to work quickly.

Classroom Training

Dislocated workers in need of replenishing their marketable skills usually are referred to either classroom training programs or, less frequently, firm-based training programs. In the case of classroom training, an eligible worker often is assigned a slot in a curriculum already developed by an institutional training provider subcontracting to the agency administering the program. An alternative approach allowing more individual choice is to provide a voucher that the client may redeem by selecting a course of study supplied by an approved post-secondary training institution.

The Dislocated Worker Demonstrations

The four dislocated worker demonstration projects described earlier all take the approach of offering eligible workers classroom training slots developed by approved institutional training providers. As noted, results obtained in the Downriver, Buffalo, and Texas WAD demonstrations indicate that classroom training generally fails to have an incremental labor market impact above that of job search assistance only. It certainly does not appear from these studies that the additional effect of CT is large enough to compensate for the higher cost of classroom training services. Authors of the major evaluation reports suggest a number of caveats for their disappointing findings. These include the difficulty of drawing reliable inferences from small sample sizes; the problem that program participants undergoing skill training have little time left to receive placement assistance (given demonstrations of fixed length); the scarcity of training providers capable of putting together high-quality, short-duration training courses on short notice; and mismatches between training curricula and client interests.

In comparison with those demonstrations, the New Jersey UI Reemployment Demonstration offers the advantages of larger samples and a wider variety of clients offered demonstration services. Corson et al. (1989) present net impact estimates for the first year following the date of filing the initial UI claim. Unlike JSA services, skill training is not expected to speed up reemployment, but it is anticipated to enhance earnings potential. For the JSA plus retraining treatment, however, there is no evidence of either expedited employment or a permanent increase in earnings measured relative to the control group. Corson et al. (1989: 14) suggest one reason for the absence of an earnings effect is that a very low take-up rate among claimants assigned to this treatment (15 percent) means that any positive effect of skill training for those who actually enrolled in a training program would be substantially diluted. In addition, they note that the one-year observation period is not long enough to accurately measure the effects of retraining.

The two available follow-up studies of the New Jersey program are useful because of their longer observation periods and the distinction they make between classroom training and OJT. Anderson, Corson, and Decker (1991) present results for a 10-quarter follow-up period, while a six-year follow-up is examined in Corson and Haimson (1995). With a focus on claimants who actually participated in a skill training program (as opposed to all claimants in the treatment group offered skill training), table 8.4 shows that classroom training significantly reduces earnings in the initial two quarters relative to the earnings of claimants receiving JSA, largely because of its depressing effect on weeks worked. This result is expected because training is

Table 8.4 ESTIMATED INCREMENTAL EFFECTS OF CLASSROOM TRAINING AND OJT ON AVERAGE EARNINGS AND WEEKS WORKED OF TRAINING RECIPIENTS IN THE NEW JERSEY UI REEMPLOYMENT DEMONSTRATION

Time Period	Classroom Training		On-the-Job Training	
	Earnings ($)	Weeks Worked	Earnings ($)	Weeks Worked
Quarter				
1	−458**	−1.00***	1,469**	2.57***
2	−635***	−1.90***	2,347***	4.98***
3	−314	−0.60	2,632***	4.55***
4	195	0.74*	2,995***	4.69**
5	384	1.27***	3,174***	4.76***
6	191	0.67*	2,480***	4.05***
7	323	0.74*	2,652***	3.88***
8	505**	0.90**	2,681***	3.81***
9	408*	0.80**	2,932***	4.55***
10	582**	0.85**	3,005***	4.38***
Year				
1	−1,212*	−2.76**	9,443***	16.79***
2	1,402	3.58***	10,987***	16.50***
3	1,561*	2.95**	14,387***	18.49***
4	1,298	2.26	11,232***	15.91***
5	1,025	2.11	10,357***	13.63***
6	1,004	1.97	11,954***	12.01***

Sources: Quarterly estimates from Anderson et al. (1991: tables III.4 and III.5); annual estimates from Corson and Haimson (1995: tables III.2 and III.3).
Note: Estimates are relative to those for claimants who received JSA-only services.
***, **, and * indicate significance at the 1 percent, 5 percent, and 10 percent levels, respectively.

likely to be ongoing during those quarters. Thereafter, CT leads to generally steadily increasing increments in quarterly earnings, rising to $582 in the 10th quarter. It is interesting to note that although the earnings gains in quarters 4 and 5 appear to be fueled by additional weeks worked, the still larger earnings increments observed in quarters 8 through 10 do not correspond to longer workweeks. This suggests that the positive earnings impacts of classroom training are associated with higher wages as well as greater numbers of weeks worked.

Estimates obtained over the six-year follow-up period indicate that the incremental effect of CT peaks in year 3 at nearly $1,600 per year in additional earnings and at about three additional weeks worked. Thereafter, permanent gains appear of about $1,000 annually in additional earnings and two weeks of additional employment.

A point to keep in mind with respect to the classroom training findings (as well as the OJT estimates) shown in table 8.4 is that individuals receiving training are self-selected, so that the evidence cannot be used to argue that training will increase earnings for a randomly chosen group of UI claimants. On-the-job training results are discussed later in this section.

THE TRADE ADJUSTMENT ASSISTANCE STUDY

In the early 1990s, the DOL initiated a major study to assess the labor market effects of extended unemployment insurance benefits called Trade Readjustment Allowances and of TAA retraining services. In contrast to the short-duration training in the New Jersey demonstration, TAA funds longer-term training aimed at developing job skills to allow dislocated workers to qualify for jobs in entirely new occupations. As noted earlier, the substantial discretion given eligible workers to select their own training programs makes TAA training a voucher-based system.

In addition to making training mandatory, the 1988 amendment to the TAA Act contains a provision designed to help eligible laid-off workers enter training earlier in their unemployment spells by providing information on TAA through EDWAA-established rapid-response teams. Corson et al. (1993: 51–54) suggest that to a moderate degree this initiative was successful. The percentage of trainees who entered training before receiving TRA (i.e., while still receiving UI benefits) rose from 52 percent in the pre-1988 sample to 60 percent in the post-1988 sample. Once training commenced, most TAA trainees were committed for a lengthy period. Among pre-1988 trainees, mean length of training was about 59 weeks. Average duration of training among post-1988 trainees was significantly longer, at

67 weeks. The long-term nature of most TAA training means that a substantial number of trainees exhausted their one year of TRA eligibility before completing their training. Among pre-1988 trainees, 44 percent were still in training more than 52 weeks after first receiving TRA, compared with 46 percent among post-1988 trainees.

The Corson et al. (1993) evaluation is based on interviews with nearly 4,800 sample members broken down into three groups: (1) recipients of TRA income maintenance benefits; (2) TAA trainees, nearly all of whom were receiving TRA benefits; and (3) a comparison sample of people who had exhausted their UI benefits and whose previous job was in manufacturing. (Decker and Corson 1995 summarize the major results of the evaluation study.) To measure the labor market effects of retraining, the authors point out that the more appropriate comparison group is TRA recipients because their characteristics are closer to those of trainees than are those of people whose UI benefits are exhausted.

The time pattern of observed earnings differences (not shown) between trainees and other TRA recipients indicates, as expected, that trainees were forgoing short-run earnings as part of their investment in skill training. However, earnings tend to rise faster for trainees, resulting in their earnings overtaking those of other TRA recipients by the 11th quarter after the initial claim. For both the pre- and post-1988 samples, table 8.5 presents estimates of the impact of training among TRA recipients for the final quarter of the 12-quarter observation period. The first row of the table shows that average

Table 8.5 ESTIMATED EFFECTS OF TRADE ADJUSTMENT ASSISTANCE TRAINING ON EARNINGS IN QUARTER 12, TRA RECIPIENTS ONLY

Sample and Inclusion of Control Variables	Pre-1988 Sample ($)	Post-1988 Sample ($)
All TRA recipients:		
No control variables ($)	228	495*
	(215)	(239)
Control variables included ($)	−416*	152
	(206)	(238)
TRA recipients excluding those still in training:		
No control variables ($)	490	777**
	(251)	(268)
Control variables included ($)	−206	353
	(235)	(250)

Source: Decker and Corson (1995: tables 3 and 4).
Note: Standard errors appear in parentheses.
** and * indicate significance at the 1 percent and 5 percent levels, respectively.

earnings of trainees are $228 per quarter higher than those of other TRA recipients in the pre-1988 sample and $495 higher in the post-1988 sample. Only the post-1988 difference is statistically significant. Estimates in the second row adjust for a variety of personal and job-related characteristics that might differ between trainees and other TRA recipients. Controlling for these other variables, the training coefficient is negative and statistically significant for the pre-1988 sample and positive but small and statistically insignificant for the post-1988 sample.

Decker and Corson (1995) point out that, even as late as the end of the 11th quarter, 5 to 10 percent of trainees were still enrolled in a training program. The final two rows of the table show training effects estimated omitting those still in training at some point two or more years after their initial UI claim. The results, as anticipated, indicate larger (or less negative) estimated effects of training. Taken at face value, the three positive earnings estimates suggest earnings gains from TAA training of from $1,400 to $3,100 per year. However, only one of the positive estimates is statistically significant at customary standards of significance. Decker and Corson (1995: 773) conclude that in the absence of more substantial evidence that training works, skill training should be made voluntary rather than mandatory for TRA recipients, with the 1988 training requirement replaced by a requirement to participate in a job search program.

THE NEW JERSEY WORKFORCE DEVELOPMENT PARTNERSHIP PROGRAM (WDPP)

A second voucher-based training program targeted to the dislocated is one of three components of the New Jersey WDPP enacted in 1992. (The other two components are extended unemployment benefits during training and grants to employers for customized training services.) Dislocated workers are defined as individuals permanently separated from their previous employers who are eligible for UI benefits and were employed in at least five of the previous seven years. Using the UI system, newly dislocated workers are processed through an elaborate series of intake steps before they are allowed to enroll in a training program. The last of these steps is a formal agreement between the client and a WDPP counselor detailing the type, length, cost, and dates of training. While in training, an individualized job placement plan is developed for each trainee.

Under the WDPP's Individual Training Grants program, the maximum training grant per person is $4,000, with an additional grant of up to $1,000 if the participant requires remedial education prior to training. Benus et al. (1996) note that most WDPP grantees proposed relatively short training programs. About half of grantees in fiscal year 1995 proposed programs of six months or less, and approximately one-third planned to enroll in training programs lasting between 6 and 12 months. Proprietary schools and community colleges are the major providers of training services.

Benus et al. (1996) supply net impact estimates for the Individual Training Grant program using a treatment group/matched comparison group evaluation design. As anticipated, initial quarterly earnings of the treatment group are considerably below those of the comparison group. However, earnings rise faster for the treatment group, with an overtaking point reached during the fifth quarter after the claim date. Average quarterly earnings of the treatment group then exceed those of the comparison group by roughly $500 to $900 through quarter nine after the claim date. Lending credibility to these preliminary but impressively large estimates is a similar pattern of prelayoff earnings for the treatment and comparison groups.

THE PENNSYLVANIA DISPLACED WORKERS EDUCATIONAL TRAINING PROGRAM (DWETP)

The final classroom training program considered here was established in Allegheny County, Pennsylvania, during the 1982–83 recession. Allegheny County includes the city of Pittsburgh. A 16.2 percent county unemployment rate plus limited assistance available from higher levels of government led the county to develop its own retraining program operated through a local community college, the Community College of Allegheny County (CCAC). Eligible dislocated workers were allowed to choose their own course of study and whether they attended the community college full-time or part-time. DWETP staff members also developed noncredit classes teaching job search skills and career development techniques.

Using administrative data on college courses and quarterly earnings, Jacobson, LaLonde, and Sullivan (1994) examine choices among different CCAC classroom programs and the impact of the programs on subsequent earnings. Their sample includes about 4,800 dislocated workers who were permanently displaced during 1978–85 from jobs lasting three years or longer. Earnings records are available for these individuals through 1991. The comparison group used in obtaining net impact estimates consists of DWETP program dropouts and no-shows for credit classes.

Several major findings emerge from the Jacobson et al. (1994) study.

- Despite having their training subsidized, most participants did not complete even a year's worth of credits. Moreover, only 23 percent of male and 29 percent of female participants earned a two-year degree or occupational certificate.
- For men, the impact on earnings of one year of training rises steadily from $100 to $300 per quarter below the earnings of the comparison group during the first postprogram year to $250 to $400 per quarter above comparison group earnings by the seventh postprogram year.
- Earnings impact estimates for females decline after the fifth post-program year and are substantially lower than those estimated for males by the seventh postprogram year.
- Enrollment in a noncredit job search assistance course boosts male earnings by about $150 per quarter. The effect of JSA for women is much lower.
- Average returns mask considerable variation across different classroom programs. The payoffs for academic courses in math and science, nursing and other health-related fields, trades and repair, and computer information systems are substantially higher than those for other vocational and academic courses.
- For both males and females, an AA degree has little effect on post-program earnings.

Wage Subsidies

Recognizing the importance of on-the-job training as an alternative to classroom training, wage subsidy programs offer employers a cash payment or tax credit to hire targeted workers and provide them with sufficient skill training to ensure their continued employment after the subsidy period ends. Relatively little evidence directly bears on the effectiveness of wage subsidy programs for dislocated workers.[10] As described earlier, the Buffalo dislocated worker demonstration offered employers a 50 percent wage subsidy for up to six months to develop OJT slots. The evaluation results reported in Corson, Long, and Maynard (1985) are mixed. On-the-job training has little impact on either average earnings or the employment rate for the target-plant sample, and it is statistically significant in increasing earnings but not employment for non-target-plant workers. Because OJT was primarily used in the Buffalo program as a placement tool, the absence of an effect on employment opportunities suggests that the OJT treatment was unnecessary.

The New Jersey UI Reemployment Demonstration offered UI claimants in the JSA-plus-retraining treatment an opportunity to enroll in an OJT or classroom training program. As in the Buffalo study, employers who agreed to provide an OJT slot received a 50 percent, six-month wage subsidy. Table 8.4 shows that the subsidy program generated what appears to be a permanent increment in annual earnings on the order of $12,000 and in weeks worked of 12 weeks per year. In interpreting such very large estimates, however, it must be emphasized that only 45 individuals actually received OJT services. Corson et al. (1989: 116) explain that it was the responsibility of the JTPA system to provide OJT referrals, and local JTPA program operators had more experience developing lower-wage job opportunities for disadvantaged workers than the higher-wage jobs thought to be appropriate for the dislocated.

Another piece of evidence relating specifically to dislocated workers is a random-assignment experiment carried out in Illinois. The Illinois Claimant Bonus Experiment that supplied a $500 cash bonus to UI claimants upon reemployment was outlined earlier. The parallel Illinois Employer Bonus Experiment made the employer of each newly hired claimant eligible for a $500 cash bonus. In contrast to the striking results for the claimant reemployment bonus, Woodbury and Spiegelman (1987) report much smaller effects for the employer bonus treatment. Those small effects primarily reflect limited participation of workers assigned to the employer experiment and the fact that most employers eligible for a bonus failed to submit their bonus vouchers for cash.

One final related study concerns the effect of a Michigan wage subsidy program on the employment stability of *employed* workers at risk of dislocation. Targeted to small manufacturing firms implementing new types of technology, the question addressed is whether the subsidy program increases specific training enough to make workers' jobs more secure and, perhaps, raise their earnings. Holzer et al. (1993) find that receipt of a training grant is associated with a one-time increase in training hours and with a more lasting reduction in scrap rates indicating a permanent effect on product quality.

Self-Employment

Rather than attempting to enhance marketable skills, the basic idea of self-employment plans is to develop the latent entrepreneurial talent possessed by at least some dislocated workers. In these initiatives, selected workers are exempted from the usual work search requirements imposed on UI recipients while they receive training in basic business skills and assistance in converting a business idea into a formal business plan. Then, with limited financial assistance, they are turned loose to establish their own small businesses.

"Evidence on Activities to Speed Up Reemployment" earlier in this chapter described a series of random-assignment experiments funded by the U.S. Department of Labor to test the effectiveness of proposed UI system reforms. The two reforms discussed earlier are enhanced JSA services and the reemployment bonus. The third of the three reforms tested is self-employment. Two self-employment experiments received DOL funding during the late 1980s and early 1990s, the first in Washington state and the second in Massachusetts. Both projects are three-year demonstrations providing early intervention services that include 20 hours of training in basic business skills, counseling, and financial assistance in the form of biweekly unemployment benefits. Along with these similarities, the projects differed in two important respects. First, the Massachusetts project was targeted to unemployed workers judged likely to exhaust their benefits. The Washington project did not impose that restriction. Second, the Washington project provided, in addition to regular payments, a lump-sum payment equal to remaining unemployment benefits to those who completed five project milestones, defined as completing a set of four business training modules, developing an acceptable business plan, opening a business bank account, satisfying all licensing requirements, and obtaining adequate funding.

Both self-employment demonstrations were evaluated using a random-assignment methodology. Over follow-up periods averaging 21 months in Washington state and 19 months in Massachusetts, Benus, Wood, and Grover (1994) report that program services sharply increased the likelihood of self-employment and accelerated its start but otherwise had little effect on self-employment earnings and wage and salary earnings. Nor did the program services appear to increase employment opportunities for nonparticipants. Perhaps the most important finding from the demonstrations is that very few UI claimants who expressed an initial interest in self-employment actually followed through by taking steps to start up their own small firms. Benus et al. (1994: ii) comment that "while many profess an interest in self-employment, relatively few choose to pursue self-employment when the opportunity arises."

Earnings Subsidies

The primary motivation for the earnings subsidy as a policy intervention is evidence showing that dislocated workers frequently suffer very large earnings losses. An earnings subsidy program works by paying reemployed workers some fraction of the gap between their pre- and postdisplacement earnings. In this way, the greatest level of assistance flows to those suffering the greatest earnings losses. In addition, the subsidy is restricted to those who find a new job, so that eligible workers have an incentive to return to work quickly.

The main sources of evidence on earnings subsidies are two random-assignment experiments currently being carried out in Canada—one targeted to the dislocated and the other to the economically disadvantaged. The dislocated workers experiment (called the Earnings Supplement Project or ESP) is based on a sample of about 8,100 new UI claimants who were permanently laid off from jobs held at least three years. Claimants in the treatment group (half the total sample) first receive an explanation of the earnings subsidy plan. They then receive the subsidy if reemployment in a full-time job (a minimum of 30 hours of work per week) with a new employer occurs within 26 weeks of the date of the subsidy offer and if the new job pays less than the predisplacement job. The subsidy offsets 75 percent of the claimant's weekly earnings loss up to a maximum of $250 per week for a period not to exceed 24 months.

Bloom, Fink, et al. (1997) discuss the following major findings in their interim report on ESP's implementation:

- ESP is functioning smoothly within the existing Canadian employment service system, and a telephone "mini-survey" of 343 dislocated workers indicates that respondents are well informed about the specifics of ESP.
- Focus group interviews indicate that ESP's main effect on the job search behavior of the dislocated is to broaden the range of jobs they are willing to consider, including jobs that initially pay less than their predisplacement jobs. ESP appears to have less influence on the speed or intensity of job search.
- Sixteen percent of dislocated workers are projected to take up the supplement offer by the end of their 26-week job search period. That is about 50 percent of the one-third of dislocated Canadian workers estimated in earlier studies to experience earnings losses upon reemployment.

Future reports will present estimates of the net impact of ESP on dislocated workers' employment, earnings, and UI benefit receipt.

Designed to encourage economically disadvantaged Canadians to find full-time employment, the Self-Sufficiency Project (SSP) provides an earnings supplement equal to half the difference between a participant's labor earnings and a target earnings level. The target earnings level is set at $37,000 in British Columbia and $30,000 in New Brunswick (in Canadian dollars)—the sites of the two demonstration projects. The final SSP evaluation will eventually follow the 6,000 eligible families included in the program over five years. However, an 18-month interim analysis by Lin et al. (1998) indicates a dramatic effect of the program on labor force attachment. As of the fifth quarter of the follow-up period, the full-time employment rate (defined as 30 hours per week) for the treatment group is 29 percent, compared with 14 percent for the control group.

SUMMARY AND POLICY IMPLICATIONS

A sizable literature exists documenting the substantial earnings losses suffered by dislocated workers. One widely cited study pegs those earnings losses, even in the fifth year after displacement, at more than $6,500 per year, or about 25 percent of predisplacement earnings (Jacobson et al. 1993b). Losses of that magnitude bring home the point that while the benefits to society of an open and technologically progressive economy are widely shared, the costs tend to be borne by a relatively small number of workers who lose jobs in which they had accumulated considerable firm-specific human capital. Some form of compensation may thus be in order for those workers.

This chapter has examined the evaluation evidence available for a variety of publicly funded programs offering assistance to the dislocated. Available forms of assistance are divided into two categories: services designed to speed up the reemployment of dislocated workers, and services intended to assist them in replacing lost earnings capacity.

Services designed to expedite reemployment include JSA, reemployment bonuses, and relocation assistance. As described in "Evidence on Activities to Speed Up Reemployment," a large volume of quantitative evidence supports the effectiveness of job search assistance services. It appears that many dislocated individuals possess sufficient marketable skills that they can find new jobs with limited, relatively low-cost assistance. JSA should be made widely available to the dislocated. Nevertheless, preliminary findings from a study of state profiling systems indicate that there are often significant delays in supplying reemployment services and that service plans are not always tailored to meet the individual needs of the dislocated.

Recent evidence for reemployment bonuses is less favorable than that for job search assistance. Bonus plans appear to expedite reemployment to about the same extent as JSA services but at much higher cost due to the bonus payments. The evidence also shows that offers of relocation assistance are seldom of interest to dislocated workers.

Activities intended to restore lost earnings capacity include classroom training, wage subsidies to encourage employers to provide OJT, and self-employment programs. Earnings subsidies paid to eligible dislocated workers couple compensation for lost earnings with an incentive to return to work quickly.

The most widely implemented of these activities is classroom training. The CT programs examined differ along a number of dimensions, including short- versus longer-duration training, designated classroom slots versus training vouchers allowing participants to make their own curriculum choices, and curriculums designed to enhance existing skills versus those intended to retool dislocated workers for entirely new occupations. Estimated earnings impacts are found to vary substantially across programs. Possibly the most reliable net earnings estimates of those discussed in "Evidence on Activities to Replace Lost Earnings Capacity" are obtained for the New Jersey UI Reemployment Demonstration and the TAA study. Even those estimates are quite varied, ranging between roughly $500 and $2,000 per year for short-term training programs and between $1,400 and $3,100 per year for longer-term training.

With annual operating costs of short-term CT programs typically falling between $2,000 and $3,000, there is room for cautious optimism regarding the potential for classroom training in helping to restore dislocated workers' lost earnings capacity. However, it is clear that a substantial expansion in classroom training expenditures would be required to make much of a dent in earnings losses on the order of $6,500 per year. There is also evidence from several of the evaluation studies, notably the New Jersey UI Reemployment Demonstration, the TAA study, and the Pennsylvania DWETP, that dislocated workers are less interested in returning to school than they are in finding new jobs.

Wage subsidy programs capitalize on dislocated workers' interest in getting back to work quickly. In addition, net impact estimates reported for the New Jersey UI demonstration are enough larger than those for corresponding CT services to indicate promise for making up a substantial fraction of earnings losses suffered by the dislocated. A technical issue is whether the New Jersey estimates are overstated due to self-selection of individuals recommended for OJT services. Another outstanding question of considerable policy importance is whether employers can be induced to provide jobs offering OJT opportunities in sufficient numbers to match the employment needs of dislocated workers.

Of the two remaining approaches to compensating dislocated workers for lost earnings, evaluations of self-employment programs carried out in Pennsylvania and Washington state indicate that self-employment is an option of limited interest to the dislocated. Earnings subsidies represent an interesting conceptual approach in that assistance is targeted to dislocated workers most in need as measured by the size of their earnings losses. A Canadian earnings subsidy experiment designed for the dislocated is currently under way to assess the likely impacts of this activity. A noteworthy finding from an interim evaluation report is that the earnings subsidy has the effect of broadening the range of jobs dislocated Canadians are willing to consider, including jobs that initially pay less than their prelayoff jobs.

Notes

Author's note: The helpful comments of Walter Corson and Paul Decker on an earlier draft of this chapter are gratefully acknowledged.

1. Hamermesh (1988) provides a useful discussion of issues involved in defining the dislocated. As he notes, definitions range from the most restrictive (limiting the dislocated to trade-displaced, long-tenure workers whose plants closed) to the least restrictive (allowing all laid-off workers to count as dislocated). His own analysis of Panel Study of Income Dynamics data defines the dislocated as those (regardless of job tenure) whose plants closed and shows, using this definition, that the rate of dislocation increased over the 1968–81 period. Hipple (1997) and Kletzer (1998) supply more recent discussions of the impact of alternative definitions for estimates of the number of dislocated workers.

2. Stevens (1997) presents evidence that the persistence of wage and earnings reductions results from repeated job losses following the initial dislocation experience.

3. Barnow and King (1996) provide a useful overview of the U.S. experience with voucher programs for training the unemployed.

4. A more detailed discussion of all four demonstration projects is found in Leigh (1990, 1995).

5. Buffalo net impact estimates are based on a complicated evaluation design. Program services were offered to two groups of dislocated workers: (1) steel and auto workers displaced during 1982 from nine area plants, and (2) a more heterogeneous group of workers permanently laid off after 1980 from more than 300 area establishments. Members of the "target-plant sample" who were offered program services (or recruited) are a random sample of all workers from six of the nine plants. The "non-target-plant sample" consists of all of the workers from the three remaining plants plus workers from the over-300 area establishments who were offered program services on a first-come, first-served basis as program slots became available. Thus, the target-plant sample offered the promise of a simple comparison of outcomes for randomly assigned

treatment and control groups. However, a very low take-up rate among recruited workers for program services (16 percent) caused the substitution of an alternative evaluation design that, controlling statistically for the program participation decision, compares actual program participants with a comparison group that includes recruited nonparticipants. Self-selection is clearly an issue in carrying out this comparison. Nevertheless, self-selection bias is likely to be even more of a problem for the non-target-plant sample in which actual program participants who had to have actively applied for program services are compared with a comparison group of nonparticipants.

6. In contrast to the Buffalo program, the take-up rate for Texas WAD services is quite high at 71 percent. This means that net impact estimates measured for actual participants are similar in size to those measured for all treatment group members.

7. In addition to the New Jersey UI Reemployment Demonstration, the job search experiments are the Nevada Claimant Placement Program, Charleston Claimant Placement and Work Test Demonstration, Nevada Claimant Employment Program, Washington Alternative Work Search Experiment, and Wisconsin Eligibility Review Pilot Project.

8. The bonus experiments are the Illinois UI Incentive Experiments, New Jersey UI Reemployment Demonstration, Pennsylvania Reemployment Bonus Demonstration, and Washington Reemployment Bonus Experiments.

9. From the perspective of the UI system, costs are administrative expenses and benefits are savings in UI payments. Benefits from the perspective of the government as a whole are reduced UI payments plus tax revenues collected on any increases in earnings. Because they are a transfer payment between the government and individuals, the social perspective excludes UI payments from the calculations. Benefits are limited to increases in claimants' earnings, and costs are administrative expenses.

10. More evidence is available on wage subsidy programs for the economically disadvantaged. Particularly noteworthy is the National JTPA Study commissioned by the U.S. Department of Labor in 1986 (see Orr et al. 1996; Bloom, Orr, et al. 1997). This is a large-scale, random-assignment evaluation of Title II-A programs supplying classroom training and OJT services to disadvantaged adults and youth. Over a 30-month follow-up period, Bloom, Orr, et al. (1997: table 4) report that a combined JSA and OJT service strategy increased treatment group earnings over those of the control group by $2,109 (9.8 percent) for adult men and $2,292 (15.3 percent) for adult women. These estimates compare to classroom training earnings effects of $1,287 (7.1 percent) for adult men and $630 (5.5 percent) for adult women. Katz (1996) surveys the experience gained in the United States and other countries with a variety of wage subsidy programs aimed at the disadvantaged.

References

Anderson, Patricia, Walter Corson, and Paul Decker. 1991. "The New Jersey Unemployment Insurance Reemployment Demonstration Project Follow-Up Report." Unemployment Insurance Occasional Paper 91-1. Washington, D.C.: U.S. Department of Labor.

Barnow, Burt S., and Christopher T. King. 1996. "The Baby and the Bath Water: Lessons for the Next Employment and Training Program."

In *Of Heart and Mind: Social Policy Essays in Honor of Sar A. Levitan*, edited by Garth Mangum and Stephen Mangum (255–82). Kalamazoo, Mich.: W.E. Upjohn Institute for Employment Research.

Benus, Jacob M., Michelle Wood, and Nelima Grover. 1994. "A Comparative Analysis of the Washington and Massachusetts UI Self-Employment Demonstrations." Cambridge, Mass.: Abt Associates. January.

Benus, Jacob M., Neelima Grover, Jane Kulik, Steven Marcus, and Michelle Ciurea. 1996. "Third Annual Assessment Report of the Workforce Development Partnership Program." Cambridge, Mass.: Abt Associates. July.

Bloom, Howard S. 1990. *Back to Work: Testing Reemployment Services for Displaced Workers.* Kalamazoo, Mich.: W.E. Upjohn Institute for Employment Research.

Bloom, Howard S., Barbara Fink, Susanna Lui-Gurr, Wendy Bancroft, and Doug Tattrie. 1997. "Implementing the Earnings Supplement Project: A Test of a Reemployment Incentive." Ottawa: Social Research and Demonstration Corporation. October.

Bloom, Howard S., Larry L. Orr, Stephen H. Bell, George Cave, Fred Doolittle, Winston Lin, and Hans Bos. 1997. "The Benefits and Costs of JTPA Title II-A Programs: Key Findings from the National JTPA Study." *Journal of Human Resources* 32 (summer): 549–76.

Corson, Walter, and Joshua Haimson. 1995. "The New Jersey Unemployment Insurance Reemployment Demonstration Project Six-Year Follow-Up and Summary Report." Unemployment Insurance Occasional Paper 95-2. Washington, D.C.: U.S. Department of Labor.

Corson, Walter, Sharon Long, and Rebecca Maynard. 1985. "An Impact Evaluation of the Buffalo Dislocated Worker Demonstration Program." Princeton, N.J.: Mathematica Policy Research. March 12.

Corson, Walter, Paul Decker, Shari Dunstan, and Stuart Kerachsky. 1989. "New Jersey Unemployment Insurance Reemployment Demonstration Project." Unemployment Insurance Occasional Paper 89-3. Washington, D.C.: U.S. Department of Labor.

Corson, Walter, Paul Decker, Phillip Gleason, and Walter Nicholson. 1993. "International Trade and Worker Dislocation: Evaluation of the Trade Adjustment Assistance Program" Princeton, N.J.: Mathematica Policy Research.

Decker, Paul T., and Walter Corson. 1995. "International Trade and Worker Displacement: Evaluation of the Trade Adjustment Assistance Program." *Industrial and Labor Relations Review* 48 (July): 758–74.

Decker, Paul T., Katherine P. Dickinson, Evelyn K. Hawkins, and Suzanne D. Kruetzer. 1996. "Implementation of Worker Profiling and Reemployment Services in Six States." Paper presented at the 18th Annual Research Conference of the Association for Public Policy Analysis and Management, Pittsburgh, Oct. 31–Nov. 1.

DOL. See U.S. Department of Labor.

Fallick, Bruce C. 1996. "A Review of the Recent Empirical Literature on Displaced Workers." *Industrial and Labor Relations Review* 50 (October): 5–16.

Farber, Henry S. 1993. "The Incidence and Costs of Job Loss, 1982–91." *Brookings Papers on Economic Activity: Microeconomics* 1: 73–119.

Flaim, Paul O., and Ellen Sehgal. 1985. "Displaced Workers of 1979–83: How Well Have They Fared?" *Monthly Labor Review* 108 (June): 3–16.

Gardner, Jennifer M. 1995. "Worker Displacement: A Decade of Change." *Monthly Labor Review* 118 (April): 45–57.

Hamermesh, Daniel S. 1987. "The Costs of Worker Displacement." *Quarterly Journal of Economics* 102 (February): 51–75.

———. 1988. "What Do We Know about Worker Displacement in the U.S.?" *Industrial Relations* 28 (winter): 51–59.

Hamermesh, Daniel S., Joseph J. Cordes, and Robert S. Goldfarb. 1987. "Compensating Displaced Workers—What, How Much, How?" In *Labor Market Adjustments in the Pacific Basin*, edited by Peter T. Chinloy and Ernst W. Stromsdorfer (243–65). Boston: Kluwer-Nijhoff.

Hipple, Steven. 1997. "Worker Displacement in an Expanding Economy." *Monthly Labor Review* 120 (December): 26–39.

Holzer, Harry J., Richard N. Block, Marcus Cheatham, and Jack H. Knott. 1993. "Are Training Subsidies for Firms Effective? The Michigan Experience." *Industrial and Labor Relations Review* 46 (July): 625–36.

Jacobson, Louis S., Robert J. LaLonde, and Daniel G. Sullivan. 1993a. "Earnings Losses of Displaced Workers." *American Economic Review* 83 (September): 685–709.

———. 1993b. *The Costs of Worker Dislocation.* Kalamazoo, Mich.: W.E. Upjohn Institute for Employment Research.

———. 1994. "The Returns from Classroom Training for Displaced Workers." Mimeo. Rockville, Md.: Westat, Inc. September.

Katz, Lawrence F. 1996. "Wage Subsidies for the Disadvantaged." NBER Working Paper No. 5679. Cambridge, Mass.: National Bureau of Economic Research.

Kletzer, Lori G. 1998. "Job Displacement." *Journal of Economic Perspectives* 12 (winter): 115–36.

Kulik, Jane, D. Alton Smith, and Ernst W. Stromsdorfer. 1984. "The Downriver Community Conference Economic Readjustment Program: Final Evaluation Report." Cambridge, Mass.: Abt Associates. May 18.

Leigh, Duane E. 1990. *Does Training Work for Displaced Workers? A Survey of Existing Evidence.* Kalamazoo, Mich.: W.E. Upjohn Institute for Employment Research.

———. 1995. *Assisting Workers Displaced by Structural Change: An International Perspective.* Kalamazoo, Mich.: W.E. Upjohn Institute for Employment Research.

Lin, Winston, Philip K. Robins, David Card, Kristen Harknett, and Susanna Lui-Gurr. 1998. "When Financial Incentives Encourage Work: Complete 18-Month Findings from the Self-Sufficiency Project." Ottawa: Social Research and Demonstration Corporation. September.

Meyer, Bruce D. 1995. "Lessons from the U.S. Unemployment Insurance Experiments." *Journal of Economic Literature* 33 (March): 91–131.

O'Leary, Christopher J., Paul Decker, and Stephen A. Wandner. 1998. "Reemployment Bonuses and Profiling." Staff Working Paper 98-51. Kalamazoo, Mich.: W.E. Upjohn Institute for Employment Research.

Orr, Larry L., Howard S. Bloom, Stephen H. Bell, Fred Doolittle, Winston Lin, and George Cave. 1996. *Does Training for the Disadvantaged Work? Evidence from the National JTPA Study.* Washington, D.C.: Urban Institute Press.

Ross, Murray N., and Ralph E. Smith. 1993. "Displaced Workers: Trends in the 1980s and Implications for the Future." Washington, D.C.: Congressional Budget Office. February.

Stevens, Ann H. 1997. "Persistent Effects of Job Displacement: The Importance of Multiple Job Losses." *Journal of Labor Economics* 15 (January): 165–88.

U.S. Department of Labor. 1986. "Economic Adjustment and Worker Dislocation in a Competitive Society." Washington, D.C.: Secretary of Labor's Task Force on Economic Adjustment and Worker Dislocation. December.

Woodbury, Stephen A., and Robert G. Spiegelman. 1987. "Bonuses to Workers and Employers to Reduce Unemployment: Randomized Trials in Illinois." *American Economic Review* 77 (September): 513–30.

Chapter Nine

METHODOLOGIES FOR DETERMINING THE EFFECTIVENESS OF TRAINING PROGRAMS[1]

Daniel Friedlander, David H. Greenberg, and Philip K. Robins

Other chapters in this volume report findings on the effects of government-sponsored training programs that are obtained from some of the numerous evaluations conducted of those programs. This chapter focuses on the evaluations themselves—specifically, how they are used to measure training program effects and issues associated with measuring those effects.

Training programs may, of course, potentially affect numerous outcomes, including earnings, welfare and unemployment compensation payments, crime rates, feelings of satisfaction, and so forth. For simplicity, we focus in this chapter on measuring training program effects on earnings, although much of what we say also applies to measuring training program effects on other outcomes. We focus on earnings effects because a major objective of all government-sponsored training programs is to increase the earnings of participants. Consequently, virtually all evaluations of training programs attempt to determine earnings effects, but many evaluations do not examine other program effects.

This chapter is intended to serve three major purposes. First, we attempt to provide guidance in interpreting the estimates of earnings effects reported in the other chapters in this book. That is not as straightforward an undertaking as it may first appear. For example, the interpretation depends upon the specific evaluation techniques used to obtain the estimates. As a result, great care must be used in comparing different estimates, even for the same program.

A second objective is to point out some of the limitations of existing estimates of the earnings effects of training programs. Thus, we indicate various biases to which they are subject and suggest the information the evaluations do and do not provide.

Third, we suggest potentially fruitful approaches that might be used in future evaluations to address some of the limitations of previous training program evaluations.

Much of the remainder of this chapter is organized around the different issues that arise in estimating earnings effects of government-sponsored training programs on three successively broader groups. Thus, "Estimating Effects on Participants" focuses on effects on the earnings of persons who receive services from an evaluated training program (that is, program participants). "Estimating Effects on Program-Eligible Target Populations" discusses estimating effects on the earnings of individuals who are eligible for the program (the target population), some of whom actually participate in the program and others of whom may not. "Estimating Effects on Those Outside the Target Population" examines potential effects on the earnings of persons who are outside the target population and, hence, ineligible for the program. A concluding section offers an agenda for future evaluations of government-funded training programs.

Many evaluations of government-sponsored training programs are not limited to estimating program effects on earnings and other outcomes. Many also include a process analysis and a cost-benefit analysis. Process analysis almost always entails reviews of whatever written material on the training program being evaluated exists and often also involves conducting interviews and surveys of program participants and administrators. Sometimes focus group discussions are also held. The goals of process analysis vary, but they can include attempting to learn about the bureaucracy set up to run the program, what sorts of people receive the training, how long they remain in training, what sorts of services they receive, the economic environment they will face when they complete the training, how decisions are made as to what sorts of people receive what sorts of services, and the availability of alternative training programs. That information can be valuable in interpreting estimates of program effects. For example, if a program is found to have little effect, that could result from its not being implemented in the manner intended, from the program's services not actually being received or not being received by those who could benefit most, or from other operational problems. Process analysis often can uncover the existence of such problems.

The objective of cost-benefit analysis is to determine whether the sum of the benefits from an evaluated training program—for example, increases in earnings—exceeds the sum of the program's costs. If it does, this suggests that the program should be continued and, perhaps, expanded. If costs exceed benefits, the program should be modified or, if necessary, discontinued.

An examination of process analysis and cost-benefit analysis is beyond the scope of this chapter. As previously indicated, we focus instead on the analysis of the effects of government training programs on earnings.

ESTIMATING EFFECTS ON PARTICIPANTS

Participant/Nonparticipant Comparisons

The fundamental strategy for estimating the effects of participating in training on earnings (as well as other outcomes) is to compare a sample of persons who receive services from a training program that is being evaluated to a sample of persons who do not. A statistical model that is often used in making the comparison is described in exhibit 9.1.

In practice, the comparison between participants and nonparticipants is made in one of two ways: a nonexperimental approach and an experimental approach. Under certain conditions, which are discussed below, the nonexperimental approach is adequate to yield an unbiased estimate of the effect of participating in training on earnings. When such conditions do not hold, the experimental approach is an alternative.

Exhibit 9.1 A FORMAL MODEL OF THE EFFECTS OF PARTICIPATION IN TRAINING

The following model has often been used to depict the behavior of participants in training programs:

$$Y_{it} = c_t X_i + b_t P_{i0} + u_{it}, t > 0, \tag{9.1a}$$

$$P_{i0} = a_0 Z_i + e_{i0}. \tag{9.1b}$$

In this model,

Y_{it} is the outcome of interest (say, earnings) for the ith person in period t, where $t = 0$ is the period in which the training occurs;

X_i and Z_i are sets of (perhaps overlapping) exogenous factors and personal characteristics for individual i (usually measured before the program begins);[2]

P_{i0} is a binary variable, with zero indicating no participation in training program activities and unity indicating participation;[3] and

u_{it} and e_{i0} are random error terms.

In this formulation, the mean effect of training program participation in period t is b_t, which may vary over time.[4] Equation (9.1b) is sometimes called an index function (Heckman and Robb 1985) or a propensity score (Heckman and Hotz 1989),[5] to denote that the decision to participate in training program activities may be made by a program administrator, a prospective trainee, or both.

Nonexperimental Evaluations

Nonexperimental evaluations usually involve the selection of a comparison group by the evaluator. The comparison group is intended to provide a counterfactual for the program participant group—that is, to indicate what would have happened to the group had it not participated in the program. Comparison groups for estimating training program effects for participants have been variously drawn from among training program applicants who dropped out or were turned away without receiving program services, target group members who did not apply for training program services, individuals outside the geographic area covered by the program, and nonparticipants drawn from national microdata sets. Training program participants also have served as their own comparison group in periods prior to participating; that is, their pre- and postprogram earnings are compared.[6]

In a nonexperimental evaluation, an estimate of the effect of training on earnings for a typical participant can be obtained by subtracting the average earnings of members of the comparison group from the average earnings of members of the participant group during some postprogram period. However, the estimate will be unbiased only if the decision to participate in training is unrelated to earnings potential. As will be explained below, if it is not, then all or part of the difference in earnings between the two groups may be due not to the effect of training, but instead to other factors. Unfortunately, in practice, participation is likely to be related to earnings potential. That relation takes the form of "selection on observables" or "selection on unobservables." The formal definition of those two possible sources of bias is given in exhibit 9.2. An explanation of the two types of biases appears in the following paragraphs.

What selection on observables generally means in practice is that program administrators are admitting applicants into a program on the basis of a set of known characteristics.[7] For example, persons might be admitted into a program if they have dropped out of high school, if they are unemployed, or if they satisfy a ranking based on

---

Exhibit 9.2 THE SOURCES OF BIASES IN NONEXPERIMENTAL EVALUATIONS

Returning to the model shown in exhibit 9.1, if $E(P_{j0}u_{it}) = 0$ in a nonexperimental evaluation, then an unbiased estimate of b_t can be obtained by regressing Y_{it} on X_i and P_{i0}. Unfortunately, there is no guarantee that this condition will hold in practice. Correlation between P_{i0} and u_{it} can arise in two ways, through Z_i or through e_{it}. If $E(Z_iu_{it}) \neq 0$, but $E(u_{it}e_{it}) = 0$, there is selection on observables (Heckman and Hotz 1989; Heckman and Robb 1985). If $E(Z_iu_{it}) = 0$, but $E(u_{it}e_{it}) \neq 0$, there is selection on unobservables.

a set of observable characteristics. Barnow, Cain, and Goldberger (1980) prove that when there is selection *only* on observables, and certain other conditions hold,[8] unbiased estimates of the effects of the program on earnings can be obtained by including the factors that are being used to select persons for a program as control variables in a regression equation. By doing that, evaluators can statistically control for differences between observables that cause the postprogram earnings of members of the program participant group and members of the comparison group to differ and, hence, isolate the effect of participating in the program on earnings.

Unfortunately, isolating the effect of participating in the program on earnings is much more difficult if there is also selection on unobservables. That can occur when individuals are prompted to participate in program activities by some underlying factor, such as motivation, that is difficult to measure. Selection on unobservables can also occur if program administrators use subjective or objective criteria to select program participants, and their ratings of individuals are not recorded.[9] This is a much more serious problem than selection on observables because solutions require strong (largely untestable) behavioral assumptions, complex nonlinear statistical estimation models, or difficult-to-obtain data.

Addressing the Problem of Selection on Observables

Early nonexperimental evaluations of voluntary training programs implicitly assumed that selection into the program was based only on observables (see Cain 1975; Goldberger 1972 for discussions). One approach taken in several early nonexperimental studies was to use an "internal" comparison group (for example, nonparticipating training program applicants) to draw inferences about the effects of a program (Borus 1964; Cain 1968; Cooley, McGuire, and Prescott 1979; Stromsdorfer 1968). It was thought that internal comparison groups were appropriate because those individuals possessed many of the same characteristics as participants.

The use of internal comparison groups never achieved great popularity because it was quickly recognized that nonparticipants are likely to be quite different from participants by virtue of the fact that they have chosen not to participate or have been excluded by program staff. Recently, Bell et al. (1995) proposed using a variant of that method, based on a statistical approach called the "regression discontinuity" model, to evaluate a training program for welfare recipients.[10] They argue that "screened out" applicants—those excluded because of decisions made by an intake staff—by definition differ from participants only on factors (both objective and subjective) observable to staff. Their regression discontinuity approach attempts to control fully for these differences using intake workers' ratings of applicant potential.

Whether the Bell et al. study will stimulate more nonexperimental evaluations using internal comparison groups remains to be seen. One alternative that has proven popular for a number of years uses "external" comparison groups, consisting of a sample of individuals whose observed characteristics resemble those of program participants, but who are drawn from a different source (often a national database, such as the Current Population Survey or the Panel Study of Income Dynamics, or special samples from geographic areas that have not implemented the program). The use of external comparison groups became prevalent in evaluating the effects of national training programs, such as the Manpower Development and Training Act (MDTA) and the Comprehensive Employment and Training Act (CETA),[11] in the 1970s and 1980s (Ashenfelter 1978; Barnow 1987), and is still under way in the 1990s (Dehejia and Wahba 1995; Heckman, Smith, and Taber 1998; Long and Wissoker 1995).[12]

The use of external comparison groups sometimes involves searching for a group of individuals who can be matched statistically to members of the program group. One procedure, known as "cell matching," was used by Bryant and Rupp (1987), among others, to evaluate the CETA program. Under that procedure, subgroups of individuals are created based on certain observed characteristics (such as age, education, and race) and are then matched to other individuals with the same characteristics. Another procedure, known as "distance function matching," matches individuals based on a weighted function of observed characteristics. The first application of distance function matching in the training program evaluation literature was by Dickinson, Johnson, and West (1986, 1987) in their evaluation of the CETA program.

Recently, Dehejia and Wahba (1995) and Heckman, Ichimura, and Todd (1997) have proposed a variant of statistical matching. Based on the methodology developed by Rosenbaum and Rubin (1983), they use the "propensity score" as the matching variable. The propensity score summarizes the information in a set of observable variables into a single index function. Program group and comparison group observations with similar propensity scores (similar predictions of being in the program group) are considered good matches for one another.[13] Dehejia and Wahba (1995) argue that the propensity score method can serve as a good approximation to a wide variety of linear and nonlinear econometric response functions when there is selection on observables.

Statistical matching is to be distinguished from econometric matching. Econometric matching denotes the standard behavioral modeling techniques and specification tests that use observed characteristics as control variables in regression models, without necessarily restricting the composition of the estimation sample through the use of matching. As noted by Friedlander and Robins (1995), statistical matching and econometric matching with the same data set can produce very similar estimates of program effects on earnings. Essentially, both methods adjust estimates of program effects for the influence of a given set of observables. Thus, they differ only in the way they specify the functional relationship between the observed characteristics and postprogram earnings.

ADDRESSING THE PROBLEM OF SELECTION ON UNOBSERVABLES

A number of early training program evaluation studies proposed methods for dealing with selection on unobservables. All of them rely on strong assumptions and somewhat complex statistical and econometric procedures. Three approaches are summarized briefly in exhibit 9.3.

One of the first and best-known attempts to deal with selection on unobservables was made by Ashenfelter (1978). Ashenfelter attempted to use earnings differences between the program participant group and the comparison group during the period before the participants entered training to control for unobservable differences between the two groups (see exhibit 9.3). One of his more important results was that training effects tend to decay or diminish over time. This finding stimulated a number of other papers, including a lively exchange between Bloom (1984) and Bassi (1987). Bloom argued that Ashenfelter failed to correct for a time-varying bias in his fixed-effect model and that when such a correction is made the estimated effects of training do not decay over time. Bassi countered that Bloom's estimates were no more credible than Ashenfelter's because they, like Ashenfelter's, were based on a set of strong assumptions about the nature of the selection on unobservables. Debates about nonexperimental evaluations such as these rarely produce a winner because there is no clear-cut way of determining whose assumptions are valid.

Experimental Evaluations

Because procedures such as those described in exhibit 9.3 are at best only partially successful in controlling for the effect of unobservables

Exhibit 9.3 METHODS FOR TREATING UNOBSERVABLES

All approaches to dealing with unobservables make certain assumptions about the nature of the dependence between u_{it} and P_{io} (or u_{it} and e_{io}).

Ashenfelter (1978) hypothesized an autoregressive model of the earnings generation process based on a simple model of human capital investment. In Ashenfelter's model, preprogram earnings histories play a crucial role in estimation.[14] The key assumption in Ashenfelter's model is that earnings contains an unobserved fixed effect that can be accounted for in estimation by making appropriate transformations of the earnings outcome data.[15]

An alternative to the fixed-effect model for addressing selection on unobservables is instrumental variables (Angrist, Imbens, and Rubin 1996; Heckman and Robb 1985). In effect, equation (9.1b) is estimated and is used to construct an instrument for P_{io} that is uncorrelated with u_{it}. Although the use of instrumental variables has sometimes proved successful, it has not been popular because of difficulties in finding an appropriate instrument—that is, a variable that influences P_{io} but not Y_{it}.[16] In addition, as discussed by Heckman (1997), the instrumental variable method has important limitations when the program effect varies across people (so-called random-coefficient models).

Another method, proposed by Barnow, Cain, and Goldberger (1980) and based on the procedure developed by Heckman (1978) to deal with censored samples, relies on the assumption that u_{it} and e_{io} are jointly normally distributed. As in the case of instrumental variables, equation (9.1b) is estimated, in this instance, using a probit model. An appropriate Mills ratio adjustment term is then constructed as a weighted average of predicted P_{io} and $1 - P_{io}$ and is included as an additional variable in equation (9.1a), which is then estimated using conventional regression techniques. The two-step method avoids the need for an instrument by relying on the functional form of (9.1b) for identification but suffers from low reliability associated with specification uncertainty.

---

on decisions to participate in training programs, use of those procedures tends to produce statistically imprecise estimates of the effect of training. In addition, a number of studies (Ashenfelter and Card 1985; Bassi 1983; Fraker and Maynard 1987; Friedlander and Robins 1995; LaLonde 1986; LaLonde and Maynard 1987) find that different nonexperimental procedures typically produce very different estimates of program effects. Moreover, the nonexperimental estimates are often different from experimentally based estimates from the same data set.[17] Recognition of this sensitivity made experimental evaluations of training programs more popular in the 1980s and 1990s.[18]

In contrast to nonexperimental evaluations, experimental evaluations are based on random assignment of individuals into a treatment (or "program") group and a control group. Because of randomization, the program and the control group will be very similar in both observables and unobservables.[19] Therefore, an unbiased estimate of the effect of training on earnings can be obtained by simply taking the difference between mean earnings of the program and control groups.[20]

In an ideal experiment, only members of the program group participate in program activities and their participation rate is 100 percent. As will be discussed later, this ideal experiment is never fully realized in actual evaluations because not all members of the program group participate in training, and some members of the control group seek out and engage in training similar to that provided by the program being evaluated.

Moreover, even an "ideal" experiment has inherent limitations. Although it provides an unbiased estimate of the program effect on the earnings of the average participant, it cannot provide unbiased estimates of the distribution of program effects across participants. Thus, an experiment cannot estimate the percentage of participants whose earnings actually increase from a training program (Clements, Heckman, and Smith 1994; Manski 1995). As Heckman and Smith (1995) point out, experimental estimates of the "average effect per sample member" cannot distinguish between two possibilities: (a) most people gained about the average, and (b) a few people gained much but most gained nothing or perhaps even lost. In addition, experimental data provide only limited information about effects on the components of earnings. For example, they can provide unbiased estimates of the effects of training programs on employment status (employed versus not employed), but not on effects that are conditional on employment status, such as the effects of training on rates of entry into or exit from employment (Card and Sullivan 1988; Ham and LaLonde 1990, 1996; Heckman and Smith 1995) or on hourly wage rates or weekly work hours. All these limitations, however, apply equally to the commonly used nonexperimental techniques. Thus, because the experimental approach solves the fundamental problem of selection on unobservables in estimating mean effects of training, many analysts now see it as the more attractive method of program evaluation.

Given the comparative attractiveness of experiments, it may seem surprising that nonexperimental evaluations of training programs continue to be conducted. One reason, discussed below, is that experimental evaluations may be inappropriate if a program is expected to have large community or macro effects, or large entry effects. In addition, experiments incur costs for implementing and monitoring randomization. These additional research costs, which are often rather modest, must be weighed against the costs of the misallocation of social resources from decisions based on less-reliable nonexperimental designs.

Finally, a nonexperimental evaluation may, in some cases, produce results faster than an experiment. For evaluations of ongoing training programs, data on earnings often can be obtained retrospectively. Data collection and statistical analysis therefore can be completed relatively quickly following the start of the evaluation, as long as researchers are interested only in a program as it operated in the immediate past. Experimental evaluations typically take much longer to complete, as the period of evaluation must include up to a year or more of sample intake during random assignment and a two- to five-year follow-up period plus the time required for data collection and analysis.

On the other hand, experimental evaluations of new training programs are not necessarily more time-consuming than nonexperimental evaluations if the evaluation is initiated as soon as the program begins. As Orr et al. (1996) suggest, even with an ongoing program, much of the relatively higher cost and lack of timeliness of an experimental evaluation can be overcome if a fraction of program applicants are randomly assigned to a control group on a continuing basis.

The Problem of External Validity

A critical issue in the evaluation of training programs is external validity. External validity refers to the extent to which estimated program effects can be generalized to different locations and populations, to different time periods, and to different variants of the program being studied. The external validity of specific estimates of program effects may be questioned for a number of reasons. Most of these have been offered recently as criticisms of experimental evaluations (Heckman and Smith 1995), but nearly all apply to nonexperimental evaluations as well.

First and most obviously, social attitudes, government institutions, the business cycle, the relative demand for unskilled and skilled labor, and other relevant factors may change in the years following an evaluation. Likewise, different locations may have dissimilar trainee characteristics, social attitudes, state and local government institutions, labor market conditions, and so forth.

Second, training program evaluations are often performed at a small number of sites that are rarely selected randomly, a situation that raises questions about how well they represent administrative capacity and other unobservables for the universe of sites (see Heckman 1992; Heckman and Smith 1995; Hotz 1992). Difficulties in

obtaining a representative sample of program sites are especially acute when the cooperation of local administrators is essential and the administrators cannot be compelled to participate in the evaluation. It has been argued, for example, that the sites participating in the recently completed national evaluation of the Job Training Partnership Act (JTPA) program,[21] which until recently was the major national training program, were not representative of all JTPA sites because many of the sites that were asked to participate in the experiment refused (Heckman and Smith 1995).[22] The evaluators (Orr et al. 1996) argue that the participating sites are representative, judging by observable characteristics. An important area of future research is to determine the degree to which site selectivity translates into bias in generalizing the estimated effects to other sites.

Third, external validity may be compromised by scale bias that may result when training program innovations are tested as small demonstrations or pilot programs, which is often the case. Garfinkel, Manski, and Michalopoulos (1992) and Manski and Garfinkel (1992) suggest that scaling up to universal participation could change community norms or combine with patterns of social interaction or affect information diffusion in ways that will feed back and influence the success of the policy innovation. Such community or macro effects, they argue, will be absent in small-scale pilot programs or partially scaled programs.[23] In addition, testing a program on a small scale may cause the composition of the program participants to differ from what it would be in an ongoing training program by inhibiting diffusion of information about the program to potential applicants; by limiting the number of program slots and thereby encouraging program administrators to restrict participation to higher-quality applicants; or, in an experiment, by discouraging risk-averse individuals from applying to a program when they could be randomly assigned to a no-services control group (see Heckman 1992; Heckman and Smith 1995; Manski 1993, 1995).[24]

At present, little is known about the practical importance of community effects, although in principle their presence could greatly multiply, or seriously impede, the effectiveness of government training programs. An important area for future theoretical and empirical research may lie in adapting methods from sociology, urban anthropology, ethnography, and community psychology to study the community effects of large-scale, permanent training programs.[25] Similarly, although the possibility of bias caused by distortion of the participant sample in small-scale selective voluntary programs has strong theoretical appeal, its empirical importance has yet to be demonstrated.[26]

One nonexperimental approach for avoiding biases caused by testing policy innovations on a small scale is to implement them on a sitewide, fully scaled basis in some locations and, for comparison, use other sites (perhaps statistically matched) that have not adopted the innovation. Although this saturation evaluation design does, in principle, allow feedback effects to be captured, the program may have to be kept in place for many years, with firm guarantees of permanence, before the effects reach full potency. Moreover, cross-site comparison designs will produce unreliable estimates of program effects if the program and comparison sites differ in ways that are inadequately controlled for in the evaluation (see Friedlander and Robins 1995; Hollister and Hill 1995). Indeed, even if sites are randomly assigned to program and control status, there may simply be too few of them to achieve statistical precision or to ensure that the two groups of sites do not differ in some unobserved way.

Fourth, it is often the case that some members of comparison groups receive services similar to those that the program group members receive. The possibility of substituting training program activities for similar activities provided elsewhere first gained empirical attention in the evaluations of WIN in the 1980s, when it was found that participation in education and training activities by a randomly assigned program group also took place among members of the comparison group (Hamilton and Friedlander 1989; Riccio et al. 1986). It was confirmed in several later evaluations, notably in the JTPA evaluation (Heckman and Smith 1995; Orr et al. 1996). Some comparison group members engaged in those activities through adult schools, community colleges, or other local institutions, and they did so without special program assistance. Moreover, to provide education and training, government-sponsored training programs often send their enrollees to the same local institutions, where they attend classes side by side with individuals who are in the target population but who are not enrolled in the government training program being studied.

Under such circumstances, simply comparing the earnings of participants in a program being evaluated with a comparison group of persons not participating in that program does not measure the pure effect of participating in training versus not participating in training. Rather, it measures the *incremental* effect of the additional receipt of training services stimulated by the program being evaluated. Although this measure is clearly policy-relevant, in interpreting results from training program evaluations, it is critical to keep firmly in mind what the findings really measure.

In addition, the fact that comparison group members, as well as program group members, engage in training is a source of at least two threats to external validity. First, not only will the evaluated program differ over time or from one place to another, but the array of activities available to comparison group members also will differ, complicating the problem of generalizing the evaluation results. Second, the very existence of the program being evaluated may change the number of training opportunities available to the comparison group. This second threat to external validity, which Heckman and Smith (1995) call "substitution bias," could occur if, by absorbing some persons who desire training, the evaluated program frees more nonprogram training slots for others who want training. Or, if the evaluated program is large enough, it may induce state and local governments to refrain from funding training activities they would normally provide in the absence of the program.

ESTIMATING EFFECTS ON PROGRAM-ELIGIBLE TARGET POPULATIONS

The Distinction between Voluntary and Mandatory

Estimates of training program effects often pertain to the entire program-eligible target population, rather than just to those who actively participate in the program. This is important because training programs almost always target more people, often many more, than actually participate. The interpretation of estimates of the effects of a training program on its target population depends importantly on whether the program is voluntary or mandatory. As will be explained, the distinction is important because it is reasonable to assume that members of a target population who did not participate, whom we refer to as "nonparticipants," were unaffected by the program if it was voluntary, but may well have been affected if it was mandatory.

Voluntary programs provide training for individuals who apply for them and meet certain criteria of need, such as having income below a certain level, lacking a high school diploma, or being permanently laid off. One example of a voluntary training program is JTPA.

Mandatory training programs, on the other hand, are directed at public assistance and unemployment compensation recipients. The most prominent current examples of mandatory training programs are the so-called welfare-to-work programs operated by state and county welfare authorities and directed at recipients of Temporary Assistance for Needy Families (TANF).[27] A training program's mandatory nature stems from its statutory authority to penalize or sanction recipients who do not cooperate by reducing (or in some cases terminating) their transfer payments.

Not all policy analysts consider the distinction between voluntary and mandatory training programs meaningful. Most of the program activities in the two kinds of programs are similar and the institutions providing the training can be the same. Local program administrators often downplay enforcement in mandatory programs, making participation seem voluntary. Additionally, the voluntary and mandatory target populations partially overlap: for example, a significant proportion of JTPA participants are public assistance recipients, and some of them are there to satisfy their training program participation obligation.

Nonetheless, despite the similarities, we believe the differences are sufficient to warrant separate treatment in discussing the effects of training programs on the eligible target population. For one, the evidence suggests that pressure to participate or to work has been increasing in recent years for enrollees in mandatory programs in many states. In addition, as previously suggested, only mandatory programs may have effects on the earnings of nonparticipants. If they do have such effects, it is because some nonparticipants are prompted to find a job to avoid what may be perceived as an onerous participation requirement. As discussed later, the possibility of program effects on nonparticipants imposes restrictions on the ways results from evaluations of mandatory programs can be interpreted.

Program Effects on the Target Population in Voluntary Programs

We mentioned earlier that often in evaluations of training programs some members of comparison groups receive services similar to those the program group members receive. Under these circumstances, the evaluated program is more accurately viewed as not providing training, but rather making an offer of training to members of the program target population. The offer consists of a bundle of services to facilitate participation in certain activities and incentives to individuals to participate in those activities. One of the services offered might be either the actual training or referral and access to training provided elsewhere in the community. Some training activities, such as remedial reading and math courses, may be virtually identical for training participants whether they are enrolled in the government training program being evaluated or in some other program. Other activities—for example, subsidized employment—will be available only to enrollees in the evaluated program. The prospective program enrollee considers whether to accept that offer, a competing offer, or none at all.

Comparisons of the postprogram earnings of those who accept the offer with the earnings of a comparison group introduce a profound conceptual issue in interpreting findings from evaluations of voluntary programs if some members of the comparison group participate in training activities similar to or identical with those received by the other acceptors. As indicated earlier, estimates of program effects based on such an approach do not measure the pure effect of training on participants.

Exhibit 9.4 modifies the model described in exhibit 9.1 to allow for the availability of training opportunities outside a voluntary training program being evaluated. The key implication of the modified model is that a voluntary training program has two different potential effects on earnings. First, persons who enroll in the program may increase their earnings as a result of the services they receive (although they might also have increased their earnings if they had received similar services through other channels). Second, the program may increase the number of members of the target population that participate in training.

An evaluated program's total effect on the target population depends on the size of each of the two factors. Thus, a training program with a large effect on the earnings of those who enroll could yield a small total program effect. That would occur, for example, if the program results in little effect on the amount of training received by members of the program target population because the enrollees would have received similar training elsewhere if the program did not exist and, consequently, enjoyed a similar increase in earnings.

Conversely, even if the program has only a modest effect on the earnings of those who enroll, it may have a substantial total effect if the program causes large numbers of additional persons in the target population to participate in training. Thus, a voluntary training program's overall effectiveness can depend critically on whether more members of the target population participate in training than would otherwise be the case.

Consequently, a full assessment of the effects of the evaluated training program requires not only an estimate of the effects of training on those enrolled in the program but also an understanding of the effects of the evaluated program on overall participation in training by

Exhibit 9.4 A MODEL OF THE EFFECT OF A TRAINING PROGRAM WHEN
TRAINING IS ALSO AVAILABLE OUTSIDE THE PROGRAM

We begin by positing that an individual, i, in the population eligible for an evaluated training program faces a number of opportunities for training, of which the program is one. Therefore, unlike the model in exhibit 9.1, participation, P_{io}, cannot be defined as unique to the program in question. Instead, P_{io} must be redefined to represent participation in any training activities similar to those offered by the evaluated program. A training participant is defined as a person engaged in one of these activities, whether enrolled in the training program being evaluated (an enrollee) or acting outside the program on his or her own initiative. The distinction between *program enrollee* and *training participant* is important and is maintained throughout the rest of this chapter.

For simplicity, we assume that P_{io} is a scalar representation of a single training activity and that there is no difference in the efficiency of similar activities obtained by enrolling in the evaluated program and obtained in other ways. We can then rewrite Model 1 as Model 2 by adding a term to the second equation:

$$Y_{it} = c_t X_i + b_t P_{io} + u_{it}, \tag{9.2a}$$

$$P_{io} = a_0 Z_i + g_0 T_i + e_{io}. \tag{9.2b}$$

In this model, T_i is a binary scalar that takes on the value of unity if the program offer of training is in effect for individual i (and, hence, the individual is a member of the program group) and zero if the offer is not in effect (and, hence, the individual is a member of the comparison group). Thus, g_0 will measure the program's incremental effect on participation—that is, the change in training participation induced by the program. Under this formulation, b_t retains its original meaning as the measure of the effect of training on participants. In this case, however, b_t applies both to those who receive training as enrollees in the evaluated program and those who receive it by other means.[28]

By substituting for P_{io} from equation (9.2b), equation (9.2a) can be rewritten as

$$Y_{it} = c_t X_i + (b_t a_0) Z_i + (b_t g_0) T_i + b_t e_{io} + u_{it}. \tag{9.2a'}$$

Thus, the total effect of the evaluated program on the average earnings of members of the program group (that is, the program target population) is $b_t g_0$, which is the product of the program's effect on the earnings of participants (b_t) and the incremental effect of the evaluated program on participation (g_0).

Hence, whenever participation in a training program mostly duplicates participation that would have occurred anyway, g_0 will be close to zero and the total effect of the program on earnings will be small, even if b_t is large and the training is, therefore, effective. On the other hand, a modest effect per participant may lead to a large total effect if a large increase in participation can be attributed to the evaluated program.

members of the target population. Together, the effects of training on those enrolled and the program effect on participation in training yield the overall effect on the program-eligible target population.

We have previously indicated that early evaluations of government-sponsored training programs usually relied upon a participant/nonparticipant design, whereas more recent evaluations have

relied upon comparison group designs, especially randomized experiments, and on comparison area designs. The two types of designs
are different, and these differences have important implications for
how evaluation findings that are based on them can be interpreted.
All members of a participant/nonparticipant design program group
actually receive training, while members of the nonparticipant group
with whom they are compared receive little or no training. On the
other hand, with a comparison group (or comparison area) design,
not all members of the program group necessarily participate in
training, while at least some members of the comparison group
receive training similar to that offered by the evaluated program.
Consequently, as we more rigorously demonstrate in exhibit 9.5, a
participant/nonparticipant design generally should yield larger estimates of program effects on earnings than a comparison group (or
comparison area) design. Moreover, as also discussed in exhibit 9.5,
when an evaluation of a voluntary training program indicates that
the program increases earnings, a comparison group design often can
provide information on whether that occurs primarily because of

Exhibit 9.5 NONCOMPARABILITY OF EVALUATION DESIGNS

The model developed in exhibit 9.4 implies that there is a fundamental noncomparability between estimated program effects that come from participant/nonparticipant
designs on one hand and from comparison group designs and comparison area designs
on the other. A participant/nonparticipant design estimates b_t in equation (9.2a) by
comparing outcomes for training participants and nonparticipants, in exactly the same
fashion as in equation (9.1a). In contrast, under comparison group designs, a program
group represents condition $T_i = 1$, and a comparison group (or comparison area sample) represents condition $T_i = 0$ in equation (9.2a'). Not all members of the program
group are participants and not all members of the comparison group are nonparticipants. The coefficient of T_i is $b_t g_0$, which represents the effect of the program on the
entire target population, not b_t. It is therefore invalid to compare the magnitude of estimated effects from the earlier participant/nonparticipant designs with those from the
later experimental designs and with other comparison group or area designs. Because
g_0 is less than unity, participant/nonparticipant designs will yield more positive estimated effects for a given program or for programs with similar activities, even when
selection bias has been corrected. The statistical significance of estimates from the two
kinds of designs may also not be comparable if g_0 is small. Only the signs should be the
same (as long as g_0 is positive).

Participant/nonparticipant designs cannot provide estimates of the program effect on
the amount of training activity, g_0. Under comparison group or area designs, g_0 can be
found by estimating equation (9.2b); that is, g_0 is the coefficient of T_i in a regression
of P_{i0} on T_i and Z_i. Current evaluation practice under such designs is to report program and comparison group levels of participation in the various activities offered by
the training program. With this information, it is often possible to determine whether
a weak total effect results from a limited program effect on participation in training
(g_0 near 0) or from a small effect of the training itself (g_0 substantially greater than 0).

the evaluated program increasing participation in training or because of the contribution of the training itself. A participant/nonparticipant design, in contrast, cannot provide information of this sort.

Program Effects on the Target Population in Mandatory Programs

Analytically, the most important aspect of mandatoriness in a training program is the possibility of program effects on the earnings of enrollees who do not actually participate in formal program activities. Such effects may be produced if individuals leave welfare and find employment to avoid pressure from program staff to comply with a time-consuming participation requirement. Alternatively, mandatory welfare-to-work programs generally permit enrollees to engage in part-time employment while they remain on welfare as a substitute for participation in a training program activity. Indeed, employment that is a substitute for participation in training may occur as often as program participation itself in some programs, especially in states where welfare grant levels are high enough to permit substantial concurrent mixing of work and welfare (see, e.g., Hamilton 1988, p. xviii). Working in lieu of participating in training under a mandatory program is often referred to as the program's "deterrent effect." In exhibit 9.6, we modify the model developed in exhibit 9.4 to allow for the possibility that the earnings of enrollees in mandatory training programs are influenced by a deterrent effect.

As suggested by exhibit 9.6, the total effect of a mandatory program on the earnings of those enrolled can potentially result from three separate effects. First, those program enrollees who receive training may enjoy increased earnings as a result. Second, the program may increase the number of persons who receive training, especially as a result of the mandatoriness of the program. Third, the earnings of those program enrollees who do not actually receive training may nonetheless increase as a result of the deterrent effect. As previously discussed, the first two effects may also result from voluntary training programs. The deterrent effect is unique to mandatory programs, however.

Consequently, as demonstrated more formally in exhibit 9.6, the estimated effects of mandatory and voluntary programs on earnings cannot be directly compared with one another. Further, as also indicated in exhibit 9.6, if a mandatory program is found to increase the earnings of enrollees, it is not possible to sort out the relative contributions of the three effects listed in the previous paragraph. Indeed, it is not usually possible even to determine whether a deterrent effect exists.

Exhibit 9.6　A MODEL OF THE DETERRENT EFFECT

To incorporate the possibility that a deterrent effect from mandatory programs influences earnings, equation system (9.2) is modified by adding an additional term to the first equation:

$$Y_{it} = c_t X_i + b_t P_{i0} + h_t T_i (1 - P_{i0}) + u_{it}, \tag{9.3a}$$

$$P_{i0} = a_0 Z_i + g_0 T_i + e_{i0}. \tag{9.3b}$$

Again, the dummy variable T_i indicates whether the program offer—or, in the mandatory case, the program requirement—is or is not in effect for individual i. The new coefficient, h_t, is the program effect on nonparticipants who are covered by the participation requirement.

As with equation system (9.2), estimating the full effect of the program in system (9.3) requires an evaluation sample that includes some individuals for whom $T_i = 1$, the program group, and others for whom $T_i = 0$, the comparison group. As before, both program and comparison groups will have participants and nonparticipants in training activities, although it is naturally assumed that with a mandatory program participation will be greater when $T_i = 1$.

The total effect of the program on individuals subject to program participation requirements can be found by substituting (9.3b) into (9.3a), evaluating Y_{it} at $T_i = 1$ and $T_i = 0$, and taking the difference (noting that $T_i \times T_i = T_i$ for the dummy variable). Hence, the total effect is

$$b_t g_0 + h_t [1 - P_{i0}(T_i = 1)], \tag{9.3c}$$

where $P_{i0}(T_i = 1)$ represents $a_0 Z_i + g_0$, the probability of participation when $T_i = 1$. An estimate of the entire expression (9.3c) can be obtained as the coefficient of T_i in a regression of Y_{it} on T_i and control variables. The first term in this expression, $b_t g_0$, is the same as the coefficient on T_i in equation (9.2a'). The new term is the program's effect on nonparticipants, h_t, multiplied by the probability of nonparticipation, $1 - P_{i0}(T_i = 1)$, among those covered by the participation requirement.

Although the entire expression (9.3c) may be estimated, unique estimates of b_t and h_t cannot be recovered, even if g_0 and $1 - P_{i0}(T_i = 1)$ have been estimated from equation (9.3b). Thus, in contrast to voluntary programs, comparison area and comparison group (including random assignment) designs for mandatory programs typically cannot provide valid estimates of the effect on earnings of participating in activities, b_t. Consequently, estimates of participation effects do not generally appear in mandatory program evaluation studies. Nor is dividing published estimates of program effects by the program participation rate a valid option, as it is for voluntary program evaluations. Direct comparisons of the estimated effects of voluntary and mandatory programs, therefore, cannot be made, even when experiments are used to evaluate both. Valid comparisons, however, can be made using estimated internal rates of return.[29]

ESTIMATING EFFECTS ON THOSE
OUTSIDE THE TARGET POPULATION

Government-funded training programs may have important effects on the earnings of some persons not eligible for a program. Two such effects, which are almost never taken into account in training program evaluations, are entry effects and displacement effects. Empirical evidence about the magnitude of both effects is limited. Our assessment of the theoretical arguments is that the importance of entry effects is somewhat speculative, whereas displacement could substantially offset the effects of training programs on the earnings of those who do enroll.

Entry and Deterrent Effects

If training program services are perceived as beneficial, then some persons who initially are not eligible to enroll may leave their jobs and reduce their earnings to qualify (an entry effect).[30] On the other hand, in mandatory programs for welfare recipients, some individuals who might otherwise have entered the welfare rolls may decide not to do so to avoid the hassle of having to participate in training (a deterrent effect).[31] As a result, the earnings of those persons may increase. Manski and Garfinkel (1992) and Moffitt (1992, 1996), among others, argue that program entry or deterrent effects could be substantial. However, the empirical evidence concerning these effects is inconsistent and inconclusive (see Friedlander, Greenberg, and Robins 1997).

Displacement Effects

Training program graduates may end up in jobs that otherwise would have been held by individuals not in the program (Johnson 1979). If those displaced individuals become unemployed or accept lower-wage jobs, their earnings will fall.

Although virtually no research quantifies the magnitude of displacement caused by training programs for the economically disadvantaged,[32] several theoretical arguments have been put forward to suggest that displacement may not seriously undermine training program effectiveness. First, it has been suggested that macroeconomic policy may be able to expand employment enough to provide jobs for those who otherwise would be displaced. Second, as Cohen (1969) and Johnson (1979) point out, if training program participants are less likely to seek employment while they are in training than they otherwise would have been, then more jobs will be open to nonparticipants, at least temporarily. Third, as emphasized by Johnson (1979) and Katz (1994), if training programs can impart skills that allow trainees to leave slack occupational labor markets for tight ones, then they can decrease the competition for job vacancies in the slack markets, thereby making it easier for those who remain in those markets to find jobs. Such a possibility could produce a result that is the opposite of a displacement effect: total employment could increase by more than the number of persons who are trained.

AN AGENDA FOR FUTURE
TRAINING PROGRAM EVALUATIONS

The methods described in this chapter have been applied to evaluations aimed at estimating the effects of training programs on summary estimates of program effectiveness, such as mean earnings. Future evaluations of this sort will continue to be necessary to monitor program performance. They will be especially important for training programs run under the Workforce Investment Act (WIA), which has recently replaced the Jobs Training Partnership Act as the major source of national funding for training programs. The WIA increases the localization of training services and will probably lead to greater program diversity across the country. Given the changes under the WIA, it is important to monitor programs it funds.

The recently completed National JTPA study was designed in a way that does not provide a very appropriate mechanism for doing this. It had difficulties in obtaining site cooperation, took more than six years to complete, and did not provide timely information to policymakers. Orr et al. (1996) suggest an alternative random-assignment evaluation design that may be particularly appropriate under the WIA funding structure in providing feedback on a timely basis. As they indicate, one problem with the JTPA design was considerable local opposition to creating a control group by denying services to some program applicants. Instead, they recommend a design in which only a few individuals at each site are randomly assigned to a control group and, thus, denied services. Such an evaluation would take place in a large number of sites, but on a rotating basis. Sites would be required to participate. This type of design would ensure a representative sample of program models and would permit frequent appraisals of program performance at the national and local levels.

While traditional black box evaluations of the sort described in this chapter will always remain useful for monitoring purposes, we are nearing the limit on what can be learned from such evaluations. Hence, we recommend that evaluation resources focus more on improving training *technique*. Closer study of training program technique means looking at approaches to training that are associated with success or failure, given the level of funding—for example, ways of increasing program participation without decreasing average earnings gains and ways of organizing skills-building activities to get the most out of them.

To do this, future evaluation designs should make greater use of direct comparisons of competing candidates for best program practice. One method for testing the effectiveness of alternative service strategies was used in the JTPA evaluation, which estimated earnings effects separately for three clusters of activities by randomizing sample members after program intake staff had recommended them for specific services. Another method, employed in some Job Opportunities and Basic Skills (JOBS) evaluation sites, was to randomly assign all program enrollees, regardless of program staff preferences, to either a rapid employment program approach or an approach that aimed for long-term skill development. Finally, some theoretical work has been undertaken to develop feasible designs for comparing program approaches across randomly assigned local offices (Greenberg, Meyer, and Wiseman 1993). None of these research designs is free of conceptual difficulties, however. The designs also present serious practical challenges, not the least of which is simply maintaining the distinctiveness of the competing service strategies and ensuring high participation rates in the activities of interest.

Under any of the designs, training techniques demonstrated to be highly effective in the study sites can be replicated and evaluated at additional sites to determine whether the original favorable results are generalizable. Some efforts along those lines are currently taking place, such as the replication and evaluation in Los Angeles (Freedman, Mitchell, and Navarro 1999) of a successful welfare-to-work program tested earlier in Riverside, California (Riccio et al. 1994) and a multisite replication and evaluation of the San Jose program that produced earnings gains for youth.

Further work in integrating experimental and nonexperimental methods is needed. Nonexperimental methods could be an important adjunct to random assignment in determining the path through which training programs influence earnings, such as through changes in educational attainment. They could also be important for increasing our understanding of the determinants and consequences of population participation rates and of substitution of activities across government and nongovernment providers, across periods of an individual's life cycle, and across episodes of nonemployment and employment.

Studying training technique requires additional and more detailed data than have been collected in most previous evaluations. To assess intensive skills-development activities, the focus must shift from short- to long-term earnings effects. As a partial substitute for long-term results, however, greater attention could be paid to measuring program effects on hourly wage rates and other terms of employment, including prospects for future on-the-job training and wage growth, which, in theory, should be improved by skills upgrading. More detailed description will be required of the nature of the training activities and the behavior of participants who engage in them, both to document that the prescribed training was received and to serve as a basis for replicating approaches that prove successful. Special consideration must be paid to measuring the extent to which services provided by the program being evaluated are substituted for training services available elsewhere in the same locality. Efforts must be directed toward determining whether trainees have actually acquired skills, and to what extent, and whether employers value the skills acquired.

To achieve the measurement objectives listed above, increasing research outlays on in-classroom observation and on relatively expensive surveys and pre- and postprogram skills tests for study participants appear unavoidable. Without detailed knowledge about the nature of the training, how it was administered, who received it, what activities it replaced, and whether it actually increased the skill level and productivity of the trainee, it will be difficult to draw firm conclusions about the relative effects of different program activities.

An important issue in studying training technique involves the degree of control that evaluators should have over the program being evaluated. In a typical training program evaluation, state or local administrators choose the array of services to be offered and, perhaps with input from participants, decide the mix of services each participant receives. The evaluator then attempts to measure the effect of the program as implemented. Such an approach can hinder the ability to study new program techniques. Innovations in technique are, by their nature, often difficult to find in practice and must sometimes be set up specifically for the purpose of study.

In addition, when evaluators control the services for which each program participant is eligible, they are better able to maintain the distinctiveness of alternative service streams and to determine the differential effect of several service combinations. Greater control over the programs to be tested, however, often can be gained only when research budgets include substantial resources to compensate local agencies for changes in their program operations.

Were additional research funding available, it could be devoted to investigating various hypotheses advanced about group dynamics in training. Those hypotheses stem from the nascent literature on potential community effects and concern influences on motivation coming from classroom peers and from the participant's social and community context. Economists have been responsible for most major evaluations of training programs, but they do not have special expertise for examining motivational issues. In this area, then, economists might find it fruitful to work more closely with measurement experts in sociology, psychology, education, and urban anthropology.

Notes

1. This chapter borrows heavily from parts of Friedlander, Greenberg, and Robins (1997).

2. In principle, X_i and Z_i can be measured during or after the program, but if this is done, they may be affected by participation and, hence, be endogenous. It is assumed that X_i and Z_i are uncorrelated with u_{it} and e_{io}, respectively.

3. Ideally, it is desirable to differentiate among several kinds of training activities, by defining P_{io} as a vector, and to account for the level and intensity of participation by defining P_{io} as a continuous variable. For one recent attempt to do the latter, see Jacobson et al. (1994).

4. In practice, b_i is also often allowed to vary over certain kinds of individuals (subgroup analysis). In addition, evaluators have recently become interested in examining effects on the entire distribution (as opposed to the mean) of the outcomes. See, for example, Björklund and Moffitt (1987); Clements, Heckman, and Smith (1994); Friedlander and Robins (1997); and Manski (1995).

5. The term "propensity score" comes from the statistics literature (Rosenbaum and Rubin 1983; Rubin 1973).

6. An overview of nonexperimental evaluation methods is given in Moffitt (1991) and Bell et al. (1995).

7. Alternatively, persons with these characteristics may disproportionately apply to the program.

8. The major condition is that the relation between variables can be represented by a simple linear regression model such as the one in equation set (1). Linearity may not be a good assumption, however, and, as described later, a number of fairly sophisticated methods have been proposed to deal with the general problem of selection on observables.

9. To a degree, making the distinction between selection on observables and selection on unobservables is artificial (and perhaps even misleading), because unobserv-

ables may represent mainly factors that are difficult, but not necessarily impossible, to measure. Heckman and Smith (1995) argue that collecting better data can minimize (and perhaps even eliminate) problems caused by selection on unobservables and thereby will reduce the evaluation problem to one of finding an appropriate method for controlling for selection on observables.

10. The "regression discontinuity" model was first proposed as an evaluation model in the field of education by Thistlewaite and Campbell (1960), but it has received scant attention in the training program evaluation literature.

11. See chapter 10 of this volume for a description of these programs.

12. Some evaluators claim to have solved the problem of selection on unobservables by using external comparison groups. External comparison groups usually are chosen on the basis of a set of observed characteristics, however, and, hence, technically their use addresses only the problem of selection on observables.

13. Dehejia and Wahba (1995) propose using "good" matches more than once (in effect, matching them to more than one program group member).

14. Ashenfelter noted that trainees tend to suffer a sharp decline in earnings just before program entry. This "preprogram dip" undoubtedly reflects adverse economic circumstances that are at least partly responsible for an individual's decision to enter training. Knowing whether the level of earnings immediately before entering the program is transitory or permanent is critical for developing an appropriate statistical model to account for selection on unobservables.

15. For example, in the case of a simple fixed effect, where $u_{it} = \mu_i$ and $e_{io} = \mu_i$ (i.e., the correlation between u_{it} and P_{io} arises from a common component, μ_i), an unbiased estimate of the program effect can be obtained by estimating a first difference model for earnings (see Barnow 1987 for details). A transitory earnings "dip," however, will make the results sensitive to the base year used to construct the first difference model.

16. Perhaps one of the more successful applications of the instrumental variable technique was performed by Mallar (1978), who used proximity to the training site as an instrument for participating in the Job Corps program.

17. LaLonde (1986) was the first to develop procedures for assessing nonexperimental estimators using experimental data.

18. An advisory panel that convened in the 1980s to make recommendations concerning how to evaluate the JTPA program, which at the time was the major federally funded training program, concluded that an experimental evaluation was the preferred method (Stromsdorfer et al. 1985). Ashenfelter and Card (1985); Barnow (1987); Burtless (1995); and Burtless and Orr (1986) reached similar conclusions regarding the preference for experimental evaluations of training programs. Eventually, the federal government decided to fund an experimental evaluation of JTPA, with an associated nonexperimental research component. The earlier generations of federal training programs (MDTA, CETA) had been evaluated exclusively using nonexperimental methods.

19. In terms of the model presented in exhibit 9.1, randomization is intended to produce zero correlation between P_{io} and X_i and between P_{io} and u_{it}, so that $E(P_{io}X_i) = E(P_{io}u_{it}) = E(u_{it}e_{it}) = a_0 = 0$.

20. In practice, the earnings effect is usually estimated using ordinary least squares. The Xs are included to increase the statistical precision of the estimates, but such gains are usually small.

21. The JTPA program is described elsewhere in this volume. In August 1998, President Clinton signed legislation that replaced the JTPA program with a "semi-block" grant, the Workforce Investment Act (WIA). WIA will maintain separate non-block-grant funding streams for adults, dislocated workers, and youth. It will attempt to improve coordination between the workforce investment system and the various pro-

grams authorized in the legislation. It will also prioritize eligibility for intensive services to those who are unsuccessful in finding work after receiving initial core services. Finally, WIA will increase customer choice of services. For more details, see chapter 1.

22. A standard argument is that only sites operating superior programs will agree to an evaluation; however, there may be only minimal correlation between local operators' self-appraisals and the results of a rigorous third-party evaluation.

23. In at least two recent instances—the Massachusetts Employment and Training Choices Program (Nightingale et al. 1991) and the Washington state Family Independence Program (Long and Wissoker 1995)—those issues were considered so important that a decision was made against using a random-assignment evaluation design that would create a no-program control group and would therefore interfere with sitewide program coverage.

24. To illustrate the potential bias caused by distortions in the participant population, Manski investigates nonparametric bounded estimators that are virtually assumption-free (see also Angrist and Imbens 1991). As Manski shows, the bounds can often be large and can be narrowed only if the evaluator is willing to impose strong and untestable assumptions about behavior of individuals outside the specific program being evaluated.

25. Hypotheses concerning community effects are currently being tested in the evaluation of the Youth Fair Chance Demonstration.

26. In a study of "creaming" in the JTPA Title IIA program, Anderson, Burkhauser, and Raymond (1993) find that the problem of nonrandom selection of participants is not as serious as some critics suggest.

27. TANF replaced the former Aid to Families with Dependent Children (AFDC) program in August 1996.

28. To generalize Model 2, T_i could be specified as an array of services and incentives characterizing training "policy." In addition, Model 2, as we have written it, makes no provision for decreasing marginal returns to training, so that b_t does not decline as the scale of the training program increases (i.e., for programs for which g_0 is large). Incorporating scale effects could be done by making b_t a function of P averaged across the population. Allowing personal characteristics to affect the returns to training and the training decision could be accomplished by making b_t a function of X_i and g_0 a function of Z_i. Finally, a further generalization of Model 2 would be to distinguish the efficiency of training participation that does or does not come through the evaluated program. This could be accomplished by creating separate P variables and b coefficients for the evaluated program and training obtained by other means.

29. For completeness, it should be noted that b_t for mandatory programs can be estimated within the context of a comparison group/area design by a nonexperimental participant/nonparticipant comparison in which nonparticipants are not subject to the program mandate (i.e., for whom $T_i = 0$), providing, of course, that selection bias can be removed. If b_t can be estimated in such a fashion, then h_t can be recovered as well.

30. Their earnings may, of course, later increase as a result of having enrolled in the program.

31. This effect is obviously similar to the deterrent effect discussed earlier. The distinction is that the earlier discussion pertained to persons already on the welfare rolls. In both instances, however, individuals seek employment to avoid training program participation requirements.

32. During the 1970s, a number of empirical studies of displacement focused on the extent to which unemployed workers absorbed by public-sector job creation programs displaced regular government workers. These findings provide little insight into displacement in the private sector that would result from training programs.

References

Anderson, Kathryn H., Richard V. Burkhauser, and Jennie E. Raymond. 1993. "The Effect of Creaming under the Job Training Partnership Act." *Industrial and Labor Relations Review* 46 (4, July): 613–24.

Angrist, Joshua D., and Guido W. Imbens. 1991. "Sources of Identifying Information in Evaluation Models." NBER Technical Working Paper 117. Cambridge, Mass.: National Bureau of Economic Research.

Angrist, Joshua D., Guido W. Imbens, and Donald Rubin. 1996. "Identification of Causal Effects Using Instrumental Variables." *Journal of the American Statistical Association* 91 (434): 444–55.

Ashenfelter, Orley. 1978. "Estimating the Effects of Training Programs on Earnings." *Review of Economics and Statistics* 60 (1, February): 47–57.

Ashenfelter, Orley, and David Card. 1985. "Using the Longitudinal Structure of Earnings to Estimate the Effects of Training Programs." *Review of Economics and Statistics*, 67 (4, November): 648–60.

Barnow, Burt S. 1987. "The Impact of CETA Programs on Earnings: A Review of the Literature." *Journal of Human Resources* 22 (2, spring): 157–93.

Barnow, Burt S., Glen G. Cain, and Arthur S. Goldberger. 1980. "Issues in the Analysis of Selectivity Bias." *Evaluation Studies* 5 (1, May): 42–59.

Bassi, Laurie J. 1983. "The Effect of CETA on the Postprogram Earnings of Participants." *Journal of Human Resources* 18 (4, fall): 539–56.

———. 1987. "Estimating the Effect of Job Training Programs Using Longitudinal Data: Ashenfelter's Findings Reconsidered, a Comment." *Journal of Human Resources* 22 (3, summer): 300–303.

Bell, Stephen, Larry L. Orr, John D. Bloomquist, and Glen G. Cain. 1995. *Program Applicants as a Comparison Group in Evaluating Training Programs.* Kalamazoo, Mich.: W.E. Upjohn Institute for Employment Research.

Björklund, Anders, and Robert Moffitt. 1987. "The Estimation of Wage Gains and Welfare Gains in Self-Selection Models." *Review of Economics and Statistics* 69 (1, February): 42–49.

Bloom, Howard. 1984. "Estimating the Effect of Job Training Programs Using Longitudinal Data: Ashenfelter's Findings Reconsidered." *Journal of Human Resources* 19 (4, fall): 544–56.

Borus, Michael E. 1964. "A Benefit-Cost Analysis of the Economic Effectiveness of Retraining the Unemployed." *Yale Economic Essays* 4 (fall): 371–430.

Bryant, Edward C., and Kalman Rupp. 1987. "Evaluating the Impact of CETA on Participant Earnings." *Evaluation Review* 11 (4, August): 473–92.

Burtless, Gary. 1995. "The Case for Social Experiments." *Journal of Economic Perspectives* 9 (2, spring): 85–110.

Burtless, Gary, and Larry L. Orr. 1986. "Are Classical Experiments Needed for Manpower Policy?" *Journal of Human Resources* 21 (4, fall): 606–39.

Cain, Glen G. 1968. "Benefit-Cost Estimates for Job Corps." Discussion Paper No. 9-68. Madison: Institute for Research on Poverty, University of Wisconsin.

———. "Regression and Selection Models to Improve Nonexperimental Comparisons." 1975. In *Evaluation and Experiment*, edited by C.A. Bennett and A.A. Lumsdaine. New York: Academic Press.

Card, David, and Larry L. Sullivan. 1988. "Measuring the Effect of Subsidized Training Programs on Movements In and Out of Employment." *Econometrica* 56 (3, May): 497–530.

Clements, Nancy, James Heckman, and James Smith. 1994. "Making the Most Out of Social Experiments: Reducing the Intrinsic Uncertainty in Evidence from Randomized Trials with an Application to the National JTPA Experiment." National Bureau of Economic Research Technical Paper 149. Cambridge, Mass.: NBER.

Cohen, Malcolm S. 1969. "The Direct Effects of Federal Manpower Programs in Reducing Unemployment." *The Journal of Human Resources* 4 (1, fall): 491–507.

Cooley, Thomas M., Timothy W. McGuire, and Edward C. Prescott. 1979. "Earnings and Employment Dynamics of Manpower Trainees: An Econometric Analysis." In *Research in Labor Economics,* edited by Farrell E. Bloch. Greenwich, Connecticut: JAI Press.

Dehejia, Rajeev H., and Sadek Wahba. 1995. "Causal Effects in Nonexperimental Studies: Re-Evaluating the Evaluation of Training Programs." Unpublished paper. Cambridge, Mass.: Harvard University.

Dickinson, Katherine, Terry Johnson, and Richard West. 1986. "An Analysis of the Impact of CETA Programs on Participants' Earnings." *Journal of Human Resources* 21 (1, winter): 64–91.

———. 1987. "The Impact of CETA Programs on Components of Participants' Earnings." *Industrial and Labor Relations Review* 40 (3, April): 430–40.

Fraker, Thomas, and Rebecca Maynard. 1987. "Evaluating Comparison Group Designs with Employment-Related Programs." *Journal of Human Resources* 22 (2, spring): 194–227.

Freedman, Stephen, Marisa Mitchell, and David Navarro. 1999. "The Los Angeles Jobs-First GAIN Evaluation: First Year Findings on Participation Patterns and Impacts," New York: Manpower Demonstration Research Corporation.

Friedlander, Daniel, and Philip K. Robins. 1995. "Evaluating Program Evaluations: New Evidence on Commonly Used Nonexperimental Methods." *American Economic Review* 85 (4, September): 923–37.

———. 1997. "The Distributional Impacts of Social Programs." *Evaluation Review* 21 (5, October): 531–53.

Friedlander, Daniel, David H. Greenberg, and Philip K. Robins. 1997. "Evaluating Government Training Programs for the Economically Disadvantaged." *Journal of Economic Literature* 35 (4, December): 1809–55.

Garfinkel, Irwin, Charles F. Manski, and Charles Michalopoulos. 1992. "Micro Experiments and Macro Effects." In *Evaluating Welfare and Training Programs*, edited by Charles F. Manski and Irwin Garfinkel (253–76). Cambridge, Mass.: Harvard University Press.

Goldberger, Arthur S. 1972. "Selection Bias in Evaluating Treatment Effects." Discussion Paper 123-72. Madison: Institute for Research on Poverty, University of Wisconsin.

Greenberg, David H., Robert H. Meyer, and Michael Wiseman. 1993. "Prying the Lid from the Black Box: Plotting Evaluation Strategy for Welfare Employment and Training Programs." Discussion Paper 989-93. Madison: Institute for Research on Poverty, University of Wisconsin.

Ham, John C., and Robert J. LaLonde. 1990. "Using Social Experiments to Estimate the Effect of Training on Transition Rates." In *Panel Data and Labor Market Studies*, edited by J. Hartog, G. Ridder, and J. Theeuwes. North Holland: Elsevier Science Publications.

———. 1996. "The Effect of Sample Selection and Initial Conditions in Duration Models: Evidence from Experimental Data on Training." *Econometrica* 64 (1, January): 175–205.

Hamilton, Gayle. 1988. "Interim Report on the Saturation Work Initiative Model in San Diego." New York: Manpower Demonstration Research Corporation.

Hamilton, Gayle, and Daniel Friedlander. 1989. "Final Report on the Saturation Work Initiative Model in San Diego." New York: Manpower Demonstration Research Corporation.

Heckman, James J. 1978. "Dummy Endogenous Variables in a Simultaneous Equation System." *Econometrica* 46 (3, July): 931–59.

———. 1992. "Randomization and Social Policy Evaluation." In *Evaluating Welfare and Training Programs*, edited by Charles F. Manski and Irwin Garfinkel (201–30). Cambridge Mass.: Harvard University Press.

———. 1996. "Randomization as an Instrumental Variable." *Review of Economics and Statistics* 78 (2): 336–41.

———. 1997. "Instrumental Variables: A Study of Implicit Behavioral Assumptions in One Widely Used Estimator." *Journal of Human Resources* 32 (3, summer): 441–61.

Heckman, James J., and V. Joseph Hotz. 1989. "Choosing among Alternative Nonexperimental Methods for Estimating the Impact of Social Programs." *Journal of the American Statistical Association* 84 (408, December): 862–74.

Heckman, James J., and Richard Robb, Jr. 1985. "Alternative Methods for Evaluating the Impact of Interventions: An Overview." *Journal of Econometrics* 30 (1–2): 239–67.

Heckman, James J., and Jeffrey A. Smith. 1995. "Assessing the Case for Social Experiments." *Journal of Economic Perspectives* 9 (2, spring): 85–110.

————. Forthcoming. "Ashenfelter's Dip and the Determinant of Program Participation in a Social Program: Implications for Simple Program Evaluation Strategies." *Economic Journal*.

————. Forthcoming. "The Sensitivity of Experimental Impact Estimates: Evidence from the National JTPA Study." In *Youth Employment and Unemployment in Advanced Countries*, edited by R. Freeman and L. Katz. Chicago, Ill.: University of Chicago Press.

Heckman, James J., H. Ichimura, and Petra Todd. 1997. "Matching as an Econometric Evaluation Estimator: Evidence from Evaluating a Job Training Program." *Review of Economic Studies* 64 (4): 605–54.

————. 1998. "Matching as an Econometric Evaluation Estimator." *Review of Economic Studies* 65 (2): 261–94.

Heckman, James J., Robert J. LaLonde, and Jeffrey A. Smith. 1999. "The Economics and Econometrics of Active Labor Market Programs." In *Handbook of Labor Economics, Volume III*, edited by Orley Ashenfelter and David Card (chapter 31). Amsterdam: North Holland Publishing Company.

Heckman, James J., Jeffrey Smith, and Nancy Clements. 1997. "Making the Most Out of Programme Evaluations and Social Experiments: Accounting for Heterogeneity in Programme Impacts." *Review of Economic Studies* 64 (4): 487–535.

Heckman, James, Jeffrey Smith, and Christopher Taber. 1998. "Accounting for Dropouts in Evaluations of Social Programs." *Review of Economics and Statistics* 80 (1): 1–14.

Heckman, James J., H. Ichimura, Jeffrey Smith, and Petra Todd. 1996. "Sources of Selection Bias in Evaluating Social Programs: An Interpretation of Conventional Measures and Evidence on the Effectiveness of Matching as a Program Evaluation Method." *Proceedings of the National Academy of Sciences* 93 (23): 13416–20.

————. 1998. "Characterizing Selection Bias Using Experimental Data." *Econometrica* 65 (5, September): 1017–98.

Hollister, Robinson G., and Jennifer Hill. 1995. "Problems in the Evaluation of Community-Wide Initiatives." In *New Approaches to Evaluating Community Initiatives: Concepts, Methods, and Contexts*, edited by James P. Connell, Anne C. Kubisch, Lisbeth B. Schorr, and Carol H. Weiss (127–72). Washington, D.C.: Aspen Institute.

Hotz, V. Joseph. 1992. "Designing an Evaluation of the Job Training Partnership Act." In *Evaluating Welfare and Training Programs*, edited by Charles F. Manski and Irwin Garfinkel (76–114). Cambridge, Mass.: Harvard University Press.

Jacobson, Louis, Robert LaLonde, and Daniel G. Sullivan. 1993. "Earnings Losses of Displaced Workers." *American Economic Review* 83 (4, September): 685–709.

Jacobson, Louis S., Robert S. LaLonde, Daniel G. Sullivan, and Robert Bednarzik. 1994. "The Returns to Classroom Training for Displaced

Workers." Macroeconomic Issues Working Paper 94-27. Chicago: Federal Reserve Bank of Chicago. October.

Johnson, George. 1979. "The Labor Market Displacement Effect in the Analysis of the Net Impact of Manpower Training Programs." In *Research in Labor Economics, Supplement 1* (227–54). Greenwich, Conn.: JAI Press.

Katz, Lawrence F. 1994. "Active Labor Market Policies to Expand Employment and Opportunity." In *Reducing Unemployment: Current Issues and Policy Options* (239–90). Proceedings from a symposium held by Federal Reserve Bank of Kansas City, Jackson Hole, Wyo. August.

LaLonde, Robert J. 1986. "Evaluating the Econometric Evaluations of Employment and Training Programs with Experimental Data." *American Economic Review* 76 (4, September): 604–20.

LaLonde, Robert J., and Rebecca Maynard. 1987. "How Precise Are Evaluations of Employment and Training Programs? Evidence from a Field Experiment." *Evaluation Review* 11 (4, August): 428–51.

Long, Sharon K., and Douglas Wissoker. 1995. "Welfare Reform at Three Years: The Case of Washington State's Family Independence Program." *Journal of Human Resources*, 30 (4, fall): 766–90.

Mallar, Charles D. 1978. "Alternative Econometric Procedures for Program Evaluations: Illustrations from an Evaluation of Job Corps." *Papers and Proceedings of the American Statistical Association, Social Statistics Section:* 317–21.

Manski, Charles F. 1993. "What Do Controlled Experiments Reveal about Outcomes When Treatments Vary?" Discussion Paper No. 1005-93. Madison: Institute for Research on Poverty, University of Wisconsin.

———. 1995. "Learning about Social Programs from Experiments with Random Assignment of Treatments." Discussion Paper No. 1061-95. Madison: Institute for Research on Poverty, University of Wisconsin.

Manski, Charles F., and Irwin Garfinkel. 1992. "Introduction." In *Evaluating Welfare and Training Programs*, edited by Charles F. Manski and Irwin Garfinkel (1–22). Cambridge, Mass.: Harvard University Press.

Moffitt, Robert A. 1991. "Program Evaluation with Nonexperimental Data." *Evaluation Review* 15 (3, June): 291–314.

———. "Evaluation Methods for Program Entry Effects." 1992. In *Evaluating Welfare and Training Programs*, edited by Charles F. Manski and Irwin Garfinkel (231–52). Cambridge, Mass.: Harvard University Press.

———. 1996. "The Effect of Employment and Training Programs on Entry and Exit from the Welfare Caseload." *Journal of Policy Analysis and Management* 15 (1, winter): 32–50.

Nightingale, Demetra Smith, Lynn C. Burbridge, Douglas Wissoker, Lee Bawden, Freya L. Sonenstein, and Neal Jeffries. 1991. *Evaluation of the Massachusetts Employment and Training (ET) Program.* Urban Institute Report 91-1. Washington, D.C.: Urban Institute Press.

Orr, Larry L., Howard S. Bloom, Stephen H. Bell, Fred Doolittle, Winston Lin, and George Cave. 1996. *Does Training for the Disadvantaged Work? Evidence from the National JTPA Study.* Washington, D.C.: Urban Institute Press.

Riccio, James, Daniel Friedlander, and Stephen Freedman. 1994. *GAIN: Benefits, Costs, and Three-Year Impacts of a Welfare-to-Work Program.* New York: Manpower Demonstration Research Corporation.

Riccio, James, George Cave, Stephen Freedman, and Marilyn Price. 1986. *Final Report on the Virginia Employment Services Program.* New York: Manpower Demonstration Research Corporation.

Rosenbaum, Paul, and Donald B. Rubin. 1983. "The Central Role of the Propensity Score in Observational Studies for Causal Effects." *Biometrika* 70 (1, April): 41–55.

Rubin, Donald B. 1973. "Matching to Remove Bias in Observational Studies." *Biometrics* 29 (1, March): 159–83.

Stromsdorfer, Ernst. 1968. "Determinants of Economic Success in Retraining the Unemployed: The West Virginia Experience." *Journal of Human Resources* 3 (2, spring): 139–58.

Stromsdorfer, Ernst, Howard Bloom, Robert Boruch, Michael Borus, Judith Gueron, Alan Gustman, Peter Rossi, Fritz Scheuren, Marshall Smith, and Frank Stafford. 1985. *Recommendations of the Job Training Longitudinal Survey Research Advisory Panel.* Washington, D.C.: Employment and Training Administration, U.S. Department of Labor.

Thistlewaite, D.L., and D.T. Campbell. 1960. "Regression-Discontinuity Analysis: An Alternative to Ex Post Facto Experiment." *Journal of Educational Psychology* 51: 309–17.

Chapter Ten

REFLECTIONS ON TRAINING POLICIES AND PROGRAMS

Garth L. Mangum

There comes a time in life when one's most useful role is to provide historical perspective—but that is at least one step up from having no useful role left. Having been involved beginning in 1963 as a Senate staffer handling the first few amendments to the 1962 Manpower Development and Training Act (MDTA) and in the U.S. Department of Labor with its early administration, followed by involvement at the national level in the design of both the Comprehensive Employment and Training Act (CETA) and the Job Training Partnership Act (JTPA), and having served on state-level advisory councils for both of the last two programs, I am grateful to the editors of this volume for an opportunity to comment on what may be useful lessons from that history.

THE NECESSITY OF OCCUPATIONAL PREPARATION

Those of us who graduated from high school in 1943 were automatically in the upper one-third of that cohort. But that did not matter very much because recruiters from a hungry steel plant nearby did not care about formal education, and military recruiters and the draft board were waiting impatiently outside the auditorium doors anyway. On the supply side of the labor market by the late 1940s, the postwar GI Bill had begun to produce a more educated workforce with which one had to compete. As a simple measure, the average years of educational attainment for the U.S. population over the age of 25 rose from 1940's 6.0 years to 6.8 years in 1950, 8.0 in 1960, 9.8 in 1970, 12.0 in 1980, and 12.4 in 1990. The demand side of the labor market also began to change to reflect substantial technological advancements, including many made in part because there was now the beginning of a more sophisticated workforce able to handle them.

Those without education, skill training, or substantial work experience were increasingly disadvantaged in job market competition.

In retrospect, the passage of MDTA in 1962 could be perceived as an emerging recognition that a first and second chance at more formal preparation for workforce participation was becoming increasingly important. That need has intensified over the subsequent 37 years so that, on average, the only people who maintained the level of their real earnings from the early 1970s to the late 1990s were those with college education, and only those with graduate degrees, again on average, experienced real increases in their standard of living (Mishel, Bernstein, and Schmitt 1999: 156). Real wages for most workers are rising in the tighter labor markets of the last half of the 1990s, but we all know who will suffer most whenever labor markets soften. While the rising real incomes of the educated and trained have been the leading edge, at the rear of the column are those who entered the working world underprepared, who were at risk of doing so, or who became displaced from reasonably satisfactory but tenuous positions somewhere up the line. They have been the targets during those 37 years of programs that have never been funded at any level capable of serving more than a small margin of those eligible but that have made significant contributions to the well-being of most of those who have completed such programs. Who has and who has not profited, how much, why, and what to do about it is a controversy toward which this volume is addressed.

PROGRAMMATIC PATTERNS

Despite the dramatic changes that have occurred in the U.S. economy over the last third of the century, the experience of these workforce development programs has been remarkably consistent.

Objectives

Within scarce resources, there has been a persistent search for balance among the concerns for disadvantaged adults and youth and dislocated experienced workers. The MDTA of 1962 targeted the technologically displaced, accompanied by minor attention to out-of-school youth. However, after the launching in 1964 of the multifaceted program called the war on poverty, it dedicated two-thirds of its resources to that cause. The youth portion grew over the years and then declined in response to discouraging results in the 1990s. Concern with the impacts of international trade kept the dislocation target alive. Globalization, geographic shifts of industry, and new technological developments elevated the dislocated worker to separate title status under JTPA in the 1980s and to superior funding compared with disadvantaged adults in the 1990s. Sporadic attempts at welfare reform added single heads of households as a new concern beginning in the late 1960s toward the close of the MDTA era. The new category grew under CETA and exploded in the partnership between JTPA and the Job Opportunities and Basic Skills (JOBS) emphasis of the Family Support Act of 1988. The Workforce Investment Act of 1998 (WIA) sharply reversed the latter emphasis. It maintained separate funding for dislocated adults and youth in that order of funding magnitude. It appropriated lesser funding for nondislocated adults and eliminated the limitation of that segment to the economically disadvantaged. It also endorsed "work first" with a vengeance. It specified that the nondislocated adults, including those newly deprived of public assistance, could receive training paid for with WIA funds only if they could not find any job, no matter how rudimentary and ill-paid, without being trained. At least those of the poor and former welfare recipients who cannot find those rudimentary jobs do get priority for that portion of funds left for training after being used for "core" and "intensive" services by populations unrestricted by economic status. One can only conjecture whether the balancing act among disadvantaged adults, disadvantaged youth, dislocated workers, and single heads of households has ended in clear victory for the nondisadvantaged.

Bipartisanship

Employment and training programs profited from bipartisan advocacy during their first quarter century but have suffered bipartisan criticism since. It was as easy for Republican Senators Jacob Javits and Winston Prouty as it was for my Democratic boss, Senator Joseph Clark, and brand-new young Senator Edward Kennedy to believe in and support MDTA (Mangum 1968: 14–19). To the liberal it meant opportunities for the unemployed and disadvantaged; to the conservative, preparation for the responsibilities of self-reliance. CETA was very much a bipartisan creation between the Republican Labor Department and the Democratic Congress in 1973. The Reagan administration secretary and assistant secretary of labor for employment and training wanted to kill CETA without replacement. JTPA was substituted through an alliance between the Republican Senate and the Democratic House and the sub rosa involvement of kitchen cabinet–level Labor Department staff. The final act in 1982 was the personal intervention of Republican Senator Orrin Hatch with White House counsel Edwin Meese to get the labor secretary overruled. The compromises necessary to save the employment and training program included ending public service employment and stipends. Without essentially changing the membership of local governing bodies, the chairing role was shifted from local elected officials to private employers. Governors were promoted from merely overseeing the rural "balance of state" to a dominant position in governing the program. A performance-driven accountability system was added for the first time in almost any federal program.

Continuing bipartisanship in a more negative mood included the Clinton administration's merely changing the name and taking over in 1993 President Bush's Job Training 2000 proposal of 1992 and Republican and Democratic proposals made but never acted upon in 1995 and 1996 until passed in 1998 as the Workforce Investment Act, purportedly to devolve employment and training responsibility to the states through federal block grants.[1] Whether the federal government or the states have the lead role is not the issue. What is needed is bipartisan recognition that the overall record of employment and training programs has been a positive one that could have been and still can be reinvigorated, though at no little cost, through being brought to consistency with the demands of current labor markets.

Parsimony

Throughout employment and training program history, Congress has been more generous with its definitions of eligibility for training than it has with its funding of training services. For many years, the rule of thumb was that funding was adequate to enroll about 5 percent of those eligible. Whether because of the general tightening of federal budgets over the past 20 years or because of the declining reputation of such programs, those entering and subsequently leaving JTPA, whether completing or dropping out, are now only about 1 percent of the number who are eligible for enrollment (table 10.1).[2]

Brevity

That discord between eligibility and funding has been the primary cause of brevity in training duration, which has in turn been the major factor leading to limited impact.[3] Among the first amendments to MDTA in the early 1960s were successive lengthenings of program authorization to allow longer training times and the addition of reme-

Table 10.1 ESTIMATED NUMBER OF 22- TO 69-YEAR-OLDS ELIGIBLE
FOR JTPA TITLE II-A IN 1997 COMPARED WITH THE NUMBER
OF 22- TO 69-YEAR-OLD JTPA TITLE II-A TERMINEES
BY GENDER AND AGE, 4/1/96–6/30/97

Demographic Group	Number of Eligibles	Number of Terminees	Terminees as Percentage of Eligibles
All	26,637,000	265,281	0.99%
Gender			
Men	10,995,000	85,191	0.77%
Women	15,642,000	180,090	1.15
Age			
22–29	6,412,000	108,138	1.69%
30–34	10,599,000	125,643	1.18
45–69	9,626,000	31,241	0.32
Age/Gender			
Men 22–29	2,583,000	30,755	1.19%
Women 22–29	3,829,000	77,383	2.02
Men 30–34	4,448,000	41,567	0.93
Women 30–34	6,151,000	84,076	1.36
Men 45–69	3,964,000	12,757	0.32
Women 45–69	5,661,000	18,484	0.33

Sources: Eligibles from March 1998 Current Population Survey (CPS), terminations
from U.S. Department of Labor. Data are from Social Policy Research Associates,
JTPA Standardized Program Information Report, Program Year (PY) 96, Public Use
File, hereinafter called SPIR 96; tabulations by Center for Labor Market Studies,
Northeastern University.

dial basic education to support it. The resulting 104 weeks of training authorized could have been long enough to obtain an associate's
degree and even make major inroads on a baccalaureate. Yet the average weeks of training for adults throughout most of this history have
been in the low 20s, lengthening recently into the 30s, while youth
have averaged no more than one week for each year of their age. During the 1980s there was a period of flirtation with job search training,
a process that, if done well, can speed the return to work but can only
help people find jobs commensurate with the skills they already have.
But in pursuit of cheap training, a few days or weeks of job search
assistance seemed an easy answer. Occupational skill training has
always provided the highest return among alternative training services, but it is also the most expensive (table 10.2).

If eligibility exceeds funding 20- to 100-fold, local administrators
find it difficult to say no to the many in order to provide meaningful
training to the few. The relationship between the duration of training
and the cost of training is an obvious one, but so is the relationship

Table 10.2 EMPLOYMENT RATES AND WAGES OF THE EMPLOYED AT TERMINATION AND FOLLOW-UP, BY SERVICES RECEIVED, TITLE II-A INDIVIDUALS WHO TERMINATED BETWEEN 1 APRIL 1996 AND 30 JUNE 1997

Type of Training	Number of Terminees	Percentage of Total	Outcomes at Termination		Outcomes at Follow-Up	
			Employed at Termination (%)	Mean Hourly Wage ($)	Employed at Follow-Up (%)	Mean Weekly Wage ($)
Total	199,730	100%	65.1%	$7.52	65.5%	$291
Basic skills only	18,613	9.3	48.8	6.43	53.2	248
Occupational skills only	93,110	46.6	67.5	8.08	67.9	313
On-the-job training (OJT) only	16,199	8.1	81.1	6.75	74.6	270
Work experience only	4,858	2.4	45.4	5.89	52.2	198
Other training only	8,975	4.5	60.2	7.12	56.9	253
Training combinations	39,653	19.9	68.6	7.27	65.7	278
Received no training	18,322	9.2	54.8	7.35	62.3	250

Source: SPIR 96.

between the duration of training and the occupational level for which one is trained and the rate of pay received by those who complete the training and are placed in a training-related job (table 10.3).

As long as 20 years ago, it was estimated that those whose CETA classroom training duration was less than 20 weeks experienced only one-sixth the earnings gains of those few who trained for more than 40 weeks (Taggart 1981: 103, 111). But funds have never been adequate for longer training durations to become the norm, and now labor market realities demand that even the 40 weeks that would have been an academic-year-equivalent duration might have to be doubled for the best results. Yet just as that fact was becoming more obvious, the 1996 welfare reform was introducing a "jobs first" philosophy while 1998's workforce development legislation sought to make training a last resort.

The requirement that WIA funding be used for training only those without access to Pell grants and other such education funding reinforces that message. Those who can undertake longer-term education and training are to do so with other education funding, while WIA funds are used first for "core" placement services and "intensive" counseling services, with whatever WIA funds are left applied to short-term training for minimal jobs. That is the implied intent of Congress. How the states will react remains to be seen.

Stipends

Training duration raises the issue of training stipends. Subsistence while in training has been a continuing issue. MDTA began with adult stipends tied to the average levels of unemployment compensation in each state, with youth stipends providing minor spending. CETA offered the equivalent of the minimum wage to its enrollees, thereby committing half the available training funds to subsistence and attracting charges that enrollees were becoming program junkies in pursuit of the stipends. Those charges required JTPA's designers to throw the baby out with the bathwater, leaving stipends available only to welfare recipients, limiting other enrollments only to those who had other earners in their families to support them, and contributing to the unduly brief training durations. WIA reopens that door by endorsing needs-based payments, but apparently only to support training that is to be the last resort within "workforce investment."

Creaming

A related constant has been complaints of "creaming." Whatever the eligibility criteria prescribed by Congress, the most aggressive

Table 10.3 TITLE II-A PLACEMENT AND FOLLOW-UP WAGES BY TRAINING DURATION, 4/1/96 TO 6/30/97 TERMINEES

Training Hours	Total Service Hours			Occupational Skill Training Hours		
	Percentage of Total	Median Termination Wage ($)	Median Follow-Up Wage ($)	Percentage of Total	Median Termination Wage ($)	Median Follow-Up Wage ($)
Total	100.0%	$7.00	$263	100.0%	$7.00	$263
Zero hours	17.3	7.00	278	43.0	6.50	250
1–479	54.2	6.90	250	36.3	7.00	260
480–639	8.7	7.00	267	5.7	7.50	280
640–799	5.0	7.00	272	3.5	7.50	280
800–959	3.4	7.00	275	2.4	7.50	280
960–1,199	3.7	7.24	280	2.7	7.72	290
1,200–1,439	2.4	7.50	300	2.0	8.00	310
1,440–1,599	1.3	8.00	300	1.2	8.00	311
1,600–1,919	1.5	8.00	320	1.2	8.15	327
1,920–2,079	0.5	8.00	320	0.4	8.13	320
2,080 and above	2.1	8.00	319	1.6	8.38	320

Source: SPIR 96 data. Wages are averages for those employed of the numbers contacted.

and most competent individuals within those criteria are the most likely to become aware of the program opportunity and be at the front of the applicant line. Recruiters and program operators are unlikely to reject those eager eligibles to beat the bushes for those with more formidable barriers—and the employers who are the ultimate determiners of program success are even less likely to insist that they do so. The issue is perpetual, and Congress has responded from time to time by toughening the requirements as to income and employment barriers. But the real cure would have been to increase appropriations so that more of those declared eligible could have been accommodated.

Related to the countertendency to enroll the most qualified of the eligible has been the tendency to abandon innovations designed to better enable the system to serve the disadvantaged in order to return constantly to the mainstream. Examples are the abandonment by the Labor Department, once it gained total domination under CETA, of two major contributions of the Department of Health, Education, and Welfare during its dual administration of MDTA. One was the Area Manpower Institutes for the Development of Staff (AMIDS), designed to train state and local vocational training staff to relate effectively to the unfamiliar new disadvantaged training population. Another was the abandonment—almost but not yet quite total—of the separately administered skills centers designed and operated to serve the disadvantaged population. Many skill center innovations such as open-entry, open-exit access and individualized and modularized curricula have been adopted by mainstream institutions. However, the willingness to start with a disadvantaged population from where they are and bring them forward step by step until they can compete in the mainstream has too often been abandoned in favor of merely paying an eligible trainee's tuition to compete with all other enrollees in ongoing vocational or technical education courses. And now WIA removes economic disadvantage from the eligibility criteria, though leaving it as a source of priority for training funds, if any funds are left at that point.

Current advocacy of training vouchers, called individual training accounts by WIA, is one more step along that road—in which direction remains to be seen. Many displaced but experienced workers may know what they want to learn and where to find it, but those who do can hardly be classified as disadvantaged (Barnow and King 1996: 255–82). Counseling and guidance with considerable coaching and mentoring are essential to the transition from disadvantagement. WIA implies funding priority for the nondisadvantaged but for other than training services. The nondisadvantaged are to look to mainstream educational funding for their skill upgrading. WIA's funds apparently are to be used first for placement and thereafter for short-term training for the unplaceable.

Outcomes

All of that led to a constancy of results throughout the 36 years between MDTA and WIA. There was consternation in the early 1990s when controlled experimental evaluations showed adult women profiting substantially; men having positive outcomes that, though larger in absolute gains, were often too small in percentage terms to be statistically significant; but youth being no better off and some-times worse off for having enrolled (Orr et al. 1996: 139–79). Despite the weaknesses in methodology examined elsewhere in this volume, many of the results did not surprise old hands in the employment and training game. Women had always experienced greater propor-tionate gains than men throughout the MDTA and CETA experience (Mangum and Walsh 1973: 28–34; Levitan and Mangum 1981: 100). Most of them were pursuing full-time employment after being out of or only sporadically in the labor force. The program provided not only training but also a priority access route into job placement. More of the earnings increase was gained from steadier employment than from higher wage rates. Most of the men had already been in the labor force, and many were really displaced workers who had fallen under the poverty incomes necessary for disadvantaged eligibility after some period of unemployment. For the latter, even retraining was unlikely to offset the loss of seniority and longevity wages. Those losses would have to be offset against the earnings gains of others for a larger absolute but lower proportionate gain for men. The youth experience will be discussed later in this chapter.

A significant factor in the sometimes disappointing returns to national investments in training the disadvantaged and the dislo-cated has been the low proportions of enrollees actually receiving training that could be expected to improve their basic employabil-ity. Table 10.4 illustrates the tendency during the 1980s to replace occupational skills training with job search training and other approaches in pursuit of low-cost placements.

PROGRAM PERFORMANCE

With that background, it is worth summarizing JTPA outcomes by target group.

Table 10.4 TYPES OF JTPA SERVICES PROVIDED AS PROPORTIONS OF TOTAL
ENROLLMENT, 1982–1995 (IN PERCENT)

Service Provided	1982	1987	1991	1994	1995
Classroom training	48%	34%	44%	59%	61%
Work experience	29	8	6	5	6
On-the-job training	12	24	15	14	9
Job search and other assistance	11	34	35	22	24

Source: Office of Policy and Research, Employment and Training Administration, U.S.
Department of Labor.

The Disadvantaged

The risks of that approach having been demonstrated by the widely
advertised results, there was a trend back toward occupational skills
training during the 1990s. Nevertheless, as table 10.5 documents,
one-fourth of those economically disadvantaged adults who termi-

Table 10.5 DISTRIBUTION OF JTPA TITLE II-A TERMINEES RECEIVING
SERVICES BY TYPE OF TRAINING RECEIVED

	Number	Percentage of Total Including Objective Assessment?	
		Yes	No
Total terminations	265,281	100.0%	
Objective assessment only	65,551	24.7	
Total beyond objective assessment	199,730	75.3	100.0%
Basic skills only	18,613	7.0	9.3
Occupational skills only	93,110	35.1	46.6
OJT only	16,199	6.1	8.1
Work experience only	4,858	1.8	2.4
Other training only	8,975	3.4	4.5
Multiple training, total	39,653	14.9	19.9
Multiple, including basic skills	24,718	9.3	12.4
Multiple, including occupational skills	32,398	12.2	16.2
Multiple, including OJT	6,322	2.4	3.2
No training	18,322	6.9	9.2
Received some basic skills training	43,331	16.3	16.9
Received some occupational skills training	125,508	47.3	62.8
Received some OJT	22,521	8.5	11.3

Source: SPIR 96 data, tabulated by the Center for Labor Market Studies, Northeastern
University.
Note: Number of terminees does not add to total because of double counting of those
receiving multiple services.

nated from JTPA Title II-A during program year 1996 had received objective assessment only. That is, they were assessed to determine their need for training but were not thereafter enrolled for training. In addition to that, another 7 percent enrolled for training but left without actually receiving training of any sort. Others received basic skills training, work experience, or other training that may have been important to the recipients but did not include occupational training to prepare them directly for employment. Fewer than half of those who received services including objective assessment and less than two-thirds (62.8 percent) of those enrolled for services beyond that assessment during that program year received any occupational skills training, while another 8 percent received on-the-job training. Postenrollment outcomes measured in employment and earnings cannot help being affected by the mix of services provided.

It is not to be expected that all of those who enroll and subsequently terminate will be promptly placed in jobs. Some will terminate without completing significant amounts of training, some will not be successful in their training courses, some will experience family or personal obstacles, jobs may not be available for some, and some may choose to remain out of the labor market for a variety of reasons. Therefore, the approximately two-thirds immediate placement rates and subsequent employment rates at 13-week follow-up have been fairly standard over the years (table 10.6). More significant are the differential wage rates. From the beginning, OJT has had the highest placement rates because all that is required is retention with the employers who have been provided with wage subsidies. However, low placement and follow-up wages are consistent with the hypothesis that what has been purchased with the subsidy has been jobs that might not have otherwise been available to those enrollees rather than training that substantially augmented their skills. The generally lower wages of those not receiving occupational skills training is also historically significant. The first year of MDTA experience revealed that a basic remedial education component was going to be essential, and that was added by the first amendment to the act. However, subsequent experience has demonstrated that such remediation is most effective when integrated with skills training rather than when provided as a freestanding component preceding occupational skills training. Job search training, which comprises most of the "other training" component, already has been cited as useful in achieving placement but as doing little to augment wage levels.

Given the positive impact of training duration on both placement rates and posttraining earnings, it is also worth noting the relationship between training durations and types of training (table 10.7).

Table 10.6 EMPLOYMENT RATES AND WAGES OF THE EMPLOYED AT TERMINATION AND FOLLOW-UP, BY SERVICES RECEIVED, TITLE II-A INDIVIDUALS WHO TERMINATED BETWEEN 1 APRIL 1996 AND 30 JUNE 1997

Type of Training	Number of Terminees	Percentage of Total	Outcomes at Termination			Outcomes at Follow-Up	
			Employed at Termination (%)	Mean Hourly Wage ($)		Employed at Follow-Up (%)	Mean Weekly Wage ($)
Total	199,730	100%	65.1%	$7.52		65.5%	$291
Basic skills only	18,613	9.3	48.8	6.43		53.2	248
Occupational skills only	93,110	46.6	67.5	8.08		67.9	313
OJT only	16,199	8.1	81.1	6.75		74.6	270
Work experience only	4,858	2.4	45.4	5.89		52.2	198
Other training only	8,975	4.5	60.2	7.12		56.9	253
Training combinations	39,653	19.9	68.6	7.27		65.7	278
Received no training	18,322	9.2	54.8	7.35		62.3	250

Source: SPIR 96.

Table 10.7 MEAN AND MEDIAN HOURS AND QUINTILE BOUNDARIES OF HOURS AND SERVICES RECEIVED BY JTPA TITLE II-A TERMINEES BY TYPE OF TRAINING RECEIVED

	Basic Skills Only	Occupational Skills Only	OJT Only	Work Experience Only	Other Only	Multiple Training
Mean hours	232	556	378	417	87	605
Median hours	120	325	320	400	20	402
Percentile						
20th	30	120	160	198	8	157
40th	80	241	276	324	17	310
60th	167	450	366	480	30	520
80th	324	864	520	499	91	900

Source: SPIR PY 96 data.

Table 10.8 EMPLOYMENT RATES AND WAGES AT TERMINATION, BY HOURS
OF SELECTED SERVICES RECEIVED, TITLE II-A INDIVIDUALS WHO
TERMINATED BETWEEN 1 APRIL 1996 AND 30 JUNE 1997

	Employed at Termination	Mean Wage	Median Wage
Total	65.1%	$7.52	$7.00
Basic skills training only			
Total	48.8%	$6.43	$6.00
Lowest hours quintile (<30)	53.5	6.70	6.25
Second lowest hours quintile (30–79)	52.5	6.27	6.00
Middle quintile (80–166)	44.5	6.43	6.00
Second highest quintile (167–324)	43.5	6.27	6.00
Highest quintile (>324)	45.9	6.26	6.00
Occupational skills training only			
Total	67.5%	$8.08	$7.50
Lowest hours quintile (<120)	58.2	7.49	7.00
Second lowest quintile (120–240)	69.1	7.96	7.50
Middle quintile (241–449)	68.3	7.82	7.30
Second highest quintile (450–864)	66.9	8.10	7.50
Highest quintile (>864)	71.9	8.65	8.00
OJT only			
Total	81.1%	$6.75	$6.50
Lowest hours quintile (<160)	63.1	6.58	6.00
Second lowest quintile (160–275)	77.8	7.01	6.50
Middle quintile (276–365)	88.2	6.84	6.50
Second highest quintile (366–520)	89.0	6.86	6.50
Highest quintile (>520)	89.9	6.68	6.50

Source: SPIR 96 data.

Being reminded that an academic year of enrollment should involve about 1,200 training hours provides another insight into the returns to training involvement that should be expected.

Interestingly, there has been strong correlation between the hours spent in occupational skills training and the wage received at placement but little such correlation for those enrolled in basic skills training or on-the-job training (table 10.8).

Because employment and training programs have been perceived primarily as antipoverty tools since midway in the MDTA experience, it is also useful to note the relationship between postplacement wages and the weekly earnings required to overcome poverty for families of various sizes. Program enrollment has been effective in raising small families out of poverty, but for larger families it has been only a route upward from deep in poverty to its upper levels (table 10.9).

Table 10.9 MEAN WEEKLY EARNINGS OF JTPA TITLE II-A TERMINEES
EMPLOYED AT TIME OF TERMINATION BY GENDER AND
FAMILY RELATIONSHIP STATUS BY NUMBER OF DEPENDENTS
(PERSONS WHO TERMINATED BETWEEN APRIL 1, 1996, AND JUNE 30, 1997)

Poverty Weekly Wage	Total	None $152	One $204	Two $256	Three $309	Four or More $361 (for four)
Gender						
Total	$280	$288	$278	$275	$274	$272
Male	310	302	325	325	331	325
Female	265	268	267	264	261	258
Family Status						
Parent in one-parent	269	287	273	268	264	261
Parent in two-parent	292	276	298	292	293	288
Other family member	278	279	275	270	286	283
Not family member	290	290	289	283	306	311

Source: PY 96 data, tabulated by the Center for Labor Market Studies, Northeastern
University.

WIA's jobs-first emphasis implies a continuation of low-wage targeting for the adult components. The struggles of employment and
training workforce development programs to overcome poverty are
provided an additional perspective in the light of the deterioration of
the official poverty standard over the years under discussion. When
the federal government launched the war on poverty in 1964, it
established a set of definitions and measures based on food costs as
a proportion of typical household expenditures to indicate who was
poor and eligible for help and to tell whether and what progress was
being made toward poverty alleviation. However, by the mid-1990s,
food costs had slipped substantially as a percentage of the budgetary
expenditures of the average low-income family while shelter
expenses had risen dramatically. In 1964, the poverty threshold for
a four-person family had been equal to 43 percent of the pretax and
50 percent of the posttax median family income. In 1996, it was only
31.3 percent of the pretax income (table 10.10). To achieve the same
relative pretax standard of living that the poverty threshold implied
in 1964, the 1996 poverty threshold for a family of four would have
to be increased by 39 percent—32 percent for a posttax median.

The meager value of the living standards attainable at current
poverty-level incomes has been implicitly recognized by policymakers at both national and state levels who provide eligibilities for a
number of antipoverty programs at incomes up to 200 percent of the
existing poverty thresholds. Table 10.11 cites the widespread recognition that the official poverty thresholds are outmoded and too low

Table 10.10 COMPARISONS OF THE 1996 PRETAX MEDIAN FAMILY INCOMES
AND WEIGHTED AVERAGE POVERTY INCOME THRESHOLDS FOR
FAMILIES CONTAINING TWO TO SIX PERSONS

Family Size	Median Income ($)	Poverty Threshold ($)	Threshold as Percentage of Median Income
2	$35,936	$10,233	.284
3	44,029	12,516	.284
4	51,242	16,036	.313
5	48,100	18,952	.394
6	41,700	21,389	.513

Source: March 1997 CPS, public use tape, tabulations by Center for Labor Market Studies, Northeastern University.

and lists some of the increases in poverty thresholds that have been advocated in the literature.

The poverty threshold as derived in 1964 for the average-sized poor family was approximately half the pretax median family income of the time, so 164 percent of the current poverty threshold

Table 10.11 ALTERNATE JUSTIFICATIONS FOR INCREASES IN THE CURRENT POVERTY THRESHOLDS

Poverty Line Multiple	Studies Advocating That Multiple
113%	National Research Council recommendation based on actual consumption expenditures by low-income families in 1990–95 (Citro and Michael 1995)
124%	1989 Gallup survey asking respondents' judgments as to the amount of income needed to avoid being poor (Schiller 1989)
136%	Food spending multiplier raised to four with expenditures that prevailed in 1988 (Ruggles 1990)
142%	Cost-of-housing-based poverty threshold based on rents paid on two-bedroom apartments at the 45th percentile, with rental expenditures limited to 30 percent of income, à la HUD Section 8 rental subsidy program before 1996 (Sum and Bahuguna, with Palma 1998)
165%	Weighted ratio of half of pretax median incomes of two- to six-person families in the United States in 1996 to existing poverty thresholds[4]
165%	Ratio of CPU-U adjusted BLS lower living standard budget for urban family of four to poverty threshold

Source: Fogg et al. (1999: 39).

would be required to provide the same relative standard of living today. That relationship is confirmed by the fact, as noted, that a similar ratio exists between the current poverty thresholds and the updated value of the BLS lower living standard budget for an urban family of four that ceased publication in 1981.[5]

Therefore, the existing poverty thresholds would have to be multiplied by something like 165 percent to maintain a meaningful income measure reflecting income changes over the 35 years since a national war on poverty was officially declared by the president of the United States. Table 10.12 provides estimates of the family incomes and consequent full-time, full-year hourly wage implied for a single earner that would comprise the poverty thresholds for families of various sizes at 100 percent, 133 percent, and 165 percent of the current poverty thresholds. The latter would be the wage results necessary if workforce development programs were currently to be the effective antipoverty tools they were originally expected to become.

One needs only to reexamine the wage results recorded in tables 10.6 and 10.9 to recognize how far behind their original antipoverty ambitions workforce development programs have fallen. The 10 occupational categories predominating throughout the history of MDTA, CETA, and JTPA—clerk/typist, secretary or word processor, electronic assembler, machinist, custodian, nurse's aide, salesperson, licensed practical nurse, accounting clerk or bookkeeper, food service worker, and computer operator—offered a substantial step forward for most enrollees during the 1960s and 1970s. They enjoy little wage advantage today.

The wages attained by many JTPA Title II-A terminees in the past do not augur well for placement at these upgraded poverty standards,

Table 10.12 1996 FEDERAL POVERTY GUIDELINES WITH 133 PERCENT AND 165 PERCENT ADJUSTMENTS

Family Size	Poverty Guideline	Hourly Wage	133% of Poverty	Hourly Wage	165% of Poverty	Hourly Wage
1	$7,890	$3.79	$10,520	$5.04	$13,019	$6.26
2	10,610	5.10	14,150	6.78	17,507	8.42
3	13,330	6.41	17,770	8.53	21,995	10.57
4	16,050	7.72	21,400	10.27	26,483	12.73
5	18,770	9.02	25,030	12.00	30,971	14.89
6	21,490	10.33	28,650	13.74	35,459	17.05
7	24,210	12.42	32,280	16.52	39,947	19.21
8	26,930	13.89	35,910	18.47	44,435	21.36

Source: Mangum et al. (1999: 24–35).

both because the training received by most terminees has not been designed to add substantially to their existing occupational skills and because the occupations chosen for training too often were not those expected to provide above-poverty wages. As noted, the most consistent shortcoming of past skill training programs for the disadvantaged and displaced has been their concentration on occupations the skills of which could be learned relatively quickly and that therefore tended to pay relatively low initial wages. The basic economics of human capital investment and occupational wage structures cannot be overturned by an act of Congress. We can only expect trainees to reap what they have sown. Though the costs may be subsidized, the expected returns to investments in training will, at best, be consistent with the resources committed.

The Dislocated

It is instructive to compare the participant characteristics and results for JTPA's Title III dislocated workers to those for Title II-A disadvantaged adults. Title II-A enrollees are, by definition, economically disadvantaged adults who by and large have limited education and work experience. Title III enrollees are more frequently workers with more substantial experience who were displaced from their regular employment by a plant closing, corporate downsizing, major technological change, or international competition. Their training has been on average of no longer duration than II-A training. They just have more skills and experience to begin with and can expect higher placement wages as a result, although often below those that they earned on the jobs from which they were displaced.

Whereas in the mid-1990s, 46 percent of II-A terminees were female family heads, 36.4 percent of Title III terminees were parents in two-parent families, 29.4 percent were not members of a family, and 21.5 percent were nonparent family members. Whereas 68 percent of those in II-A were female, probably as a consequence of pressure to reduce public assistance rolls, males were 54 percent in Title III. Three-quarters in Title III were non-Hispanic whites, compared with one-half for Title II-A. On the other hand, 56 percent of Title II-A terminees had high school educations and 21 percent some postsecondary schooling, compared with 47 percent high school graduates and 13 percent with college diplomas in Title III. One-third of those in II-A were AFDC recipients, with a total of 41 percent being public assistance recipients with general assistance and Supplemental Security Income added, compared with essentially none in Title III. One-third of II-A enrollees lacked significant work histories, 58 percent were deficient in basic education skills, and 14 percent had been convicted as public offenders. By definition, all of those in Title III had been in the labor force, with over half making more than $10 an hour at the time of displacement. Less than one-third of Title III enrollees have been poor or near poor, in contrast with all of those in Title II-A.

Data on most dislocated worker programs reflect a population that has been steadily employed and needs primarily to be restored to employment. The workers are anxious to return to jobs to support their families, not to spend time in school. Although one-fifth of enrollees had not completed their high school education, a factor related more to their age than to their predilections, they have made little use of remedial help—only 1 in 20 participants receive basic education instruction. As many participants had substantial skills, local project operators have emphasized short-term, low-cost assistance designed to get them back to work without additional training. Once enrolled, nearly half the dislocated worker enrollees as contrasted with about 10 percent of disadvantaged adults engaged in neither remedial education nor skills training, concerning themselves primarily with job search assistance. The superior position of those who did not appear to need occupational retraining was indicated by the fact that their prelayoff wage had averaged $12.52, compared with $11.45 for the 1995 classroom skills training group. Nevertheless, skills training seems to have paid off for those who received it. Whereas the placement wage of those Title III enrollees forgoing training in program year 1995 was $10.23 and their average wage at 13-week follow-up was $11.34, those who undertook classroom skills training were placed at $10.36 and were earning $10.65 at follow-up, despite their lower prelayoff earnings. This was the result of an average of only 223 hours of occupational skills training. In further contrast, those who undertook basic skills training only were placed at $9.12 and were down to $9.06 at follow-up, with those undertaking on-the-job training receiving only $8.86 and $9.08, respectively. Those retained had a placement rate at termination of 76 percent and a wage recovery rate of 93.6 percent, compared with 63 percent and 86.2 percent, respectively, for those Title III participants not retrained.

Unlike JTPA Title II-A disadvantaged adults, Title III placement rates and placement wages have not been positively correlated with their length of training, being more dependent upon their current skills. The finding that average placement wages were less than pre-displacement wages is an indication of the losses from displacement and the difficulty of catching up with the gains of longevity despite additional training. According to one estimate, the average displaced worker loses $80,000 in lifetime earnings. The authors concluded that retraining of at least two years' duration—equivalent to an associate's degree—would be necessary to restore their previous earning power (Jacobson, LaLonde, and Sullivan 1993).

Table 10.13 returns to the issue of the antipoverty potency of JTPA placement wages, comparing them for Titles II-A and III in relation to various multiples of the current poverty guidelines. Though a substantially higher proportion of Title III than Title II-A terminees were enabled to overcome poverty by various definitions, these dislocated workers, too, fell far short of the 1964 equivalent income targets, especially as their numbers of dependents rose.

Another of the positive aspects of the Workforce Investment Act is its potential for better integration between the employment and training services provided under Title I and the adult basic education and literacy programs under Title II. The new act continues to provide separate funding for adult basic education and literacy programs. However, it at least calls for coordination and integration of services between Titles I and II and with other employment and training activities within a state through joint planning and oversight by state and local Workforce Investment Boards. There is clear evidence from the national Labor Department databases that a high fraction of the participants in JTPA Titles II-A and III programs in recent years have lacked even rudimentary reading and math proficiencies

Table 10.13 PERCENTAGE OF EMPLOYED JTPA TITLE II-A AND TITLE III TERMINEES WITH GROSS WEEKLY EARNINGS AT OR ABOVE SELECTED EARNINGS THRESHOLDS, BY NUMBER OF DEPENDENTS (PERSONS WHO TERMINATED BETWEEN APRIL 1, 1996, AND JUNE 30, 1997)

Earnings Level	One Dependent	Two Dependents	Three Dependents
Title II-A			
100% of poverty	74.4	55.7	29.4
133% of poverty	46.8	23.8	9.0
150% of poverty	31.9	15.4	5.8
175% of poverty	19.1	8.4	2.6
Title III			
100% of poverty	85.2	77.2	57.5
133% of poverty	69.2	53.7	31.7
150% of poverty	57.8	44.3	25.0
175% of poverty	45.4	32.4	17.4

Source: SPIR 96 data, tabulations by Center for Labor Market Studies, Northeastern University, p. 27.

at the time of enrollment (table 10.14). For instance, during PY 1996, 14 percent of Title II-A terminees who received services beyond objective assessment had reading proficiencies below the seventh-grade level, and 24 percent performed below the seventh-grade level in math. Those who did not continue beyond objective assessment were even worse off, with 18 percent and 30 percent, respectively, lacking reading and math proficiencies equal to the seventh-grade level. High school dropouts among the terminees had entered the JTPA system with 29 percent performing below seventh-grade level in reading and 46 percent below in math. The literacy proficiencies of Title III terminees have been somewhat stronger, with 10 percent reading below the seventh-grade level and 17 percent performing below the seventh-grade level in math. That was partly true because their average educational background was superior, with only 11 percent lacking a high school diploma compared with 23 percent of Title II-A terminees. Of those Title III enrollees without a high school diploma, 32 percent fell below the seventh-grade level in reading and 47 percent in math, slightly higher than their Title II-A counterparts.

Table 10.14 READING AND MATH SKILLS OF JTPA TITLE II-A AND III TERMINEES BY SELECTED CHARACTERISTICS

| | Percentage below Seventh-Grade Level | | | |
| | Title II-A | | Title III | |
	Reading	Math	Reading	Math
Total	14.8	25.4	9.9	16.8
Objective assessment only	17.7	30.4	—	—
Received services	13.9	23.8	—	—
Male	16.5	25.7	9.8	14.7
Female	14.0	25.3	10.0	18.7
White, non-Hispanic	7.9	18.1	5.4	11.7
Black, non-Hispanic	19.7	32.1	19.2	31.1
Hispanic	22.0	32.1	22.4	27.6
American Indian/Alaskan	15.4	29.0	10.4	19.2
Asian, Pacific Islander	35.1	24.7	26.1	21.7
Under 25	13.0	19.9	9.9	14.2
25–44	14.9	26.3	9.9	17.1
45 and above	16.7	28.0	9.9	17.0
Less than high school	29.2	46.0	32.2	47.2
H.S. graduation or equivalent	12.2	22.2	10.0	18.5
Some college	6.4	12.6	5.8	10.6
Bachelor's and above	7.7	7.5	2.8	3.2

Source: SPIR 96 data, persons who terminated between April 1, 1996, and June 30, 1997.

Yet, despite this high incidence of severe literacy and numeracy deficiencies, only about one out of every five Title II-A enrollees and 1 of 10 Title III enrollees received any remedial education. In fact, only one of three Title II-A enrollees and one of five of those Title III enrollees with reading and math skills below the seventh-grade level received such services (table 10.15). However, only about half those enrolled in basic skills training were also engaged in occupational skills training (48 percent for Title II-A and 56 percent for Title III), suggesting limited integration between the dual training aspects required for higher-level and better-paid occupations.

Also, the placement and wage outcomes for basic education terminees have been quite low. Only half of the Title II-A terminees receiving basic skills education entered employment upon termination from the local JTPA system, compared with 7 of 10 of those receiving a combination of basic skills education and either classroom occupational training or on-the-job training (table 10.16). One could conjecture that either little remediation actually occurred or that which did had little labor market value, absent accompanying occupational skills preparation. The long-term lesson seems yet to be learned that remedial basic education is essential to upgrade the employability of most disadvantaged workers but to be effective it must be integrated with, rather than apart from, occupational skills training.

Table 10.15 PERCENTAGE OF JTPA TERMINEES WHO RECEIVED BASIC SKILLS TRAINING AMONG THOSE WHO TERMINATED BETWEEN 1 APRIL 1996 AND 30 JUNE 1997

	Title II-A	Title III
All terminees	22%	11%
Reading skills below seventh-grade level	37	19
Reading skills at or above seventh-grade level	19	12
Reading skills missing	20	5
Math skills below seventh-grade level	34	19
Math skills at or above seventh-grade level	18	11
Math skills missing	19	5
Basic skills deficient	29	17
Not basic skills deficient	12	10
Reading or math skills missing	19	5

Source: SPIR 96 data, tabulations by Center for Labor Market Studies, Northeastern University, p. 39.

Table 10.16 EMPLOYMENT RATES AND MEAN HOURLY PLACEMENT WAGES
OF JTPA TITLE II-A TERMINEES BY THEIR BASIC SKILLS TRAINING
STATUS

Trainee Group	Entering Employment Rate (%)	Mean Hourly Wage ($)
All terminees	65.1%	$7.52
Received basic skills only	49.0	6.43
Received basic skills plus classroom training or OJT	69.7	7.26
Received no basic skills training	66.7	7.68

Source: PY 96 SPIR data, tabulations by Center for Labor Market Studies, Northeastern
University.

Disadvantaged Youth

Current disillusionment with the youth program results also has a
long history. A major difference is that less was expected in earlier
days. Enrolled youth often made less earnings progress than those
not enrolled, a situation that goes back to the Neighborhood Youth
Corps that paralleled MDTA during the 1960s. Such programs were
often described as "aging vats" in which to park the youth until they
either went back to school or became old enough to become better
employed or to disappear. There were always some successful youth
programs, but they were never run-of-the-mill. Note that most youth
programs are still primarily work experience programs rather than
skills training programs, though they have become enriched in recent
years with some basic remedial education. Average youth enrollment
durations have been around 15 weeks throughout the employment
and training experience.

The Title II-C terminees of the mid-90s were composed of a heavily minority population—only 38 percent being non-Hispanic whites
and three-quarters not high school graduates. Despite their youth,
about 20 percent in PY 1995 were single parents, 31 percent were
welfare recipients, and 42 percent had received food stamps. Two-
thirds were not in the active labor force and had no significant preen-
rollment work history, 71 percent were deficient in basic skills,
28 percent were pregnant or parenting youth, and one of nine was a
public offender. During their enrollment, only 113,563 of the 130,116
PY 95 youthful terminees had received any service beyond objective assessment. Of those, one-half were provided with basic skills
training during their enrollment, a quarter underwent some occupational skills training, and a similar portion obtained some work experience. Four of five were involved in the program for no more than

500 hours, with an average training duration of 330 hours. Not surprisingly, only about one-third entered employment at termination, and a little over half were calculated to have attained employability enhancements of some type such as improved basic skills or a general equivalency diploma. Only 2 percent of those previously out of school returned to school, while 15 percent were in school and remained. Average hourly wages for those entering employment rose from $5.07 in PY 91 to $5.81 in PY 95, but this only matched the rise in the consumer price index over the same period.

Although JTPA allowed local administrators to offer participants a variety of services, the summer youth employment program funded primarily work experience. Most enrollees worked 32 hours a week at government agencies, schools, or community organizations for seven weeks at the federal hourly minimum wage. The law required local sponsors to assess the reading and math skills of participants and to allocate at least some funding to teaching the 3 Rs. The summer and year-round youth programs were designed to offer work experience and earnings as an incentive to stay in or return to school, as well as a source of needed income. Requirements to include basic remedial education were introduced in 1986 and then intensified after the devastating reports of the early 1990s. Thereafter, about half the summer youth enrollees received academic enrichment as well as work experience. Half the year-round enrollees received basic skills training and 25 percent entered job skills training, thereby raising the total employability enhancement rate from 39 percent in 1990 to 54 percent in 1994. Nevertheless, the limited time spent in either remedial education, skills training, or work experience could hardly be expected to substantially improve the learning and earning experience of youth confronting major barriers to employment.

The vaunted gains for the Job Corps have always been generated by the minority who remain in residence long enough to make a substantial difference in their conduct as well as their skills, and those gains come more from postprogram employment stability than wage increases. Despite the "nothing works for disadvantaged youth" aura of the prevailing discussions, WIA portends a reinvigorated youth program under the direction of the newly required Youth Council within every local Workforce Investment Board. The MDTA, CETA, and JTPA experience confirms its need.

COMMENTARY

The necessity of formal occupational preparation has been documented increasingly over the years. The second-chance workforce development programs that were among the first products of that

recognition have made substantial contributions. Nevertheless, they
have maintained too many of their initial characteristics and have not
kept up with the march of time. Now even that weak commitment
appears to have disappeared in favor of WIA's jobs-first preference.

Budgetary Consequences

The publicity about negative evaluations throughout the late 1980s
and early 1990s could only lessen enthusiasm for employment and
training programs on behalf of adults and create the conviction that
nothing works for out-of-school and at-risk youth. Amendments to
JTPA in 1992 insisted that most enrollees have other identified
employment barriers than merely low incomes in order to qualify
for JTPA enrollment as disadvantaged and also minimized the use
of job search training unaccompanied by skills improvement. But
those amendments only indicated the concern of the friends of
employment and training who had persisted in their support as the
years went by (Pines 1989a, 1989b). Greater animosity was demonstrated by the recisions of already appropriated but as yet unspent
budgets that occurred following the 1994 election.

By PY 1997, with replacement of JTPA under discussion, the total
budget for what had been known as employment and training programs but now are designated more appropriately as workforce
development programs was nearly back to its PY 1995 level, not
accounting for inflation. However, the reallocation involved reflected
congressional program judgments as well as political pressures. For
JTPA, Title II-A was still below recision levels, though it was creep-
ing back up from the further cuts in PY 1996. Funding for Title II-B
Summer Youth was even above pre-recision levels, the result of considerable lobbying but probably also a reflection of a preference for
keeping in-school youth off the streets during the summer. Funding
to train out-of-school youth through the Title II-C Year-Round Youth
program was cut drastically and remained down. Title III and Trade
Adjustment Act dislocated worker funds were restored in a reflection
of the desire to divert opposition to various reductions in foreign
trade barriers. The Job Corps experienced modest gains. Other JTPA
expenditures declined even further in the years following the PY
1995 recisions. Always politically potent older workers got their
money back and then some. On the other hand, programs for out-of-
school youth, the funding for which was $8.5 billion in 1979 if
counted in 1997 dollars, had declined to $1.5 billion by the latter
year. The superior balance of power of secondary over postsecondary
vocational education was reflected in which programs recovered and

which did not. The introduction of programs such as School-to-Work and Goals 2000 Education Reform reflected the greater concern evident for the in-school mainstream as contrasted with the out-of-school poor. That includes Pell grants with appropriations approximately double those of JTPA. Pell grants are accessed for the most part by low-income college students. WIA continues these trends in its first year by allocating $1.4 billion to dislocated worker services but only $955 million for all other adults; it keeps funding for disadvantaged youth stable at $1 billion but adds $250 million for pilot efforts in selected troubled cities.

SHALL WE REJOICE?

What should one conclude concerning the results of more than one-third of a century of second-chance workforce development programs? Was the $2,165 per adult participant, $2,108 per youth participant, $7,378 per adult who entered employment, and $4,764 per youth positive termination in program year 1994, for instance, a worthwhile investment? First, there are reasons to think that the cost per adult participant is higher and the cost per adult who entered employment lower than those official figures.[6] But taking those costs at face value, let us compare the costs to the results. Going in, 51 percent of disadvantaged adults in PY 95 had not worked for more than 26 weeks; 14 percent earned less than $5.00 an hour, 25 percent $5.00 to $7.49, and 11 percent $7.50 or more. Coming out, two-thirds were employed, and of those 11 percent earned less than $5.00 an hour, 19 percent between $5.00 and $5.99, 32 percent between $6.00 and $7.49, 24 percent between $7.50 and $9.99, and 13 percent $10.00 or more, for an average hourly wage of $7.25. But full-time, full-year employment at that average wage would bring a four-member family only to the federal poverty line. That phenomenon has a long history: MDTA and CETA also brought their average participants from deep in poverty to its upper edges. But at least the posttraining wages of JTPA's economically disadvantaged enrollees exceeded their pretraining wages, which was not true for the Title III dislocated workers.

As noted earlier, training duration always has been a major factor influencing training outcomes. It was not surprising, therefore, that during the late 1980s, when the average training duration had shrunk to less than 24 weeks, a comparison between the subsequent earnings of adult JTPA participants (many of whom had not actually received training) and a control group (who had not been enrolled in JTPA but might have been enrolled elsewhere) showed only modest gains for adults and no positive returns for youth, whose enrollment was even briefer (Bloom et al. 1993).

However, even though the average duration of JTPA training lengthened from 24 weeks in the 1980s to 34 weeks in the 1990s, the graduates of the program suffered from the same economic forces that widened the earnings advantages of college graduates over all of those with less education and training and dictated that only those with postgraduate training were, on average, able to keep their real incomes from declining. The continued positive relationship between training duration and placement and retention wages has already been demonstrated, though the margin was by no means as great under JTPA as it had been under CETA. Given the extended periods of job preparation manifested by the population at large, second-chance skill training programs will either have to extend their duration longer or increase their intensity to even regain the CETA impacts.

Interestingly, the consistent increase in average wages with enroll-ment duration does not prevail for either on-the-job training or basic education, a fact that supports the view that subsidizing on-the-job training under JTPA often buys a job rather than training. Neither does it hold true for Title III, where the degree of convergence of the prior skills and experience of the dislocated worker with labor mar-ket need is the determining factor. The number of youthful trainees engaged in any long-term training under JTPA has been too few to measure the differential results.

But time as such is not the telling factor. It is to what purpose the time is dedicated and what is done in the time allocated. Better-paying jobs are characterized by longer preparation times or more work experience. Longer training durations for disadvantaged adults open doors to more rewarding occupations. The same can be said for youth. There are successful programs for out-of-school and at-risk youth, but they require more commitment and invest-ment than has generally been found in run-of-the-mill JTPA youth programs. The school-to-work movement has concentrated on the in-school population and, as WIA was replacing JTPA, was just beginning to widen its attention to include those already on the out-side. The few programs that had demonstrated success with the at-risk and out-of-school youth population have been characterized by at least a year's enrollment duration; integrated combinations of basic education, skills training, and on-the-job experience; visible connection to jobs of promise; mentoring by respected adults; opportunities for high-profile community service; and the possibilities of further educational advancement upon demonstrated success (Walker 1997: 76). The youth in these programs have shared decisionmaking responsibilities within their programs and have gained a greater sense of empowerment than that available through antisocial activities. There is no reason to expect greater success with lesser commitment.

There is little reason to doubt the worthwhileness of the 36-year investment in remedial skills training for many disadvantaged adults. It could have been done better, but the evidence is that the investment has paid off as well as any human capital investment. James Heckman (1996: 326) has estimated that the average mainstream investment in human capital pays off at a rate no greater than 10 percent. Robert LaLonde (1995: 156), here and elsewhere, has reviewed the evaluation literature and concluded that MDTA and CETA, and by implication JTPA, have raised the annual earnings of their participants by $1,000 to $2,000. Even with costs per participant entering employment alleged to be $7,368, it would only be necessary to increase the annual earnings of those placed by $737 in perpetuity to equal a rate of return calculated on the basis of college education and employer-sponsored training as well as public second-chance programs. The perpetuity is the challenge because the durability of the earnings differential is an unknown.

The struggle is to keep up with the race between education, training, and the job market. As noted earlier, between 1973 and 1997 only the college educated were able, on average, to avoid deterioration of their real earnings and only those with education beyond the baccalaureate degree have enjoyed real increases in their living standards. As also noted earlier, the 10 occupational categories predominating throughout the employment and training program history— clerk/typist, secretary or word processor, electronic assembler, machinist, custodian, nurse's aide, salesperson, licensed practical nurse, accounting clerk or bookkeeper, food service worker, and computer operator—offered a substantial step forward for most enrollees during the 1960s and 1970s but enjoyed little or no wage advantage in the 1990s. As Bennici, Mangum, and Sum have already demonstrated in this volume, giving a meaningful second labor market chance to a disadvantaged adult in the 1990s and beyond requires both more intensive and extensive preparation. The key issue is whether the nation is willing to make the necessary human resource investments.

WHITHER WIA?

Being possessed of little institutional memory, Congress embodied in its Workforce Investment Act of 1998 few of the lessons learned from the previous 36 years of workforce development experience. After several years of promising (or threatening) to consolidate what were described as a plethora of workforce development programs and devolve them to the states in the form of relatively unfettered block grants, Congress provided little of either consolidation or added state discretion in the WIA. WIA does broaden the membership required of the state and local Workforce Investment Boards that replace the State Job Training Coordinating Councils and Private Industry Councils of JTPA, though not beyond what many states had already done on their own. That may enhance the joint across-program consideration of issues. Though the Adult Education and Literacy provisions of WIA's Title II are not integrated with the Workforce Investment Systems of Title I—the focus of this treatise—their joint appearance in the same legislation might invite their education and job training sponsors to at least consider their potential compatibility. The individual training accounts required by the act represent a congressional preference for vouchers, though there is no evidence that they have been effective for disadvantaged populations. The five-year plan requirements of WIA Title I should extend time horizons somewhat. Though not required, most promising is Title V's invitation for states to undertake unified planning of most federally funded employment, training, and public assistance programs, thereby promoting coordination across and among those programs. Those states with the political will to do so could add an array of state-sponsored programs to that mix, including appropriate educational components. WIA makes universal the still unproven but promising one-stop career centers. WIA's individual training accounts, though perceived as vouchers, could be used to enable well-counseled individuals to choose and tailor employment and training services to individual need. The act calls for negotiated state and local performance criteria and more rigorous and systematic measurement of outcomes. WIA's youth provisions in Chapter 4 of Title I are really commendable, involving Youth Councils within Workforce Investment Boards in the design of a more comprehensive employment development system for both in-school and out-of-school youth and young adults, with additional funding for exemplary programs in heavily impacted poverty areas.

This mix of weaknesses and strengths is further burdened by exalting a "work first" philosophy to the extent that training is relegated to the position of service of last resort. Adults without limitation as to socioeconomic status are made eligible for those "core services" that one would expect to see offered by a well-run public employment service:

- Eligibility determination;
- Outreach, intake, and orientation;
- Assessment of skills, aptitudes, abilities, and supportive service needs;
- Job search and placement assistance and career counseling;
- Labor market information;
- Information concerning the effectiveness of alternative service providers;
- Information concerning the availability of supportive services;
- Information about and assistance in filing for other related services; and
- Follow-up services.

If those core services are not sufficient to enable an unemployed applicant to obtain or retain employment or an employed one to attain or retain a job at a pay rate adequate to "allow for self-sufficiency," the applicant—again, without socioeconomic limitation—becomes eligible for "intensive services" that include the following:

- Diagnostic testing and assessment,
- Identification of employment barriers and appropriate employment goals,
- Development of an individual employment plan,
- Individual and group counseling and career planning,
- Case management for those seeking training, and
- Short-term prevocational services, including development of learning skills, interviewing skills, punctuality, personal maintenance skills, and professional conduct to prepare individuals for unsubsidized employment or training.

The appropriations for dislocated adults and all other adults are separate for all of these core and intensive training purposes so that funding for services to either group could well be exhausted before the core and intensive hurdles are surmounted.

But even if funds for training are available, they may not be accessible to the unskilled individual. WIA provides that "funds allocated to a local area . . . shall be used to provide training services to adults and dislocated workers . . . who have met the eligibility requirements for intensive services . . . and who are unable to obtain or retain employment through such services." In straightforward language, those who as a result of core services cannot obtain a job paying enough to provide self-sufficiency are eligible for intensive services, but, apparently, only those who cannot find any job of any kind following intensive services can receive skills training under the Workforce Investment Act. The act contains no provisos about the quality, work hours, pay, or working conditions of the jobs involved. Whether the job provides wages consistent with self-sufficiency appears to be irrelevant as a criterion for referral to training. The only issue is whether the individual has or has not been able to "obtain or retain employment" in the absence of the training in question. When confronted by a situation in which employment does not appear possible without some training, it does not seem likely that program administrators are then going to introduce that individual to a training sequence long enough to lift him or her to the advocated median income wage. The jobs-first focus would more likely argue for just enough training to enable the earliest possible job placement.

But that is not all. To be eligible for Workforce Investment Act training, one must also be "unable to obtain other grant assistance for such services, including Federal Pell Grants or require assistance beyond the assistance made available under other grant assistance programs, including Federal Pell Grants." WIA is, therefore, the trainer of last resort, with funds available for training only for those who cannot otherwise find jobs or alternative sources of training. Thus, spending priorities under the act are consistent with the "work first" or "jobs first" priority. As noted, access by adults to core, intensive, and training services is not restricted to those who are economically disadvantaged. However, if funds are limited compared to the demands for services, as they ordinarily are and certainly will be under WIA, priority among nondislocated adults is to be given to "recipients of public assistance and other low income individuals for intensive services and training services." A welfare reform priority is implied, though the economically disadvantaged not receiving public assistance are included in the priority. Dislocated workers have access to their own funding and do not face this competition. Nevertheless, for those who can surmount these numerous hurdles, the act declares that training services may include

- Occupational skills training, including training for nontraditional employment;

- On-the-job training;
- Combinations of workplace training and related instruction, including cooperative education (apprenticeship is not cited but should fit the description);
- Private-sector-provided training;
- Skill upgrading and retraining;
- Entrepreneurial training;
- Job readiness training;
- Adult education and literacy; and
- Customized training conducted for employers with employment guarantees upon successful completion.

This list of training options seems highly diverse and sophisticated, considering its apparent last-resort nature. However, it is consistent with the hypothesis that little training will occur for disadvantaged adults, more will be available to dislocated workers, and the designation of skill upgrading and retraining will open the option of training incumbent workers, few of whom could meet the definition of disadvantagement. How to justify the training of incumbent workers with funds from an act restricting training to those unable to obtain or retain employment remains a mystery to which we return later. Perhaps the key will be to declare the incumbent workers to be in danger of losing their jobs in the absence of further training.

APPLYING THE LESSONS OF EXPERIENCE

But Congress is not the only body charged with learning and applying the lessons from 37 years of workforce development program experience. Just as Congress has advertised its legislative product as a block grant devolving further authority and discretion to states and localities, those entities now have the responsibility to confront the challenge in innovative ways that may not have been contemplated at the federal level. Overall, states have tended to care for mainstream populations but ignore the needs of those on the political periphery. Historically, a few states have stepped up to the various challenges others have ignored. Federal sponsorship and funding have generally been necessary to entice states to serve those who are politically weak at the local and state levels but in the aggregate have been able to win support at the national level. Even then, increasing numbers of states fail to meet the matching requirements that would bring them substantial additional federal funds to serve needy state citizens. MDTA was modeled after a Pennsylvania retraining program, but only national legislation carried the concept cross-country. The 1964 declaration of war on poverty assumed the necessity of bypassing state and local governments in favor of partnership between the federal government and community-based organizations because the governments in between had shown little enthusiasm for the challenge. But the federal partner having lost momentum in recent years, increasing numbers of states have begun to exert new initiatives. The Workforce Investment Act is an invitation to do exactly that for those disadvantaged and dislocated workers—adults and youth—who have been the 37-year targets of programs designed to give them a second chance at employability. Despite the new act's limitations, a truly committed state can offer a realistic second chance if it is willing to use federal funds as a supplement to its own designed and funded programs.

What would that realistic second chance look like? It would serve variously the economically disadvantaged, the welfare reform target, and the displaced experienced worker. Within those broad groupings, it would be individually focused, combining the preferences of the client and the guidance of a knowledgeable case manager in an individualized rehabilitative plan. It would recognize that simply having a job is not sufficient. There must be the realistic promise of a family-supporting wage within a reasonable time period. Even being able to earn one's way out of poverty is not enough. Today's poverty thresholds would have to be increased sufficiently to offer the same standard of living as that provided by the poverty thresholds of 1964, as King et al. demonstrate in this volume. But the poverty threshold should be only the beginning, not the end. Once committed to help, case managers of workforce development programs should not abandon an applicant until he/she has been able to achieve a family-supporting income.

The single head of household, upon successful completion of a workforce development program, should be able to count on placement at a wage rate at least equal to the poverty threshold for full-time, full-year work, accompanied by Earned Income Tax Credits or some other form of income subsidy leading upward toward the 165 percent of the current poverty threshold that would equate with the 1964 promise. The responsible case manager should continue to counsel potential earners in a family as long as that family accepts and responds to the challenge until an hourly wage is attained that would allow a one-earner family to reach that income target through full-time, full-year earnings. Child care assistance and Medicaid should be guaranteed as needed until that target is met. A two-parent family should be entitled to do even better if one wants to work full-time and the other part-time while sharing parenting duties, but society should make the single-earner choice a viable one for those willing to undertake the requisite workforce development.

How could all of this be accomplished in a second-chance program? For out-of-school but ill-prepared youth, that would depend upon an out-of-school equivalent to the school-to-work program as derived by the Levitan Youth Policy Network, described in *A Generation of Challenge: Pathways to Success for Urban Youth* and available from the Sar Levitan Center for Social Policy Studies at Johns Hopkins University. For family heads, those target wages are around the median for those occupations in Bennici, Mangum, and Sum's table 2.8, requiring an associate degree, substantial on-the-job training, or long work experience. How can a program that has taken 36 years to get to a 34-week average training duration shift to that level of accomplishment? That is where local-level ingenuity unimpeded by detailed federal rules can (but not necessarily will) manifest itself. As noted, though 104 weeks of training has been legally allowable almost from the beginning of the workforce development experiences, funding has never been adequate to justify spending such a high proportion of scarce resources on so few. Also, the trainee and dependents must be supported during the training. As also noted, one of CETA's limitations was that more than half its training appropriations went into stipends. Under JTPA, only Aid to Families with Dependent Children (AFDC) recipients have had stipends available. The same must be said for child care assistance and health insurance. Add to the dilemma the fact that employers often say to training completers, "Your training is great, but where is your work experience? How do I know you can do the job?" But all of that can fit together, given flexibility, ingenuity, and dollars.

Imagine a competent case manager employed in a one-stop career center or one of the new state workforce development departments arising across the nation (see Pines and Callahan 1997; Lazerus et al. 1998). She/he opens the state's equivalent of BLS Bulletin 2472, *Employment Outlook: 1994–2005 Job Quality and Other Aspects of Projected Employment Growth,* prepared by the state's labor market information unit, and shares it with the client sitting comfortably across the table.[7] They turn to the state counterpart of table B-1 and mark all of the occupations designated for earnings quartiles 2 and 3 and designating associate degree or long-term and moderate-term

OJT as the most significant source of training. They leave out the work experience category because the client cannot wait that long, even if he/she could get a foot onto the work experience ladder. They now have before them a long list of technician, administrative support and precision production, craft and repair, and operative and fabrication occupations and a few service occupations.

Now imagine this knowledgeable case manager learning the client's background, experience, interests, capabilities, and financial situation. *If* the client is a former AFDC recipient now making the transition to TANF and *if* the state's welfare administrators are not too enamored of the "jobs first" philosophy, she has two years of education and training time available, accompanied by child care assistance and transitional Medicaid. *If* she does not require remedial education before entering an associate's degree program and *if* that is her best choice, then she is on her way. However, "jobs first" is not a threat if used as a work experience step on an upward ladder because, receiving no public assistance while employed, the client is not eating up the valued 60-month lifetime public assistance limit. Client preference or the need for remedial education may suggest a shorter-term program or an alternating mix of classroom and on-the-job training. But the case manager stays committed and involved as long as the client chooses continued effort until the 165 percent poverty target is attained.

For those without access to welfare assistance, more ingenuity is required but the possibilities are still there. Being able to undertake and complete an uninterrupted two-year classroom program is unlikely and often undesirable. The devolved WIA funds will help, but they were inadequate before and will remain so. There is no legitimate reason that a state cannot supplement that federal funding to pay tuition at its own postsecondary institutions for those declared eligible. The new federal legislation encourages a work-first approach, allowing federally funded training beyond core services only if eligible individuals cannot be placed in employment on the basis of their existing skills, regardless of the inadequacy of the wage level. How vigorously that requirement will be imposed remains to be seen. Bringing a family's income to the current poverty guideline may offer subsistence but hardly self-sufficiency. Work first may make sense if perceived as a work experience step followed by classroom and/or on-the-job training thereafter. If not, it will merely transfer the welfare poor to the ranks of the working poor.

If a state can justify use of federal training funds or provide its own, the sticking point becomes subsistence during the training process for those not eligible for welfare assistance. Some of the displaced may be eligible for Trade Adjustment Act or other foreign trade protection. For the rest, the preferred approach may be to intersperse classroom training with on-the-job training and work experience. That would be preferable pedagogically at any rate. Classrooms and laboratories serve well for concentration on either facts or skills but always suffer from artificiality. Sooner or later the abstract learning must be applied and tested in a realistic on-the-job setting.

Back to our case manager example. As in most U.S. job markets in 1999, labor is in demand and employers are cooperative. Once client and case manager have agreed upon a training occupation, an initial classroom sequence is undertaken combining introduction to the hands-on skills with related academic instruction. Congress has unwisely forbidden the combined use of Workforce Investment Act funds and Pell grants for subsistence purposes. However, needs-related payments are allowed under the WIA, though they further reduce the scarce training moneys available. Still, wise use of such funds for subsistence purposes is better than enforced restriction to ineffectively short training durations. And there is no reason that states in their current budgetary situations should not supply their own subsistence supplements for classroom sequences. With subsistence provided from either federal or state sources, the classroom sequence melds into on-the-job training, with a cooperating employer receiving a subsidy of half the wage for, say, three months. Then, perhaps, there will be another classroom sequence followed by another OJT period, or, if the trainee's skills have become sufficient to be worth it, the next period may be an internship fully paid by the employer. Each OJT sequence or internship should involve mentorship by fellow employees who can help with personal conduct and with adaption to the workplace society as well as job performance. Part-time employment may also be used for income supplementation during classroom periods, preferably but not necessarily in a training-related occupation.

The final certification may be an associate's degree or lesser completion certificate, but equally important will be the OJT/internship employer's recommendation—and often those will have changed into a permanent job offer from the training employer. None of this is new. It has been going on sub rosa in individual circumstances all along. But running programs by the book kept it from becoming the norm. JTPA administrators have sent JTPA trainees to schools to be entered in the schools' ongoing programs. School financial aid offices administered Pell grants, but JTPA trainees did not normally go through those offices. The classroom and OJT components of JTPA were administered at the local level by different agencies with no significant cooperation between them. OJT wage reimbursement was used to "buy" a job, usually without being concerned whether and how much training occurred. Postsecondary vocational and technical schools and community colleges have long maintained internship relationships with cooperating employers but have treated JTPA and employers as separate customers without mixing them. Placing JTPA graduates generally has been the responsibility of the JTPA administrators and public employment services rather than that of the schools that trained them. Now it becomes the case manager's task to bring all those forces to bear on the trainee's future, with the additional handicap of forced choice between Workforce Investment Act and Pell grant and other funding.

But neither the alternative training funding limitation nor the prohibition against training the placeable need thwart the imaginative and committed state. WIA funds can concentrate on the core and intensive services, supplementing the scarce Wagner-Peyser Act support for the public employment service through the new one-stop centers, while occupational skills training is supported by Pell grant, federal, and state vocational and other education funding. Or, while the latter sources pay for training, the needs-based payments provisions of WIA might be used for subsistence stipends. The Title I listing of incumbent worker training and skill upgrading among "allowable statewide employment and training activities" and "local employment and training activities," along with the exception of on-the-job training and customized training from eligible provider of training service and one-stop delivery system and individual training account requirements, all suggest the possibility of using WIA funding in cooperation with employers while education funding supports classroom training. Also the adult education and literacy provisions of WIA Title II and the Rehabilitation Act Amendments of Title IV may enable tradeoffs between education and employment and training funds. The ultimate in state discretion would be to seek Title V authorization for unified planning of all WIA titles along with the Carl Perkins Vocational and Applied Technology Education Act, the training provisions of the Food Stamp Act, various trade acts, the Wagner-Peyser Act, other public employment service provisions, unemployment insurance, the Older Americans Act, training activities of the Department of Housing and Urban Development, and the Community Services Block Grant, but not to stop there. Nothing in WIA or any other known federal or state legislation would prohibit a state from including in that unified planning process all other federal and state education support, public assistance programs, and any other relevant matter, as long as the specific requirements of all of the governing acts were honored. In short, the state that sets its own workforce development targets is free to pick and choose among whatever federal provisions apply and that offer usable resources to accomplish those state and local objectives.

MDTA, CETA, and JTPA have been in many ways a historical continuum—for both better and worse. Devolution from federal to state and local responsibility has been another element of that 36-year continuum. Further devolution will have mixed results, but those states that really care can have a better shot at bringing their displaced and disadvantaged out of poverty into the middle class as always intended. Longer-duration training will increase per capita costs and require either reduced enrollments or enlarged budgets. There is no reason that second-chance training should be totally a federal responsibility. Dislocated worker funding began as a matching program, and the whole of workforce development could return to that premise by state choice, merely by providing state funding to bring enrollments and performance to levels dictated by local economic circumstance and job market outlook.

For over 20 years, most American workers have had to run faster and faster to stand still in living standards. There is no reason to think that trend has subsided. Our 37 years of workforce development experience should have taught us something about how to enable those needing a second chance to keep up the pace. The challenge will be for states to apply that long experience to continually changing circumstances.

Notes

1. The Workforce Investment Act is critiqued, among other sources, in Mangum et al. (1999).

2. Tables in this section have been published previously in Mangum et al. (1999).

3. W. Norton Grubb (1996: 91–104) sees this as just one of many reasons for JTPA's modest successes. I consider it the primary one. The rest could be reasonably accommodated if there were time to do so.

4. These findings are based on the March 1997 CPS, tabulations by the Center for Labor Market Studies, Northeastern University, Boston.

5. The Bureau of Labor Statistics discontinued publication of the family budget series in 1981. The calculation herein was accomplished by multiplying the 1981 budget costs by the changes in the consumer price index for all urban consumers (CPI.U). The BLS lower living standards for the years they were published were in excess of the official poverty thresholds.

6. Those enrolled in a previous program year and carried over into the present one are counted in the enrollment for the current program year, but the dollars spent on them during the previous program year are not. Hence the costs per participant are underestimated to that extent. On the other hand, many terminees are listed by the states as having received "objective assessment only" (for instance, 26 percent of those terminating in program year 1994). They are counted as participants and therefore help keep the cost per participant down. But even though the moneys spent on them are counted in program expenditures, the individuals are not followed up to find out whether or not they obtained employment thereafter. Because substantial numbers of them eventually would, the expenditures are enlarged but the number entering employment is undercounted, with a resulting unknown exaggeration in the cost per adult entering employment.

7. This approach is described more fully in Mangum et al. (1998).

References

Barnow, Burt S., and Christopher T. King. 1996. "The Baby and the Bath Water: Lessons for the Next Employment and Training Program." In *Of Heart and Mind: Social Policy Essays in Honor of Sar A. Levitan,* edited by Garth Mangum and Stephen Mangum. Kalamazoo, Mich.: W.E. Upjohn Institute for Employment Research.

Bloom, Howard S., Larry L. Orr, George Cave, Stephen H. Bell, and Fred Doolittle. 1993. *National JTPA Study: Title II-A Impacts on Earnings and Employment at 18 Months.* Bethesda, Md.: Abt Associates, Inc.

Citro, Constance F., and Robert T. Michael, eds. 1995. *Measuring Poverty: A New Approach.* Washington, D.C.: National Academy Press.

Fogg, Neal, Andrew Sum, and Garth Mangum, with Neeta Fogg and Sheila Palma. 1999. *Poverty Ain't What It Used to Be: The Case for and Consequences of Redefining Poverty.* Policy Issues Monograph 99-03. Baltimore: Sar Levitan Center for Social Policy Studies, Johns Hopkins University. June.

Grubb, W. Norton. 1996. *Learning to Work: The Case for Reintegrating Job Training and Education.* New York: Russell Sage Foundation.

Heckman, James J. 1996. "What Should Be Our Human Capital Investment Policy?" In *Of Heart and Mind: Social Policy Essays in Honor of Sar A. Levitan,* edited by Garth Mangum and Stephen Mangum. Kalamazoo, Mich.: W.E. Upjohn Institute for Employment Research.

Jacobson, Louis, Robert LaLonde, and Daniel Sullivan. 1993. *The Cost of Worker Dislocation,* Kalamazoo, Mich.: W.E. Upjohn Institute for Employment Research.

LaLonde, Robert J. 1995. "The Promise of Public Sector-Sponsored Training Programs." *Journal of Economic Perspectives* 9 (2, spring): 156.

Lazerus, Scott, Garth Mangum, Stephen Mangum, and Judith Tansky. 1998. *The Public Employment Service in a One-Stop World.* Policy Issues Monograph 98-02. Baltimore: Sar Levitan Center for Social Policy Studies, Johns Hopkins University. July.

Levitan, Sar, and Garth Mangum, eds. 1981. *The T in CETA*. Kalamazoo, Mich.: W.E. Upjohn Institute for Employment Research.

Mangum, Garth. 1968. *MDTA: The Foundation of Federal Manpower Policy*. Baltimore: Johns Hopkins University Press.

Mangum, Garth, and John Walsh. 1973. *A Decade of Manpower Development and Training*. Salt Lake City: Olympus Publishing Company.

Mangum, Garth, Stephen Mangum, and Andrew Sum. 1998. *A Fourth Chance for Second Chance Programs: Lessons from the Old for the New*. Baltimore: Sar Levitan Center for Social Policy Studies, Johns Hopkins University. January.

Mangum, Garth, Stephen Mangum, Andrew Sum, James Callahan, and Neal Fogg. 1999. *A Second Chance for the Fourth Chance: A Critique of the Workforce Investment Act of 1998*. Policy Issues Monograph 99-01. Baltimore: Sar Levitan Center for Social Policy Studies, Johns Hopkins University. January.

Mishel, Lawrence, Jared Bernstein, and John Schmitt. 1999. *The State of Working America, 1998–99*. Washington, D.C.: Economic Policy Institute.

Orr, Larry L., Howard S. Bloom, Stephen H. Bell, Fred Doolittle, Winston Lin, and George Cave. 1996. *Does Training for the Disadvantaged Work? Evidence from the National JTPA Study*. Washington, D.C.: Urban Institute Press.

Pines, Marion. 1989a. *Working Capital: JTPA Investments for the 90's*. Washington, D.C.: Employment and Training Administration, U.S. Department of Labor. March.

_____. 1989b. *Working Capital: Coordinated Human Investment Directions for the 90's*. Washington, D.C.: Employment and Training Administration, U.S. Department of Labor. October.

Pines, Marion, and Jim Callahan. 1997. *The Emerging Workforce Development System*. Baltimore: Sar Levitan Center for Social Policy Studies, Johns Hopkins University. March.

Ruggles, Patricia. 1990. *Drawing the Line: Alternative Poverty Measures and Their Implications for Public Policy*. Washington, D.C.: Urban Institute Press.

Schiller, Bradley R. 1989. *The Economics of Poverty and Discrimination*, 5th ed. Englewood Cliffs, N.J.: Prentice Hall.

Sum, Andrew, and Anwiti Bahuguna, with Sheila Palma. 1998. *Rethinking Poverty Measures: Local Housing Costs, Adjusted Poverty Lines, and Their Consequences for Massachusetts*. Report prepared for the Massachusetts Institute for a New Commonwealth, Boston.

Taggart, Robert. 1981. "A Review of CETA Training." In *The T in CETA*, edited by Sar Levitan and Garth Mangum. Kalamazoo, Mich.: W.E. Upjohn Institute for Employment Research.

Walker, Gary. 1997. "Out of School and Unemployed: Principles for More Effective Policies and Programs." In *A Generation of Challenge: Pathways to Success for Urban Youth*, by Andrew Sum et al. Baltimore: Sar Levitan Center for Social Policy Studies, Johns Hopkins University.

Chapter Eleven

STRATEGIES FOR IMPROVING THE ODDS

Burt S. Barnow and Christopher T. King

Many of the chapters in this volume have focused on what is known about alternative training strategies for major target groups in the U.S. labor market—welfare recipients, disadvantaged youth, disadvantaged adults, and dislocated workers. This chapter outlines a series of strategies for improving the odds of success in publicly funded employment and training, based on the research that forms the main part of the book.

Although most of the book was written before the enactment of the Workforce Investment Act (WIA), neither it nor other recent legislation is likely to alter significantly the capacity of the nation's employment and training system to implement the recommendations made in this volume. For the most part, as noted in the first chapter in this volume, WIA maintains separate funding for target groups of interest, permits a variety of training and training-related services, and contains oversight provisions similar to the provisions of the Job Training Partnership Act (JTPA). As this book was being written, the WIA regulations had not been issued, so it is too soon to know how the Department of Labor will interpret various provisions of the act. Some features of particular interest include these:

- *The establishment of one-stop service centers.* The requirement that most major programs co-locate at one-stop centers could foster improved coordination among programs. On the other hand, welfare programs are *not* required to participate in one-stop centers, and in some states early implementation of one-stop centers has shown mixed results.
- *Encouragement for longer-term, unified planning across major employment, training, and related programs.* WIA encourages states to develop and submit five-year, unified plans for many programs, including job training, vocational education, adult education and family literacy, and others. To what extent states will avail themselves of that option remains to be seen. However, more comprehensive planning across the major programs affecting the

target populations also has the potential for improving program
service delivery and ultimately outcomes as well.

- *Universal eligibility for core services and less targeting on those
  with substantial barriers.* Local WIA programs are required to
  offer services such as eligibility determination, labor market
  information, job search and placement assistance, and follow-up
  postemployment services. In addition, WIA contains no provisions similar to those in JTPA that required that 65 percent of
  those served had to have one of seven barriers to employment.
  Although the universal access provision could enhance the image
  of WIA relative to JTPA, the reduced emphasis on targeting could
  reduce access for those with the greatest needs.
- *Most training must be provided through individual training
  accounts (ITAs).* We have written elsewhere (Barnow and King
  1996) about the dangers of using "pure" vouchers in targeted
  training programs, but "individual referrals," where training
  decisions are made jointly by participants and staff, can be effective. In addition, the WIA legislation makes exceptions for customized training and on-the-job training, two of the strategies that
  the authors of this volume have found to be especially effective.

In sum, the environment for training programs is likely to be
largely similar to what has existed in recent years. States and localities are going to be devoting considerable time and energy addressing
the new requirements and provisions of WIA, as well as those contained in the Adult Education and Family Literacy Act and the Rehabilitation Act (Titles II and IV of WIA, respectively) and the Carl D.
Perkins Vocational and Technical Education Act of 1998, or Perkins
III, as it has already been dubbed. As they begin to address these new
provisions, policymakers and program administrators may be open
to considering strategies for more effectively delivering publicly
funded training services in their states and local communities.

RECOMMENDED STRATEGIES

Seven basic strategies are offered for consideration by national, state,
and local policymakers and program administrators. There is nothing magic about the number seven; it is simply the tally of strategies
that were identified as having promise for improving the odds of success in publicly funded training programs.

individual vs market

1. *Publicly funded training programs should be driven by labor market demand.* Regardless of the group being served or the location of the particular program, one of the most important ways to improve the odds of success is to link the training being provided tightly to the needs of the local labor market. Local programs must have access to up-to-date labor market information (LMI), which tends to be developed with the active support of federal and state governments (e.g., the National and State Occupational Information Coordinating Committees), as well as to more informal sources of information about new and emerging occupations and better-paying jobs that might be gathered from employer groups, labor market experts, union representatives, and others. States can assist in the process by developing and making available tools for analyzing LMI to identify high-growth and emerging occupations, especially those that pay higher wages, offer desired benefits, and provide for career advancement via career paths, and encouraging their use in selecting occupations for training (as Florida and Texas have done so well). In addition, local programs can take this one step further by pursuing a "constrained choice" approach to training selection with participants, one in which they are encouraged to train in whatever occupation they wish, but with public funds only underwriting those with the requisite growth, pay, and advancement characteristics. The chapter by Bennici, Mangum, and Sum documents the importance of focusing on occupations with robust demand if the participants are to earn a reasonable wage afterward. In their analysis of successful local training programs, King et al. point to the importance of good labor market information and focus on high-demand occupations as an important factor in the longer-term success of local programs.

2. *Employment and training programs targeted on disadvantaged groups should focus on occupational training rather than immediate employment, and the training should be intensive rather than short-term in nature.* Local programs and their state administrators should recognize that, while labor force attachment approaches (e.g., WorkFirst, job search assistance) are associated with significant increases in employment and earnings (and reduced welfare receipt), such benefits tend to be short-lived. Longer-lasting impacts of the sort needed for real productivity growth and economic prosperity tend to be associated with human capital development in the form of more intensive occupational skills training. Mangum makes this point forcefully in

his chapter, referring to the "essentiality of occupational preparation." We recognize that this recommendation is contrary to current trends in employment and training policy, but in our view, the current emphasis on quick fixes and work first represents for the most part the triumph of hope over evidence.

All the chapters in this volume have stressed the need for focusing programs on substantial training rather than quick-fix job search strategies.[1] If funding is limited, it is probably better to serve fewer people than to spread the resources too thinly among participants. Note that greater intensity is more important than longer-duration training; with increasing global interdependence and high dropout rates from training, we cannot simply advocate for longer-term training. Instead, we must find better ways of achieving skill gains in ever shorter time periods. In part, this means putting pressure on community and technical colleges to be more receptive to nontraditional, open-entry/open-exit course offerings; in part, it may entail pressure on the demand side, to push employers into providing greater and continuing access to on-the-job training. Moreover, training should be provided in occupations that show real promise in compensation overall, or at least career paths that can be documented as leading to career and pay advancement in a reasonable time.

3. *Programs should integrate basic skills with occupational skills training for workers with considerable basic skills deficits.* As Bennici, Mangum, and Sum point out in their chapter, the economic rewards for education are at a historic high, so providing further education to participants is a sensible strategy. Unfortunately, the literature shows limited returns to programs that provide education alone to disadvantaged adults (e.g., Fishman et al. 1999; Burghardt and Gordon 1990), but providing basic skills in context holds more promise. Such learning by doing tends to be more effective than basic skills followed sequentially by occupational training, a lengthy process that fosters high dropout rates (e.g., the Job Corps). Moreover, training also can be linked to work itself in a more enlightened approach to the usual WorkFirst strategies.

Programs also should pay serious attention to training in what are known widely as the SCANS (or "soft") skills as well, after the various nonoccupational skills identified by employers via the Secretary's Commission on Achieving Necessary Skills as essential for employment and retention (SCANS 1991). Such skills include thinking skills, individual responsibility, self-management, sociability, and integrity. Occupational skills will be of little value to employers or the individual workers themselves unless they are accompanied by the soft skills required to adapt and perform in today's workplace.

4. *Employers should be solidly engaged in publicly funded training programs.* Labor, economists are fond of saying, is a derived demand. Employers control the jobs and dictate the requirements for both initial employment and retention on the job. Without serious employer engagement in curriculum design, equipment, the provision of training or at least trainers, and assistance in identifying emerging occupations and employment opportunities, training cannot be expected to perform successfully. Employers also can be asked to make up-front hiring commitments to trainees. One efficient and apparently effective way of engaging employers, an approach that gets programs around the "free-rider" concerns of individual employers, is relying on employer consortia or industry associations.[2] Customized training programs are perhaps the ultimate example of employer participation and, at their best, as shown in the chapter by Isbell, Trutko, and Barnow, can lead to significant benefits for participants, employers, and training programs. WIA acknowledges the unique features of customized training programs and exempts them from the requirement that training be provided through individual training accounts. The bottom line is that employer engagement must mean more than simply serving on an advisory committee.

5. *Programs with universal eligibility must be structured so that those with the greatest needs are adequately served.* We have noted how emphasis in employment and training programs has shifted over time between serving disadvantaged groups and more experienced, dislocated workers. The Workforce Investment Act requires universal access to all members of the labor force— the disadvantaged, dislocated workers, and the general population seeking labor market information and job leads. It is important for programs to balance the needs of various groups and ensure that those with the greatest needs are enrolled in sufficient numbers and that they are provided with appropriate services. In some instances, this may simply mean offering them job search assistance and access to information about labor market opportunities; in others, it will entail providing them with occupational training and the support required to take full advantage of it.

6. *Programs should offer a full range of supportive services as part of their program mix.* Supportive services—including need-based training payments, access to affordable child care and trans-

portation, and individualized case management and various postemployment services—should be an integral part of publicly funded training programs. Not all participants will require such services, but when they are needed, they may be the difference between success and failure of the effort, regardless of the quality of the training or the level of demand for the skill being trained for. Welfare recipients in particular often face many serious barriers to work, including child care, transportation, and lack of health insurance.

In addition, employers also must consider the extent to which they should adopt policies supporting workers, including such beneficial work/family policies as flexible work schedules, access to so-called flex accounts (for favorable tax treatment of medical and child care expenses), pay-period rather than end-of-year Earned Income Tax Credit reimbursement, and ongoing access to and financing of employee training, not just for high-level professionals but for other skilled and semi-skilled occupations as well.

7. *Local programs also should firmly embrace substantive performance management practices, but care must be taken to send the right messages and to avoid rewarding or sanctioning programs for factors beyond their control.* Performance standards (both outcomes and process oriented), incentives, and sanctions now occupy a regular place in the program administration at all levels and across most education and training offerings. However, it is unclear whether such approaches are sufficient to get the job done.[3] As King's chapter points out, most of the "success stories" visited in Illinois and Texas made no reference to performance standards; they spoke instead about a host of more concrete performance management practices. Real day-to-day performance management to ensure results—greater impacts on employment and earnings, and reduced welfare receipt—is likely to require pursuing individual referrals to training rather than more traditional standing contracts,[4] much greater attention to occupations to be trained for and their particular training requirements instead of simply who receives the training funds, and timely monitoring and assessing of performance at the local level where it counts. In addition, experience with performance standards in JTPA and other programs shows that if the outcomes and standards are not set wisely, the system can lead to incentives for creaming or providing inexpensive and inefficient services. Moreover, some studies indicate that the JTPA standards are only weakly correlated with program impacts, so care must be exercised to avoid sanctioning programs when the poor measured

performance is not an accurate measure of actual program performance (Barnow 2000a). As states and localities address the emerging cross-program accountability requirements of WIA, Perkins III, and related programs, these issues will become even more important and complex.

FUTURE RESEARCH AGENDA

An agenda for future research is also suggested by the chapters in this volume. Just as surely as we begin to get answers to some of the more vexing workforce policy questions, others are sure to arise. We hope that, through some combination of federal and state funding, progress on this agenda can be made in the next few years.

Key items on this future research agenda are as follows:

- *Systematic—either experimental or carefully designed and implemented quasi-experimental—evaluations of customized training of the type reviewed by Isbell, Trutko, and Barnow.* Such training is fast becoming the preferred route for employers seeking public partners in workforce development, much more so than is now provided through JTPA and related programs. California's Employment and Training Panel, Texas's Smart Jobs and Skills Development Funds, and other programs are operating now in four of five states. In some states, expenditures from these funds now rival in magnitude those from their combined JTPA Title II-A and II-C programs. Yet few of them have been subjected to the same level of scrutiny or held to the same standards of accountability as mainline, publicly funded job skills training or vocational education.

- *Net impact research to further explore the determinants of levels of labor market outcomes (i.e., employment and earnings) documented by King et al.* Most impact evaluations in employment and training have focused on the increase in earnings resulting from training, but King et al. focus on the level (adequacy) of earnings for trainees in the postprogram period. Time limits on welfare and similar limits on other assistance programs point to the need for evaluations to focus more on attaining adequate levels of earnings as well as the size of the increases.

- *Continuing youth demonstrations to find interventions that work, especially drawing on European experiences and testing promising ones domestically.* Robert Lerman's chapter points out how poorly our various programs for youth have performed, but he also identifies promising approaches. Sum et al. (1997) are more optimistic, arguing that many youth programs can be effective if properly implemented. Careful tests of the most promising approaches for youth programs—accompanied by rigorous process and impact evaluations—are clearly needed.

- *Systematic research on vouchers, particularly given the new workforce legislation's emphasis on their use.* As Barnow (2000b) points out, vouchers can range from simply providing people with voucher certificates and perhaps some information on occupations and providers and then turning them loose to a system where the voucher recipient is required to receive assessment and counseling before using the voucher. The latter approach may sometimes more appropriately be characterized as an individual referral approach. Research and demonstrations are needed to determine the conditions under which voucher and referral systems are most effective for various population groups in need of workforce services.

- *Continuing research and demonstration initiatives to identify effective teaching and training methods that can produce skills gains through intensive—as distinct from longer-term—training.* Few evaluations of workforce development interventions have given much more than lip service to determining which teaching/training methods are truly effective for which population groups.[5] Such pedagogical issues have traditionally been left to educators. Moreover, it is clear that too many of those who appear to need skills development drop out well before they have completed training for whatever reason. Much more can be done here by way of research, especially focusing on community and technical colleges and other training provider networks.[6]

- *Identifying "best practices" for effectively combining work and further education and training.* Although the authors of the chapters in this volume conclude that the evidence indicates that the human capital approach is preferable to the WorkFirst approach,[7] the reality is that WorkFirst is the way the nation's employment and training system is going to operate, at least for the near future. Unfortunately, there is little research available on ways training can be combined with work for welfare recipients and other disadvantaged persons placed in low-paying jobs. Demonstrations testing promising strategies for combining work with training and education would be extremely valuable.

- *Expanding basic research on incumbent worker training.* Because of the rapid pace of technological change and increased global competition in markets, both employers and workers must place far greater emphasis on training and skills acquisition throughout the work life. Further research is needed on incumbent worker training. Issues to be investigated include whether adequate training is taking place, which firms are providing it and for whom, the extent to which unions are involved, whether the government should offer firms or workers additional incentives to train incumbent workers, and, if so, what the most appropriate incentives are.

- *Identifying effective job creation and work experience strategies.* Although the 1996 Temporary Assistance for Needy Families legislation has made it more difficult for states and localities to provide work-related education and training for welfare recipients, creating public-sector jobs and offering work experience are encouraged. Research is needed on how such jobs can best be structured, and possibly combined with training and education, to lead to unsubsidized private-sector employment. A subtopic to be examined is which job creation strategies appear to lead to jobs capable of making those families economically self-sufficient.

- *Exploring ways to greatly improve occupational data reporting and collection in support of labor market research at all levels.* Despite the fact that workforce education and training efforts are geared in large part to addressing occupational skills deficits, as a nation our occupational data collection and reporting systems are not well suited to supporting them. We have very little systematic knowledge about career pathways for adults and youth or about the requirements for securing and maintaining employment in a given field. Such data, when they exist, are typically out of date, incomplete, and unavailable to those who have the most pressing needs for them, namely, program planners and counselors in local boards, training providers, and community and technical colleges, among others. A major improvement would be for states to add occupational identifiers, as well as employment site codes, to their employers' existing unemployment insurance wage records, so that we might have access to something beyond workers' quarterly earnings and industry of employment.[8] Such data would support the development of more-effective tools for targeting training offerings at the local level.

- *Testing the effectiveness of community-based investment approaches.* In recent years, some policy analysts have claimed that interventions should be focused at the community rather than the individual level. The Youth Fair Chance Demonstration sought to test that concept for disadvantaged youth, and the empowerment zones seek to provide intensive investments at the community level. Further research is needed to compare the more macro place-based approaches to individually focused programs.

- *Examining more systematically what is actually inside the "black box."* In their chapter, Friedlander, Greenberg, and Robins have pointed to the need for future evaluations to focus more on the reasons for the impacts we observe from our training programs. Systematic and rigorous differential impact evaluations are needed to help us understand what aspects of various training programs make them more or less effective.

Our look at the nation's employment and training programs indicates that, on the whole, those programs are successful at improving the employment and earnings of participants. With the exception of disadvantaged out-of-school youth, the programs generally lead to modest but significant increases in the outcomes of interest; for youth, the evidence is less positive, but some potentially positive approaches have been identified. But we are not where we want to be. As noted, the gains from most programs are modest. Further development of programs with greater payoffs for the most-disadvantaged members of the labor force is clearly needed.

Notes

1. Scrivener et al. (1998) provide additional evidence concerning the value of investing in training over simple labor force attachment.

2. For another supportive take on this subject, see two July 1998 segments produced by Hedrick Smith on the Public Broadcasting System's *The NewsHour with Jim Lehrer*, "Austin's [TX] High-Tech Labor."

3. See Barnow and King (1996) and Barnow (2000a) for more on this topic.

4. In Texas, 1995's House Bill 1863 mandated separation between workforce boards and actual service provision and the use of individual referrals to training. National workforce development legislation now sitting in conference committee embodies much the same approach.

5. This point is also made by Grubb et al. (1999) in their review of state and local workforce development initiatives.

6. One example of an innovative approach to training is provided by the EnterTech training project being developed and implemented by the University of Texas at Austin's IC². EnterTech has worked closely with area employers to identify both the hard and soft skills required in a series of entry-level occupations offering good compensation and promising career paths. They are also designing intensive, contextually based, multimedia training to be delivered over weeks rather than months through a variety of modes in the community.

7. The Manpower Demonstration Research Corporation's very recent longer-term impact findings from its Portland, Oregon, welfare-to-work site are some of the most promising yet (Scrivener et al. 1998).

8. The America's Labor Market Information System (or ALMIS) project, sponsored by the U.S. Department of Labor, has supported useful state efforts along these lines.

References

Barnow, Burt S. 2000a. "Exploring the Relationship between Performance Management and Program Impact: A Case Study of the Job Training Partnership Act." *Journal of Policy Analysis and Management* 19 (1): 118–41.

———. 2000b. "Vouchers for Federal Targeted Training Program." In *Vouchers and Related Delivery Mechanisms: Consumer Choice in the Provision of Public Services*, edited by Eugene Steuerle and Robert Reischauer. Washington, D.C.: Brookings Institution Press. Forthcoming.

Barnow, Burt S., and Christopher T. King. 1996. "The Baby and the Bath Water: Lessons for the Next Employment and Training Program." In *Of Heart and Mind: Social Policy Essays in Honor of Sar A. Levitan*, edited by Garth Mangum and Stephen Mangum. Kalamazoo, Mich.: W.E. Upjohn Institute for Employment Research.

Burghardt, John, and Anne Gordon. 1990. *More Jobs and Higher Pay: How an Integrated Program Compares with Traditional Programs.* New York: The Rockefeller Foundation, The Minority Female Single Parent Demonstration.

Fishman, Michael E., Burt S. Barnow, Karen N. Gardiner, Barbara J. Murphy, and Stephanie A. Laud. 1999. *Job Retention and Advancement among Welfare Recipients: Challenges and Opportunities. Research Synthesis.* Washington, D.C.: Administration for Children and Families, U.S. Department of Health and Human Services. January.

Grubb, W. Norton, Norena Badway, Denise Bell, Bernadette Chi, Chris King, Julie Herr, Heath Prince, Richard Kazis, Lisa Hicks, and Judith Taylor. 1999. *Toward Order from Chaos: State Efforts to Reform Workforce Development Systems.* MDS-1249. Berkeley, Calif.: National Center for Research in Vocational Education.

SCANS. See Secretary's Commission on Achieving Necessary Skills.

Scrivener, Susan, Gayle Hamilton, Mary Farrell, Stephen Freedman, Daniel Friedlander, Marisa Mitchell, Jodi Nudelman, and Christine Schwartz. 1998. "Implementation, Participation Patterns, Costs, and Two-Year Impacts of the Portland (Oregon) Welfare-to-Work Program: Executive Summary, National Evaluation of Welfare-to-Work Strategies." Washington, D.C.: U.S. Department of Health and Human Services, Administration for Children and Families and Office of the Assistant Secretary for Planning and Evaluation; and U.S. Department of Education, Office of the Under Secretary and Office of Vocational and Adult Education. May.

Secretary's Commission on Achieving Necessary Skills. 1991. *What Work Requires of Schools: A SCANS Report for America 2000.* Washington, D.C.: U.S. Department of Labor. June.

Sum, Andrew, Stephen Mangum, Edward DeJesus, Gary Walker, David Gruber, Marion Pines, and William Spring. 1997. *A Generation of Challenge: Pathways to Success for Urban Youth.* Baltimore: Sar Levitan Center for Social Policy Studies, Johns Hopkins University.

348   *Index*

basic, 64, 66, 67, 71, 72, 115
offered in welfare employment
    programs, 72–74
postsecondary, 64, 67, 71, 72
projected change in
    employment by, 33, 34
remedial, 72, 321
eligibility, 216, 336, 338
"employability security," 22
employer performance measures,
    15n.9
employers. *See also* customized
    training for employers
    engagement in publicly funded
        training programs, 339
employment
    commitments for, 224
    future projected
        by industry and occupation,
            26–30
        training and projected change
            in, 33, 34
employment programs, history of
    public, 1
employment rates, at termination
    and follow-up, 304, 305,
    307
employment relationship, altered,
    21–22
employment success
    of disadvantaged adults and
        youth, 148, 151–153
    gender differences in, 140–142,
        153, 154, 156, 157
enrollees, 276
entry effects, 280

F

Fallick, Bruce C., 229
family demands, 166
Family Support Act of 1988, 51
FAST TRACK, 202–203
federal education, for out-of-
    school youth, 186
federal government, involvement
    in training programs, 1, 325
federal policy, regarding welfare
    employment programs, 51–53
federal programs
    challenges facing, 39–40

for dislocated workers, 231–233
    strategies for, 40–42
federal welfare provisions,
    waivers from, 52–53
feedback, 224–225
Fink, Barbara, 252
firm size, and amount of training
    received, 37–39
Florida, reforms in workforce
    programs in 1990s, 10
Friedlander, Daniel, vi, 132

G

Garfinkel, Irwin, 271, 280
gender comparisons and
    disparities, 297
    in employment success of
        disadvantaged persons,
        140–142, 153, 154, 156,
        157
general equivalency diploma
    (GED), 72, 73
Glazer, Nathan, 91
globalization, 20–21
Goldberger, Arthur S., 265, 268
grants, training, 2, 247–248
Greater Avenues for Independence
    (GAIN), 54, 56, 68, 69. *See
    also* California GAIN
Greenberg, David H., 132
Grover, Nelima, 251
Gueron, Judith, 56, 65, 68

H

Hamermesh, Daniel S., 230–231,
    255n.1
Harrington Hospital, 212, 214
hiring commitments, company,
    218
hiring vouchers, 231
Hispanic people, 43n.9
Homemaker/Home Health Aide
    Demonstrations, 54, 56, 66,
    69, 70, 84–86
HOPE program, 202, 203
human capital development
    (HCD) model, 57, 66, 70
human resource concerns,
    current, 22–23

ABOUT THE EDITORS

Burt S. Barnow is interim associate director for research and principal research scientist at the Institute for Policy Studies at Johns Hopkins University. Dr. Barnow has over 25 years of experience as an economist and manager of research projects in the fields of labor economics, employment and training programs, and welfare programs. Dr. Barnow joined the Institute for Policy Studies in 1992 after working for eight years at the Lewin Group, where he was vice president in charge of research on human resource issues, and nearly nine years of experience in the U.S. Department of Labor, where he was a member of the Senior Executive Service and directed the research, development, and evaluation program for the department's largest agency. Dr. Barnow has published widely in the fields of labor economics, program evaluation, and employment and training. He chairs the Performance Management Committee for the Maryland Governor's Workforce Investment Board and is vice chair of the National Academy of Science's Information Technology Workforce Committee.

Christopher T. King is director of the Ray Marshall Center for the Study of Human Resources and a lecturer at the University of Texas at Austin's Lyndon B. Johnson School of Public Affairs. His recent publications include *Toward Order from Chaos: State Efforts to Reform Workforce Development Systems* (National Center for Research in Vocational Education 1999, with W. Norton Grubb and others) and "Public Labor Market Policies for the 21st Century" (with Bob McPherson and Donald Long) in *Back to Shared Prosperity: The Growing Inequality of Wealth and Income in America*, edited by Ray Marshall (M.E. Sharpe 2000). Dr. King is conducting a multi-state study of urban welfare-to-work transitions for the U.S. Department of Labor and the Upjohn Institute, examining welfare and workforce devolution in 20 states as part of the State Capacity Project. Dr. King was principal editor of the Secretary of Labor's 1989 Job Training Partnership Act (JTPA) Advisory Committee report *Working Capital* and served on the Technical Advisory Panel for the National JTPA Evaluation from 1986 to 1993.

ABOUT THE CONTRIBUTORS

John Baj is currently a senior research associate in the Human Resource Policy Program at the Center for Governmental Studies. He has been involved in numerous projects focusing on the assessment of workforce development programs and has extensive experience with a variety of administrative databases and reporting systems. He is the author of several publications, including *Building State Systems Based on Performance: The Workforce Development Experience—A Guide for States* (National Governors' Association 1996), which he coauthored with Charles Trott.

Frank Bennici is a labor economist and senior research analyst at Westat. His research has focused on education, employment, training, welfare, disability, and vocational rehabilitation. He has been an author and coauthor on many technical reports from Westat to several federal agencies; his publications include *Managing Expectations for Welfare to Work: The Realities of Servicing the Hardest to Serve* (Westat 1999).

Daniel Friedlander was a labor economist who spent his entire 20-year professional career with the Manpower Demonstration Research Corporation (MDRC) as a program evaluator. He published over 50 reports, books, and articles during his tenure at MDRC. His most recent coauthored book was *Five Years After: The Long-Term Effects of Welfare-to-Work Programs* (Russell Sage Foundation 1996). He was a pioneer in multistage experimental designs and popularized the now-standard "subgroup analysis" that appears in almost every evaluation study. He was also an expert in developing performance standards for employment and training programs.

David H. Greenberg is a labor economist at the University of Maryland–Baltimore Campus (UMBC). Before coming to UMBC in 1982, he worked for the Rand Corporation, SRI International, and the U.S. Department of Health and Human Services. Much of his research focuses on the evaluation of government programs that are targeted at the low-income population, especially public assistance, employment, and training programs. He recently completed a guide for conducting and using cost analyses of employment and training programs, and he is the coauthor of both the *Digest of Social Experiments* (Urban Institute Press 1998) and a textbook on cost-benefit analysis. He is currently coauthoring a supplement to the *Digest.*

Kellie Isbell is a research associate at Aguirre International in Bethesda, Maryland. Her publications include "Involving Employers in Training: Best Practices" for the U.S. Department of Labor Evaluation Series and "Social Sector Reform Activity: Labor Market Reform and Private Pension Reform in Bulgaria" for the U.S. Agency for International Development. She is currently researching the effects of the transition to democracy and market economies on social benefits in Central and Eastern Europe.

Leslie O. Lawson currently serves as a partnership specialist for the U.S. Bureau of the Census, coordinating Census 2000 outreach and promotions in central Texas. Before joining the Census Bureau partnership team in 1998, Ms. Lawson conducted quantitative social welfare policy analysis and program evaluation with the Ray Marshall Center for the Study of Human Resources and the Bureau of Business Research at the University of Texas at Austin. She has published on public assistance utilization patterns and policy, changing family demographics, and the labor force participation of women.

Duane E. Leigh is a professor of economics and the economics department chair at Washington State University, Pullman, Washington. He has held teaching and research positions at the University of Wisconsin–Madison and the University of Virginia. In recent years, his research has centered on the training needs of two groups of adult workers: dislocated workers who require retraining to qualify for new jobs, and downsizing survivors who require retraining to cope with increased workplace responsibilities in their old jobs.

Robert I. Lerman is the director of the Human Resources Policy Center at the Urban Institute and professor of economics at American University. His research focuses on welfare programs, income inequality, child support, youth employment programs, fatherhood, and family structure. His recent article, "Reassessing the Trends in U.S. Earnings Inequality" (*Monthly Labor Review* 1997), was cowinner of the Lawrence Klein award.

Garth L. Mangum is Max McGraw Professor of Economics and Management Emeritus at the University of Utah. He served as research director of the Senate Subcommittee on Employment and Manpower and as executive director of the President's Committee on Manpower during the Kennedy and Johnson administrations and was involved in the passage and early administration of the anti-poverty and workforce development legislation of that era. He was an originator of the National Council on Employment Policy, served as its chairman for a time, and is currently its secretary-treasurer. He was cofounder with Sar Levitan of the Center for Social Policy Studies at George Washington University, director of the Institute for Human Resource Management at the University of Utah, and is currently a fellow of the Sar Levitan Center for Social Policy Studies at the Johns Hopkins University.

Stephen Mangum is senior associate dean for academic programs and professor of management and human resources at the Max M. Fisher College of Business, Ohio State University. He has produced several publications, including *Programs in Aid of the Poor* (Johns Hopkins University Press 1997) and *With Heart and Mind: Social Policy Essays in Honor of Sar A. Levitan* (W.E. Upjohn 1996), both of which he coedited with Sar A. Levitan and Garth L. Mangum.

Demetra Smith Nightingale is a principal research associate in the Human Resources Policy Center at the Urban Institute, where she is director of the Welfare and Training Research Program. She is a nationally recognized expert in social policy and has for over 20 years focused her research on issues related to poverty and the alleviation of poverty. She serves on numerous advisory boards and task forces at the national, state, and local levels. She is coeditor with Robert Haveman of *The Work Alternative: Welfare Reform and the Realities of the Job Market* (Urban Institute Press 1995), and coauthor with C. Eugene Steuerle, Edward N. Gramlich, and Hugh Heclo of *The Government We Deserve: Responsive Democracy and Changing Expectations* (Urban Institute Press 1998).

Jodi Nudelman is currently a project leader with the Office of Inspector General in the U.S. Department of Health and Human Services. She has conducted numerous short-term sudies about the efficiency and effectiveness of the department's programs and policies. Her primary research interests include health care and welfare issues. Prior to this, she was a research analyst at the Manpower Demonstration Research Corporation.

Jerome A. Olson is a research scientist and chief economist at the Ray Marshall Center for the Study of Human Resources at the University of Texas at Austin, where he provides quantitative and statistical expertise. Prior to coming to the Center in 1994, Dr. Olson was the associate director of the Bureau of Business Research at the University of Texas, where he developed databases and statistical procedures for analyzing changes in the Texas economy. Dr. Olson's research has been published in *Texas Business Review, The Journal of Econometrics*, and *Technological Forecasting and Social Change*.

Lisa Plimpton is a policy analyst at the Center for Law and Social Policy (CLASP), where she works on workforce development issues and tracks welfare policies in the 50 states and Washington, D.C. Prior to joining CLASP in 1997, she worked as a research assistant at the Johns Hopkins Institute for Policy Studies and at Abt Associates, Inc. She has worked on program evaluations and policy analyses of welfare reform, workforce development, community development, and housing.

Philip K. Robins is a professor of economics at the University of Miami. He is a widely published specialist in labor economics and the economics of family behavior and is considered an expert on the economic evaluation of social programs for low-income families. He is a research affiliate with the Institute for Research on Poverty at the University of Wisconsin–Madison and a consultant to the Manpower Demonstration Research Corporation. His current research includes studying the economic effects of financial incentive programs for welfare recipients. Before coming to the University of Miami in 1982, he worked for SRI International and the Federal Reserve Bank of Chicago.

Andrew M. Sum is a professor of economics at Northeastern University and the director of the Center for Labor Market Studies in Boston. He has been involved with employment and training policy-making, planning, and evaluation at the local, state, and national levels for nearly three decades. His recent research publications in this field include *Literacy in the Labor Force* (National Center for Education Statistics 1999); *Poverty Ain't What It Used to Be: The*

Case for and Consequences of Redefining Poverty, with Neal Fogg and Garth Mangum (Sar Levitan Center for Social Policy Studies 1999); and *The Road Ahead: Emerging Threats to Workers, Families, and the Massachusetts Economy* (Teresa and H. John Heinz III Foundation 1999).

Charles E. "Pete" Trott, the current director of the Center for Governmental Studies at Northern Illinois University, has been engaged in employment and training policy research for over 30 years. He started with studies of metropolitan labor markets with the Federal Reserve Bank of Cleveland and moved into studies of workforce migration with the Bureau of Economic Analysis, U.S. Department of Commerce. He shifted into issues of performance management of publicly funded programs under CETA, continued under JTPA, and is now involved with assisting the state of Illinois under WIA. He is also very active in the skill standards arena.

John Trutko, a senior consultant to the Urban Institute and president of Capital Research Corporation, has worked for over 20 years as a policy analyst and program evaluation specialist. Mr. Trutko specializes in research studies in the employment, training, and welfare fields. He has directed a wide variety of program evaluation studies for federal and state agencies, as well as a number of leading foundations.

Improving the Odds:
Increasing the Effectiveness of Publicly Funded Training
Burt S. Barnow and Christopher T. King, editors

"*Improving the Odds* is a blend of previously unpublished research, literature reviews on training for groups ranging from welfare recipients to incumbent workers, and prescriptions for improving training policies and programs written by some of the leading researchers in the field. The authors offer policy-makers, administrators, and researchers alike timely, practical insights on ways to improve the success of training programs at all levels in the context of rapidly changing global markets. The policy implications and recommendations contained in this volume carry well beyond the programs now being implemented under the Workforce Investment and the Carl D. Perkins Acts. This is an excellent collection that anyone with an interest in the workforce enterprise should have on his or her desk."

—Ray Marshall, Audre and Bernard Rapoport Centennial Chair in Economics and Public Affairs, Lyndon B. Johnson School of Public Affairs, University of Texas at Austin, U.S. Secretary of Labor, 1977–1981

"This is an incredibly well-timed book. A new federal law for employment and training programs was just passed and is being implemented right now. Barnow and King are two of the nation's leading experts on the subject, and they have included chapters by respected colleagues—which makes this an essential book for everyone who works in the field of job training."

—Richard P. Nathan, Director, Nelson A. Rockefeller Institute of Government, SUNY, Albany

"One of the most difficult questions in the world of public policy is what can be done to help the workforce left behind by the recent economic prosperity. *Improving the Odds* offers solid conclusions about what works—and what doesn't work—in government training programs."

—Peter Cappelli, Director, Center for Human Resources, The Wharton School, University of Pennsylvania

"*Improving the Odds* provides a valuable series of papers summarizing the vast literature on publicly funded training and recommending improvements in short-term training programs, including those for welfare recipients, disadvantaged and dislocated workers, out-of-school youth, and incumbent workers. The breadth and completeness of these contributions make them fitting commentaries on almost forty years of experimentation."

—W. Norton Grubb, David Gardner Chair in Higher Education, University of California, Berkeley

The Urban Institute Press

9 780877 666899

Cover design: Lisa Carey / Matthew Hirschmann
Cover illustration: Bryan Leister, Alexandria, VA